# BRISTOL
## for families

## 10<sup>th</sup> edition

**Editor**

**Lindsey Potter**

## Titch Hikers' Guide, Bristol for families

10th Edition

## Published by

Freedom Guides Limited
PO Box 296, Bristol BS99 7LR

## Published

April 2006

## ISBN

978-09534648-4-5

## Cover design

karen painter designs
www.karenpainterdesigns.co.uk

## Printed by

AST Print Group Ltd
www.astprint.com

## Cover photographs courtesy of

Waterbabies (swimming baby)
Tim Potter (harbour)
Nick Turner, www.sustrans.org.uk (cyclist)
Tim Potter (suspension bridge)
Martin Chainey, At-Bristol (coral reef)

## Special thanks to

- Destination Bristol for their support and loan of maps
- Sport Services, Bristol City Council
- Children's Information Service
- Our advertisers
- See also the acknowledgements at the back of the book, pg 289

## Book orders

Email: books@titchhikers.co.uk
Tel: 0117 914 4867

First Published as Titch Hikers' Guide to Bristol by The National Childbirth Trust (Bristol Branch): First Edition 1983, revised editions 1985, 1987, 1989, 1992, 1994,

Seventh Edition published by Titch Hikers' Guide Limited, 1998, revised edition 2001.

Ninth Edition published by Titch Hikers' Guide (UK) Limited, 2004

# CONTENTS

## How to navigate

- Symbol keys pg 132
- Maps pgs 130, 134, 138
- Fast Index pg 304

## Welcome

I can't believe it's two years since our last edition. Time has flown, but then that is something which seems to happen to all busy parents.

However, this book is all about giving you more time and making that time better with your children. And let's face it, such times are priceless, making this book very good value!

Our 10th Edition marks 25 years of this unique publication which, like a baton, has been passed from one team of Bristol parents to another. The content over the years has grown, making this a bumper edition — we hope it isn't too heavy for your bag!

Our researchers have left no stone unturned when it comes to updating our listings and finding new ones. There is so much, whether you have babes-in-arms or kids in the thick of football boots and skipping ropes.

What makes the book so good is your feedback: the listings are there because our Titch Hikers' readers say they should be. So please keep sending us news on what's hot and what's not, to:

info@titchhikers.co.uk or www.titchhikers.co.uk or PO Box 296, Bristol BS99 7LR

Let us guide you to great places to eat, cycle, walk, chill or go wild. Dip into any of the chapters and you will find something to inspire you.

We hope you enjoy using this book and tell your friends about it.

*Lindsey*

Lindsey Potter
Editor

PS We no longer include a Teenguide, as due to popular demand we have created a book just for them: The Freedom Guide to Bristol for Young People aged 10-18, to help them find their freedom and to help you let go.

# OUT & ABOUT IN BRISTOL

**Alex Reed**

## CONTENTS

## INTRODUCTION

Bristol is brimming with activities, attractions and services for families to enjoy. But for many of us, immersed in the business of bringing up children, it's hard to keep up with the exciting activities and events on offer.

This chapter offers plenty of ideas on local outings, both outdoor for those bright, sunny days, and indoor escapes from the rain and winter chill. The great thing about Bristol is that much of these destinations are close to hand and you can often leave the car behind.

Libraries, parks and museums put on a wide variety of events, many of which are free. See the maps in the reference section and look up the annual events listings for details.

Keep us posted on city excursions you've enjoyed and tell us your views on Bristol, when it comes to getting out and about.

## VISITOR INFORMATION CENTRE

Bristol has an excellent tourist information office, known as Destination Bristol. Their website has excellent coverage of seasonal events. There are four visitor information points with the harbourside centre being the largest. They offer advice, accommodation booking, maps, guides, leaflets and brochures.

### Bristol Visitor Information Harbourside

Wildwalk-At-Bristol, Harbourside, Bristol, BS1 5DB
0906 711 2191 (50p/min)
www.visitbristol.co.uk
Mon-Fri: 10am-5pm, Sat-Sun & sch hols: 10am-6pm

### Bristol Visitor Information City Centre

Travel Bristol Centre, 11 Colston Ave, BS1 4UB
Mon-Fri: 10.30am-5.30pm, Sat: 10am-1pm

Self serve terminal, booking hotline, leaflets and brochures

### Bristol Visitor Information Points

Ground Floor, The Mall Galleries &
Bristol City Museum & Art Gallery, Queens Rd, Clifton

## Bristol City Sightseeing Tour

0870 4440654 information hotline
www.bristolvisitor.co.uk, www.city-sightseeing.com
Easter-Sep: 10am-5pm
Call for prices, U5's free, one child free per adult passenger

Tickets can be bought on the bus or from Bristol Tourist Information Centre and the Travel Bristol Information Centre. This open-top, live guide sightseeing bus takes in all the major attractions: including at-Bristol, Bristol Zoo, SS Great Britain, Clifton Village and the British Empire and Commonwealth Museum. Discounts on a number of attractions on presentation of your bus ticket. You can hop on and off the bus at any of the 20 stops en route. Children fun packs available. See advertisement in the Colour Reference Section, pg 133.

Planning a day out in town?
Check out our Eating Out chapter see pg 63.

# LANDMARKS

## Bristol Cathedral

College Green, Bristol
0117 926 4879
www.bristol-cathedral.co.uk
Daily 8am-6pm
Free (donations welcome)

Bristol Cathedral welcomes visitors young and old, and a look-in holds more for children than you might first expect. The awesome size of the building is impressive and the animals, stain glass windows and gruesome gargoyles provide plenty of entertainment. A children's guide is available. The cathedral staff encourage kids to draw many of the features and also hold regular brass rubbing events and other workshops, including music, drama, environmental science and craft.

## Cabot Tower

Brandon Hill Park, off Park Street, Bristol
Daily 8am-½hr before dusk
Free

At over 32.4 metres high on top of a high hill, this tower offers one of the best panoramic views of Bristol. It was built in 1897 to celebrate John Cabot's voyage to America in 1497. There is a winding staircase that takes you to the top. Very young children may find the climb tricky but there are secure viewing areas. The gardens are great for exploring.

## Clifton Suspension Bridge

0117 974 4664
www.clifton-suspension-bridge.org.uk
Guided tours from £2.50 pp

One of the world's greatest bridges and it's on our doorstep. It was designed by the Victorian engineer Isambard Kingdom Brunel, although he never lived to see it finished in 1864. Its spectacular setting over the Avon Gorge have made it the symbol of Bristol and the subject of many school projects! Bridge tours for groups are available by arrangement. Visit the website or phone for details.

## Concorde at Filton

Location 09L, Airbus UK, Filton, BS99 7AR
0870 3000 578 booking line
0117 936 5485 visitor centre
www.concordeatfilton.org.uk
Wed-Sun 4 guided tours each day
£12.50 adult, £7 child 5-14yrs, U5's not admitted,
children must be accompanied

Concorde 216 flew home to Bristol on
November 26th 2003. It's on loan from British
Airways but the hope is that a permanent
visitor centre can be funded to celebrate
this remarkable piece of aviation history. All
visitors need to pre-book the guided tours in
advance. Parking at BAWA then a coach will
take you through the Airbus site.

## Doors Open Day

www.bristoldoorsopenday.org

This annual event held in the autumn is your
chance to see for free inside some of Bristol's
most architecturally and historically important
buildings, many of which are not normally
open to the general public.

# ZOO

## Bristol Zoo Gardens

Clifton, Bristol, BS8 3HA
0117 974 7399
www.bristolzoo.org.uk
Daily 9am-5.30pm, 4.30pm winter
£11 adult, £7 child 3-14yrs, free U3's
These are Gift Aid Visitor prices which include a
voluntary contribution of approx 10% above normal
admission prices. Good annual membership deals.
Follow the brown tourist signs from the M5 J17 or
from Bristol city centre

New for summer 2006, Monkey Jungle,
featuring "meet the lemurs". This offers an
immersive forest experience where monkeys
mingle with gorillas and visitors enjoy close-
up, walk through, encounters with lemurs.
Senses will be filled with the sights, sounds
and smells of the forest.

There is also the award winning Seal &
Penguin Coasts where you come face to face
with seals and penguins through transparent
underwater walkways. Discover other
favourites including Gorilla Island, Twilight
World, Bug World and the Reptile House.

From the smallest and rarest tortoise in the
world, to the largest ape, there are over 400
exotic and endangered species to experience.
Regular animal encounters are held every day.

# THE DOCKSIDE

This is a fascinating and lively area of Bristol
which has a lot to offer parents and children
of all ages. The city has a distinguished
history of maritime activity and attractions
such as the Industrial Museum and the ss
Great Britain. This largely traffic-free area
makes it ideal for walking and family cycling.
Parking is ample and located at the Industrial
Museum, ss Great Britain and At-Bristol. There
are cafes and restaurants on both side of the
harbour.

## Bristol Harbour Railway

Princes Wharf, Wapping Rd, Bristol, BS1 4RN
0117 925 1470
Apr-Nov selected w/e's
£1 single, £2 rtn, £3.50 Family, free U6's

This train steams along the dockside from
the Bristol Industrial Museum to the SS Great
Britain. Locally built engines (Henbury or
Portbury) pull the wagons which once ran at
the Avonmouth Docks.

## Bristol Industrial Museum

See Museums' section - overleaf

## Brunel's ss Great Britain

Great Western Dock Yard, Gas Ferry Road, BS1 6TY
0117 929 1843 information line
0117 926 0680 enquiries & bookings
www.ssgreatbritain.org
Apr-Oct: 10am-5.30pm, Nov-Mar: 4.30pm
£9 adult, £5 child, £25 family ticket (2+2)

Brunel's masterpiece of ship design has been wonderfully restored throughout and appears to float in her original dry dock. Go "under water", to stand below the ship's impressive hull and propeller. Step back in time in the Dockyard Museum and try your hand at preparing the ship for sail, steering her on a westerly course, or climbing above the rigging to the crow's nest.

On board, explore cabins and crew quarters and try your hand at controlling the ship's massive recreated engine. A choice of audio guides bring the ship to life. Holiday activities available. See advertisement, pg 130.

### The Matthew

A replica of the ship built in the 15th century in which John Cabot sailed from Bristol across the Atlantic to discover Newfoundland in 1497. Disabled and buggy access is limited.

# FERRIES

## The Bristol Ferry Boat Company

MB Tempora, Welsh Back, Bristol, BS1 4SP
0117 927 3416
www.bristolferryboat.co.uk
Daily 10.30am-6.10pm (charters can run later)

This friendly company operates a waterbus service from the city centre which runs every 40 minutes, covering the middle and western end of the harbour. During Apr-Oct and in the school holidays the service covers the middle and eastern end of the harbour up to Temple Meads Station. There are many stops allowing access to tourist attractions along with cafes, restaurants and pubs. Chartered trips which go beyond the harbour to the river and gorge run Apr-Oct. There are two heated boats in the fleet, look out for their popular Sail with Santa on weekends in December.

## The Hotwells Ferry

Daily 10.30am-6.10pm
Single £1.50 adult, £1.20 child,
Round trip £4.30 adult, £2.80 child

The Hotwells Ferry is in operation around the harbour between Hotwells and the city centre. The 40 minute round trip includes the ss Great Britain.

### The Temple Meads Ferry

Apr-Sept Sat-Sun/daily during the school holidays
Round Trip £4.30 adult, £2.80 child, £12 family (2+2) shorter fares available

Operates between Temple Meads and the City Centre. This is a 60-minute round trip that includes the ss Great Britain and Castle Park.

## Bristol Packet

SS Great Britain Car Park, Wapping Wharf, BS1 6UN
0117 9268157
www.bristolpacket.co.uk
Open all year, daily in school holidays, weekends only during term-time

Bristol Packet offers a variety of educational-based river adventures on one of their four boats. These include city dock tours with commentary, trips under the Clifton Suspension Bridge and lunch and afternoon tea cruises to local, child friendly pubs and Beese's tea gardens.

# MUSEUMS & GALLERIES

## Arnolfini

16 Narrow Quay, Bristol, BS1 4QA
0117 917 2300
www.arnolfini.org.uk
Open daily, galleries & bookshop: 10am-8pm,
cafebar & cinema: 10am-11pm
Entry to galleries, bookshop and exhibitions are free

This is Bristol's centre for the contemporary arts. It has recently undergone refurbishment making it very pushchair friendly. An ever-changing programme provides lots to see including exhibitions, live art and performance, dance and cinema. There are regular family-friendly events, activities and workshops on offer.

## At-Bristol

Anchor Rd, Harbourside, Bristol, BS1 5DB
0845 345 1235
www.at-bristol.org.uk
Daily 10am-5pm, 6pm weekends & sch hols
From £6.50 adults, £4.50 child, free U3's, £19 family
ticket, various ticket combinations available
Membership includes free entry to Explore and
Wildwalk and £1 off each IMAX film.

### Explore-At-Bristol

Experience the everyday and the
extraordinary in this interactive science and
discovery centre. You can make a programme
in a TV studio, experience a walk-in tornado
or watch a computer-generated film on the
journey of a sperm! New for 2006/07 is a
series of exhibitions for U8's. There is also a
planetarium.

### Wildwalk-At-Bristol

A fascinating journey through the plant and
animal kingdoms. Now with a new live events
area and People and the Planet exhibition.

### IMAX Theatre-At-Bristol

Showing 2D, 3D and some feature films on
a screen that is four storeys high, this is the
ultimate film experience!

## Blaise Castle House Museum

Blaise Castle Estate, Henbury Rd, BS10 7QS
0117 903 9818
Sat-Wed 10am-5pm
Admission free

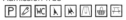

Social history collections, exhibiting domestic
furnishings, costumes, textiles and toys.

## Bristol City Museum & Art Gallery

Queens Rd, Clifton, BS8 1RL
0117 922 3571
www.bristol-city.gov.uk/museums
Daily 10am-5pm
Admission free

Many interesting and varied exhibits appealing
to children including stuffed animals, a
bi-plane suspended from the ceiling in the
entrance hall and a Romany caravan. Older
children and adults can request a gallery

trail. Toys and play-things are provided at
some exhibitions. Ask staff for toddler steps
if required. Holiday activities and workshops.
Family fun days first Sunday of the month.

## Bristol Industrial Museum

Princes Wharf, Wapping Rd, Bristol, BS1 4RN
0117 925 1470
Sat-Wed: 10am-5pm
Admission free

The ground floor has displays of motorised
and horse-drawn vehicles and a model railway
(20p to operate). The first floor chronicles
Bristol's aerospace and maritime history. At
the weekends there is sometimes a chance
to try your hand at printing. Also, the steam
crane may be operational: climb on it, get
oily, then watch it move. On the harbour,
half-hour boat trips are sometimes available,
and you might be lucky enough to see the
Pyronaut fireboat's water cannon in action.
For information on the Harbour Railway, see
The Dockside above.

### British Empire & Commonwealth Museum

Clock Tower Yard, Temple Meads, Bristol, BS1 6QH
0117 925 4980
www.empiremuseum.co.uk
bookings@empiremuseum.co.uk
Daily: 10am-5pm
£6.95 adult, £3.95 child, £16 family, free U5's
Paying full price on your admission ticket allows you
free entry for 12mths

P V WC 👤 👥 🏠 ✂ 🧺 🚂 🚌 ♿

Housed next to Temple Meads Station, the museum charts the 500 year history of the British Empire. A visit includes entry to the hands-on, family-friendly exhibition Pow Wow, plus a range of exciting children's activities during the school holidays.

A new tour in celebration of the 200th anniversary of the birth of Isambard Kingdom Brunel will be available twice a month on Sundays (until 10/06). The tour will include the original railway buildings adjacent to the current station. An expert guide will take you through the passenger sheds, cavernous vaults and the mock-Gothic railway boardroom. There have been ghostly sightings of Brunel so watch out! Pre-booking required.

### CREATE Environment Centre

Smeaton Rd, Spike Island, Bristol, BS1 6XN
0117 925 0505
Mon-Fri 9am-5pm

WC 👤 👥 ☕ 🏠 ♿

CREATE is a riverside centre focusing on ecology and the environment, in particular recycling. The recycling exhibition demonstrates what happens to waste material and has a smiley face trail for kids to follow. The centre also has a demonstration eco-home, made of salvaged, recycled and natural materials and using energy saving systems (open 12pm-3pm). The centre is probably of most interest to teens. The recommended café is open 9am-2pm and has high chairs. The centre encourages the use of public transport, the no. 500 bus or a ferry ride. There is limited parking.

### Georgian House

7 Great George Street, Bristol, BS1 5RR
0117 921 1362
Apr-Oct: Sat-Wed 10am-5pm
Admission free

WC

The lovely Georgian House was built in 1790 and is furnished in period style. No buggies in the house but they can be stored.

### Red Lodge

Park Row, Bristol, BS1 5LJ
0117 921 1360
Apr-Oct: Sat-Wed 10am-5pm
Admission free

P WC

Beautiful Elizabethan house with panelled rooms and a Tudor knot garden. No buggies in the house but they can be stored.

### Royal West of England Academy

Queens Rd, Bristol, BS8 1PX
0117 973 5129
www.rwa.org.uk
Mon-Sat: 10am-5.30pm, Sun 2pm-5pm
Ground floor exhibition free,
1st floor £3 adult, free U16's

P ✏ WC ✂ 👤 🏠 ✂ 🏛 🚌

The RWA welcomes parents with young children and prams, although many of the exhibitions are of more interest to the older child. The exhibitions on the first floor change six times a year. Those on the ground floor change monthly. There are gallery tours and educational worksheets (suitable for 9+yrs). Keep an eye on their website for an exhibition that appeals to you.

# VISITOR CENTRES

## Ashton Court Visitor Centre

Stable Court Yard, Ashton Court Mansion, Long
Ashton, Bristol, BS41 9JN
0117 963 9174
www.bristol-city.gov.uk/ccm
Apr-Oct: Sat-Sun 10.30am-5.30pm, staffed some
weekdays during summer
Nov-Mar: Sun 11am-4pm

Gives the history of the estate and information
on how it is managed. Walking, nature trails
and orienteering maps available. They also
run holiday and half term events for children,
8-12yrs, such as mountain biking.

## Clifton Observatory and Caves

Clifton Down, Bristol
0117 924 1379
Mon-Fri: 11.30am-5pm summer only, Sat-Sun
10.30am-5pm occasionally closed due to adverse
weather, phone first
£1 adults, 50p children (£2 and £1 for both Obscura
and Caves)
Access from the Clifton side

The Observatory houses a Camera Obscura
installed in 1829. In fine weather a rotating
mirror in the roof reflects the panorama
outside. From the Observatory a steep
stepped passage through the rock leads to a
viewing platform which give splendid views of
the Bridge and Gorge. Buggies can be left at
the kiosk, which sells ice creams.

# THEATRES

## Bristol Old Vic

King Street, Bristol, BS1 4ED
0117 987 7877
www.bristol-old-vic.co.uk
From £4 child (£1.50 U5's sessions), concession and
seasonal family tickets available

Bristol Old Vic presents a varied and critically-
acclaimed theatre programme. Children's
shows often take place around school holidays
and U5's sessions take place most Friday
mornings. Telephone the box office or visit
the website for details of the current season's
productions.

**Back stage tours**
Fri & Sat at 11.30am

Take a tour of the oldest continually working
theatre in the country. Booking required

## Colston Hall

Colston Street, BS1 5AR
0117 922 3686
www.colstonhall.org, www.remix-music.org
boxoffice@colstonhall.org

Bristol's largest concert hall. The Colston Hall
Education Project organises workshops for
young people and family days (from classical
to reggae). It also attracts well-known
musicians who encourage enjoyment of and
interaction with music for youngsters. Colston
Hall is connected to REMIX, the Bristol Youth
Music Action Zone, which provides music-
making opportunities for U18's, from DJ
workshops to jazz sessions.

## Redgrave Theatre

Percival Rd, Clifton, Bristol, BS8 3LE
0117 3157 666
www.cliftoncollege.uk
For details of upcoming performances take a look at
the school's website or phone for details

A purpose-built school theatre attached to
Clifton College that stages productions by
school groups and local performing groups.

11

Seasonal shows for a younger audience and productions from Clifton upper school, prep school and pre-school. The Old Vic Theatre School also performs at the Redgrave.

## The Bristol Hippodrome

St Augustine's Parade, Bristol, BS1 4UZ
0117 3023333 (enquiries) 0870 6077500 (bookings)
www.getlive.co.uk/bristol

The Hippodrome is Bristol's west end theatre. Its large stage allows for spectacular productions. The theatre hosts regular children's productions particularly around Christmas and in the summer holidays. Efficient online booking service. Parking nearby at NCP car park.

## The Tobacco Factory

Raleigh Rd, Southville, Bristol, BS3 1TF
0117 902 0344
www.tobaccofactory.com
tickets@tobaccofactory.com

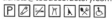

The Tobacco Factory strives to offer productions that are innovative and unusual. Not all performances are suitable for family viewing but they do stage critically acclaimed children's productions every year around Christmas time and children's shows around Easter, see website for details. Children welcome in the Green Room area of the café bar and in the theatre bar.

# CINEMAS

## Broadmead Odeon

Union Street, Bristol, BS1 2DS
0117 929 0884 Cinema office,
08712 244 007 Bookings
www.odeon.co.uk
Family Tickets £14 anytime (2+2 or 3+1)

Birthday parties can be held with drink & popcorn as part of the price. Phone for more detail. Buggies can be stored.

## Cineworld the Movies

Hengrove Leisure Park, Hengrove, Bristol, BS14 0LH
0871 220 8000
Kids Club Sat 10am
£1 child, free accompanying adult

Kids club includes half an hour of fun and games, then a choice of three films. Suitable for U11's, U11's must be supervised. Phone for details of parties.

## IMAX

Harbourside, Bristol, BS1 5DB
www.at-bristol.org.uk

Showing 2D, 3D and some feature films on a screen that is four storeys high.

## Orpheus Cinema

7 Northumbria Drive, Henleaze, Bristol, BS
017 962 3301 cinema office, 0845 1662381 film info

Particularly caters for families at the weekends with lots of child friendly films. Discount tickets on Mondays, £2.50 per person

## Showcase

Avon Meads, St Philips Causeway, Bristol, BS2 0SP
0117 972 3434
www.showcasecinemas.co.uk

## Vue

The Venue, Cribbs Causeway Leisure Complex, Merlin Rd, BS10 7SR
08712 240240
&
Aspect Leisure Park, Longwell Green, Bristol, BS15 9LA
08712 240240

Child booster seats available.

## Watershed

1 Canons Rd, Bristol, BS1 5TX
0117 927 5100
www.watershed.co.uk

See also Cinekids, special events for 8-12yr olds, see pg 112.

# FARMS

## Avon Valley Country Park

Pixash Lane, Bath Rd, Keynsham, BS31 1TS
0117 986 4929
www.avonvalleycountrypark.co.uk
Apr-Oct: Tue-Sun, B/H's 10am-6pm, daily in sch hols
£5 adult, £4 child, free U2's
Winter w/e's: play barn £3.50 per child
A4 towards Bath, follow brown signs

Farm trail leads through several fields of farm animals and rare breeds. Other attractions include bottle feeding the lambs in the spring, a land train, a miniature ride-on railway, large adventure playground, a barn accommodating soft play and impressive slides, quad bikes for any age (additional cost, U4's accompanied) and a duck pond with boats for hire. Lovely walk along the river. "Energy busting indoor play area — great on wet days."

## Hartcliffe Community Farm

Lampton Ave, Hartcliffe, Bristol, BS13 0QH
0117 978 2014
Daily 9.00am-4.30pm
Admission free (donations welcome)
Signposts from Bishport Ave

The main site is 35 acres of pasture with a collection of the usual farm animals. Kiddies Corner contains goats, rabbits and ducks. The farm now has its own aviary with budgies, canaries, cockatiels and peacocks.

## HorseWorld

Staunton Lane, Whitchurch, Bristol, BS14 0QJ
01275 540173
www.horseworld.org.uk
Easter to Oct & school holidays: daily 10am-5pm
Oct to Easter: Tues-Sun 10am-4pm
£5.75 adult, £4.75 child (under 3's free), £19.50 family ticket (2+2)
Access: Just off the A37

Horseworld is an equine welfare charity. Learn about the rescue, rehabilitation and re-homing work undertaken. Great opportunity for children to meet horses, donkeys and ponies. Museum with audio-visual presentation, nature trails, pony rides and pony and pet handling make for a good family day out.

## Lawrence Weston Community Farm

Saltmarsh Drive, Lawrence Weston, BS11 0ND
0117 938 1128
Tue-Sun 8.30am-5.30pm, winter 4.30pm
Admission free (donations welcome)

A city farm set in 6 acres of land, sheep, goats, pigs, chickens and rabbits. Some rare breeds. Events include Easter activities, and play schemes in the holidays for U11's. Also a bee-keeping club, educational projects and a volunteer programme. Refreshments available.

## St Werburgh's City Farm

Watercress Rd, St Werburgh's, Bristol, BS2 9YJ
0117 942 8241
Daily 9am-5pm (summer) 9am-4pm (winter)
Admission free (donations welcome)

This is a small community farm set among allotments. Animals include pigs, goats, rabbits, guinea pigs, ducks, geese, sheep and chickens and sometimes lambs and kids. The site includes a large pond and farm shop selling plants and organic produce. Teens (13-19yrs) can learn community farm skills by joining their environmental youth work programme. Other attractions are the adventure playground for U8's, café (closed Mon/Tues) and a children's homeopathic

13

clinic, see Healthcare. A community building next to the café can be hired out for kids birthday parties at £6 per hour.

## Windmill Hill City Farm

Philip Street, Bedminster, Bristol, BS3 4EA
0117 963 3252
www.windmillhillcityfarm.org.uk
Tue-Sun: 9am-dusk
Admission free (donations welcome)

Well laid out paved farmyard with animal enclosures. Wide paths lead to paddocks, a small nature reserve, gardens and allotments. The Play Centre is for 1-5's, with indoor and outdoor areas. Adventure playground for 5-11's. U8's must be accompanied by an adult. Holiday activities and events. Educational group visits to the farm can be arranged.

# LIBRARIES

Libraries are an excellent community resource for all ages, easy to join and free! The children's sections are often brightly decorated and welcoming, providing a fun and stimulating environment to encourage your child's love of books. As well as story books, there are children's non-fiction books, music and story tapes, CDs, DVDs, videos and jigsaw puzzles which may be borrowed or used in the library. Most libraries offer pre-school storytimes, sometimes followed by a craft activity. They are also a great source of information on local groups for children and parents. All libraries have wheelchair access, although some are trickier to negotiate than others.

See advertisement in Colour Reference Section, pg 136..

**Please note:**

• Bristol City libraries allow you to borrow and return books from different libraries.

• Library opening hours are subject to change, please check Bristol City Council's website for details www.bristol-city.gov.uk.

## Library Services for Children

Bristol's Children/Young People's Librarian Janet Randall 0117 903 8565
&
South Gloucestershire Children/Young People's Librarian Wendy Nicholls 01454 868451

## Avonmouth Library

Avonmouth Rd, Avonmouth, Bristol, BS11 9EN
0117 903 8580
Mon 2pm-5pm, Fri 2pm-6pm, Sat 9.30am-12.30pm

Storytime Fridays 2.15pm, term time only. Story tapes & puzzles available.

## Bedminster Library

4 St Peters Court, Bedminster Parade, BS3 4AQ
0117 903 8529
Mon/Fri/Sat 9.30am-5pm,Tue/Thu 9.30am-7.30pm

Storytime Fri 10.30am, term time only. Story tapes, videos & puzzles available. Internet access and computer facilities available. Please contact library for details of children's activities during school holidays. Car parking & toilets in Asda nearby.

## Bishopsworth Library

Bishopsworth Rd, Bishopsworth, Bristol, BS13 7LN
0117 903 8566
Mon 9.30am-1pm & 2pm-7pm Tue/Thu/Fri/Sat 9.30am-1pm & 2-5pm

Storytime Tue 2.15pm, term time only. Story/ music tapes, videos and puzzles.

## Bradley Stoke Library

Bradley Stoke Leisure Centre & Library, Fiddlers Wood Lane, Bradley Stoke, BS32 9BS
01454 865 723
Mon/Thu 10.30am-6pm, Tue/Fri 10.30am-8pm, Sat 9.30am-5pm, Sun 11am-3pm

Storytime Mon 11am with craft activity, term time only. Story/music tapes and videos. Toy box.

## Bristol Central Library

College Green, Bristol, BS1 5TL
0117 903 7215
Mon/Tue 9.30am-7.30pm, Wed 10am-5pm,
Thu 9.30am-1pm, Fri/Sat 9.30am-5pm,
Sun 1pm-5pm

Storytime Wed 2pm and Chatterbooks
(8-10yrs) monthly Sat am. Also Baby Bounce
and Rhyme Wed 10am. Story/music tapes,
videos, lots of board/picture books. A few
toys. The disabled entrance is to the right. An
excellent library for student research. PCs for
children with safe internet access.

## Bristol Mobile Library

C/o Outreach Services, Units 1&2, Bristol Vale
Trading Estate, Hartcliffe Way, Bedminster, BS3 5RJ
0117 903 8531

Branch library on wheels with good adult and
children's books and tapes. Runs fortnightly
service around Bristol (phone for stops).
Residential service for housebound in Bristol.

## Cadbury Heath Library

School Rd, Cadbury Heath, Bristol, BS30 8EN
01454 865 711
Mon/Thu 9.30am-7pm, Fri/Sat 9.30am-5pm

Storytime Fri 2.15pm, termtime only, with
story-related craft activity afterwards.
Chatterbooks Sat am, monthly. Story tapes
and puzzles.

## Cheltenham Rd Library

Cheltenham Rd, Cotham, Bristol, BS6 5QX
0117 903 8562
www.bristol-city.gov.uk
Mon/Wed/Fri 10am-1pm & 2pm-5pm,
Sat 10am-1pm & 2pm-4pm

Storytime Fri 2.15pm, term time only. Story
tapes and a few toys and puzzles to use in
library. Public toilets 150m away.

## Chipping Sodbury Library

High Street, Chipping Sodbury, BS37 6AH
01454 865 719
Tue/Fri 9.30am-5pm, Thurs 9am-1pm,
Sat 9.30am-12.30pm
Closes lunchtime 12.30pm-1.30pm

Story/music tapes and videos. Rhyme-Time
first Fri of every month 2.15pm.

## Clifton Library

Princess Victoria Street, Clifton, Bristol, BS8 4BX
0117 903 8572
Mon/Wed/Fri 10am-1pm & 2pm-5pm,
Sat 10am-1pm & 2pm-4pm

Storytime Mon 10.30am with colouring, term
time only. Tea, coffee and squash 30p. Story
tapes & puzzles. Playpen and toys.

## Downend Library

Buckingham Gardens, Downend, Bristol, BS16 5TW
01454 865 666
Mon/Thu 9.30am-7pm, Wed/Fri 9.30am-5pm,
Sat 9.30am-5pm

Storytime Fri 2.15pm, term time only, with
story related crafts. Rhyme-Time Wed
10.30am. Chatterbooks first Thu of every
month 5pm. Key available for public toilet.
Tapes and videos.

## Eastville Library

Muller Rd, Eastville, Bristol, BS5 6XP
0117 903 8578
Mon/Wed/Fri 10am-1pm & 2pm-5pm,
Sat 10am-1pm & 2pm-4pm

Storytime Mondays 2.15pm, term time only,
with craft activity. Tapes and puzzles.

## Emersons Green Library

Emersons Way, Emersons Green, BS16 7AP
01454 865680
Tue/Thu 10.30am-8pm, Fri 10.30am-6pm
Sat 9.30am-5pm

Storytime Tue 2.15pm, term time only. Also
teen group 2nd Tue of each month, 7.30pm
(term time only), and Rhyme-Time Thu 2pm.

## Filton Library

The Shield Retail Park, Link Rd, Filton, BS34 7BR
01454 865 670
Mon/Thu 9.30am-7pm, Tues/Fri/Sat 9.30am-5pm

Storytime Tue 2pm, term time only, with story related craft activity. Chatterbooks Sat 2.30pm monthly. Tapes, videos & computer games.

## Filwood Library

Filwood Broadway, Bristol, BS4 1JN
0117 966 1671
Mon/Tues/Wed/Fri 9.30am-1pm & 2pm-5pm,
Sat 9.30am-1pm

Storytime Mon 2.15pm, term time only, with colouring activity afterwards. Homework club Mon and Fri 3.45pm. Story/music tapes available. Puzzles to use in library.

## Fishponds Library

Fishponds Rd, Fishponds, Bristol, BS16 3UH
0117 9038560
Mon/Tue/Fri/Sat 9.30am-5pm, Thu 9.30am-7pm

Storytime Tue 2pm, term time only, with nursery rhymes, craft activity, drink & biscuit (50p), booking advisable. Coffee mornings Fri 9.30am-12pm. Story/music tapes, CDs and videos. Car parking and public toilets in Safeway opposite the library.

## Hanham Library

High Street, Hanham, Bristol, BS15 3EJ
01454 865 678
www.southglos.gov.uk
Mon/Fri/Sat 9.30am-5pm Tues/Thu 9.30-7pm

Storytime Thu 2.15pm with craft activity afterwards. Bounce and Rhyme monthly. Lots of story tapes and videos.

Do your kids love stories? Visit the Old Vic on Friday mornings for songs and shows, see pg 110.

## Hartcliffe Library

Peterson Square, Hartcliffe, Bristol, BS13 0EE
0117 903 8568
Mon/Thu/Fri 9.30am-1pm & 2pm-5pm,
Sat 9.30am-1pm

Storytime Fri 10am, in partnership with Play Days, with simple craft activities. Story and music tapes.

## Henbury Library

Crow Lane, Henbury, Bristol, BS10 7DR
0117 903 8522
Mon/Tue/Thu/Sat 9.30am-1pm & 2pm-5pm,
Fri 9.30am-1pm & 2pm-7pm

Storytime Tue 2.30pm, including school holidays. Tapes & videos available. Puzzles to borrow once you have donated one!

## Henleaze Library

Northumbria Drive, Henleaze, Bristol, BS9 4HP
0117 903 8541
Mon/Fri 9.30am-7pm, Tue/Thu 9.30am-5pm,
Sat 9.30am-5pm

Storytime Thu 10.45 with songs. Tapes,videos, games, DVDs & educational CD-Roms. Puzzles to use in library. Toilets are available at Waitrose across the road.

## Hillfields Library

Summerleaze, Hillfields, Bristol, BS16 4HL
0117 903 8576
Mon/Wed/Fri 10am-1pm & 2pm-5pm,
Sat 10pm-1pm & 2pm-4pm

Storytime Wed 10.15. A few story tapes and puzzles available.

## Horfield Library

Filton Avenue, Horfield, Bristol, BS7 0BD
0117 903 8538
Mon 9.30am-1pm & 2pm-7pm,
Tue/Thu/Sat 9.30am-1pm & 2pm-5pm

Storytime Tue 10.30am. Story tapes & videos available. Homework club Mon 3.45 pm, Fri 3.45pm.

## Kingswood Library

High Street, Kingswood, Bristol, BS15 4AR
01454 865 650
Mon/Tue 9.30am-5pm, Wed/Fri 9.30am-7pm,
Sat 9.30am-5pm

Storytime Tue 2.15-3pm with activity, term
time only. Tapes, videos, & CD-Roms.

## Knowle Library

Redcatch Rd, Knowle, Bristol, BS4 2EP
0117 903 8585

Storytime first Sat of each month 4pm. Story/
music tapes, videos, toys and puzzles.

## Lawrence Weston Library

Broadlands Drive, Lawrence Weston, BS11 0NT
0117 904 5696
Mon-Fri 9.30am-5pm, Sat 9.30am-1pm

Storytime Fri 9.30am. Story tapes, puzzles
and a few toys.

## Marksbury Road Library

Marksbury Rd, Bedminster, Bristol, BS3 5LG
0117 903 8574
Mon 10am-1pm & 2pm-7pm,
Wed/Fri 10am-1pm & 2pm-5pm, Sat 10am-1pm

Storytime for pre-schoolers Wed 10.45am,
term time only, in children's area with small
chairs & toys. Tapes & puzzles. After school
club every other Mon, booking necessary.

## Patchway Library

Rodway Rd, Patchway, Bristol, BS34 5PE
01454 865 674
Mon/Wed 9.30am-7pm, Fri/Sat 9.30am-5pm

Storytime Wed 2pm with story related craft
activity afterwards. Story tapes, videos,
music CDs, DVDs, computer games & puzzles
available. Phone for details of activities during
school holidays. Public toilets next door.

## Redland Library

Whiteladies Rd, Redland, Bristol, BS8 2PY
0117 903 8549
Mon/Tue/Fri/Sat 9.30am-5pm, Thu 9.30am-7pm,
Sun 1pm-4pm

Storytime Mon 2.30pm with related craft
activity. Videos available. Soft toys & puzzles
in library. Disabled access at side. Toilets at
Clifton Down Shopping Centre.

## Sea Mills Library

Sylvan Way, Sea Mills, Bristol, BS9 2NA
0117 903 8555
Mon/Thu/Sat 9am-1pm & 2-5pm,
Tue/Wed/Fri 9am-1pm

Storytime Thu 11.45am. Tapes, videos and
puzzles.

## Shirehampton Library

Station Rd, Shirehampton, Bristol, BS11 9TU
0117 903 8570
Mon/Wed/Fri 10am-1pm & 2pm-5pm,
Sat 10am-1pm & 2pm-4pm

Story/music tapes and puzzles.

## South Gloucester Mobile Library

C/o Yate Library, 44 West Walk, Yate, BS37 4AX
07881 813292

Wide range of adult and children's books and
videos. Story tapes, CDs and internet access.
Runs fortnightly service all around South
Gloucester, phone for stops.

## Southmead Library

Greystoke Ave, Southmead, Bristol, BS10 6AS
0117 903 8583
Mon/Wed/Fri 9.30am-1pm & 2pm-5pm,
Sat 9.30am-1pm

Storytime Mon 2.15pm. Story tapes and
puzzles to use in library. Wooden train that
children can sit in! Toilets and car park in Aldi.

## St George Library

Church Rd, St George, Bristol, BS5 8AL
0117 903 8523
Mon 9.30am-1pm & 2pm-7pm,
Tue/Wed/Fri/Sat: 9.30am-1pm & 2pm-5pm.

Storytime Tue 2.15pm including singing and craft activity (50p) term time only, booking necessary. Story tapes and videos.

## St Pauls Library

Grosvenor Rd, St Pauls, Bristol, BS2 8XJ
0117 9145489
Mon/Thu 1pm-7.30pm, Tue/Fri 10am-1pm, Wed 1pm-5pm, Sat 10am-12pm & 1pm-5pm

Storytime Tue 11am. DVDs and story tapes for children and adults, and internet with high security access for children to surf safely.

## Staple Hill Library

The Square, Broad St, Staple Hill, BS16 5LR
01454 865 715
www.southglos.gov.uk/libraries
Tues/ Fri 9.30am-7pm, Thu/Sat 9.30am-5pm

Storytime Fri 11am with story related craft activity, term time only. Good selection of story tapes. Small collection of DVDs and videos for hire. Activities for older children during school holidays. Disabled toilet.

## Stockwood Library

Stockwood Rd, Bristol, BS14 8PL
0117 903 8546
Mon/Thu/Fri/Sat 9.30am-1pm & 2pm-5pm,
Tue 9.30am-1pm & 2pm-7pm

Storytime Fri 9.30am term time only. Large colourful children's area. Story/music tapes, videos & puzzles.

## Thornbury Library

St. Mary Street, Thornbury, South Glos, BS35 2AA
01454 865 657
Mon/Tue 9.30am-5pm, Wed/Fri 9.30am-7pm,
Sat 9.30am-5pm

Storytime Mon 2.15pm with rhymes, singing and craft activity. Story tapes, videos, DVDs and free internet access. Phone for details of holiday activities. Toilets opposite Safeway.

## Trinity Road Library

Trinity Rd, St Philips, Bristol, BS2 0NW
0117 9038543
Mon/Wed/Fri 10am-1pm & 2pm-5.30pm,
Sat 10am-1pm & 2pm-5pm.

Storytime Fri 10.30am, term time only. Collection of story tapes, puzzles, picture books and videos. Wide range of childrens' and adult books, including many in Asian languages. Refurbished children's area with new stock of picture books and videos.

## Westbury-on-Trym Library

Falcondale Rd, Westbury-on-Trym, Bristol, BS9 3JZ
0117 903 8552
Mon/Tue/Wed/Sat 9.30am-5pm, Fri 9.30am-7pm

Storytime Mon 2.15pm with activity, term time only. Story tapes, videos & puzzles.

## Wick Road Library

Wick Rd, Brislington, Bristol, BS4 4HE
0117 903 8557
Mon 9.30am-1pm & 2pm-7pm,
Tue/Wed/Fri/Sat 9.30am-1pm & 2pm-5pm

Storytime Fri 9.30am with craft activity (20p), term time only. After school club Mon 4.45pm for 6-9yrs. Tapes, videos and puzzles.

## Winterbourne Library

Flax Pits Lane, Winterbourne, South Glos BS36 1LA
01454 865 654
Tue/Fri 9.30am-7pm, Wed/Sat 9.30am-5pm

Storytime Wed 2.15pm with craft activity, term time only. Story and music tapes.

## Yate Library

44 West Walk, Yate, BS37 4AX
01454 865 661
www.southglos.gov.uk/libs.htm
Mon/Tue/Thu/Fri 9.30am-7pm, Sat 9.30am-5pm,
Sun 11am-3pm

P 🖊 🔾 🔾

Storytime Tue 2.15pm with colouring and craft, term time only. Chatterbooks reading club every 4th Sat, 2pm. Wide selection of story tapes, videos and DVDs.

# TOY LIBRARIES

For a small fee, you can borrow toys from toy libraries, often with the opportunity to meet other parents and carers. These libraries often share facilities with other groups, so opening times may vary. Toys are generally suitable for children up to 6yrs. For children with special needs, there are toy libraries run by social services and voluntary organisations. Contact the National Association of Toy Libraries for more information and venues.

**National Association of Toy Libraries**
0207 2554600
www.natil.org.uk

## Downend Toy Library

Mangotsfield United Reform Church, Cossham St
0117 985 9929
Fri 9.30am-11.30am

P WC 🔾 Pp

This toy library is also a weekly toddler group, and is open to anyone from Downend, Kingswood, Warmley, Staple Hill and Mangotsfield. For £1.50 you can borrow 4 toys. Range available for 0-6yrs including a play kitchen, ride-on toys and videos.

## Freshways Toy Library

Lawrence Weston Resource Centre, Knovill Close,
Lawrence Weston, BS11 0SA
0117 923 5353
Mon-Fri 10.30am-4pm

WC 🔾

Lifetime membership costs £1 and toy hire is

then 25p per toy for a fortnight. This is a large library with toys for 0-5yrs and games for older children and those with special needs.

## Footprints Children's Centre

Daventry Rd, Knowle, Bristol, BS4 1QD
0117 903 9781
Fri 9.30am-12pm
£1 refundable deposit per item, £5 membership fee

Toy library service available for members of Children's Centre and also local childminders and early years practitioners. A variety of outdoor play items, games, dressing up clothes and puppets. Maximum of three items can be borrowed for a 2 week period.

## Play Days Toy Library

Hartcliffe Methodist Church Hall, Mowcroft Rd,
Hartcliffe, BS13 0LT
0117 902 0265
Mon: 12.30pm-2.30pm

WC 🖊 🔾 🔾 🔾 🔾 🔾

This toy library runs in conjunction with a parent and toddler group. No membership fee is charged, and toys cost 10p-20p to hire once you have been visiting the group for 6 weeks. Play sessions with simple crafts, soft play and action songs.

# PARKS AND PLAY AREAS

## Bristol City Council Parks, Estates and Sport

Department of Culture and Leisure Services, Colston House, Colston St, BS1 5AQ
0117 922 3719
www.bristol-city.gov.uk/parks

Call the above number for information about your nearest park or play area.

## Park events

The parks service runs a programme of events and activities, many taking place during the school holidays. See their news and events guide produced twice a year called Park Life. It can be obtained in local libraries, the museums or by phoning the above number. Also take a look at the website. Examples of activities for younger children include: play days, craft days and teddy bear's picnics. For older children, there are wildlife discovery events, deer feed rambles and sports activities. If you would like to organise your own community event in one of Bristol's 200 parks, call the Events Team: 0117 922 3808.

## Blaise Castle Estate BS10

0117 3532266
Entrance and car park off the B4057 Kingsweston Rd

You will find the largest play area in North Bristol at Blaise. It attracts children of all ages from all over the city. There is a play area for toddlers and one for older children. Parents/carers must accompany their children. There is a café which has toilets. The spacious grass areas are great for picnics and ball games, while recently resurfaced drives offer the opportunity to explore woodlands and water features. The Castle Folly is open on most summer Sunday afternoons. Also take a look in the museum near the play area.

## Brandon Hill BS8

Entrances on Great George St (off Park St), Jacobs Wells Rd, Upper Byron Place and Queens Parade

Climb Cabot Tower's many steps and see superb views across the city. The opening times vary, normally 8am until half an hour before dusk. From the tower, there is a network of pathways and steps with waterfalls, ponds and trees. Toilets are on the middle terrace. Fenced in play area with toddler swings, sand pit and climbing structure for older children.

## Canford Park BS10

Entrance on Canford Lane, Westbury-on-Trym.

This is an attractive well-kept park, with a fenced play area providing a good variety of play equipment. The park itself has a large, flat lawn, excellent for ball games and picnics. There is also a sunken rose garden with a pond. The circular path around the park perimeter is popular for learning to cycle and skate. Tennis courts for hire by the hour.

## Clifton Down BS8

Off the Suspension Bridge Rd

This is an unfenced play area with a good mixture of assault course style wooden climbing equipment including slides, swings as well as natural rock faces — great for budding mountaineers. Toilets are on Bridge Road. Close to the Observatory and bridge.

## Cotham Gardens BS6

Entrance on Redland Grove, Nr Redland train station

A small friendly park. Spacious fenced play area with large sand pit, swings and climbing apparatus. Also a grassed area for ball games and picnics. Great views of the trains passing on the railway line alongside.

## The Downs BS8

Park anywhere along Ladies Mile

The Downs are made up of Clifton Down and Durdham Down. They are Bristol's most famous open space with grassland and some wooded areas. They are very popular with footballers, joggers, kite flyers and dog walkers. The Circular Road offers dramatic views of the Gorge and the Suspension Bridge. Toilets can be found near the viewpoint on the Sea Walls and at the Water Tower/The Downs Tea Room (see pg 70).The Downs usually hosts annual events such as the Children's Festival, circuses and a superb fireworks display in November.

**Avon Gorge & Downs Wildlife Project**
c/o Education Department, Bristol Zoo Gardens, Bristol, BS8 3HA
0117 903 0609
www.bristolzoo.org.uk/conservation/avongorge

Set up in partnership with several groups to protect the wildlife and nature of the Avon Gorge and Downs. They run holiday activities, parent & toddler story telling picnics, wildlife trails and the popular Gorgeous Wildlife Family Fun Day, held each summer. For further information, pick up leaflets from the Downs Tea Rooms or at the Zoo.

## Easton Play Park BS5

Main entrance on Chelsea Rd next to The Mission

This exciting and imaginative playground is really worth a visit. It is compact without being overcrowded, which makes it relatively easy to keep an eye on the children. There are climbing frames, slides, swings and a marvellous seesaw suitable for all ages. There is also an all-weather 5-a-side football pitch and a small area for picnics. The Bristol-Bath cycle path runs alongside.

## Eastville Park BS16

Alongside Fishponds Rd(A432) & adjacent to M32 J2

A large area of grassland ideal for running about. There are two play areas, one of which is fenced and has a sandpit. Take a walk down to the lake, or walk through the woodland and along the river towards Oldbury Court.

Don't let the wet weather stop you going outside. See Raindrops outdoor clothing on pg 266.

## Hengrove Play Park BS14

01275 836946
Entrance off Hengrove Way

Next door to the leisure park on the site of the old Whitchurch airfield. It features the innovative play dome, a 12 metre high domed frame with enclosing chutes and walkways. There is a skateboard/BMX zone, an area for sand and water play for younger children. There is plenty of open space plus seating, a café and toilets. Staffed during the day.

## Monks Park BS7

Entrances off Lyddington Rd, Kenmore Crescent and Biddestone Rd.

Built on the former Monks Park School playing fields. There are two equipped play areas catering for children of different ages, and plenty of green open space.

## Oldbury Court Estate & Snuff Mills BS16

Entrances at Oldbury Court Rd and Riverview (cul-de-sac off Broom Hill)

Both entrances have car parks. This is a large park that extends from Snuff Mills to Frenchay, with the River Frome in its grounds. There is a large, well equipped, fenced off play area near the Oldbury Court Road entrance. Equipment includes a 9.6m high tower unit with tubular slides, several sand play areas, swings, long slides, trains, castles, a crows nest and lots more. There are pleasant walks by the river and woodland to explore. Toilets and a small café are situated by the Broom Hill entrance. There are also toilets next to the play area.

## Redcatch Park BS4

Main entrance on Redcatch Rd and Broadwalk

A pleasant, quiet park with a fenced play area. The park offers plenty of green space and also has tennis courts on-site which can be hired by the hour in season.

## Redland Green BS6

Entrances on Redland Green Rd and Cossins Rd

Lovely green with a fenced play area. There are swings and a whirligig for older children and a low-level climbing structure set over a large sandpit, which is particularly suited to toddlers but enjoyed by all.

## Shirehampton Park BS11

Entrance off Shirehampton Rd

Open parkland and wooded areas with walks to Penpole Wood and Kingsweston Down. Good views of both Severn Bridge crossings and of Kings Weston House. There are good connecting paths to Blaise Castle.

## St Andrews Park BS6

Entrances on Effingham Rd, Leopold Rd, Maurice Rd, Somerville Rd and Melita Rd

The play area has good play equipment and an area of grass for ball games or picnics. The park also boasts Bristol's only functioning paddling pool. During hot weather the attraction of the pool makes the park extremely crowded. It hosts Music in the Park in June, a fun family afternoon.

## St George Park BS5

Entrances on Church Rd (A420), Park Crescent and Park View, with a car park off Chalks Rd

A large popular Victorian park with plenty of open space, as well as a lake with ducks and swans. There is a fenced play area with a variety of equipment, and a Wheel Park for skateboarding, roller-skating and BMX biking.

## Victoria Park BS3

Entrances from Fraser St, Somerset Terrace, Nutgrove Avenue, Hill Ave, St. Luke's Rd and Windmill Close

Plenty of open space with views over Bristol from the top of the hill. Small fenced playground with equipment for very small children set on a safety surface. There is a basketball backboard for older children, and a planned multi-sport facility off St Luke's Rd. The water maze is fun so bring your wellies! There are toilets next to Somerset Terrace.

# WALKS

There are some great walks all over the city. Below are a few of our favourites. However, if you are looking to discover new places check out the websites of the organisations below or your local book shop for family walking guide books. For walks further afield, see Walks in our chapter Out & About in the West Country.

### Forest of Avon

Ashton Court Visitor Centre, Bristol, BS41 9JN
0117 953 2141
www.forestofavon.org.uk

This is an excellent website giving an extensive guide to local woodlands within the Forest of Avon.

### Avon Wildlife Trust

32 Jacobs Well Rd, Bristol, BS8 1DR
0117 917 7270
www.avonwildlifetrust.org.uk

This charity is dedicated to protecting wildlife. It has two centres, one at Folly Farm, Chew Valley and one at Willsbridge Mill, Keynsham. They offer activities and walks for families.

## Ashton Court Estate

Long Ashton, BS41 9JN
0117 9639174
2 entrances off the A369, one at Kennel Lodge Rd and one at Clifton Lodge (opp. Bridge Rd). Third entrance off A370 at Church Lodge (opp. Long Ashton)

[P] [WC] [⅄] [⅄]

Ashton Court Estate is a huge heritage estate with woodland, grassland and meadowland to explore. There are many tracks that are suitable for toddlers or for walking with a backpack, and some suitable for buggies. For more information visit the Ashton Court Visitor Centre, in the Stable Court Yard of Ashton Court Mansion.

The deer herd is popular with children and the deer keeper runs regular deer feeding rambles, phone for details. Take a ride on the miniature railway (see Transport chapter) or have a game of golf on one of the two pitch-and-putt courses. A small café and toilets are available at the golf kiosk. Many large events such as the Bristol International Balloon

Fiesta, International Kite Festival and Bristol Community Festival take place on the estate, see Annual Events and Festivals.

## Blaise Castle Estate

Henbury Rd, Henbury, Bristol, BS10 7QS

See Parks and Play Areas section above. Park at Blaise Castle Estate car park on Kings Weston Road. Pleasant wooded walks through the grounds, leading up to the castle folly and beyond into Coombe Dingle. Can be muddy and since it is popular with dog walkers, watch your step!

## Eastville Park

Opposite the Royate Hill Turn off on the A432, Fishponds Rd

Once in the park, descend the hill to the lake, then turn right and continue along the banks of the Frome for 1½ miles to Snuff Mills. This walk is suitable for pushchairs but parts of it can be muddy. See also Oldbury Court Estate in Parks and Play areas above.

## Floating Harbour Walk

This walk can be combined with a ferry trip, see The Dockside section above. It is possible to walk a complete circuit around the Floating Harbour (west of Prince Street Bridge), taking in the ss Great Britain, Industrial Museum, Arnolfini, Watershed, At-Bristol, Lloyds TSB building and the skateboarders! This walk is flat, so great for pushchairs and cyclists but watch the harbour edge with toddlers. A good place to start from is the car park at the ss Great Britain. The Floating Harbour extends beyond Prince Street Bridge, along Welsh Back towards Temple Meads.

## Kings Weston Wood & House

Kings Weston Lane, Shirehampton, BS11 0UR
0117 938 2299
www.kingswestonhouse.co.uk
7 mins walk to house from the car park opposite Shirehampton Golf Course

Paths through the woods lead to the grotto and to Kings Weston House, a Palladian mansion built in 1710. Pleasant grounds for picnics and paths are suitable for pushchairs. It has a tea room open Mon-Fri: 9am-5.30pm, Sat-Sun and bank holidays 10am-4pm.

## Leigh Woods

The National Trust, Valley Rd, Leigh Woods, BS8 3PZ
0117 9731645
leighwoods@nationaltrust.org.uk
Open all year round
From Clifton take A369 towards Portishead, after the traffic lights there is a large old archway on the right, take right turn almost immediately after this, car park ½km on the left

The Purple Trail which begins and ends at the car park is a fully accessible 2½ km circular route, hard-surfaced, mostly level and suitable for pushchairs and wheelchairs. There are also other hard-surfaced paths leading from the Purple Trail which are marked on the board in the car park and on a free leaflet available from the Reserve Office on Valley Road. However, not all are waymarked on the ground like the Purple Trail. Don't miss the bluebells in April and May.

## Willsbridge Mill

Avon Wildlife Trust, Willsbridge Hill, Bristol, BS30 6EX
0117 932 6885
www.avonwildlifetrust.org.uk
Nature Reserve open all year, mill seasonal
Free admission
A431 Bristol to Bath road, turn into Long Beach Road, car park on left

This converted mill housing hands-on wildlife and conservation displays is currently only open when schools are visiting, but there is plenty to do outside. The Valley Nature Reserve which includes a Heritage Sculpture Trail, a Wild Waste Garden and plenty of lovely sculptural seating areas for picnics is open all year. Pond dipping equipment available for hire. All paths pushchair friendly.

**Rainy day?**
There are eight indoor soft play venues in Bristol, see Activities pg 106

## ANNUAL EVENTS & FESTIVALS

There are a huge number of annual events across the West, many of which are free. For more information, check the local press or go to these websites: www.titchhikers.co.uk or www.visitbristol.co.uk.

## MAY

**Bath International Music Festival**
www.bathmusicfest.org.uk

## JUNE

**Bristol Harbour Fun Run**
www.thisisbristol.co.uk
For all ages, in aid of British Heart Foundation.

**Bristol's Biggest Bike Ride**
www.bristol-city.gov.uk/bristolbikeride
Fun, traffic-free cycling on Durdham Downs.

**Bristol Bike Fest**
www.bristolbikefest.com
Mountain bike event at Ashton Court Estate.

**Bristol Festival of Nature**
www.thisisbristol.co.uk
Films, animal encounters, walks and more.

**Bristol Motor and Classic Car Show**
www.thisisbristol.co.uk

**Cheltenham Festival of Science**
www.cheltenhamfestivals.co.uk
Fun event for budding scientists.

**Glastonbury Festival**
www.glastonburyfestivals.co.uk
The biggest and best and it's on our doorstep!

**Westonbirt Festival of Gardens**
www.forestry.gov.uk/westonbirt

**Royal Bath & West Show**
www.bathandwest.co.uk
Animal action at Shepton Mallet Showground.

## JULY

**St Paul's Carnival**
www.netgates.co.uk
Spectacular carnival, music and great food.

**Truckfest**
www.truckfest.co.uk
Trucking heaven at Shepton Mallet.

**Ashton Court Festival**
www.ashtoncourtfestival.com
The best music, theatre and arts from Bristol.

## AUGUST

**Bristol Children's Festival**
www.childrensworldcharity.org
Fun activities for under 12's at Bristol Downs.

**Bristol Harbour Festival**
www.bristol-city.gov.uk/harbourfestival
The city's most spectacular waterside event.

**Bristol International Balloon Fiesta**
www.bristolfiesta.co.uk
150 hot air balloons go up at 6am and 6pm.

## SEPTEMBER

**Bristol International Kite Festival**
www.kite-festival.org
Colourful kites at Ashton Court Estate.

**Bristol Half Marathon**
www.bristolhalfmarathon.co.uk

**Doors Open Day**
www.bristoldoorsopenday.org
Peek inside Bristol's most interesting buildings.

**Organic Food Festival**
www.organicfoodfairs.co.uk
Harbourside event with tempting treats!

## NOVEMBER

**Encounters**
www.encounters-festival.org.uk
Short film festival including animation.

**Firework Fiesta**
www.visitbristol.co.uk
Bonfire and fireworks at Bristol Downs.

**Somerset Carnivals**
www.somersetcarnivals.co.uk
Impressive illuminated processions

# OUT & ABOUT IN THE WEST COUNTRY

**Nicola O'Brien**

## CONTENTS

# INTRODUCTION

Bristol is incredibly well-placed for families that like to get out at the weekends. Whether you like messing about on beaches, getting on your bikes or exploring museums, there is a wide choice of places to visit within an hour's drive of the city. No matter what your kids are into or how old they are, there is something for everyone and many attractions are free.

The entries in the first part of the chapter are places of interest, listed by location, starting at Portishead, moving down the coast to Burnham, and then anticlockwise past Bath, up through Gloucestershire and ending up in Cardiff. The rest of the chapter lists attractions by type, such as castles, farms, Roman Britain and so on. Once you've picked your destination, don't forget to cross-reference chapters such as Eating Out to find a good spot for lunch or check out Farmers' Shops and Markets for other excursion ideas.

# PORTISHEAD

Drive 20 minutes from Bristol's city centre and you'll discover a peaceful escape with something for all ages. There is a new marina with working lock; the lake grounds are right on the coast, although you cannot swim from the beach (it's mud!), however there's a wonderful open air pool, see below, and an excellent leisure centre, see Colour Reference Section.

## Lake Grounds

Portishead
Follow brown signs from town centre

WC | 🧍 | 🧍 | ✂

Spacious seafront park with boating lake, playground, seasonal bouncy castle and donkey rides.

## Portishead Open Air Pool

Esplanade Rd, Portishead, BS20 7HD
01275 843454
May-Sep

Heated open air swimming pool with separate toddler pool. Indoor changing rooms, showers and sunbathing terraces. U8's must be accompanied by an adult. 1:1 ratio for U5's. See Colour Reference Section.

# CLEVEDON

This Victorian seaside town has a seafront promenade ideal for walks with toddlers and pushchairs. With older children, the rocky foreshore is good for fossil hunting! At the opposite end of the promenade to the pier is Salt House Fields where there are separate enclosed play areas for toddlers and older children. In season, there is also a bouncy castle, miniature railway, crazy golf and snack bar. There are various coastal walks around the area, see Walks and Days Outside pg 60.

## Clevedon Tourist Information Centre

Clevedon Library, 37 Old Church Road, BS21 6NN
01275 873498
www.somersetcoast.com
Mon/Thu/Sat 9.30am-5pm, Tue/Fri 9.30am-7pm, Wed/Sun closed

## Clevedon Craft Centre

Moor Lane, off Court Lane, Clevedon, BS21 6TD
01275 872 149
Daily 10am-5pm, but most workshops closed on Mon
Admission free
M5 J20, follow brown signs, Court Lane is off B3130 (Tickenham Rd).

P | WC | 🧍 | 🧍 | 🏛

Craft studios demonstrating a variety of skills. Jewellery, pottery, illustrations, hand-carved leather goods and stained glass are just some of the items made and sold here. There is a pond where children can feed the ducks and chickens. Refreshments are available in one of the studios.

## Clevedon Heritage Centre

4 The Beach, Clevedon, BS21 7QU
01275 341 196
Daily 10.30am-4.30pm, seasonal variations
Admission Free

Photographic history of Clevedon.

## Clevedon Pier

The Toll House, Clevedon Pier, Clevedon, BS21 7QU
01275 878 846
Mon-Wed 10am-6pm, Thu-Sun 9am-6pm
£1 adult, 50p child, free U3's

Grade 1 listed pier, a fine example of Victorian architecture. Summer sailings to islands, phone for timetable, see Transport chapter.

# WESTON-SUPER-MARE

Seaside town, offering a vast expanse of safe, flat, sandy beach. If you want to paddle, the tide is always in at Marine Lake at the North end of the seafront; rock pooling at Anchor Head. Seasonal seafront land train, bouncy castles, crazy golf, miniature railway, putting green and a horse drawn Thomas the Tank engine. If it rains, check out the pier, the Helicopter Museum, the model train layout in Model Masters and soft play places for toddlers, see also Shopping pg 265.

### Weston-super-Mare Tourist Information

Beach Lawns, Weston-super-Mare, BS23 1AT
01934 888 800
www.somersetcoast.com
touristinfo@n-somerset.gov.uk
Daily exc Sundays in winter

## North Somerset Museum

Burlington St, Weston-super-Mare BS23 1PR
01934 621 028
www.n-somerset.gov.uk/museum
Mon-Sat 10am-4.30pm
£3.75 adult, accompanied children free

Child-friendly displays, Victorian dressing up clothes, interactive computers, passport trail, U5's activity corner and holiday events.

## Seaquarium

Marine Parade, Weston-super-Mare, BS23 1BE
01934 613361
www.seaquariumweston.co.uk
Daily 10am-4pm
£5.50 adult, £4.50 child, £18 family (2+2), free U4's
Reduction of £1 on presentation of this book.

Built on its own pier, the aquarium has a wide variety of marine life and an underwater walk through a tunnel. Opportunities to handle the creatures.

## The Grand Pier

Marine Parade, Weston-super-Mare BS23 1AL
01934 620 238
www.grandpierwsm.co.uk
Feb-Nov: daily 10am-dusk
At north end of seafront

Covered amusement park over the sea, including bowling, dodgems, haunted house, ride simulators and fairground rides. Large soft play area upstairs.

## Wacky Warehouse/The Bucket and Spade Pub

Yew Tree Drive, Weston-super-Mare, BS22 8PD
01934 521 235
Daily 11.30am-10pm, £2/hour
Mon-Fri 9.30am-11.30am toddler sessions £2.50
Situated on the A370 dual carriageway into Weston.

Three levels of soft play, with swings, tunnels, slides and ball pools designed for U12's (145cm). Separate play area for U5's. The Bucket and Spade pub next door serves a wide range of meals.

# BERROW & BREAN

Berrow has a sandy beach and sand dunes which can be reached from the nature reserve (parking free). Brean's beach car park is inexpensive. At the North end, a steep climb will take you to Brean Down, a rocky National Trust headland with great views.

## Animal Farm Country Park

Red Road, Berrow, Nr Burnham-on-Sea, TA8 2RW
01278 751 628
www.animal-farm.co.uk
Daily 10am-5.30pm, closes 4.30pm in winter
£5.50 adults & child, free U2's, bag of animal feed with presentation of this book
Annual: £19.50

Large variety of animals, including rare breeds, set in 25 acres of countryside. Opportunities to cuddle and feed the animals. Huge indoor and outdoor play areas with toddler zones. Treasure hunts in the holidays.

## Brean Down Tropical Bird Garden

Brean Down, Brean, Somerset, TA8 2RS
01278 751 209
www.burnham-on-sea.co.uk/brean_bird_garden
Mar-Oct: daily 10am-4pm
Nov-Mar: Sat-Sun 10am-4pm
Phone for school holiday openings
£1.95 adult, 95p child

Located at the foot of Brean Down. Largest selection of tropical parrots in the West!

## Brean Leisure Park

Coast Road, Brean, Somerset, TA8 2QY
01278 751 595
www.brean.com
Mar-Oct, phone for details,
May-Sep outdoor pool
Pool complex £3/session, U3's free,
£17.99 wrist band for unlimited rides

Fun park with over 40 rides and attractions including go-karts, laserquest and rollercoasters. Indoor and outdoor pools with water shutes (U5's must be accompanied). One child per adult. Attraction has more appeal to older children.

# BURNHAM-ON-SEA

Seven miles of sandy beach stretches from Burnham to Brean. Sandcastles, walking, kite flying, picnics and seasonal donkey rides. Swimming restrictions due to hazardous tides. Esplanade, pier and amusement arcade.

### Burnham-on-Sea Tourist Information

South Esplanade, Burnham-on-Sea, TA8 1BU
01278 787 852
www.somersetbythesea.co.uk
Mon-Sat 9.30am-4.30pm (closed 1-2pm), open Sundays in summer

### Apex Leisure and Wildlife Park

Marine Drive, Burnham-on-Sea
Sedgemoor Parks Dept: 01278 435435

42-acre park, walks, ducks, skate park, BMX biking (members only) and a play area.

### Play Centre

Pier Street, Burnham-on-Sea, Somerset, TA8 1BT
01278 784 693
Daily 10am-4pm (closed Mon/Tue during term time)
Child £2.50, U4's £2.10

Small indoor play area for 1-8yrs. Party packages available including electric car racing on a 70ft track. See Parties pg 127.

# STREET

Clarks Village is a great day out for shopaholics with an eye for a bargain. And there's fun stuff for the rest of the family too! See Shopping chapter.

## Greenbank Outdoor Pool

Wilfrid Road, Street, Somerset, BA16 0EU
01458 442468
www.greenbankpool.co.uk
May-mid Sept: Mon-Fri 12am-6.45pm term time
Sat-Sun 10am-6.45pm, summer hols 10am-6pm
£4 adult, £3 child, U2's free. Ring or see website for details of season tickets

This pleasant heated outdoor pool surrounded by grass is less than 5 minutes walk from Clark's Village. There's a separate children's area, a new Wet Play Area and refreshments.

## The Shoe Museum

40 High Street, Street, BA16 0YA
01458 842169
Mon-Fri 10am-4.45pm, Sat 10am-5pm
Sun 11am-5pm
Admission free

Traces the history of shoes and shoe making from Roman times to today. Many exhibits are on the first floor — lift only on weekdays.

# BATH

Bath is a beautiful and compact city with lots to do for families. It only takes 15 minutes on the train from Temple Meads to Bath Spa. If driving, there are Park & Rides at Newbridge (A4) and Lansdown (A46) or the Charlotte Street car park in the centre is convenient if coming in from the A4. You could also cycle on the Bristol to Bath cycleway! See also the Eating Out and Shopping chapters which have lots of listings in the Bath area.

## Bath Tourist Information Centre

Abbey Chambers, Abbey Church Yard, BA1 1LY
0906 711 2000 (50p/minute)
www.visitbath.co.uk
Mon-Sat 9.30am-6pm, Sun 10am-4pm

## Bath Open Top Bus Tour

Bath Bus Company Ltd, 1 Pierrepont Street, BA1 1LB
01225 330444
www.bathbuscompany.com or
www.citysightseeing.co.uk for online sales
Daily 10am-5pm, reduced service in winter
£9.50 adult, £6 child (6-12), free U6's,
family discount available

Tickets for this 45-min trip are are valid for two days and can be bought on the bus, at the tourist office, online or from the train station. Tours start on High St, Grand Parade. Free kids passport, tips, puzzles and games.

## Roman Baths and Pump Room

Pump Room, Stall Street, Bath, BA1 1LZ
01225 477 785
www.romanbaths.co.uk
Daily 9am-5pm, seasonal variations
£10 adult, £6 child, U6's free, £28 family (2+4)
Combined tickets to costume museum and Roman Baths are good value and valid for 7 days

One of the best preserved Roman sites in Northern Europe, this spa is a fine example of ancient engineering. The spring produces over a million litres of hot water a day. Taste it for yourself! Special events during school holidays. Unsuitable for pushchairs but back packs available.

## The Museum of Costume

Assembly Rooms, Bennett Street, Bath, BA1 2QH
01225 477789
www.museumofcostume.co.uk
Daily 11am-6pm, winter 5pm
£6.50 adult, £4.50 child, £18 family (2+4), U5's free
Combined tickets to museum and Roman Baths are good value and valid for 7 days

Clothing from the late 16th century to today, with interactive exhibitions, audio guide and activity trolley. Child carriers for babies/ toddlers available. Children's activities during the school holidays.

## Royal Victoria Park

Upper Bristol Rd, Bath
01225 477010
Take A4 into Bath, about a mile before city centre

Families tend to visit this park for its massive well-equipped playground for all ages, including skateboarders. There are also beautiful botanical gardens and a duck pond.

## Theatre Royal

Sawclose, Bath, BA1 1ET
01225 448844
www.theatreroyal.org.uk

One of the oldest working theatres in the country. An impressive range of kid's shows and workshops in half terms and holidays.

## Victoria Art Gallery

Pulteney Bridge, Bath, BA2 4AT
01225 477233
www.victoriagal.org.uk
Tue-Sat 10am-5pm, Sun 2pm-5pm, some B/H's
Free admission

An excellent audio guide and an art trolley for children in the gallery displaying the permanent collection. Two other galleries have changing exhibitions.

## Bath Postal Museum

8 Broad Street, Bath, BA1 5LJ
01225 460333
www.bathpostalmuseum.org
Mon-Sat 11am-5pm, winter 4.30pm
£2.90 adult, £1.50 child, £6.90 family, free U5's

The only museum in the country telling the story of the Postal Service. Children can have fun in a reconstructed 1930s post office weighing items, stamping forms and sorting letters. Educational videos, discovery trails, jigsaws, typewriters and computer games. The museum is moving in summer 2006, check website for updates.

## Museum of East Asian Art

12 Bennett Street, Bath, BA1 2QJ
01225 464640
www.meaa.org.uk
Tue-Sat 10am-5pm, Sun & B/H's 12pm-5pm
£4 adult, £1.50 child U12's, free U6's, £9 family
Opposite the Assembly Rooms

This museum is situated in a restored Georgian house and houses a fine collection of ceramics, jades, bronzes and other artifacts from China, Japan, Korea and Southeast Asia. They welcome young visitors of all ages. For the very young there are movable footstools, magnifying glasses and dressing up boxes. There is a family learning area and an activity trolley with Origami, word searches and colouring sheets. The Museum offers an education and handling service to schools as well as private children's parties.

## Bath Boating Station

Forester Rd, Bathwick, Bath, BA2 6QE
01225 312 900
Apr-Oct: daily 10am-6pm
£6 adult, £3 child, free U5's
Follow A36 through Bath. Just after big roundabout at Sydney Gardens, Forester Rd is 1st on left

A couple of miles NE of the centre you'll find this Victorian boating station with rowing boats and punts for hire. They also operate boat trips to Bathampton taking about 1 hour.

## American Museum

Claverton Manor, Bath, BA2 7BD
01225 460 503
www.americanmuseum.org
Museum: Mar-Oct Tue-Sun 12pm-5pm, some B/H's
Gardens & exhibitions 12pm-5pm
Dec: Tue-Sun 1pm-4pm, Wed 5.30pm-7.30pm
£6.50 adult, £3.50 child (all areas)
£4 adult, £2.50 child (gardens and galleries)
Take A36 Warminster road out of Bath, follow signs

Displays of American decorative art spanning 17th to 19th Century. Authentically furnished rooms showing the American way of life from colonial times to the eve of the Civil War. No prams in the house. Beautiful terraced gardens, lovely for children to run around in but not very suitable for buggies. Museum re-opens for a few weeks during Nov/Dec with the rooms decorated according to the period they represent for Christmas. Seasonal exhibitions often have child-friendly themes, see thier website for details.

## Museums of the Bath Preservation Trust

www.bath-preservation-trust.org.uk

The Trust works to save listed buildings from demolition and to preserve the historic beauty of Bath. It runs four museums which, due to restrictive planning, do not allow for disabled facilities (and are difficult for prams). Three of the museums have fully illustrated trails, £1.50 (also available on their website).

### Beckford's Tower

Lansdown Road, Bath
01225 422212
Easter-Oct: Sat/Sun/B/H's 10.30am-5pm

This 120ft tower, 2 miles north of Bath, has great views of the countryside.

### Building of Bath Museum

The Countess of Huntingdon's Chapel,
The Vineyards, Bath, BA1 5NA
01225 333 895
Mid Feb-Nov: Tue-Sun & B/H's 10.30am-5pm
£4 adult, £2.50 child, £10 family (2+2), free U5's

This museum describes how the city of Bath was designed and built. Join Mr Macheath, an illustrated rat, for a drawing trail and hands-on activities. Interactive play house (U5's), dressing up clothes and handling boxes. Buggies possible, back carriers preferable.

### Number 1 Royal Crescent

1 Royal Crescent, Bath, BA1 2LR
01225 428 126
Tue-Sun & B/H's 10.30am-5pm, winter 4pm
Dec-Feb closed
Open B/H's & Mondays of Bath Festival
£4 adult, £2.50 child, £12 family (2+2), U5's free

First house built on the Royal Crescent in 1767. Restored as a grand town-house of the period. Join Lily the cat on an illustrated family trail to find out how people lived in the house over 200 years ago. Drawing trail, handling boxes and dressing up clothes.

### William Herschel Museum

19 New King Street, Bath, BA1 2BL
01225 446865
www.bath-preservation-trust.org.uk
Mid Jan-Mid Dec: 1pm-5pm, Sat-Sun 11am-5pm
£3.50 adult, £2 child, £7.50 family (2+2), free U5's

For budding young astronomers. It was the home of William Herschel, who discovered the planet Uranus in 1781. An auditorium shows programmes on space travel and astromany. Follow the family trail with Sirius the dog star, or an audio guide. Part of Spaced Out UK, a large scale model of the solar system built across the UK with fantastic sculptures.

# BRADFORD-ON-AVON AND KENNET AND AVON CANAL

It only takes half an hour to get to this attractive old wool town by train from Temple Meads, but it feels a world apart from Bristol. The canal, which played such an important role 200 years ago allowing goods to be transported to and from London, has been restored and offers lots of recreational opportunities. The stretch between Bath and Devizes is one of the most attractive. Colourful narrowboats, ducks and waterside pubs make cycling, walking or boating fun for everyone. There is a car park at the station.

### Bradford-on-Avon Tourist Information

50 St. Margarets Street, Bradford-on-Avon BA15 1DE
01225 865797
www.bradfordonavontown.co.uk
10am-5pm, Sun 11am-3pm

This helpful office has new premises in Westbury Gardens — look for the flag pole.

## Barton Farm Country Park and The Tithe Barn

www.wiltshire.gov.uk
The Country Park is always open.
B3109 just out of town centre, past station

This park, created on land belonging to the ancient Manor Farm, is set in the wooded valley off the River Avon, stretching 1.5 miles between Bradford and the hamlet of Avoncliff. See walks below.

### 14th Century Tithe Barn

English Heritage
www.english-heritage.co.uk
Apr-Oct 10am-6pm, winter 4pm, admission free

On the edge of the park is this impressive barn, once used to store the Abbey's tithes. The granary and old cow byres have been restored as craftshops and galleries. There are also tea gardens and a childrens play area.

### Brass Knocker Basin

Brass Knocker Basin, Monkton Combe, BA2 7JD
01225 722292
www.bathcanal.com
Daily 8am-dusk, with seasonal variations
Take A36 south of Bath, at Monkton Combe turn left at lights onto B3108

This is a good point from which to orientate yourself whether you're walking, cycling or boating. The visitor centre here has displays and information about the canal. The Angelfish restaurant, see Eating Out, is a scenic and child friendly option for lunch.

### Kennet & Avon cycling & boating

The canal offers bike and canoe hire as well as relaxing narrow boat trips. See Lock Inn and Bath & Dundas Canal Co. in the Transport chapter pg 90.

# THE COTSWOLDS

The Cotswolds are within easy reach of Bristol and cover a large area. There are plenty of attractions, see Cheltenham Tourist Office which also has guides for family/pushchair walks in the Cotswolds.

### Butts Farm

Nr South Cerney, Cirencester, GL7 5QE
01285 862205
Easter-Oct: Wed-Sun 11am-5pm, daily sch holidays
£4 adult, £3 child, U3's free
3 miles east of Cirencester on the old A419 towards Swindon, follow brown tourist signs

Near Cotswold Water Park, this is a very hands-on farm, which specialises in rare breeds. A schedule of activities takes place and children earn stickers for their participation. They can milk goats, bottle-feed young animals, ride ponies, cuddle the smaller animals and go on a tractor-trailer safari. New farm shop selling local produce.

### Cotswold Farm Park

Guiting Power, Nr Stow-on-the-Wold, GL54 5UG
01451 850307
www.cotswoldfarmpark.co.uk
Mar-Sep: daily 10.30am-5pm
Sep Oct: w/e's only (daily in autumn ½ term)
£5.50 adult, £4.50 chlid, £18 family (2+2), U3's free,
Annual: £27.50 adult, £22.50 child
Follow brown signs from Bourton-on-the-Water.

Rare British breeds, informative animal audio guide, seasonal demonstrations of lambing, shearing and milking. Children may cuddle and feed animals in the touch barn. Battery-powered Tractor Driving School (3-12yrs), pedal tractors for toddlers. Tractor trailer rides, woodland walks, nature trails, adventure playground and indoor play area. The campsite gives reduced rates to the park.

## Cotswold Wildlife Park

Burford, Oxfordshire, OX18 4JW
01993 823 006
www.cotswoldwildlifepark.co.uk
Daily 10am-6pm, Oct-Feb 10am-dusk
£9 adult, £6.50 child, U3's free
Annual: £45 adult, £32.50 child
Jct 15 M4, A419, A361, from Lechlade follow brown
tourist signs.

Spacious enclosures with rhinos, zebras,
leopards, emus, wallabies, lions and more.
Other attractions include children's farmyard,
adventure playground, miniature railway,
reptile house and animal encounters — feed
the penguins, ducks and big cat. See their
advertisement in the Colour Reference
Section, pg 132.

## Prinknash Bird and Deer Park

Cranham, Gloucestershire, GL4 8EX
01452 812727
www.prinknash-bird-and-deerpark.com
jem@surfleader.com
Daily 10am-5pm, 4pm winter
£4.40 adult, £3 child, U3's free
M5 J11a, on the A46 between Cheltenham and
Stroud, follow brown tourist signs

Set in the grounds of a working abbey, the
bird park has aviaries housing exotic birds,
and a lake. Many birds including ducks, mute
swans, black swans, peacocks and cranes
wander freely and will feed out of your hand,
as will tame deer and pygmy goats. There is a
tearoom and playground by the Abbey, and an
80 year old 2-storey Tudor style wendy house.

## Cotswold Water Park

Spratsgate Lane, Shorncote, Cirencester, GL7 6DF
01285 861459
www.waterpark.org
Keynes Country Park open daily 9am-5pm, with
seasonal variations

Britain's largest water park with over 130
lakes. Water sports, walking, nature spotting
or just relaxing on the beach.

### Gateway Information Centre (and café)
01285 862962
At the A419 entrance to the park
For accommodation, family activities and
eating out information.

### Keynes Country Park
The larger of the two country parks. Here
you will find: the millenium visitor centre and
a bathing beach (Jun-Sep 1pm-5pm); two
large play areas; lakeside walks and cycling;
a boardwalk café and picnic/barbeque areas.
Boats (pedalos to surfbikes) and bicycles can
be hired here (phone 07970 419208)

### Adventure Zone
01285 861459
or email: advzone@waterpark.org
Based at Keynes, the Adventure Zone, offers
a range of activities for 8-16yrs including
waterskiing, windsurfing, kayaking, sailing and
horseriding. Pre-booking essential.

### Waterland
01285 861202
An outdoor pursuit centre offering sailing,
windsurfing, canoeing and kayaking, archery
and raft building.

### Neigh Bridge Country Park
Smaller park with picnic site, play area and
lakeside walk.

### Hobourne Holiday Park (camping)
See Family Holidays & Weekends Away
pg 149.

# BOURTON-ON-THE-WATER

## Birdland Park and Gardens

Rissington Road, Bourton-on-the-Water, GL54 2BN
01451 820480
www.birdland.co.uk
Apr-Oct: 10am-6pm, Nov-Mar: 4pm
£4.75 adult, £3 child, £14.50 family (2+2), free U4's,
annual: £19 adult, £11 child

Over 500 birds can be seen in a natural
setting of woodland and gardens. The River
Windrush runs through the park forming a
natural habitat for flamingos, pelicans, storks
and waterfowl. The colony of penguins is fun

to watch at feeding time (2.30pm). Over 50 aviaries contain exotic birds. Nice picnic spots, play area and café (open w/e's only in winter).

## Bourton Model Railway

Box Bush, High Street, Bourton-on-the-Water, GL54
01451 820686
www.bourtonmodelrailway.co.uk
Apr-Sep: daily 11am-5pm
£2.25 adult, £1.75 child, £7 family (2+2)
Oct-Mar: Sat-Sun 11am-5pm only
Limited opening in Jan

Over 500 sq ft of scenic model railway layouts. 40 British and continental trains run through realistic and detailed scenery; some are interactive. There is a well-stocked model and toy shop, with extended opening hours.

## Fundays Playbarn

Unit 8, Willow Court, Bourton-on-the-Water Industrial Park, Gloucestershire, GL54 2HQ
01451 822999
www.fundaysplaybarn.com
Daily 10am-6pm, B/H's 10.30am-5pm
Hols & w/e's £1 adult, £3.50 child (1-3yrs) £4 child (4-11yrs) £1 (U1's), lower prices during term-time
A429 north of Bourton, sign on right after Coach & Horses pub.

Large indoor playbarn for 1-11's. Separate toddler zone. Outdoor area open in the summer with go-carts and giant chess.

## Bourton-on-the-Water

Visitor Information Centre: 01451 820211

Further attractions accessible from its main car park:

### The Dragonfly Maze
01451 822251

Use clues found on journey through maze to help you find the golden dragonfly.

### The Model Village
01451 820467
www.theoldnewinn.co.uk

Detailed replica of the village built from Cotswold stone in one-ninth scale.

### Cotswold Motoring and Toy Museum
See Wheels and Wings pg 53.

# STROUD

A mixture of old and new, this is one of the larger towns in the Cotswolds, and it has much to offer families in terms of shops, cafés, restaurants and things to do. It also benefits from good public transport links. The town has a cinema, leisure centre and a large park. Regular events include a farmers' market and the Stroud Fringe Festival, held in September. Many of the surrounding villages, set in picturesque countryside, offer child-friendly venues.

**Stroud Tourist Information Centre**
The Subscription Rooms, George Street, Stroud, GL5
01453 760960
Mon-Sat 10am-5pm

## Coaley Peak

Nr Nympsfield, Stroud, Gloucesteshire
01452 425666/863170
www.gloucestershire.gov.uk
On the B4066 Stroud-Uley Rd, about ½ mile from Nympsfield

Picnic site on the edge of the Cotswold escarpment with panoramic views towards the Forest of Dean – on a clear day, you can see the Black Mountains in Wales. The 12-acre area has been reclaimed as a wildflower meadow (at its best in summer) with picnic tables and open grassland good for flying kites. It also includes Nympsfield long barrow, a neolithic burial chamber. The Cotswold Way runs the length of the site, and you can stroll through the adjacent Stanley Woods.

## Minchinhampton Common

Stroud, Gloucestershire
01452 814213
www.nationaltrust.org
South of Stroud, between Minchinhampton and Nailsworth

A large open space on a hill-top plateau of the Cotswolds with dramatic views over the surrounding countryside. Great for picnics, walks and flying kites. The common has a special mix of wildflowers, including cowslips and orchids, as well as a diversity of birds, butterflies and other insects. It's also one of the most important archaeological sites in Britain, with prehistoric field systems, a Neolithic long barrow, medieval roads and military defences from the Second World War.

## Museum in the Park

Stratford Park, Stratford Road, GL5 4AF
01453 763394
www.stroud.gov.uk
Tue-Fri 10am-5pm, Sat-Sun and B/H's 11am, seasonal variations
Admission free
M5 J13, A419 follow signs to Stratford Park

Set in beautiful parkland, this family-oriented museum has plenty for all ages with colourful interactive displays. Younger ones will enjoy finding Thomas the Tank Engine, doing a puzzle or having a story. Displays include local history and a room devoted to childhood over the years. There are quiz trails (30p), seasonal Family Activity Packs (£1.50) and holiday workshops. Free car parking at Stratford Park Leisure Centre (café, indoor and outdoor pools).

## Owlpen Manor

Nr Uley, Gloucestershire, GL11 5BZ
01453 860261
www.owlpen.com
May-Sep, Tue/Thu & Sun
House 2pm-5pm
Restaurant & gardens 10.30am-5pm
£4.80 adults, £2 child (4-14yrs), £13.50 family
Gardens & grounds £2.80 adults, £1 child
1 mile east of Uley, off B4066 Dursley-Stroud road

A romantic Tudor manor house with formal terraced yew gardens set in a beautiful Cotswolds valley. Contains family portraits and collections, 17th-century wall hangings and Cotswold Arts and Crafts furniture. Grounds include medieval buildings, a mill pond and early Georgian mill. The Cyder House Restaurant offers light lunches and cream teas (as well as formal dinners). The large, 300-year-old oak cider press in the corner was once used for cider feasts.

## Ruskin Mill

Old Bristol Rd, Nailsworth, Gloucestershire, GL6 0LA
01453 837537 events, 01453 837514 coffee shop
www.ruskin-mill.org.uk
Gallery daily 10am-5pm (closed Thu pm)
Coffee shop 11am-4pm, lunch fr 12.45pm, not Sun

Coffee shop and gallery with a programme of art and craft exhibitions, events and workshops, including, in term time, monthly storytelling for children (4+yrs). Park at Horsley Mill car park (the next turning on the left towards Horsley) and enjoy the 10-minute walk back along the pretty Nailsworth valley – suitable for single buggies. Parking at Ruskin Mill is for disabled visitors only.

## Stratford Park Leisure Centre

Stratford Rd, Stroud, Gloucestershire, GL5 4AF
01453 766771
www.leisure-centre.com
Outdoor pool end May-1st w/e Sept
Leisure Centre all year
£3.10 adult, £1.70 child, £5.60 family (2+2)
See Museum in the Park

Set in 32 acres of parkland, this leisure centre provides indoor and outdoor facilities for a variety of sports. The outdoor pool is popular in summer, with grass sunbathing areas. There are crèche and party facilities available.

**Looking for lunch?**
See Hobbs House Bakery and Woodruffs in Stroud, pg 76.

## Stroud Farmers' Market

Cornhill Market Place, Stroud, Gloucestershire
01453 758060
www.madeinstroud.org/markets
1st & 3rd Sat every month: 9am-2pm

Award-winning farmers' market with up to 60 stalls, offering a wide range of local produce and local crafts. A tempting range of hot food available. Entertainment from local musicians adds to the atmosphere. Seasonal events include Apple Day festivities in the autumn and Christmas activities in December.

### Woodchester Park Mansion

Nympsfield, Stroud, Gloucestershire, GL10 3TS
01452 814213 park, 01453 861541 mansion
www.woodchestermansion.org.uk
Mansion: Easter-End Oct Sun 11am-5pm & 1st Sat's
in mth, daily Jul-Aug & B/H w/e's
Park open all year 9am-dusk
£1.50 parking
Nympsfield Rd 300m from the junction with he
B4066 Uley-Stroud. Car park is a mile from the
mansion, with regular bus transfer

National Trust-owned park in a secluded
Cotswold valley with trails through scenic
woodland, parkland and around lakes. The
Mansion, a Grade 1 listed building, was built
in the 19th-century in the French Gothic
revival style but never finished. Rare bats use
the roof spaces in summer. See them from the
observatory or join a bat-watching evening.

well-marked tree-lined paths, most of them
suitable for pushchairs. The Old Arboretum
is dog free. The area is especially beautiful in
the autumn and hence busier. Ring for details
of seasonal events such as Christmas lights.
Shop with information and plants for sale.

### The Lavender Garden

Ashcroft Nurseries, Kingscote, Tetbury, GL8 8YF
01453 860356
Mar-Nov Sat-Sun & B/H's 11am-5pm, weekdays hrs
vary phone for details

A specialist plant nursery that developed
from an interest in butterflies and the plants
that attract them. More than 100 varieties
of lavender displayed in a Victorian walled
garden, plus a large collection of buddlejas
and other plants popular with bees and
butterflies.

# TETBURY

A pretty Cotswold town designated an
Outstanding Conservation Area due to its
many listed buildings.

The centre of the town is lined with Cotswold
stone buildings dating from the 17th and
18th centuries, many of which are now
antique shops. At one end, the pillared Market
House (c1655) is still in regular use as a
market. Beyond it, St Mary the Virgin is a fine
Georgian Gothic church.

Also worth checking out are Gumstool Hill,
one of Tetbury's most ancient streets and the
Old Court House museum at 63 Long Street.

### Westonbirt Arboretum

Nr Tetbury, Gloucestershire, GL8 8QS
01666 880220
www.forestry.gov.uk/england
westonbirt@forestry.gsi.gov.uk
Daily 10am-5pm (or dusk if earlier)
£7.50 adult (£6 winter), £1 child, free U5's,
Annual family: £42
M4 J18, take A46 towards Tetbury, follow brown
tourist signs.

The Arboretum consists of miles of beautiful,

# WOTTON-UNDER-EDGE

True to its name, this ancient wool town
is still a settlement by a wood under the
Cotswold Edge, and together with the
surrounding villages and countryside, it has
plenty to attract families. The characterful
high street has a range of shops and cafés;
tea and cake is served at the Town Hall on
Sunday afternoons from spring to autumn.
There's also a small swimming pool (open in
summer), with a larger year-round pool at the
leisure centre in nearby Dursley. The Heritage
Centre in the Chipping includes a tourist
information point and local history displays.

**Under the Edge Arts**
www.undertheedgearts.org.uk

Organises events and activities for children.

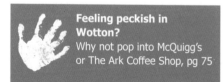

**Feeling peckish in Wotton?**
Why not pop into McQuigg's
or The Ark Coffee Shop, pg 75

## Megamaze

Kingswood, Wotton-under-Edge, Gloucestershire
01453 843120
www.megamaze.co.uk
Mid Jul-Mid Sept: daily 10am-5pm
£4 adult, £3 child (up to 12yrs), £12 family (2+2),
U3's free
About ½ mile out of Kingswood on the Hillesled Rd,
go past the Dinneywicks pub and continue to the
find the maze on the left-hand side just after the
turn to Wortley (Nind Lane)

A seasonal maze with more than two miles
of paths carved through five acres of maize.
The maize reaches more than six feet tall and
is harvested in early autumn. Also on site is
a mini-maze, large sandpit with toys, giant
haystack for climbing, trampoline and pedal
karts. There are outdoor and covered picnic
areas, and a small range of refreshments.

## Newark Park

Ozleworth, Wotton-under-Edge, GL12 7PZ
01453 842644
www.nationaltrust.org.uk
Apr-May: Wed/Thu 11am-5pm
Jun-Oct: Wed/Thu, Sat-Sun, B/H's 11am-5pm
£5 adult, £2.50 children, £13 family

National Trust property, high on a limestone
cliff, with far-reaching views. It started life as
a hunting lodge in the 1550s. Disabled and
buggy access only on ground floor. You can
stroll in the deer park and gardens, renowned
for their snowdrops in spring, or follow a
longer circular walk through the Lower Lodge
Woods, see Walks pg 57.

## The Tortworth Chestnut

Next to St Leonard's Church, Tortworth, Wotton-
under-Edge
Turn off the B4509 Tortworth-Wotton at the
crossroads just east of Tortworth Primary School,
following signs to Damery and Wick. The tree is on
the right, about ¼ mile from the junction, in a field
next to St Leonard's Church.

Park outside the church and follow a path to
the right across the field. Here you will find
a sweet chestnut tree thought to be at least
1,100 years old, with a huge, twisted main
trunk and branches that have touched the
ground and rooted, creating a mini-woodland.

Now fenced for its protection, the tree is one
of the 50 Great British Trees. Photos of the
tree are displayed in the neighbouring St
Leonard's Church, also worth a look.

## Tortworth Estate Shop

Box Walk, Tortworth, Wotton-under-Edge
01454 261633
Mon-Sat: 9am-5.30pm, closed B/H's

Farm shop with locally produced, home-made
and speciality foods. Large meat counter and
well-stocked freezer cabinets. Mini-baskets for
children to help with shopping.

## Wotton Farm Shop

Gloucester Row, Wotton-under-Edge, GL12 7DY
01453 521546
www.wottonfarmshop.co.uk
Apr-Dec: Mon-Sat 9am-4.30pm, Sun 10am-1pm

Farm shop, pick-your-own and nursery, selling
fruit and veg grown on site and locally, as
well as other products. The nursery provides
a hanging-basket re-filling service and sells
new baskets and plants. New facilities include
a farm kitchen for take-away home-cooked
food, toilets, picnic and play area.

# THORNBURY

A small market town about 12 miles north of Bristol. It boasts an attractive high street, a 14th century castle (now a hotel and restaurant), and a church (St Mary's), which dates from the 12th-century. The leisure centre offers lots of activities for children see tables in Colour Reference Section.

Regular events in Thornbury include a Saturday market, summer carnival and an arts festival. Information on the town's history is available from Thornbury Museum on Chapel Street, www.thornburymuseum.org.uk.

## Eastwood Garden Plant Centre

Eastwood Park, Falfield, Thornbury, GL12 8DA
01454 260288
www.eastwoodgardencentre.co.uk
Mon-Sat 9am-5.30pm, Sun 9.30am-5.30pm
Tea shop 9.30am-4.30pm
About a mile from the M5 junction 14, on the A38 just south of Falfield

Family-run, independent garden centre situated in what was the Victorian walled kitchen garden that served Eastwood Park country house. Play area with swings and climbing equipment near to tea shop. Small display gardens, pet enclosures with rabbits, guinea pigs, goats, chickens and ducks.

## Mundy Playing Fields

Kington Lane, Thornbury, BS35 2AR
Open all year
Off Castle St, just west of the High St (B4061)

# GLOUCESTER

## Gloucester Tourist Information

28 Southgate Street, Gloucester, GL1 2DP
01452 396 572
www.gloucester.gov.uk/tourism
tourism@gloucester.gov.uk
Mon-Sat: 10am-5pm, Jul/Aug: Sun 11am-3pm

There is also a tourist information point at the National Waterways Museum, see below.

## Gloucester Folk Museum

99-103 Westgate Street, Gloucester, GL1 2PG
01452 396 868
www.gloucester.gov.uk
Tue-Sat 10am-5pm
Admission free

Child-friendly museum of social history. In the Toy Gallery, there is a wendy house, a puppet theatre and toy cupboard. The portal ICT gallery has quizzes for all ages. There are toys in the garden which has farm animals in the summer. Free half-term and holiday activities, and free kids club Sat 11-3pm.

## National Waterways Museum

Llanthony Warehouse, Gloucester Docks, GL1 2EH
01452 318200
www.nwm.org.uk
bookingsnwm@thewaterwaystrust.org
Daily 10am-5pm
£5.95 adult, £4.75 child, £17.50 family, U5's free
M5 J12 follow brown tourist signs to Historic Docks

This award-winning museum is housed in a listed Victorian warehouse within the historic Gloucester Docks. Exhibits range from touch-screen computers to interactive pulleys, to portray the history of canals and rivers in a hands-on way. Outside, you can watch a blacksmith at work or board historic boats.

### Queen Boadicea II

From Easter to Oct: 12pm-4pm
£4.50 adult, £3.50 child

This Dunkirk little ship makes 45 minute trips along the canal.

## Nature in Art

Wallsworth Hall, Main A38 Twigworth, GL2 9PA
0845 4500 233
www.nature-in-art.org.uk
Tue-Sun & B/H's 10am-5pm
£3.60 adult, £3 child, U8's free
M5 J11A, take A417 and A40 to A38 north. Brown/
green sign at entrance

This museum is full of art inspired by
nature. Sculptures, tapestries, ceramics and
paintings. Feb-Nov, visiting artists can be
seen demonstrating skills ranging from oil
painting to chainsaw sculpting. There is an
activity room with jigsaws and brass rubbings.
Handling boxes in some of the galleries. Half
day activities run during school holidays.
These need to be booked in advance, U8's
must be accompanied by an adult.

# CHELTENHAM

## Cheltenham Tourist Information

77 Promenade, Cheltenham, GL50 1PP
01242 522878
www.visitcheltenham.info
Mon-Sat 9.30am-5.15pm, Wed 10am,
B/H's 9.30am-1.30pm

## Cheltenham Art Gallery and Museum

Clarence Street, Cheltenham, GL50 3JT
01242 237431
www.cheltenhammuseum.org.uk
Mon-Sat 10am-5.20pm, closed Sun & B/H's
Admission free

The collections relate to the Arts and Crafts
Movement with fine examples of furniture,
silver, jewellery, ceramics and textiles. Other
displays include oriental art, a history of
Cheltenham, sparkling costume accessories,
archaeology and natural history. Discovery
trails and handling tables for all ages, and
activities and colouring sheets for U5's.

## Pittville Park Playground

Evesham Rd, Cheltenham
01242 250019
Free

Designed to bring able-bodied and physically
disabled children together (1-11yrs).
Equipment is fenced in and includes a sound
sculpture for children to hit and touch, a sand
pit, hexagonal swing, springies and a climbing
unit. There are cages full of rabbits, chickens
and chipmunks. Refreshment kiosk in summer.

## Sandford Parks Lido

Keynsham Road, Cheltenham, GL53 7PU
01242 524430
www.sandfordparkslido.org.uk
Mid Apr-Sep: daily 11am-7.30pm
Ring for details of early morning adult swims
£3 adult, £4.20 family (1+1) or £6.80 (1+2) or £8.20
(2+2), U5's free
Various season tickets available
M5 J11, A40 to Cheltenham then follow tourist signs.
It's next door to Gen. Hospital

Large heated outdoor pool set in landscaped
gardens with spacious terraces for sunbathing
and a café. Separate children's pool for
U8's, paddling pool for toddlers and slides.
Two children's play areas, table tennis and
basketball. Lockers in the heated changing
rooms. Pay and display car park next door.

# THE FOREST OF DEAN & WYE RIVER

## THE FOREST OF DEAN

The Forest of Dean is one of the few remaining ancient oak forests. It covers 35 square miles between the Rivers Wye and Severn on the borders of England and Wales. If you are looking for a peaceful day but one to exhaust your children this has to be one of the top locations! From Bristol, it's less than an hour's drive, unfortunately public transport is not at its best in the area. The forest has a huge amount to offer families of all ages, such as cycling, walking, orienteering, bird watching, archery, canoeing and climbing.

### Coleford Tourist Information Centre
High Street, Coleford, GL16 8HG
01594 812388
www.forestofdean.gov.uk
Mon-Sat 10am-5pm, some seasonal variations

Contact them for information on seasonal activities. Also information on places to stay, outdoor pursuits, walks and llama trekking!

### Forest of Dean Forestry Commission
Bank House, Bank Street, Coleford, GL16 8BA
01594 833057
www.forestry.gov.uk
dean@forestry.gsi.gov.uk
Mon-Thu 8.30am-5pm, Fri 8.30am-4pm

Many useful leaflets and information on special events such as deer and bird spotting.

### Cycling in the Forest of Dean
A great place to cycle, cycle hire available, see Transport chapter pg 88.

## Beechenhurst Lodge
Speech House Hill, Near Coleford, GL16 7EG
01594 827357
www.beechenhurstlodge.co.uk
Daily 10am-6pm, winter 10am-dusk, Jan w/e's only
B4226 between Coleford and Cinderford

This is a good base to start familiarising yourself with the forest. There's plenty of parking (£2/day) and it's the starting point for

The Sculpture Trail as well as a good place to pick up the circular 12-mile family cycle route. Next to the information centre, there is a café, picnic and BBQ area and play equipment.

## Forest of Dean Sculpture Trail
01594 833057
www.forestofdean-sculpture.org.uk
Open daily dawn-dusk
Admission free
B4226 between Cinderford and Coleford, follow brown tourist signs

This walk features sculptures, inspired by the forest, located along a trail through beautiful woodland. It has a magical feel to it and is good fun for young children with wonderful views. The route is about 3½ miles long, a shorter loop is possible. Pushchair accessible, although back carriers will be easier.

## Clearwell Caves
Near Coleford, Royal Forest of Dean, GL16 8JR
01594 832535
www.clearwellcaves.com
Feb-Oct & Dec: daily 10am-5pm
£4.50 adult, £2.80 child, £12.90 family, U5's free
Christmas special: £5.50 adult/child inc. gift for U14's
From Coleford take B4228 south for 1 mile, turn right at Lambsquay Hotel

These natural caves have had iron ore mined from them for thousands of years (by children as young as 6yrs). Nine caverns are open to the public and miners' tools and equipment are displayed. There are no steps and single buggies can be taken into the caves. See website for special events.

## Dean Heritage Centre
Soudley, Cinderford, Gloucestershire, GL14 2UB
01594 824024/822170
www.deanheritagemuseum.com
Daily 10am-5.30pm, 4pm winter
£4.50 adult, £2.50 child, £13 family (2+4) free U5's
B4227 between Blakeney and Cinderford

History of the forest and its people in this newly refurbished museum. Children can take woodblock rubbings of forest scenes. In the grounds there is a reconstructed Victorian foresters cottage with Gloucester Old Spot pig and chickens. Adventure playground with a hurdle maze and a BBQ area. Some woodland walks from here are accessible by pushchair and wheelchair. A deck at the café overlooks the millpond with working waterwheel.

## Dick Whittington Mohair Countryside Centre

Little London, Longhope, Gloucestershire, GL17 0PH
01452 831137
www.royal-forest-of-dean.com/mohair
Tue-Sun 10am-5pm term time, daily sch hols
£3.50 adult & 10+yrs, £4.50 child, £3.50 U3's,
Free U1's
Take A40 from Gloucester towards Ross-On-Wye, take a left turn in Huntley and follow brown tourist signs

Farm park set in secluded valley. Adventure barn with five different soft play units suitable from toddlers to age 10 yrs. Outside a big sandpit, play area, pets corner, tractor rides, nature trail and picnic area. You can see pigs and goats in the paddocks, or visit the Aquarium Room which also houses an Ant Colony. See website for special events.

## Hopewell Colliery Museum

Cannop Hill, Coleford
01594 810706
www.hopewellcoalmine.co.uk
Mar-Oct: daily 10am-4pm, Dec: Santa Specials
Underground tours £3.50 adult, £2.50 child
On B4226 Cinderford to Coleford road, a mile west of Beechenhurst Lodge

Local miners will take you underground to show you around the old mine workings (45min trip). The descent into the mine is steep (as is the exit) but the route through it is level (just over ½ mile). Not suitable for pushchairs or back-carriers, children of walking age are welcome and will be kitted out with safety helmets and lamps. Practical footwear and warm clothing recommended. There's a tea room, picnic and play area and narrow gauge railway.

## Puzzle Wood

Near Coleford, GL16 8QD
01594 833187
Easter-Sep: Tue-Sun 11am-5pm, Oct: 11am-4pm
Also open B/H's & Feb ½ term
£4 adult, £2.80 child
B4228 0.5 mile south of Coleford

Originally a pre-Roman open cast iron ore mine. A tangle of pathways laid out in the early 1800's, as an unusual maze, has been resurfaced to provide a mile of pathways through deep ravines, trailing vines and moss covered rocks. Really weird scenery, great for hide and seek and getting lost in! Not suitable for pushchairs. There are also farm animals, an indoor wood puzzle and a tea room.

# WYE RIVER

## Symonds Yat Rock

Log Cabin Symonds Yat, Near Coleford
01594 833057
www.forestry.gov.uk
Log cabin: Mar-Oct 9.30am-dusk
Nov-Feb: limited opening
Take B4432 north of Coleford

Fantastic viewpoint high above the River Wye. Log cabin with snack bar, information, souvenirs and picnic area. Waymarked walks start from here. A pair of peregrine falcons nest on the nearby cliffs and from mid April to August, staff from the RSPB (see below) can tell you all about the fastest birds in the world and hopefully help spot them with telescopes (10am-6pm). If you're walking, there are two useful hand ferries (seasonal) which run from The Olde Ferrie Inne on the west bank of the Wye to the base of the Rock, and from Saracen's Head Inn on the east bank.

## Royal Society for the Protection of Birds

The Puffins, New Road, Parkend, Lydney, GL15 4JA
01594 562852
www.rspb.org.uk

The RSPB organises events in and around the Forest of Dean. These included badger watching, pond-dipping, evening bat walks and making nest boxes and bird feeders. They'll help you spot peregrine falcons at Symonds Yat rock (see above). You can also visit their two nature reserves at Nagshead and Highnam Woods, phone for details.

### King Fisher Cruises

Symonds Yat East
01600 891063

If you'd like to see the area from the water but don't fancy paddling yourself along, take a 35 minute river trip

## WYE RIVER OUTDOOR PURSUITS

There are age restrictions on many of the outdoor pursuits so please phone to avoid disappointed children!

### Symonds Yat Canoe Hire

Symonds Yat West, Herefordshire, HR9 6BY
01600 891069
www.canoehire.com
Mar-Oct: daily 9am-6pm

Located on the opposite bank of the River Wye from Symonds Yat Rock. Canoes and kayaks can be rented from 1 hour to a week. They can also transport boats up river so you can just paddle down. Camping available.

### Wye Pursuits

Riverside House, Kerne Bridge, Nr Ross, HR9 5QX
01600 891199
www.wye-pursuits.co.uk

Large range of outdoor activities on offer as well as canoe and kayak hire. Activities for groups of 8, families welcome. On offer: climbing, abseiling, caving and white water rafting. For all water activities you must be able to swim 25 metres.

### Wyedean Canoe and Adventure Centre

Holly Barn, Symonds Yat Rock, Coleford, GL16 7NZ
01594 833238
www.wyedean.co.uk
Easter-Oct: daily 8.30am-5pm, winter by appt.

As well as offering canoe and kayak hire, this outdoor centre has a vast range of activities for adults and children aged 8+. Canoeing, kayaking, raft building, abseiling, climbing, high and low rope courses, team building,

caving and archery. They cater for individuals and groups (schools, youth groups, guides and scouts). It is essential to book in advance.

## CARDIFF

45 minutes from Bristol Parkway to Cardiff Central, short walk to centre

Cardiff has undergone a complete transformation over the past twenty years. New landmarks such as Cardiff Bay, the Millennium Stadium and modern shopping centres alongside Victorian arcades make it a pleasant city to visit. If you're hoping to combine a visit to the city centre and Bay area, the Bay Xpress runs every 15 minutes between Cardiff Central station and the Bay. The Cardiff festival takes place in mid July with theatre, music and fairground entertainment. There is usually an outdoor ice rink outside City Hall during December and January.

## CITY CENTRE ATTRACTIONS

### Cardiff Gateway Visitor Centre

The Old Library, The Hayes, Cardiff, CF10 1ES
029 2022 7281
www.visitcardiff.info
visitor@thecardiffinitiative.co.uk
Mon-Sat 9.30am-6pm, Sun 10am-4pm

### Cardiff Open Top Bus Tour

01708 866000
www.citysightseeing.co.uk
info@city-sightseeing.com
Apr-Oct: Daily from 10am-4pm
Nov-Dec: Sat-Sun 10.30am-3.30pm
£7.50 adult, £3 child (5-15), £18 family (2+2), Free U5's

Good for getting an idea of the layout of the main attractions, from the Millennium Stadium to the new Bay area with a pre-recorded commentary. Tickets, valid for 24 hours, can be bought from the driver, tourist info or online. Tour starts at Cardiff Castle and lasts about 50 minutes; local fares available. Kids Passport, puzzles, games and felt tip pens.

## Cardiff Castle

Castle Street, Cardiff, CF10 3RB
029 2087 8100
www.cardiffcastle.com
cardiffcastle@cardiff.gov.uk
Mar-Oct: daily 9.30am-6pm, Nov-Feb: 9.30am-5pm
£6.80 adult, £4.20 child, £22 family (2+3 or 1+4),
free U5's

Situated in the town centre, Cardiff Castle
spans a 2000 year history from its Roman
remains, to the Norman keep and its opulent
Victorian interior. Guided tours, suitable for
5+yrs, start at 10am and last 50 minutes, no
buggies. Large green for picnicking; peacocks
and ducks wander freely.

## Millennium Stadium

029 2082 2228
www.millenniumstadium.com
Mon-Sat 10am-5pm, Sun & B/H's 10am-4pm.
Restaurant open event days only.
£5.50 adult, £3 child, £17 family (2+3), free U5's.

All sports fans will enjoy a tour of this huge
stadium and even the less sporty members
of the family can't fail to be impressed by
the largest retractable roof in Europe! The
pushchair-friendly tour includes a chance to
run down the players tunnel and sit in the
Royal Box. Pre-booking advisable, no tours on
match days.

## National Museum and Gallery

Cathays Park, Cardiff, CF10 3NP
029 2039 7951
www.nmgw.ac.uk
post@nmgw.ac.uk
Tues-Sun 10am-5pm & B/H's
Admission free
Follow signs to Cardiff city centre, nr to University

Superb range of art (best collection of
Impressionists in Europe outside Paris),
natural history and science. Exhibitions on the
evolution of Wales, with life size dinosaurs
and Ice Age creatures. The Glanely Gallery is
an interactive area enabling children to touch
items not normally on display. Steps up to the
main entrance, sloped access at side gate.

# CARDIFF BAY

Car Park: Stuart St, opposite Techniquest
From Central Station: Bay Xpress bus service

Cardiff was once the busiest coal exporting
port in the world, so the decline in the coal
and steel industries had a devastating effect
on the docks. Over recent years the ambitious
regeneration of 2,700 acres of docklands, and
the construction of the barrage has resulted
in the new Cardiff Bay with its cultural
attractions, interesting places to eat, shops,
leisure areas and summer Harbour Festival.

### Mermaid Quay

029 2048 0077
A shopping and leisure complex with plenty of
places to eat.

### Roald Dahl Plass

A large oval space used for outdoor events
and performances. It's all pedestrianised
here and great for the kids to run around.
Following the shore line you'll see:

### The Norwegian Church Arts Centre

029 2045 4899
Originally built in 1868 as a mission for
Scandinavian seamen, this has been restored
as an arts and music centre with café. The
author Roald Dahl was baptised here. Beyond
here is:

### The Goleulong 2000 Lightship

029 2048 7609
www.lightship2000.org.uk
Daily Mon-Sat 10am-5pm, Sun 2-5pm
Free
Originally positioned off the Gower coast to
warn off ships. Fun for children to explore the
engine room, light tower and cabins. There is
also a café.

## Cardiff Bay Visitor Centre

The Tube, Harbour Drive, Cardiff Bay, CF10 4PA
029 2046 3833
www.visitcardiff.info
Daily 9am-5pm summer, 10am-5pm winter
10 min walk for Mermaid Quay along waterfront

Easily recognised by its award winning tubular
design. Has a vast scale model of The Bay.

## Cardiff Bay Barrage

Harbour Authority: 029 2087 7900
Open daily, summer closes 7pm, winter 4pm

One of the most ambitious engineering projects in Europe. The barrage, across the bay entrance is over 1km long. It provides a 500 acre freshwater lake, fed by the Taff and Ely rivers. Visiting the barrage with its locks, sluice gates and fish pass (allowing fish access from the sea to the rivers to spawn) is fascinating. Penarth Marina is on the other side, an easy stroll from the locks. Access to the barrage, where there are toilets and refreshments, is by land train or boat or on foot from the Penarth end car park.

## Cardiff Barrage Road Train

029 2051 2729
www.cardiffroadtrain.com
keeftrain@ntlworld.com
April-Oct: daily 11am-5pm frm Stuart St.
Return ticket: £3 adult, £2 child
Leaves from behind Techniquest

There's a live commentary on the land train. It takes 20 minutes to reach the Barrage where there is a 10 minute stop before returning. Alternatively you could stay longer and take a later trip back, or return by boat.

## Cardiff Bay Water Bus

07940 42409
www.cardiffcats.com
yotty@msn.com
Easter-Oct: daily 10.30am-6pm
Nov- Easter: W/ends only but daily in school hols
Summer return trip: £4 adult, £2 child. Winter: £2 adult, £2 child, family discount available.

Cardiff Cats offer 40 minute cruises of the Bay with the opportunity to land at the Barrage, leaving from Mermaid Quay. The water on this side of the Barrage is usually calm. Tickets can be bought in advance from the quay information points. There are a variety of services, check website for more details.

**Fascinated by castles?**
Wales has plenty, see Caerphilly, Castell Coch and Cheptow on pg 48

## Cardiff Bay Cruises

029 2047 2004
www.cardiffbaycruises.com
cardiffbaycruise@aol.com
Seasonal cruises, phone for times
1hr cruise: £6 adult, £3 child, free U3's. ½ hour cruise: £3 adult, £1.50 child, free U3's

Cruise up the Taff, along the River Ely or around the Bay with full commentary. Boats, including the new restaurant boat, leave from in front of the Pierhead building. Pushchair access, pre-booking advisable.

## Bay Island Voyages

029 2048 4110/01446 420692 out of hours
www.bayisland.co.uk
Run all year dependent on weather and demand
Fast Bay Cruise: £6 adult, £3 child U14's. Bristol Channel: £18.50 adult, £10 child

Thrill seekers need look no further than a high speed trip on the Celtic Ranger powered by two 225hp engines and travelling at up to 60mph! This is going to appeal more to older children although babies and toddlers can be taken. The most popular option with younger children (from about 6yrs) is the half hour Fast Bay Cruise which tends to be calmer. For those with stronger sea-legs there are tours lasting between 1 and 2 hours which go up the coast or around Flat Holm and Steep Holm. The boat carries 12 passengers, waterproofs and life jackets are provided. Pre-booking advisable.

## Cardiff Bay Tours

029 2070 7882
www.cardiffbaytours.com
cardiffbaytours@hotmail.com
Easter-Oct: daily 10am-4pm
£4 adult, £1.50 child

Informative 1½ hour walking tours of the Bay starting at the Tube Visitors Centre and ending at St Davids Hotel. Of interest to older children although the route is pushchair-accessible. There is a free information pack, pre-booking advisable.

## Techniquest

Stuart Street, Cardiff, CF10 5BW
029 2047 5475
www.techniquest.org
info@techniquest.org
Mon-Fri 9.30am-4.30pm, Sat-Sun and B/Hols
10.30am-5pm, School Hols 9.30am-5pm.
£6.90 adult, £4.80 child, £20 family (2+3), free U4's,
Annual Family: £47

On the waterfront, this large Science Discovery Centre for children has over 150 hands-on exhibits. There is an interactive Science Theatre Show and Planetarium. For younger children there are curiousity boxes in the Discovery Room.

## Craft in the Bay

The Flourish, Lloyd George Avenue, Cardiff, CF10
029 2049 1136
www.makersguildinwales.org.uk
Daily 10.30am-5.30pm
Free admission
Five minutes walk from Mermaid Quay, also Bay
Xpress bus stop outside

Retail gallery set in old maritime warehouse displaying crafts made by members of the Makers Guild in Wales. Ceramics, jewellery, textiles, glass, furniture and paper. Café serving mainly vegetarian food.

## BEYOND THE CENTRE

### Roath Park Gardens and Lake

Lake Rd West, Roath, Cardiff
Open dawn-dusk

A 15-minute drive or bus ride from the city centre will bring you to a large park with plenty to see and do. It stretches for nearly 1½ miles but the best place to head for is between Lake Roads East and West (on-street parking). Here you'll find the lake with a wide variety of hungry waterfowl! In season, you can hire rowing and pedal boats. There's a well-equipped play area and flower gardens with a stream running through it to a huge hothouse containing tropical fish and plants. Seasonal café, toilets at boat stage.

**Want to explore Wales more?** See some of the fabulous places to stay in our Holidays and Weekends Away chapter, pg 147

## St Fagan's Museum

St Fagans, Cardiff, CF5 6XB
029 2057 3500
www.nmgw.ac.uk
Daily 10am-5pm
Admission free
M4 J33, follow tourist signs, bus from city centre

A village chronicling the history of Wales. A whole day is needed to see everything. Over 40 buildings have been transported here from all over Wales and rebuilt in attractive parkland. They give a fascinating insight into how people lived, worked and spent their leisure time over the past 500 years. Children will enjoy comparing a row of ironworker's houses each furnished from a different decade, sitting in a Victorian classroom and seeing traditional crafts. Also a large indoor museum, and a variety of places to eat.

## FARMS

When visiting farms, zoos and wildlife centres, it's wise to take precautions to avoid "zoonoses" — diseases spread to humans via animal carriers. The risk is easily controlled by making sure your children wash their hands after contact with animals. If you are pregnant, or think you may be pregnant, avoid contact with pregnant ewes and newborn lambs.

### Avon Valley Country Park

Pixash Lane, Bath Rd, Keynsham, BS31 1TS
0117 986 4929

See advertisement and listing in Out & About in Bristol pg 13.

## Court Farm Country Park

Wolvershill Rd, Banwell, Weston-super-Mare, BS29
01934 822 383
www.courtfarmcountrypark.co.uk
Mar-Nov: daily 10am-5.30pm, winter: 10am-4.30pm
£4.95 adult, £3.75 child, £16 family (2+2), free U3's
ATV rides: £2 adult, £1.50 child
Season ticket: £24 adult, £18 child
M5 J21 the follow brown tourist signs

A working farm with massive undercover fun area and an outdoor Adventure Land play area with aerial skyway and trampolines. Also tractor rides, pony rides, bottle feeding lambs, handling the pets and white knuckle ATV rides for the brave at heart! Maize maze from mid July to end Sept. Holiday activities include Easter egg and treasure hunts.

## Greenmeadow Community Farm

Greenforge Way, Cwmbran, Gwent, NP44 5AJ
01633 862 202
Daily 10am-6pm, winter 10am-4.30pm, closed Jan
£4 adult, £3 child, free U2's
M4 J26, go north to Cwmbran following brown signs

Farm animals in paddocks and barns. Tractor and trailer rides, machine milking viewed from glassed in area, adventure playground for ages 7+yrs and a large sandpit and tractor play area for U5's. Paddling pool with water-spurting dragon in summer.

## Noah's Ark Zoo Farm

Failand Rd, Wraxall, Bristol, BS48 1PG
01275 852606
www.noahsarkzoofarm.co.uk
Feb-Oct: Tue-Sat, B/H's 10.30am-5pm
Open on Mon sch hols
£8 adult, £6 child, £25 family (2+2) or £23 (1+3), U2's free
Annual: £40 adult, £30 child, £125 family (2+2) or £115 (1+3)
Bristol to Clevedon road via Failand ( B3128 ). Or M5 J 20. Follow brown tourist signs.

This farm creatively combines religious and agricultural themes. A full day's activity with 80 different kinds of animal from chicks to rhinos and the chance to see lambs being born around Easter time. There are tractor and trailer rides, a huge variety of indoor and outdoor play equipment, a straw den with rope swings and several adventure trails. The theme of this farm (Noah's Ark and the creationist view of evolution) is explored in exhibitions, during the tractor ride and whilst feeding and handling the animals in the barn. There is an indoor maze; a lookout tower offering stunning views across the Severn Estuary to Wales and the longest hedge maze in the world.

## Norwood Farm

Bath Rd, Norton St Philip, Bath, BA2 7LP
01373 834356
www.norwoodfarm.co.uk
Apr-Sep: daily 10.30am-5.30am
£5 adult, £3.50 child, free U3's
Annual: £20 adult, £14 child
B3110 between Bath and Frome. Hourly bus service (No 267) from Bath

This environmentally aware working farm, set in lovely countryside is the only Organic Rare Breeds Centre in the region. The farm opens in spring with the lambing of 12 different native breeds. A variety of goats, ponies, poultry, pigs and cattle can be stroked and fed. There are farm walks, gardens to picnic in, separate play areas for U12's and toddlers and a new organic veg and plant centre.

## Cattle Country Adventure Park

Berkeley Heath Farm, Berkeley, GL13 9EW
01453 810 510
www.cattlecountry.co.uk
Easter-Sep: Sat-Sun 10am-5pm, daily sch hols
Some winter openings, call for details
£5-£6.50 adult/child, free U2's, prices seasonal
M5 J14 take A38 and follow brown tourist signs.

This is a good family day out for U15's. Lots of indoor and outdoor play equipment where parents can join in too. Two dedicated play areas for U7's. A farm trail passes a willow maze and a herd of American bison. A miniature railway offering rides through the park. Private party bookings available.

# WILDLIFE

## Avon Wildlife Trust

32 Jacobs Well Rd, Bristol, BS8 1DR
0117 917 7270
www.avonwildlifetrust.org.uk

This charity is dedicated to the promoting and protecting of wildlife. It has two centres at Folly Farm in the Chew Valley and Willsbridge Mill in Keynsham. They offer activities and walks for the whole family, and events in the school holidays, all listed on their website. See Walks pg 59.

## Longleat

Nr Warminster, Wiltshire, BA12 7NW
01985 844 400
www.longleat.co.uk
Safari Park: Apr-Nov daily 10am-4pm
w/e's, B/H's & summer hols 10am-5pm
House opening/tours phone or check website
Passport ticket: £19 adult, £15 child, free U3's
(available for one season, online booking available)
A37 (Wells Road) south to Farrington Gurney, left onto A362, through Frome and follow brown signs

Longleat comprises a stately home, safari park, and other attractions. Drive through the safari park (soft top cars not permitted) and see giraffes, zebras, tigers and lions in their enclosures. The monkey jungle is optional as they will clamber on your car, so not recommended for the car proud but children will love it. Please note Modeo's seem to come off particularly badly! (Safari bus available). The other attractions include Postman Pat's Village, Butterfly Garden, King Arthur's Mirror Maze, Blue Peter maze, miniature steam railway, pets corner, a large adventure playground, a safari boat trip where you can see hippos and sea lions. Not all areas are buggy friendly.

## The National Birds of Prey Centre

Newent, Gloucestershire, GL18 1JJ
0870 990 1992
www.nbpc.co.uk
Feb-Oct: daily 10.30am-5.30pm
£8 adult, £5.50 child, £22 family (2+2), free U4's
M5 J11a, A40 Ross-on-Wye, B4215 to Newent, follow brown tourist signs.

The centre houses one of the most significant collections of birds of prey in the UK. Over 60 species of birds, including eagles, falcons and buzzards with flying displays three times daily.

## Tropiquaria

Washford Cross, Watchet, West Somerset, TA23 0QB
01984 640 688
www.tropiquaria.co.uk
Apr-mid Sep: daily 10am-6pm,
Mid Sep-Oct: 11am-5pm
Nov-Mar: w/e's & sch hols only
£6.95 adult, £5.95 child, £24.95 family (2+2)
free U3's
M5 J23, take A39 twds Minehead. It's between Williton and Washford

Housed in the old BBC transmitting station, this colourful aquarium is home to frogs, snakes, lizards, birds and spiders. Outside there are lemurs, wallabies and chipmunks. Other attractions include: The Shadowstring Puppet Theatre, Wireless in the West Museum (a history of broadcasting), an adventure playground with two life-size galleon ships, a playground for the U5's and an indoor play castle with café.

## WWT Slimbridge

The Wildfowl and Wetlands Centre, Slimbridge, GL2
0870 334 4000
www.wwt.org.uk
Daily 9.30am-5.30pm, winter 9.30am-5pm
£6.75 adult, £4 child, £18.50 family (2+2), free U4's
M5 Jct 13 or 14, follow brown tourist signs. Nearest
station Cam & Dursley.

Spacious landscaped grounds offer the chance
to get very close to and feed, exotic, rare and
endangered water birds. You can also view
from hides and towers. Humming birds can be
seen at close range in the Tropical House. The
visitor centre includes the Hanson Discovery
Centre, a cinema and great views over the
River Severn from the Sloane Observation
Tower. There is also a wildlife art gallery.

# CASTLES

## Berkeley Castle & Butterfly Farm

Berkeley, Gloucestershire, GL13 9BQ
01453 810332
www.berkeley-castle.com
Apr-Sep: Tue-Sat & B/H's 11am-4pm, Sun 2pm-5pm
Oct: Sun only, Nov-Apr: closed
£7.50 adult, £4.50 child, free U5's
Garden only (avail Tue-Fri) £4 adult, £2 child
On A38 between Bristol and Gloucester.

Twenty four generations of the Berkeley
family have lived here since 1153 in what is
England's oldest inhabited castle. It has been
transformed over the years from a Norman
fortress to a stately home full of paintings,
tapestries and treasures. Lawns and terraced
gardens surround the castle. Admission price
includes an optional 1 hour guided tour plus
entry to the Butterfly Farm (Apr-Sep). Many
steps mean pushchairs can't be used in the
castle and baby backpacks are preferable
outside. Tea rooms and plant centre.

## Caerphilly Castle

Castle Street, Caerphilly, CF83 1JD
029 2088 3143
www.cadw.wales.gov.uk
Daily 9.30am-5pm, seasonal variations
£3 adult, £2.50 child, £8.50 family (2+3), free U5's
M4 J28 direction 'Risca' then A468 to Caerphilly

This huge castle built in the 13th century is
the second biggest in Britain after Windsor.
It's a classic castle with high towers, moats,
banqueting hall, working replica siege-engines
and a leaning tower to make the people of
Pisa green with envy! Pushchair accessible
apart from the two exhibition towers.
Excellent re-enactment days through spring
and summer, ring for details.

## Caldicot Castle and Country Park

Church Road, Caldicot, Monmouthshire, NP 26 4HU
01291 420241
www.caldicotcastle.co.uk
Mar-Oct: daily 11am-5pm
Castle: £3.50 adult, £2 child, £10 family (2+3)
Admissions to Country Park: free
Annual: £27.50 family (2+3)
M4 to M48 J2 for Chepstow then A48 twd Newport
then B4245, follow signs

Although founded during Norman times,
the castle was restored in the Victorian
period and inhabited until the 1960s. Some
furnished rooms remain in the towers. Adult
and children's audio guide and discovery
sheets. The surrounding country park has
buggy-friendly trails and a wildlife pond with
dipping platform. There is also a family-
friendly orienteering course in the grounds.
The castle hosts a wide variety of events and
re-enactments.

## Castell Coch

Tongwynlais, Cardiff, CF15 7JS
029 2081 0101
www.cadw.wales.gov.uk
Apr-Oct: daily 9.30am-5pm, summer 9.30am-6pm
Nov-Mar: Mon-Sat 9.30am-4pm, Sun 11am-4pm
Jan-Feb: closed
£3 adult, £2.50 child, £8.50 family (2+3), U5's free
M4 J32, take A470 north, follow signs

Hidden in woodland, this fairytale castle, complete with conical roofed towers, working portcullis and drawbridge, looks convincingly medieval. It was, however, built in the late 19th century for the Marquis of Bute. The inside remains faithful to the Victorian era being richly furnished and decorated. Worksheet (50p) for children in shop and audio guide (£1) available, suitable for 8+yrs. Woodland trail around castle not suitable for buggies. Coffee shop open Apr-Sep.

## Chepstow Castle

Bridge St, Chepstow, Monmouthshire, NP16 5EY
01291 624065
www.cadw.wales.gov.uk
Mar-Oct: daily 9.30am-5pm, summer 6pm
Nov-Mar: Mon-Sat 9.30am-4pm, Sun 11am-4pm
£3 adult, £2 child, £8.50 family (2+3), free U5's
M4 J21 to M48 J2, then A466 and follow signs.

One of Britain's first stone-built strongholds. Building started not long after the Battle of Hastings in 1066 and the castle was significantly extended over the following centuries. Today the well-preserved ruins perch above the River Wye offering an insight into life in a Norman castle and plenty of scope for exploring. Steep slope from car park (toilets) to castle entrance.

## Farleigh Hungerford Castle

Farleigh Hungerford, Nr. Bath, BA2 7RS
01225 754 026
www.english-heritage.org.uk/farleighhungerford
Apr-Sep: daily 10am-5pm
Oct-Mar: Sun only, 10am-4pm
£3.30 adult, £1.70 child, free U5's
3½ miles west of Trowbridge on A366

Ruins of a 14th century castle and chapel with museum. Audio guide and programme of events for children, including exhibitions, medieval pageants. Pushchairs can be used but backpacks are preferable.

## Sudeley Castle

Winchcombe, Cheltenham, GL54 5JD
01242 602308
www.sudeleycastle.co.uk
Feb-Oct: daily 10.30am-5.30pm
Castle & Gardens: £7.20 adult, £4.20 child
£20.80 family (2+2), free U5's, seasonal variations
M5 J9 take A46 then B4077 then signs to Winchcombe

The castle can boast many royal visitors, including Anne Boleyn, Queen Elizabeth I and Henry VIII. Much of the impressive collection of furniture and paintings is from the Tudor and Victorian periods and school-children will enjoy the Six Wives at Sudeley exhibition. Attractive gardens surround the castle, the highpoint for children being Fort Sudeley, a large imaginatively-designed play area for 5+yrs. Separate small area for toddlers. (£1.50/child, free U5's. )

# STATELY HOMES

## Bowood House & Gardens

Derry Hill, Calne, Wiltshire, SN11 0L2
01249 812102
www.bowood.org
Apr-Oct: daily 11am-6pm
£7.50 adult, £5 child (5-15yrs)
£3.80 child (2-4yrs), free U2's, £22.50 family (2+2)
Annual: £33 adult, £18-£22 child
Off A4, Derry Hill village, midway between Calne and Chippenham.

Capability Brown designed the beautiful park in which Bowood stands. The huge grounds include a lake, waterfall, cave, Doric temple and ample space for games and picnics. More formal gardens can be found in front of the stately home itself, which contains displays of furniture, art, costumes and family heirlooms. There is also a woodland garden of azaleas and rhododendrons (separate entrance off the A342) which is open for 6 wks during the flowering season (May and June).

Bowood also has a superb outdoor adventure playground for children under 12 with a life-size pirate ship, high level rope-walks, giant slides, shutes, trampolines and an indoor soft play palace for younger children.

## NATIONAL TRUST PROPERTIES

National Trust properties are becoming increasingly child friendly, with many making provision for baby changing, feeding and transportation requirements. Often, trails, quiz sheets and activities are on offer for older children. Around Bristol, we're spoilt for choice, the latest Trust acquisition being Tyntesfield.

The four listed below are all over an hour's drive from Bristol, but well worth a day trip:

**Stourhead**, Wiltshire (01747 841152) Superb landscaped garden and house, with temples and mature woodland set around large lake.

**Avebury,** Wiltshire (01672 539250) A huge megalithic stone circle encompassing part of the village of Avebury.

**Dunster Castle**, Somerset (01643 821314) Impressive castle atop a wooded hill set in attractive gardens.

**Hidcote Manor Garden,** Gloucestershire (01386 438333). A gorgeous garden designed as a series of outdoor rooms.

**The National Trust**
Po Box 39, Warrington, WA5 7WD
0870 458 4000
01985 843600 (Wessex branch)
www.nationaltrust.org.uk
Details of all the Trusts properties can be found on the website. Becoming a member of the National Trust can be cost effective if you plan to visit several properties during the year.

**Feeling hungry?** Read our recommendations of the best places to eat in the West Country, see pg 73.

## Clevedon Court

Tickenham Rd, Clevedon, N. Somerset, BS21 6QU
01275 872257
www.nationaltrust.org.uk
enquiries@thenationaltrust.org.uk
Apr-Sep: Wed/Thu/Sun & B/H's 2pm-5pm
£5 adult, £2.50 child, free U5's
B3130 1½ mile east of Clevedon

P WC ☕ 🚌

This 14th-century manor house has been home to the Elton family since 1709. Eltonware pots and vases and a collection of Nailsea glass are on display. Attractive terraced garden — not suitable for buggies but lovely slopes for rolling down. Children's guidebook and nursery rhyme trail available.

## Dyrham Park

Dyrham, nr. Chippenham, Gloucestershire, SN14 8ER
0117 937 2501
www.nationaltrust.org.uk
dyrhampark@nationaltrust.org.uk
Park: daily 11am-5.30pm
House & Garden: Mar-Oct Fri-Tue 12pm-4pm
Phone for winter opening times
Garden and house: £9 adult, £4.50 child, £22.50 family (2+3)
Garden and Park: £3.50 adult, £1.80 child, £8 family (2+3), free U5's
M4 J18, take A46 towards Bath for 2 miles

P ✏ WC 🔱 CP ☕ ✕ 🚽 🚻 ♿

House and gardens built at the turn of the 18th century, with most of the original furnishings. Family activity pack and children's guidebook available. No prams in house, baby slings and hip-carrying infant seats for loan. Spacious grounds and deer park.

## King John's Hunting Lodge

The Square, Axbridge, Somerset, BS26 2AP
01934 732012
www.nationaltrust.org.uk
Daily Apr-Sept 1pm-4pm
Oct-Mar 1st Sat of mth (coincides with Farmers' Market)
Free (donations welcome), not essential

Immaculately restored Early Tudor wool-merchant's house owned by the National Trust, home to a local history museum run by Axbridge and District Museum Trust. Upper floors accessed via steep spiral staircases. Occasional walking tours of the historic town of Axbridge start here (phone for details).

## Lacock Abbey, Fox Talbot Museum & Village

Lacock, Nr Chippenham, Wiltshire, SN15 2LG
01249 730459
www.nationaltrust.org.uk/lacock
Museum, cloisters and garden:
Mar-Oct daily 11am-5.30pm
Abbey: Mar-Oct Wed-Mon 1pm-5.30pm
Museum (only) open winter w/e's, 11am-4pm
Abbey, museum, cloisters and garden:
£7.40 adult, £3.70 child, £18.90 family (2+3),
Free U5's
Other ticket variations available
M4 J17, take A350, 3 miles S of Chippenham

The Abbey was founded in 1232 as a nunnery and transformed into a family home in the 16th century. Children's quiz and spacious grounds to explore. Front-carrying baby slings for loan. The Museum of Photography commemorates the life of William Henry Fox Talbot who made the earliest known photographic negative. The upper gallery has changing exhibitions. The medieval village with its many lime washed half-timbered houses has been used as a location for several period dramas such as Pride and Prejudice. The Abbey was also used to film parts of the Harry Potter films. There is a small children's play area opposite the museum and lots of places to eat in the village.

## Tyntesfield

Wraxall, North Somerset, BS48 1NT
Gardens Mid Mar-Oct
House Mid Apr-Oct Mon, Wed, Sat & Sun:
10am-4pm, Gardens 5.30pm
House, chapel and gardens: £9 adult, £4.50 child,
£22.50 family (2+3)
Gardens only: £4.50 adult, £2.25 child, £11.25 family
7 miles SW of Bristol on B3128

Spectacular Victorian Gothic-Revival country house and 500-acre estate, recently acquired by the National Trust. Situated on a ridge overlooking the beautiful Yeo Valley, the mansion bristles with towers and turrets and contains an unrivalled collection of Victorian decorative arts. Still in the early stages of development, facilities on the site are limited. There are quiz trails for over 8's and more provision for younger children is planned.

Pre-booked guided tours are available. Timed tickets in operation (no guaranteed entry on very busy days). No buggies or back packs are allowed in the house, but there is free loan of hipster carriers. There's a private chapel, formal gardens and a working walled kitchen garden. If you forget your picnic, there is a kiosk for hot drinks and sandwiches.

# SEVERN ADVENTURES

The Severn Estuary has the second highest tidal range in the world — it can be as much as 50 feet. This contributes to the great natural spectacle of the Severn Bore, details below. The estuary itself can be explored by steamships Waverly and Balmoral, see Transport chapter. See also Bay Island Voyage, Cardiff Bay.

Flat Holm and Steep Holm, the two islands between Cardiff and Weston-super-Mare, are wildlife havens with fascinating histories and well worth visiting.

Although there's no pedestrian access to the new Severn Crossing you can still walk or cycle across the old bridge away from the traffic (park at Aust Services off J1 M48).

## Severn Bridges Visitor Centre

Shaft Rd, Off Green Lane, Severn Beach, BS35 4HW
01454 633511
www.onbridges.com
Easter-Oct: Sat,Sun & B/H's 11am-4pm, pre-booked group winter visits
£1 adults, 75p child
M5 J17 take B4055 through Pilning. Continue straight on. At mini-r'about follow Green Lane over M49. Right at lights into Shaft Rd.

Educational exhibition showing history of the River Severn crossing and the construction of the two road bridges. There is a video which is quite technical for children but staff offer child-friendly information.

## The Severn Bore

www.severn-bore.co.uk

The Severn Bore is a large surge wave in the estuary of the River Severn which makes a truly spectacular sight at its best. It occurs because of the shape of the estuary — it narrows from 5 miles wide at Avonmouth, to less than 100 yards wide by Minsterworth. As the water is funnelled into an increasingly narrow channel, a large wave is formed. This occurs at least once during most months of the year, but the Bore is largest around equinoxes. Surfing the Bore has become a competitive sport. See website for timetable and viewing points. Get there early, as the Bore can arrive up to half an hour either side of the scheduled time.

## Flat Holm Project

The Pier Head, Barry Docks, Barry, CF62 5QS
01446 747661
www.cardiff-info.com/flatholm
Trips run from end Mar-Oct, tide & weather dependant
£13.75 adult, £6.75 child, £35 family (2+2), U4's not permitted

A day trip to this tiny island in the Bristol Channel gives you three hours on the island and includes a guided walk. The crossing takes 30 minutes. Since the Dark Ages, the island has been used as a retreat for monks, then as a sanctuary for Vikings, Anglo Saxons, smugglers and cholera victims. Fortified in Victorian times and WW2, it is now a haven for wildlife, home to a large colony of gulls, shelducks, slow worms, goats, sheep and tame rabbits. It's best to take a picnic as the tuck shop only sells snacks.

## Steep Holm Nature Reserve

Knightstone Causeway, Marine Lake, BS22 8EA
01934 632307
www.steepholm.freeserve.co.uk
Trips run Apr-Sept, tide & weather dependent
£18 adult, £9 child accompanied (5-16), no U5's due to life jacket restrictions
M5 J21, take A370 to seafront then head north up to Knightstone

Visiting Steep Holm on a ferry from Weston-super-Mare is also possible. There are great views from the Severn Bridges as far down the coast as North Devon. There is a variety of wildlife including muntjac deer, cormorants and gulls. In summer you may see grey seals fishing. Fortifications include Victorian cannons. Visitors need to be reasonably fit as there is no landing stage on the island and the paths are steep in places. The visitor centre has toilets and offers light refreshments and souvenirs. You should have around six hours on the island depending on the tides and there's a trail guide ( £1.70 ) to help you navigate the sights. Take a torch to explore underground ammunition stores, binoculars, camera, non-slip shoes and a picnic.

## Oldbury Power Station Visitor Centre

Oldbury-on-Severn, South Glos, BS35 1RQ
01454 893500
Mar-Oct: daily 10am-4pm, pre-booked winter visits
Admission free
A38 north, take B4061 through Thornbury, then left to Oldbury-on-Severn and follow signs

Find out how a nuclear power station works with interactive displays and videos. Outdoor play area & nature trail.

# ROMAN BRITAIN

As well as the Roman Baths, see Bath section, there are several other Roman sites near Bristol worth a visit. Always useful for bringing that school project to life!

## Chedworth Roman Villa

Yanworth, Near Cheltenham, Glos, GL54 3LJ
01242 890256
www.nationaltrust.org.uk
Mar-Nov: Tue-Sun & B/H's 11am-4pm
Summer 10am-5pm
£5.50 adult, £3 child, £14.50 family (2+3), free U5's
M5 J11A take A417 east, A436 then right via
Withington, follow signs

Owned by the National Trust, this is one of the best examples of a Roman Villa in England. The remains of this substantial dwelling indicate that it would have been inhabited by a very wealthy family. There are two well-preserved bathhouses, hypocausts demonstrating how the Roman invention of under-floor heating worked, beautiful mosaics, a latrine, and a museum housing objects from the villa. Entertaining audio guide for children, 6+yrs. If you can, coincide your visit with one of the Living History Days where you can join in with demonstrations of day-to-day Roman life. Children's activities during the holidays. Pushchairs are admitted but there are some steps.There are good walks in Chedworth Woods and along the disused railway track.

## National Roman Legion Museum

High Street, Caerleon, Gwent, NP18 1AE
01633 423134
www.nmgw.ac.uk
Museum: Mon-Sat 10am-5pm, Sun 2pm-5pm
Fortress baths: Mon-Sat 9.30am-5pm
Free admission
Museum, Barracks and Amphitheatre: £2.90 adult, £2.50 child, £8.30 family (2+3)
M4 J24 follow signs to Caerleon and Museum

Nearly 2000 years ago, the Romans established a fortress at Caerleon. In the museum you can discover how the Roman soldiers lived, fought, and worshipped. At weekends and during the holidays, a barrack room can be visited where you can try on replica suits of armour and take part in the daily activities of a soldier. Also the remains of the Fortress Baths, with video, sound and light displays. A short walk from the museum is Britain's best example of a Roman Amphitheatre where gladiators battled to the death. Impressive re-enactments are held here every June (ring 01633 430041).

### Caerwent

10 miles from Caerleon on the A48 or from Bristol M4 then M48 J2

Having visited the museum at Caerleon you could stop off at the wonderfully-preserved town of Caerwent where the remains of shops, a courtyard house, temple and forum can be seen. In the 4th century, when the Romans were struggling to retain power, a high wall was built around the town, most of which still stands today.

# WHEELS & WINGS

Many children go through a stage of being fascinated with transport, be it wheeled or winged. The places listed below all display the life-sized article. If you fancy something smaller, there's Bourton Model Railway, see Cotswolds, and for the hands-on approach try Diggerland, see Fun Stuff.

## Cotswold Motoring Museum and Toy Collection

The Old Mill, Bourton-on-the-Water, Glos, GL54 2BY
01451 821 255
www.cotswold-motor-museum.com
Feb-Oct: daily 10am-6pm
£3.50 adult, £2.45 child, £10.85 family (2+2),
Free U4's

Impressive car collection dating back to the 1920s, and the museum has lots of other transport memorabilia including over 800 enamel signs. Also includes a big toy collection (including children's pedal cars and dinky toys), a workshop based on a 1920s village garage, a blacksmith's and this is also where Brum the little car lives. Children's quizzes, puzzles and jigsaws.

## Haynes Motor Museum

Sparkford, Nr Yeovil, Somerset, BA22 7LH
01963 440804
www.haynesmotormuseum.co.uk
Daily 9.30am-5.30pm, some seasonal variations
£6.50 adult, £3.50 child, £8.50-£19 family, free U5's
M5 J25 then A358 & A303 to Sparkford. Or A37
south to A303.

[icons]

If you've got a car fanatic in your household, Britain's most extensive car collection on permanent display should keep them happy, although it is more look than touch. Hundreds of cars, ranging from the Chevrolet Corvette to the Sinclair C5. There is also a Hall of Motor Sport, motorbike display, a bus full of soft play equipment (open sch summer hols), an indoor children's activity centre and a themed outdoor play area.

## STEAM

Kemble Drive, Swindon, SN2 2TA
01793 466646
www.steam-museum.org.uk
Mon-Sat 10am-5pm, Sun 11am-5pm
£5.95 adult, £3.95 child, £15.20-£18.30 family
free U5's
M4 J16, follow signs to Outlet Centre

[icons]

The Museum of the Great Western Railway gives you an idea of what it was like to work on and use the GWR with lots of hands-on exhibits. Reconstructed platforms, a cab simulator, and family activities during the school holidays. Special appearances by Thomas the Tank Engine and engines in steam, help bring history to life.

## The Helicopter Museum

The Heliport, Locking Moor Road,
Weston-super-Mare, BS24 8PP
01934 635 227
www.helicoptermuseum.co.uk
Wed-Sun, B/H's 10am-5.30pm, winter variations
Daily Easter and summer hols
£4.95 adult, £2.95 child, £13 family (2+2)
M5 J21, on the A368/A371, follow signs

[icons]

The world's largest dedicated helicopter museum housing the world's oldest, fastest and ugliest helicopters! Themed play area. Special events include Helicopter Experience Flights and the annual Heliday (usually the last weekend in July), a static helicopter display on Beach Lawns, the seafront. This features civil and military helicopters and pleasure flights from the beach.

## Fleet Air Arm Museum

RNAS Yeovilton, Ilchester, Somerset, BA22 8HT
01935 840565
www.fleetairarm.com
Apr-Oct: daily 10am-5.30pm
Nov-Mar: Wed-Sun 10am-4.30pm
£10 adult, £7 child, £30 family (2+3), free U5's
Take the A37 south of Bristol (50mins)

[icons]

Displaying the largest collection of Naval aircraft in Europe, this museum will appeal to children of 6+yrs along with aircraft-enthusiast toddlers. Follow the development of British aircraft from wooden bi-planes through to Concorde. You can sit in the cockpit of a jet fighter, or even experience life aboard an aircraft carrier, arriving on the flight deck via a simulated helicopter ride. Being next to the air base, there's a good chance of seeing Sea Harriers and helicopters going through their manoeuvres outside.

## RNAS Yeovilton Airday

www.yeoviltonairday.co.uk

Entertainment on the ground as well as flying displays at this annual event. See website for details.

## Royal International Air Tattoo

RAF Fairford, Gloucestershire, GL7 4NA
01285 713 456
www.airtattoo.com
M4 J15, follow signs

This fascinating, huge aircraft fest takes place annually at RAF Fairford in mid July. Check website for further details.

# GOING UNDERGROUND

Going down into a mine or through caves can leave a lasting impression on a child, entering a fantasy world in the semi-darkness.

## Big Pit National Mining Museum

Blaenafon, Torfaen, Nr. Newport, NP4 9XP
01495 790311
www.nmgw.ac.uk/bigpit
Mid Feb-Nov: daily 9.30am-5pm, underground tours from 10am-3.30pm
Free admission
J 25a M4 follow brown signs.

Blaenafon has World Heritage status. Walk around this coal mine and find out how men, women and children worked here for over 200 years. Children over 1 metre tall can go underground, and wear hard hats. New museum exhibitions in the original pithead baths and multi-media displays of modern mining will help to answer all their questions! Allow four hours for visit.

## Cheddar Caves & Gorge

Cheddar, Somerset, BS27 3QF
01934 742 343
www.cheddarcaves.co.uk
Daily 10am-5pm, minor seasonal variations
£11.50 adult, £8.50 child, £31.50 family (2+2) free U5's
SW of Bristol on the A371, between A38 & A37

Impressive caves located in spectacular gorge. The two main caves to explore are Gough's with its cathedral-like caverns and Cox's with its stunning formations and colours. Excellent explorer audio guide of Gough's cave (5+yrs). Buggies can be taken into the caves, although they will have to be left in certain places and picked up later. Baby back packs are fine, watch the head room. Also: The Cheddar Man museum which looks at Stone Age man and cannibalism (during the summer there are outside demonstrations of stone age survival techniques); The Crystal Quest — discover dimly-lit caves inhabited by wizards, goblins,

fairy princesses and dragons; an open top bus tour of the Gorge during summer; Jacobs Ladder — a 274 step climb to the top of the gorge with fantastic views of the Mendips from the lookout tower. From here there is a 3-mile waymarked circular walk around the Gorge. The caves also offer caving, climbing and abseiling for 11+yrs, see website for details. Further down the Gorge you can watch the famous cheese being made.

## Wookey Hole

Wookey Hole, Wells, Somerset, BA5 1BB
01749 672 243
www.wookey.co.uk
Daily 10am-5pm, winter 4pm
£10.90 adult, £8.50 child, free U4's
2 miles north west of Wells, follow brown signs.

A guided tour (approx 40 mins) takes you through this impressive series of caves carved out by the River Axe. The route is not suitable for pushchairs, there is enough headroom for child back packs. For those that cannot access the caves there is now a virtual reality tour of the caves and valley. Recently opened is a Valley of the Dinosaurs where you can stroll among full-sized dinosaurs. Other attractions include a museum, an interactive Victorian paper mill, a mirror maze, magic shows in the Wizard's Theatre, a collection of playable Edwardian Penny Arcade machines and two play barns for U10's.

# FUN STUFF

You'll find other similar ideas listed under the place/town in which they're located. These were simply geographically isolated.

## Boomerang

Bowerhill, Melksham, Wiltshire, SN12 6TJ
01225 702000
www.boomeranguk.co.uk
Daily 9.30am-6pm (Sat 7pm)
Unlimited play time (1.5hr restriction when full)
£3.20 child 2-11yrs, £2.10 child 1-2yr
Call for peak times and pricing
M4 J17, A350 to Melksham then follow signs for Bowerhill & Sports Centre.

[P] [V] [✎] [WC] [✗] [ᴪ] [CP] [↖] [↗] [✐] [TA] [⚲] [✗] [⊞] [♿]

Huge area of softplay equipment for U11's or 1.5m offering unlimited playtime when not full. Separate room for U1's with activity centres, play mats, bottle warmers etc.

Disco Mania, last Friday of the month for 5-11yrs. Also a variety of party packages, see website for details. Also party equipment for hire, bouncy castles, sumo wrestling kit etc.

## Diggerland

Verbeer Manor, Cullompton, Devon, EX15 2PE
08700 344437
www.diggerland.com
Feb-Nov: w/e's, B/H's & daily sch hols, 10am-5pm
£2.50pp, free U2's
Online booking available
Buy credits for riding/driving motorised diggers
M5 J27 take A38 east, follow signs for 3 miles

[P] [✎] [WC] [✗] [ᴪ] [CP] [♟] [↖] [↗] [◸] [TA] [✗] [⚲] [⊞] [♿]

In this large adventure park, children and adults can ride in, and drive different types of construction machinery including dumper trucks and diggers, all under strict supervision. Age limits apply. Other attractions include pedal power diggers, a digger sandpit, bouncy castle and computer digger games. Play area for younger children.

## Magicland

Meadow Rd, Circencester, Glos, GL7 1YA
01285 885570
www.magicland.co.uk
Daily 10am-6pm
£1 adults, £4 child 5-12yrs, £3.50 child 1-4yrs
free U1's
Off peak prices available

[P] [WC] [✎] [ᴪ] [CP] [✗] [⊞]

Magicland offers a 13,000sq foot arena containing soft play structures, slides, a 70ft astra slide and cannon arena. This area contains four pneumatically powered cannons that allow you to shoot foam balls at various targets including other visitors! There is a safe toddler areas, a five-a-side football pitch and café overlooking the play area. Party packages available.

# WALKS & DAYS OUTSIDE

Thanks to Jane Wisbey and Peter Stonham for their contributions to this section.

With the appropriate outdoor clothes and some parental enthusiasm, it is possible to avoid family cabin fever by getting out for a walk. Although the suggestion of a walk is not always initially met with boundless enthusiasm!

You don't have to drive very far out of Bristol to find a variety of places to stretch your legs, whether it's a gentle potter with toddlers or a proper hike you're after. Below you'll find a few ideas, some requiring basic map reading skills, others just being nice places to wander around. Where possible we've tried to give an indication of age/pushchair suitability.

## NORTH EAST OF BRISTOL

### Brackenbury Ditches, Cotswolds

OS Map 162 Gloucester & Forest of Dean.
Access: Parking on roadside 1 mile north of Wotton-under-Edge at 757943 or at 754941.

A fairly level walk of 2-4 miles through mixed woodland, some mature beech areas, plus some great views. Suitable for all-terrain buggies and children, but toddlers might struggle. Trainers OK as long as no recent rain. Mind you don't loose your bearings in the woods! Take the track going north west, or the footpath across the fields depending on where you parked. Take your pick of the tracks through the woods, but aim for the fort and Nibley Knoll in a north westerly direction for the better woodland and views.

## Lasborough Park, Cotswolds

OS Map 162 Gloucester & Forest of Dean.
Access: 5 miles east of Wotton-under-Edge. Parking on wide grass verge by Chapel in Newington Bagpath at 815948.

A 4-mile circular walk through delightful Cotswold valleys. Enjoy it during crisp frost in winter, lambs, buds and flowers in spring, warm summer afternoons, or autumn colours, grouse and blackberries. Stout footware and compass required, wellies if recent rain. Not suitable for buggies or pre-school children. Ideal if babies in back-packs and for school age children. Behind the chapel, pick up footpath west to Bagpath (across the field towards the transmission mast). At the lane, turn left going south for 300 metres and take the footpath by the drive of Seaton House. Cross the fields and down into the woods, to the stream at the bottom. Turn left (south) and follow the stream for 1km across several fields. Cross to the west bank when convenient as you approach the derelict stone bridge in the trees. Follow the track as it swings right then take a left along the track alongside the woods below Ozleworth Park. Continue into the woods, then after 200 metres take the track on the left, going due east along the stream. After 1km, take the path into the left valley going north east. There are fishing lakes in this area so keep an eye on young children. After the large lake, take the gate into Lasborough Park, walking below the house and through the park to the gate at the top corner, and the path rises towards the chapel where you started.

## Leyhill Arboretum

HMP Leyhill, Tortworth, Wotton-under-Edge, GL12
01454 264345
Daily 9am-4m
½ mile from M5, J12, on B4509 towards Wotton

An interesting collection of trees and ornamental gardens managed by Leyhill prison (regular exhibitor at Chelsea Flower Show), adjacent to the Tortworth Court Hotel – an impressive Victorian mansion. Several short, circular walks on small paths through the arboretum (not buggy friendly). The adjacent visitor centre is no longer open.

## Lower Lodge Woods

Ozleworth, Wotton-under-Edge, Gloucestershire
01452 383333
www.gloucestershirewildlifetrust.co.uk
From Wotton on the Wortley rd turn left in Wortley at the sign to Ozleworth and continue for about 1 ½ miles along this lane. Limited parking is available on the left in front of Newark Park's Lower Lodge

A nature reserve owned by Gloucestershire Wildlife Trust, this small ancient woodland, especially pretty in spring, is a haven for wildflowers and birds. Walk through the gate, past Lower Lodge, to find the map of a circular walk about a mile long. Half way round in a clockwise direction, you can either take the track to your right, which leads back to where you started, or continue to the left (a further ½ mile uphill) to Newark Park, the National Trust house just visible through the trees (see separate entry).

## Lower Woods

Wickwar, Wotton-under-Edge, Gloucestershire
01452 383333
www.gloucestershirewldlifetrust.co.uk
Approach from Wickwar or Hawkesbury Upton
via Inglestone Common. Take the track opposite
Inglestone Farm, which leads to the car park by
Lower Woods Lodge

A nature reserve owned by Gloucestershire
Wildlife Trust, this ancient woodland is
one of England's largest oak-ash woods on
heavy clay soils. The area has been wooded
since prehistoric times and, as a result, is
very rich in wildlife, including wildflowers,
butterflies, dormice and birds. There are three
waymarked trails of different lengths (up
to two miles), which take you through the
woods along paths, ancient grassy trenches
and rides. The trails are clearly signposted,
and free maps are available at the car park.
Sturdy footwear is advisable all year round;
not suitable for buggies.

## Splatts Wood, Cotswolds

OS Map 172 Bristol & Bath
Access: 2 miles North of Hawkesbury Upton. Parking
on verge between Hawkesbury Upton and Hillesley
at 772880. Alternatively, park in Hawkesbury Upton
and adjust the route accordingly

A gentle 2-3 mile walk through peaceful,
lush meadows beneath wooded ridges and
woodland, including a stretch of the Cotswold
Way. Suitable for babies in backpacks and
children. Take the right hand of the two tracks
going north, which bears right as it goes into
the woods. Follow it round to north east, into
the meadows below Splatts Wood. Continue
for 1.5 km to the lane at the bottom and
turn right. Turn right after 100 metres up the
track on the right and continue back to the
car through woods and fields. Alternatively,
continue South East along the lane, fork right
and take the footpath on the right 300 metres
after the fork. Walk up the valley taking a
choice of footpaths towards Hawkesbury
Upton. At the lane either turn right 1.5km
back to the car, past the Monument or
wander through the village to the pub on the
crossroads then back to the car.

# EAST OF BRISTOL

## Weston Big Wood

Nr Portishead, North Somerset
0117 917 7270
www.avonwildlifetrust.org.uk
mail@avonwildlifetrust.org.uk
Open all year
From the B3124 Clevedon-Portishead road, turn into
Valley Road just north of Weston-in-Gordano. Park
in the lay-by 300m on the right, and walk up the hill.
Steps lead into the wood from the road

One of the area's largest ancient woodlands,
dating back to the last Ice Age, this Avon
Wildlife Trust nature reserve is rich in wildlife,
including butterflies, woodpeckers, tawny
owls, bats and numerous badger setts. In
spring, the ground is covered with wood
anemones, violets and masses of bluebells.
The old stones, ditches and banks are thought
to be medieval boundaries used to divide
the wood into sectors. The reserve is criss-
crossed with a network of (sometimes muddy)
footpaths; keep away from the quarry sides.

## SOUTH EAST OF BRISTOL

### Bradford-on-Avon to Avoncliff

Access: Bradford-upon-Avon Station car park.

A canal-side walk between two villages. Take the path at the end of Bradford-on-Avon Station car park that leads into Barton Country Park. Follow the river until it joins the towpath. Walk along this for a mile or so past narrow boats, until you come to Avoncliff. Here you will find the Madhatter café, see Eating Out and The Cross Guns Pub.

### Brokers Wood Country Park

Brokerswood, Nr. Westbury, Wiltshire, BA13 4EH
01373 822 238
www.brokerswood.co.uk
woodland.park@virgin.net
Daily from 10am, closing times seasonal
£3 adult, £1.50 child, free U5's. Train 75p.
A36 12 miles south Bath, follow brown tourist signs

Attractive woodland country park, with a lake (fishing possible) and miles of paths to explore, many pushchair accessible. Narrow gauge railway operates Easter-Oct, w/e and school holidays (Santa Special in Dec). There are two outdoor adventure playgrounds for 2+yrs and an undercover play area for U7's. Caravan/camping available in the park.

### Willsbridge Mill

Avon Wildlife Trust, Willsbridge Hill, Bristol, BS30 6EX
0117 932 6885
www.avonwildlifetrust.org.uk
ruthworsley@avonwildlifetrust.org.uk
Nature Reserve open all year, mill seasonal
Admission free
A431 Bristol to Bath road, turn into Long Beach Road. Car park on left.

This converted mill housing hands-on wildlife and conservation displays is currently only open when schools are visiting, but there is plenty to do outside. The Valley Nature Reserve which includes a Heritage Sculpture Trail, a Wild Waste Garden and plenty of lovely sculptural seating areas for picnics is open all year. Pond dipping equipment available for hire. All paths pushchair friendly.

### Dundas Aqueduct to Avoncliff

Access: Take A36 from Bath to Monkton Combe, turn left on B3108 and park at Canal Visitor Centre

This walk starts at Brass Knocker Basin, see Bradford-on-Avon. It passes through pretty cuttings and embankments. Take towpath and follow the signs to Avoncliff. Lots of wild flowers, ducks and cyclists. Fordside Tea Gardens is about ¾ miles from the start of the walk, open daily, see below. The walk to Avoncliff Aqueduct is about four miles. There are many other walks that are possible along the Kennet and Avon canal and it's easy for family cycling (novice cyclists watch the edge). In the other direction, it is about 4 miles to Bathampton where The George is a child-friendly pub for lunch.

Fordside Tea Gardens is a gem of a place, welcoming families and offering cream teas, homemade cakes and sandwiches.

## SOUTH OF BRISTOL

### Folly Farm

Nr Bishop Sutton, Bath & NE Somerset
0117 917 7270
www.avonwildlifetrust.org.uk
mail@avonwildlifetrust.org.uk
Open all year
Follow the A368 west from the A37 for about 1.5 miles. Folly Farm is signposted up a track to the left

A large nature reserve owned by Avon Wildlife Trust including wildflower meadows, ancient woodland and 17th-century farm buildings (being restored to provide visitor facilities), with spectacular views over Chew Valley Lake and the Mendips. Visit in spring to see woodland carpets of bluebells and primroses or in summer for butterflies and meadows brimming with flowers such as ox-eye daisies and orchids. An Access for All trail through the woodland is waymarked from the car park. You could bring a picnic or visit the nearby Carpenters Arms at Stanton Wick, see pg 77.

## SOUTH WEST OF BRISTOL

### Ashton Hill, Failand

OS Map 172 Bristol and Bath
Access: The car-park is on the B3129 at the
southern tip of Failand village

A beautiful walk through woodland areas,
don't miss it in the autumn. There are several
walks of up to a couple of miles, through
mature woodland. The terrain is rough
and can get very muddy, unsuitable for
pushchairs.

### Blagdon Lake

Blagdon Visitor Centre, Blagdon Lake
Visitor Centre, May-Aug: Sun 2pm-5pm

Peaceful and pretty woodland walk along the
banks of the lake — but beware fishermen
casting. Good walking for toddlers. Park on
bridge abutting lake.

### Brockley Wood, Cleeve

OS Map 172 Bristol and Bath
Access: Take A370 towards Congresbury, turning left
in Cleeve immediately before the Lord Nelson pub,
down Cleeve Hill Road. Continue for approximately
600 yards and turn left into Goblin Coombe car park

Many pretty walks of up to four miles through
the woods, beautiful in autumn. No toilets,
but the Lord Nelson pub on the A370 is
close by.

### Burrington Coombe, near Churchill

OS Map 172 Bristol and Bath
Access: From A368 (Churchill to Blagdon) take the
B3134. Drive up the valley for nearly 2 miles to the
plateau and there is a car-park on the left

A great starting point on the Mendips for
young children. Fantastic views, wonderful
heathland vegetation (wild grassy meadows,
heather, bracken, gorse, silver birch etc.) and
wildlife. Whether it's a quiet picnic, a gentle
stroll or a few miles with the back-pack, there
are lots of options available. For picnics and
short walks take the path at the back of the
car-park (north, towards Bristol) up 10 yards
of rocky path and onto grassy meadow. For
longer walks, walk up the road 30 yards and

take the track on the right (going south) onto
Beacon Batch and head right towards the
peak. Continue west through Black Down,
into Rowberrow Warren, Dolebury Warren
to the Ancient Hill Fort above Churchill then
back along the ridge in the direction of the
car-park. This is about a seven mile circuit but
can be shortened and there are other access
points from Churchill and Shipham areas.

### Chew Valley Lake

Chew Valley Lake Information Centre, Chew Stoke,
BS40 8TF
01275 333345
www.bristolwater.co.uk
trevor.prideaux@bristolwater.co.uk
Daily 10.30am-5.30pm, 4.30pm winter
Parking £1.20

This beautiful lake with wonderful views is a
haven for birds, insects and animals. There
are two lakeside trails suitable for buggies and
wheelchairs. Park at the visitor centre where
there are walk details, gift and tea shop see
Eating Out pg 77. Dogs on leads allowed.

**New Manor Farm Shop**

North Widcombe, West Harptree, Bristol, BS40 6HW
01761 220067
Nr Chew Valley Lake

Worth checking out if you are passing.

### Clevedon Poet's Walk

Access: Pay & Display at Salt House Fields or street
parking

A wonderful, easy-going, short walk (about
1.5 miles) around the headland with good
views across the Severn. Suitable for
pushchairs (two flights of steps) with a nice
clean public toilet. Start at the Salt House
Fields car park, walk along the Front towards
the headland, up the first flight of steps,
and along the path. Continue along the
undulating, fenced tarmac path on the top of
the cliff to St Andrews Church. On the right
hand side of the church you should see a sign
for the walk, follow the path back towards
your starting point.

## Dolebury Warren

Nr Churchill, North Somerset
0117 917 7270
www.avonwildlifetrust.org.uk
mail@avonwildlifetrust.org.uk
Open all year
Follow the A38 south from Churchill; take the first left after the traffic lights into Dolebury Bottom, and follow the lane to the small car park

The site of an imposing Iron Age hill fort, this nature reserve owned by the National Trust and managed by Avon Wildlife Trust offers fantastic views across North Somerset and the Mendips. Late May to August is the best time to visit for rare wildflowers and butterflies, but you can enjoy the views and the feeling of wildness all year round. The site includes the remains of the fort's double ramparts and a medieval rabbit warren. Follow the footpaths from the car park to the summit (strenuous in places; not suitable for buggies).

## Long Wood

Nr Cheddar, Somerset
01823 652400
www.somersetwildlife.org
enquiries@somersetwildlife.org
Open all year
Off the Charterhouse-Shipham road, about ½ mile west of Charterhouse

An ancient woodland in a valley just north of Cheddar Gorge owned by Somerset Wildlife Trust. Check the information board at the entrance, and follow the circular nature trail (about 1½ miles and often muddy). If you visit in late spring, you'll see carpets of bluebells, wild garlic and other flowers. Look out for orchids in the grassland near the entrance. A stream runs through the northern end of the reserve, disappearing underground into the cave of Longwood Swallet (access controlled by Charterhouse Caving Company).

## Glastonbury Tor

Tor is open 365 days/year.
Access: 15 minute walk from village to bottom of Tor.
From Easter-Sept a tour bus costing approx £1 runs every half hour from the carpark by the Abbey and you can just hop off at the Tor.

This steep hill is a striking feature of the local landscape offering stunning views over Somerset, Dorset and Wiltshire. Renovated in 2003, the 15th century tower on top of the Tor is all that remains of a mediaeval church. Up there you get a sense of why this place is a focus for legend and superstition. The Tor is 158m high and a steep climb, but well worth the effort. Completely unsuitable for pushchairs but determined toddlers will make it to the top.

## BEACHES

Tide times: www.easytide.ukho.gov.uk

If you fancy a change from the mud of the severn estuary, then travel a little further afield for golden sands and blue sea. South Wales is about an 1¼ hr's drive from Bristol, North Devon takes just under two hours. You'll find some beautiful beaches with rock pools and good surf. For a great day out, just pack a picnic and head off! The beaches below are all recommended by the Marine Conservation Society for their clean water see: www.goodbeachguide.co.uk

## Ogmore-by-Sea

Bridgend, Vale of Glamorgan, South Wales
M4 J35, follows signs for Porthcawl, Pen y Bont, then
B4524 to Ogmore-by-Sea

P ✐ WC ✖ 👜 ⌂

Huge, popular, west facing beach with good surfing and rock pooling. Beach is accessed over pebbles, with large sandy beach at low tide – back packs preferable to buggies. Toilets and kiosk for snacks, but no other facilities. Lovely walk along cliff top, with extensive grassy areas to sit and enjoy the views. No beach at high tide. Nearby Southerndown beach (approx ½ mile beyond Ogmore) has flat, easy access from the car park, across a road and consequently gets very busy in summer.

## Rest Bay

Porthcawl, Vale of Glamorgan, South Wales
M4 J37, take A4229 to Porthcawl, follow signs to
Rest Bay

P ✐ WC ⛾ ✖ 👜 ⌂

About a mile from Porthcawl, this large, sandy beach is backed by low cliffs and rocks that are just begging to be explored! Faces south west, so excellent surfing. Plenty of space, even during summer months – just keep walking along the beach. Easy access with buggies. Very limited beach at low tide. Large grassy area next to car park and café to sit and watch the sun set. Beach lifeguard service May-September. Lost child centre.

## Woolacombe Beach and Barricane Bay

Woolacombe, North Devon
M5 J27, take the third exit and follow signs for
A361 to Barnstaple. Follow signs for Ilfracombe
and Braunton. Stay on A361 to Mullacott Cross
roundabout, take the first exit and follow signs to
Woolacombe

P ✐ WC ✖ 👜 ⌂

The village beach is a vast expanse of golden sand, backed by sandy hills. Excellent for sandcastles, paddling and surfing. Zoned areas for water sports. In summer, miniature train rides and bouncy castle. Woolacombe village at north end of beach. MCS recommended. Lost child centre. Professional

lifeguard service during summer months. Three large car parks in Woolacombe. Barricane Bay is a lovely sand and shingle beach, smaller and quieter than the village beach. Safe swimming and a great place to find unusual shells. MCS recommended. Car park next to beach. Toilets at Village beach.

## Croyde Bay

nr Saunton, North Devon
Leave M5 at junction 27 and follow A361 to
Braunton. From Braunton follow the signs for
Croyde. There is a car park next to beach allowing
easy access

P ✐ WC ✖ 👜 ⌂

Pretty, small bay, with a lovely sandy beach, backed by sand dunes. Good rock pools to explore. Popular with surfers. Enjoyable walk with spectacular views, to nearby Baggy Point. MCS recommended. Lost child centre. Beach lifeguard service May-September. Very busy in summer.

## Crooklets and Summerleaze beaches – Bude

Bude, North Cornwall
M5 J31, take A30, turn off at Okehampton, along
the A3079 and then the A3072. Bude is signposted
on the A39

P ✐ WC ✖ 🚻

Summerleaze is a huge sandy beach, ideal for sandcastles, rock pooling and paddling. Close to the town and its facilities. There is a seawater pool at low tide. Gets very busy in summer. Crooklets is a safe, sandy beach, surrounded by sand dunes, with rocks to explore. Smaller and quieter than nearby Summerleaze beach, which can also be reached at low tide. Popular with surfers. MCS recommended. Beach lifeguard service end April to end September. Lost child centre.

# EATING OUT IN BRISTOL & THE WEST

Diana Beavon

## CONTENTS

## INTRODUCTION

It used to be that having kids severely cramped your style when it came to eating out. Thankfully, that has changed, especially in Bristol, where there are lots of great places to eat where the kids are genuinely welcome and the menu has something for everyone.

This chapter is testament to the wide choice of eateries suitable for families in the city and beyond. We highlight the places where you can get half portions, kids' menus and even free food for your kids. We also tell you which restaurants and cafés have activities for kids to while away the time between ordering and eating, always a stressful time for parents!

The chapter is organised geographically (see Central Reference Section maps), so you can find a good place for lunch wherever you are planning your day out. And there are options for all tastes and budgets, whether you want a quick snack or something fancier.

# CENTRAL BRISTOL

## HARBOURSIDE

### Brunel's Buttery

Wapping Wharf, Bristol, BS1 6UD
0117 929 1696
Mon-Fri 8am-4pm, Sat & Sun 8-5pm

P WC CP ⟨⟩ ⟨⟩

End of old dock railway beyond the Industrial Museum. Basic outdoor kiosk with tables next to the harbour. Chips, bacon butties, coffee and lots more available. Lovely views.

### Firehouse Rotisserie

Anchor Square, Harbourside, Bristol, BS1 5DB
0117 915 7323
www.firehouserotisserie.co.uk
Mon-Sun 12pm-3pm & 5pm-9.30pm

P V ⟨⟩ WC ⟨⟩ ⟨⟩ CP ⟨⟩ ⟨⟩ ⟨⟩

California-style cooking served in casual restaurant next to @Bristol, overlooking Millennium Square, with outside tables. Will accept bookings for lunch, and very popular on Sundays. Separate children's menu offers choice of pizza or chicken.

### Riverstation

The Grove, Bristol, BS1 4RB
0117 914 4434
www.riverstation.co.uk
Mon-Thu 9am-10.30pm, Fri & Sat 9am-11pm,
Sun 9am-9pm

P V ⟨⟩ WC ⟨⟩ ⟨⟩ ⟨⟩ ⟨⟩ ⟨⟩

Two-storey bar and restaurant on the waterfront with decking. The kitchen downstairs now serves coffees and pastries from 9am most days, with tapas/bistro food available lunchtime onwards. Upstairs the restaurant offers a variety of fresh food with a brunch menu on Sundays. Happy to cater for children, but no specific menu.

### Quayside Restaurant

Jury's Bristol Hotel, Prince St, Bristol, BS1 4QF
0117 923 0333
www.jurysdoyle.com
Carvery daily 12.30pm-2.30pm, 6.30pm-10.30pm

P V ⟨⟩ WC ⟨⟩ ⟨⟩ CP ⟨⟩ ⟨⟩ ⟨⟩ ⟨⟩ ⟨⟩ ⟨⟩

Based in Jury's Hotel by the Harbourside, you can enjoy a light snack in the pub or lounge at any time of day. Serves a carvery menu, including a separate children's menu. Sunday is very popular, bookings is advised.

### Severnshed Restaurant

Grove Harbourside, Bristol, BS1 4RB
0117 925 1212
Mon-Sun 12pm-3pm, 6pm-10.30pm

⟨⟩ WC ⟨⟩ ⟨⟩ ⟨⟩ ⟨⟩

Buzzing harbourside restaurant with outdoor seating. Serving an eclectic seasonal menu of meat and fish. Children's menu includes freshly prepared fish and chips, sausage and mash etc. Special offers mean that family eating out needn't break the bank.

### Watershed Café Bar

1 Canons Rd, Harbourside, Bristol, BS1 5TX
0117 927 5101
www.watershed.co.uk
Mon 11am-11pm, Tue-Fri 9.30am-11pm,
Sat 10am-11pm, Sun 10am-10.30pm

P V ⟨⟩ WC ⟨⟩ ⟨⟩ CP ⟨⟩ ⟨⟩ ⟨⟩ ⟨⟩ ⟨⟩

Daily changing menu offering a variety of tapas and Mediterranean, Indian, Moroccan inspired dishes. Does have a children's menu as well as favourites of baked potatoes and sandwiches. Relaxed atmosphere with dockside views, but can get very busy.

# BROADMEAD & CITY CENTRE

### Arnolfini

16 Narrow Quay, Bristol, BS1 4QA
0117 917 2300
Mon-Sun 10am-11pm
Entry to galleries, bookshop and exhibitions are free

The café bar serves coffee and pastries from 10am, food from 12pm-9pm. Popular w/e brunch 10am-4pm and Sunday roast 12pm-4pm. Waterfront seating.

## Bella Italia

8-10 Baldwin St, Bristol, BS1 1SA
0117 929 3278
Mon-Thu 10am-11pm, Fri & Sat 10am-11.30pm,
Sun 10am-10.30pm

Formerly Bella Pasta. Open for coffees from 10am-12pm. Offers good children's menu with a choice of pizza, pasta or chicken.

## Bottelino's Restaurant

22 Bond Street, Bristol, BS1
0117 926 8054
Mon-Fri 11.30am-2.30pm, 5pm-11pm,
Sat 11.30pm-11pm

Nice Italian restaurant with lunchtime fixed price special offers Mon-Sat on pizza and pasta. Best to call to reserve a table.

## Bristol Old Vic

King Street, Bristol, BS1 4ED
0117 987 7877
www.bristol-old-vic.co.uk
Mon-Sun 10am-7pm

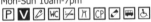

A galleried seated area overlooking the main foyer. It has a great atmosphere with a goodvalue menu.

## Deep Pan Pizza

Unit 15, Silver St, Broadmead, BS1 2DU
0117 929 8014
www.deeppanpizza.co.uk
Mon-Sun 11.30am-9pm

This efficient chain serves an inclusive children's menu of pizza, pasta or sausage and chips with desert, drink and puzzle book.

## Pizza Hut

23-25 St Augustines Parade, Bristol, BS1 4UL
0117 925 2755

Clean efficient pizza chain.

## Queen Square Dining Room & Bar

63 Queen Square, Bristol, BS1 4JZ
0117 929 0700
Mon-Sat 10am-11pm, Sun 10am-4pm

This is a large, airy and informal place to eat. British and European dishes updated daily. Recommended for family Sunday lunches with a roast joint cooked and ready to carve at your table (order joint by Fri 12pm). Popular w/e brunch from 10am.

## The Commercial Rooms

43 Corn Street, Bristol, BS1 1HT
0117 927 9681
Mon-Sun 8am-9pm

A no smoking Wetherspoons pub open from 8am for breakfast. Special children's menu includes a bag of fruit and activity bag. No bookings necessary.

## The Galleries Food Court

Galleries, 25 Union Gallery, Broadmead, BS1 3XD
0117 929 0569 Gallery Management
www.themall.co.uk
Mon-Sat 8.30am-5.30pm, Thu 8.30am-6.30pm,
Sun 10.30am-4.30pm

Food court including many popular chains, choose from B&B Coffee & Muffins, Burger King, Café Nescafe, Fat Jackets, Fruit Sticks, Movenpick, Hickory Grill, Puccinos, Singapore Sam or Zacks Deli.

## The Hole in the Wall

2 The Grove, Queens Sq, Bristol, BS1 4QZ
0117 926 5967
www.beefeater.co.uk
Mon-Sat 12pm-11pm, Sun 12pm-10.30pm

Good pub near waterfront including a Beefeater restaurant upstairs with waitress service, staff happy to help with buggies.

## PARK ST & TRIANGLE

### Boston Tea Party

75 Park St, Bristol, BS1 5PF
0117 929 8601
www.thebostonteaparty.co.uk
Mon-Wed 7am-7.30pm, Thu-Sat 7am-10pm,
Sun 9am-7.30pm

Relaxed café with terraced garden. Serves fresh rustic food including an all-day breakfast, paninis, soups, salads and daily specials. No specific children's menu, but happy to do smaller portions.

### Browns Restaurant & Bar

38 Queens Rd, Clifton, Bristol, BS8 1RE
0117 930 4777
www.browns-restaurant.com
Mon-Sat 12pm-11pm, Sun 12pm-10.30pm

Large attractive licensed refectory, very popular with families. Good extensive menu and a separate children's menu. Will only take bookings for parties of five or more. Buggy entrance at the side door. Happy to have babies sleeping in pushchair in the evenings.

### Danby's Café

Queens Road, Clifton, BS8 1RL
0117 922 3571
Sun & Mon 10.30am-4.30pm, Tue-Sat 10am-4.30pm

Based in Bristol City Museum and Art Gallery, this is a good place to stop and give the kids a treat after running around the musuem. Serves hot snacks, cakes and a children's menu of fish fingers and jacket potatoes.

### Fresh & Wild

The Triangle, 85 Queen's Road, Clifton
0117 910 5930
Mon-Fri 8am-8pm, Sat 9am-7.30pm,
Sun 12pm-5.30pm, winter Sun 11am-4.30pm

Organic supermaket with great café serving salads, sandwiches, soups and juices, plus great cakes and muffins. Food served by weight and child size juices or smoothies available. Happy to offer free Baby Cino's (frothy milk). Ramp access for buggies.

### Krishna's Inn

4, Byron Place, Triangle South, Bristol, BS8 1JT
0117 927 6864
Mon-Thu/Sun 12pm-3pm, 6pm-11pm,
Fri/Sat 12pm-3pm, 6pm-12pm

Specialists in Kerala cuisine very popular with families. No children's menu but happy to adapt any dish, children may like Dosas, a South Indian pancake.

### Le Monde

The Pavillion, Triangle West, Bristol
0117 934 0999
Mon-Sat 12pm-10.30pm, Sun 12-4pm

Large airy restaurant serving a wide choice of grilled meats or fish where children can eat free Mon-Sat between 12pm-6pm. On Sundays, there is a set price roast lunch, although children have a choice of this or the children's menu. Bookings accepted for parties of eight people or more. Restaurant only has two highchairs, so advisable to bring own.

### Nando's

49 Park Street, Bristol
0117 929 9263
Mon-Fri 12pm-11pm, Sat & Sun 12pm-12am

Chicken restaurant serving great hot wings and chips! Children's menu and vegetarian options available. You pay up front and kids can help themselves to refills of drinks and frozen yoghurts. Bookings only accepted for parties of eight or more.

### Pizza Express

31 Berkeley Square, Bristol, BS8 1HP
0117 926 0300
Mon-Sat 11.30am-12am, Sun 11.30-11.30pm

A firm favourite with families. Smart, lively and comfortable. Added attraction of watching the chefs make the pizzas.

## Zizzi

7 Triangle South, Bristol
0117 929 8700
Mon-Sun 12pm-11pm

New location on the triangle, same great Italian food. Will do children's portions of pizza or pasta.

## WHITELADIES RD

### Henry Africa's Hot House

65 Whiteladies Rd, Bristol, BS8 2LY
0117 923 8300
Fri-Sun12pm-11pm, Mon-Thu 4pm-11pm

Relaxed and friendly licensed contemporary American restaurant upstairs offering lunchtime express menu on Fri & Sat served from 12pm-7pm. Also has children's menu, but check to see if they are offering one adult pays full price and a child eats free deal.

### Café Gusto

Clifton Metro, Whiteladies Rd, Bristol, BS8 2NP
&
Unit 3, Clifton Down Shopping Centre
Mon-Sun 7am-6pm

Coffee bars selling sandwiches, baguettes and cakes. Fruit smoothies, popular with kids. No smoking at lunch time.

### Planet Pizza

83 Whiteladies Rd, Bristol, BS8 2NT
0117 907 7112
Mon-Sun 11am-11pm

Pleasant & cosy pizza restaurant. No separate children's menu — happy to offer a quarter slice or plain pizza and does have crayons.

### Top Drawer @ Maskreys

62 Whiteladies Rd, Bristol, BS8 2QA
0117 973 8401
Mon-Sat 9.30am-5pm

Revamped coffee shop on second floor of Maskrey's reached by lift with pleasant outdoor terrace. Good selection of tray bakes and lunchtime snacks including toasties, sandwiches, no separate children's menu.

## CLIFTON VILLAGE

### Aruba

6 Clifton Down Rd, Bristol, BS8 4AD
0117 974 4633
Mon-Fri 8am-4.30pm, Sat 9am-4pm, Sun 10-2.30pm

Licensed café with friendly and helpful staff serving homemade food. Special children's lunchbox available or smaller portions from main menu. Spacious patio area for supervised play.

### Avon Gorge Hotel

Sion Hill, Bristol, BS8 4LD
0117 973 8955
Mon-Sun 11am-11pm

Based in the Avon Gorge Hotel, the White Lion has the added advantage of a large sun terrace with magnificent views of the Suspension Bridge. Open daily for cakes and coffees from 11am, hot bar food served from 12pm-10pm. Ask for children's menu.

### Emmanus House

Clifton Hill, Bristol, BS8 1BN
0117 907 9954
www.emmanus-house.co.uk
Mon-Sun 12pm-2pm, recommend booking

Beautiful house in heart of Clifton which caters for conferences and weddings. It is possible to enjoy the à la carte 3-course meal when there is availability, phone to check if there is space. Offers fantastic views over Bristol with a terraced lawn where most of the produce is grown. Happy to accommodate children, no special menu.

## Madisons

1 Princess Victoria Street, Clifton Village, Bristol
0117 973 4790
Mon-Fri 8am-5.30pm, Sat 8am-6pm, Sun 10am-4pm

Airy café serving light snacks including paninis, toasties and good cakes. Very popular with young mums, but can only have two push chairs inside at one time.

## Pizza Express

2-10 Regent St, Bristol, BS8 4HG
0117 974 4259
Mon-Sat 11.30am-11pm, Sun 12-10.30pm

One of the most recommended restaurants for families offers children's menu and a Piccolo Pack of crayons and activities. Can get busy, so booking recommended. Children enjoy watching the chefs make the pizzas.

## Primrose Café & Bistro

1 Boyces Avenue, Clifton, Bristol
0117 946 6577
Mon-Sat 10am-5pm, Sun 10.30am-3pm

Great place to people watch from their outside tables. Can get very busy and buggies are restricted. Also open in the evening but this is a more grown-up affair!

## Rainbow Café

10 Waterloo St, Bristol, BS8 4BT
0117 973 8937
Mon-Sat 10am-5.30pm

Small, friendly, licensed café, serving excellent homemade whole-food lunches, snacks and teas with child-friendly cups and beakers. Limited parking in the street.

## Splinters Coffee House

66 Clifton Down Rd, Bristol, BS8 4AD
0117 973 4193
Mon-Sat 8am-6pm, Sun & B/H's 10am-5.30pm

Traditional-style licensed café with friendly staff. All food homemade, small portions available, baby food heated. Spacious patio.

## The Lansdown

8 Clifton Rd, Bristol, BS8 1AF
0117 973 4949
Mon-Fri 4pm-11pm, Sat- Sun 12pm-11pm

Friendly small pub on edge of Clifton village, children allowed in pub garden only, except Sundays when they can use the dining room. Good pub menu including choice of roasts or lighter snacks on Sundays, will accept bookings. Happy to offer children's portions, take own child seating.

## Zizzi

29 Princess Victoria Street, Bristol
0117 317 9842
Mon-Sun 12pm-11pm

Popular Italian restaurant. Will do children's portions of pizza or pasta as required. Can only book for parties of eight or more.

# NORTH WEST BRISTOL

## HENBURY

## Blaise Tea Rooms

Blaise Castle Estate, Henbury Road, Bristol
0117 904 1897
Mon-Sun 8.30am-7pm, closes 4pm winter

Adjacent to children's play area, the café serves hot drinks and snacks, including a limited children's menu of fish fingers and chicken nuggets and chips.

**Time to shop on Gloucester Road?**
Check out all the charity shops for kids' clothes and toys.

# NORTH BRISTOL

## GLOUCESTER RD

### 2-3-2

232 Gloucester Road, Bishopston, Bristol
0117 924 9736
Tue-Sat 9am-10pm

Café bistro serving breakfast from 9am-12pm, with a lunchtime menu of home-cooked meals salads, burgers and toasties from 12pm-3pm, but can serve sandwiches and cakes until 6pm when it becomes a bistro. No separate children's menu, but plenty to tempt.

### The Annex

Seymour Road, Bishopston, Bristol
0117 949 3931
Mon-Sat 11.30am-3pm, 5pm-7pm, Sun 12-11pm

Local pub with no smoking conservatory where children are allowed. In summer months, children can play in the enclosed back garden. On Sundays, full adult and children's menu is served until 3pm. When the kitchen is closed, you can buy pizza.

### Café Delight

189 Gloucester Road, Bishopton, Bristol
0117 944 1133
Mon-Sat 9am-5.30pm, Sun 9.30am-4pm, Tue-Sat open evenings

Laid-back licensed café serving good variety of snacks and Medi-themed home cooking with great special's board. Has separate children's menu.

### Café Unlimited

209 Gloucester Road, Bishopston, BS7 8NN
0117 924 0035
Mon-Sat 9am-4.30pm

Large downstairs family room (help down steps with buggies provided). Designated play area with books and drawing material for distraction. Healthy kids food. Fair trade produce used. Gluten and dairy free options. Premises can be hired out for parties for the young and old!

### Halo Restaurant & Bar

141 Gloucester Road, Bristol
0117 944 2504
Mon-Fri 12pm-11pm, Sat 10am-11pm, Sun 12pm-11am

Popular café, bar, restaurant open every day serving breakfasts till 4pm, also wide range of snacks, salads and burgers. No separate children's menu but happy to do smaller portions. In the summer, the large garden is a great sun trap and a firm favourite with the children. Advisable to reserve a table if you want to eat.

### La Ruca

89 Gloucester Road, Bristol
0117 944 6810
Mon-Sat 9am-5.30pm

Health food shop also selling wide range of home cooked food and cakes. Room downstairs to leave buggies.

## ST WERBURGH'S

### St Werburgh's City Farm Café

Watercress Rd, Bristol, BS2 5YJ
0781 395 4933
Wed-Sun 10am-5pm, Fri 7pm-10pm

Lively and unusual tree house café overlooking children's play area. Serving locally produced food. Now open for evening meals with BYO option, best to book in winter, whilst in summer, just turn up. Also offers internet access from 5pm for 15 mins.

## THE DOWNS

### Downs Tea Room

Next to the Water Tower, Durdham Downs, Bristol
0117 923 8186
Mon-Sun 8.30am-5pm

Right on the edge of the Downs near the large Water Tower, this pleasant café is open daily for breakfasts, cakes and coffees and serves a great lunchtime menu. Also good choice of children's menu served all day. Lots of tables outside, so you can relax while your kids run around.

## WESTBURY-ON-TRYM & HENLEAZE

### Café Breeze

105 Henleaze Road, Henleaze, Bristol
0117 962 8230
Mon-Fri 8.30am-5pm, Sat 9am-4pm

Recently refurbished to include a small seating area popular with pregnant ladies! Very child friendly, serves light meals and snacks, plus great coffees and children's menu.

### Smith's Patisserie

7 Charlecombe Court, Stoke Lane, Westbury on Trym
0117 962 1892
Mon-Fri 8am-4.30pm, Sat 8am-1pm

Small café serving light snacks and drinks and a selective children's menu. Great place for a postnatal catch up but limited space for buggies. Seating available on pavement.

## FILTON

### The Mill House

115 Gloucester Rd Nth, Bristol, BS34 7PY
0117 931 2706
www.millhouseinns.co.uk
Mon-Sat 11am-11pm, Sun12pm-11pm

Near the roundabout by British Aerospace, a comfortable pub with restaurant. Children are only allowed in the restaurant area where they have a good choice of food.

## CRIBBS CAUSEWAY

### Harry Ramsden's

Catbrain Lane, Cribbs Causeway, Bristol, BS10 7TQ
0117 959 4100
www.harryramsdens.co.uk
Mon-Sat 12pm-9pm, Sun 12pm-7pm

Large famous fish and chip chain restaurant near the Mall, eat in or take away, does offer more than just fish! Children very welcome, each child's menu includes a play pack. Special themed events held for children and adults — call for more details.

### Nando's

Unit 208, Cribbs Causeway Retail Park, Bristol
0117 959 0146
Mon-Fri 11am-9pm, Sat 11am-7pm, Sun 11am-5pm

Chicken restaurant serving great hot wings and chips! Children's menu and vegetarian options. You pay up front and kids can get their own refills of drinks and frozen yoghurts.

### TGI Fridays

The Venue, Cribbs Causeway, Bristol
0117 959 1987
www.tgifridays.co.uk
Mon-Thu 12pm- 10.30pm, Fri & Sat 12pm-11.30pm, Sun 12pm-10.30pm

Large American-style restaurant popular with children who love all the showmanship of the staff! Free baby food and a good selection on children's menu, plus all children are given a play pack. Will accept bookings.

## The Lamb & Flag

Harvester Restaurant, Cribbs Causeway, BS10 7TL
0117 950 1490
Mon-Sat 11am-11pm, Sun 11am-10.30pm

Harvester restaurant with garden and imaginative farm-like interior. Active policy to welcome family groups; early bird menus and offers (eg. 30% off)

## The Mall Food Court

The Mall, Cribbs Causeway, Bristol, BS34 5QU
0117 903 0303 Cribbs Management
Mon-Fri 10am-9pm, Sat 9am-7pm, Sun 11am-5pm

There are many fast food outlets situated on the second floor — choose from Arkwrights (Fish & Chips) Bakers Oven, Burger King, KFC, Singapore Sam Express, Druckers and Spud U Like. Starbucks, Pizza Hut & Nando's have their own seating. Also look for Costa Coffee, near John Lewis or Café Giardino, near M&S.

# NORTH EAST BRISTOL

## EASTON

### Café Maitreya

89 St. Marks Road, Easton, Bristol
0117 951 0100
thesnug@cafemaitreya.co.uk
Fri 11am-3pm, Sat & Sun 11am-3.30pm,
Tue-Sat 7pm-11pm

Good vegetarian food in light airy surroundings. Menus clearly marked to show vegan, wheat/gluten free and dairy free items. Kids' menu includes mini soup of the day and cheesy soldiers.

# STAPLE HILL

## Staple Hill Oak

Staple Hill, BS16 5HN
0117 956 8543
Mon-Sun 9am-9pm

Popular Wetherspoons pub where children are well catered for — all children's meals include a drink, meal, fruit and activity pack. Open for breakfast from 9am.

# EMERSONS GREEN

## The Beefeater Emersons Green

200/202 Westerleigh Rd, Bristol, BS16 7AN
0117 956 4755
Mon-Sat 11am-11pm, Sun 12pm-9pm

Modern pub in village setting with a Beefeater restaurant.

## The Mill House

The Village, Emersons Green, Bristol, BS16 7AE
0117 970 2023
www.millhouseinns.co.uk
Mon-Sat 9am-11pm, Sat 11am, Sun 12pm

Popular family pub located on commercial estate. Open for coffees from 9am weekdays, food served daily from lunchtime onwards, good choice including separate children's menu. Children love Pirate Pete's Indoor Playpen where they can play for an hour for £1.75 (height and age restrictions apply)

## Willy Wicket

Badminton Road, Downend, BS16 7EQ
0117 956 7308
Mon-Sat 12pm-11pm, Sun 12pm-10.30pm

Popular dining pub near Emersons Green in a converted nineteenth century farmhouse offering a small children's menu. No bookings necessary. The name, by the way, comes from a slang term for a Common Sandpiper.

# EAST BRISTOL

## KINGSWOOD

### Bar Celona

91 Regent Street, Kingswood, Bristol
0117 961 9311
Mon-Sun 11am-11pm

Friendly local restaurant offering range of pizza, pasta and tapas with child portions.

### Kingswood Colliers

94-96 Regent Street, Kingswood, BS15 8HP
0117 967 2247
Mon-Sun 9am-9pm

Part of the Wetherspoons chain, good for breakfast, lunch or evening meals, where children are welcome and have their own menu including a drink, meal, fruit and activity bag.

### The Crown

126 Bath Rd, Longwell Green, Bristol, BS15 6DE
0117 932 2846
Mon-Sat 11am-11pm, Sun 12pm-10.30pm

Harvester restaurant with an imaginative farm-like interior and a beer garden with play equipment.

### Wishing Well

Longwell Green, Kingswood, Bristol
0117 947 5341
Mon-Sun 11am-9pm
£2.50 for one hour in Wacky Warehouse

Part of the Wacky Warehouse group with indoor soft play area attached to the pub with separate area for U5's and another for U2's, parents must remain to supervise. The restaurant offers good family dining including an all-day family feast & two-for-one offers.

# SOUTH EAST BRISTOL

## KEYNSHAM

### The Brass Mill

Avon Mill Lane, Keynsham, BS31 2UG
0117 986 7280
Mon-Sat 11am-11pm, Sun 12pm-10.30pm

A Brewers Fare pub tucked away near Keynsham especially designed for families with scenic location by the river Avon. Large outside beer garden great for summer, plus there is a free indoor ball park (height restrictions apply).

# SOUTH BRISTOL

## BEDMINSTER

### Windmill Hill City Farm Café

Philip St, Bedminster, Bristol, BS3 4EA
0117 963 3252
Tue-Sat 9am-5pm, Sun 10am-6pm, Fri closes 7pm
Tue-Thu hot food until 2pm, Fri-Sun hot food all day

Nice café serving healthy, organic food, open to all, whether you visit the farm or not.

## SOUTHVILLE

### Oasis Café

Southville Centre, Beauley Rd, Bristol, BS3 1QG
0117 923 1039
www.southville.org.uk
Mon 9.30am-5.30pm, Tue-Fri 9.30am-3.45pm

Based in the Southville centre, popular, spacious community café serving wholesome inexpensive menu including children's portions. Not open at weekends.

### The Riverside Garden Centre Café

Clifthouse Road, Southville, Bristol, BS3 1RX
0117 966 7535
Mon-Fri 9.30am-4.30pm, Sat 9.30am-4pm,
Sun 11am-4pm

Popular garden centre café with homemade meals and childrens portions. There is an outside play area including a wendy house.

## SOUTH WEST BRISTOL

### The Dovecote

Ashton Road, Bristol, BS41 9LX
01275 392245
Mon-Sat 12pm-11pm, Sun 12pm-10.30pm

Vintage Inn chain restaurant next to Ashton Court. Large garden with open views. On Sunday's there's a choice of several roasts, no bookings accepted.

### The Stables Café

Ashton Court Visitor Centre, Bristol, BS41 9JN
0117 963 3438
Mon-Sun 10am-5pm, winter Mon-Sun 11am-4pm

Courtyard café in the old stables of Ashton Court Visitor Centre. Serves hot food and light snacks, eat inside or alfresco.

## THE WEST COUNTRY

## NORTH OF BRISTOL

### AROUND THORNBURY

### Almondsbury Garden Centre

Over Lane, Almondsbury
01454 457300
Mon-Fri 9am-5pm, Sat 9.30am-5pm,
Sun 10.30am-4pm, closes earlier in winter

Intimate café serving a variety of snacks, cakes and hot meals including jacket potatoes and paninis. No separate children's menu, but high chairs are provided. Good place to take grandparents for tea and cake!

### Bowl Inn

Church Road, Lower Almondsbury, BS32 4DT
01454 612757
www.theoldbowlinn.co.uk

Traditional village pub with à la carte restaurant and bar menu. The restaurant offers children's food and half portions, it's very popular so book a table. On warmer days you can sit outside next to the pretty church.

### Lamb Inn

Wotton Road, Iron Acton, BS37 9UZ
01454 228265
Mon-Sat 12pm-11pm, Sun 12pm-10.30pm

Quiet, cosy historic village pub with small family dining area. Attractive shaded grassy garden and covered patio. Large function room available for hire.

73

### The Mason's Arms

94 Gloucester Rd, Rudgeway, BS35 3QJ
01454 412370
Mon-Sat 11am-11pm, Sun 12pm-10.30pm

P V ✏ WC ✂ 🔥 CP ⊘ 🍸 🔦 ✈ ♿

A popular, no smoking family-friendly pub and restaurant. Children very welcome.

### The Swan

Tockington Green, Tockington, BS32 4NJ
01454 614800
Mon-Sat 11am-3pm & 6pm-11pm,
Sun 12pm-10.30pm

P V WC ✂ 🔥 CP 🍸 🔦 ✈ ♿

Atmospheric village pub, with child-friendly area and large garden.

### The White Hart

Littleton-on-Severn, Nr Thornbury, BS35 1NR
01454 412275
Mon-Sar 12pm-2.30pm (Sat 3pm) & 6pm-11pm,
Sun 12pm-4pm & 7pm-10.30pm

P WC ✂ 🔥 CP 🍸 🔦 ✈

A lovely old country pub with good beer and great food. No bookings, so it's best to go early! Children's menu and a large attractive family room with plenty of high chairs. There is a large garden but no play equipment.

## FRAMPTON COTTERELL

### The Golden Heart

Down Rd, Winterbourne, BS36 1AU
01454 773152
Sun-Thu 12pm-11pm, Fri-Sat 12pm-12pm

P V ✏ WC ✂ 🔥 CP ⊘ 🍸 🔦 ✈ 🚭

Quaint old pub with restaurant serving a range of home cooked food. Large garden with play equipment

### The Golden Lion

Beesmoor Rd, Frampton Cotterell, BS36 2JN
01454 773348
Mon-Fri 12pm-11pm, Sun 10.30pm, Sat 11am-12am

P V WC ✂ 🔥 CP 🚹 ♿

Traditional, spacious family pub, offering an extensive menu.

## BERKELEY

### Salmon Inn

Wanswell, Berkeley, GL13 9SE
01453 811306
Mon-Sat 11am-11pm, Sun 12pm-10.30pm

P ✏ ✂ 🔥 CP 🚭

Oak-beamed village pub with a few nooks and crannies, bare floorboards and a piano. A large section of the pub is given over to diners, and children are welcome if eating. The front garden, with slides and swings, also seems to double up as the village green. There is a children's tuck shop in the garden where children can purchase reasonably priced crisps and drinks.

# NORTH EAST OF BRISTOL

## FRENCHAY

### Snuff Mill Harvester

207 Frenchay Park Rd, Frenchay, BS16 1LF
0117 956 6560
Mon-Sat 12pm-10pm, Sun 12pm-10.30pm

P V ✏ WC ✂ 🔥 CP ⊘ 🔦 ✈ ♿

Imaginative farm like interior including a central indoor pond stocked with fish!

## CHIPPING SODBURY

### Chatties

16B Horse St, Chipping Sodbury, BS17
01454 321121
Mon-Sat 9.30am-5pm

P V WC ✂ 🔥 CP 🔦 ✈

A comfortable coffee shop with inexpensive meals and smaller childrens portions.

## Codrington Arms

Wapley Rd, Codrington, BS17 6RY
01454 313 145
Mon-Sat 11.30am-3pm & 6pm-11pm,
Sun 12pm-3pm & 6pm-10.30pm

A comfortable, unspoilt family country pub with a large attractive garden. Friendly staff and an extensive menu. Food outside until 8pm only. Book for indoor tables at the weekends.

## The Compass Inn

Nr Badminton, Tormarton, GL9 1JB
01454 218242
www.compass-inn.co.uk
Mon-Sat 7am-11pm, Sun 8am-10.30pm

A family-run pub with a large, pleasant family conservatory and à la carte restaurant. The pub is on a busy road.

## The Cottage Tea Rooms

16B Horse St, Chipping Sodbury, BS17
01454 321121
Mon-Sat 9.30am-5pm

A comfortable coffee shop, with inexpensive meals and smaller children's portions.

## The Dog Inn

Badminton Rd, Chipping Sodbury, BS37 6LZ
01454 312006
Open all day, every day
Food served Mon-Sun 12pm-2.30pm &
Mon-Sat 6pm-9.30pm, Sun 7pm-9pm

A busy pub with a large garden. They have an adventurous selection including a fun menu of good food for children. Quiz night Sun & Mon.

# WOTTON-UNDER-EDGE

## McQuigg's

44 Long St, Wotton-under-Edge, Glos
01453 844108
Mon-Sat 9am-5pm (meals to 3pm),
Fri-Sat 7pm-9pm (last orders)

Café serving drinks, cakes, a variety of light lunches and more substantial specials. On Friday and Saturday evenings, there's a licensed restaurant. Tables in the small garden at the back, with toys for toddlers.

## The Ark Coffee Shop

43 Long Street, Wotton-under-Edge, Glos, GL12 7BX
01453 521838
Mon-Fri 9am-12pm, 12.45pm-4.15pm,
Sat 9.30am-12.30pm

Ecumenical coffee shop run by volunteers that promote fair trade. Serves drinks and a variety of home-made cakes and biscuits. Lidded cups available for young children. Small, partitioned toddler play area with toys and books. Also sells cards and books, mostly Christian, and some fair trade products.

# STROUD & TETBURY

## Gumstool Inn

Calcot Manor, Nr Tetbury, Glos, GL8 8YJ
01666 890391
www.calcotmanor.co.uk
Sat-Sun 12pm-9pm, Mon-Fri 12pm-2pm & 7pm-9pm
On the B4135 Dursley-Tetbury, at the junction with the A46

A gastropub that positively welcomes families. Part of the luxury Calcot Manor country hotel (which has a similarly child-friendly reputation), the inn is situated in a former farmhouse set around a courtyard of lime trees, ancient stone barns and stables dating back to the 14th century. Depending on the weather, you can enjoy the terrace with sunshades outside or cosy log fires inside. There are good menus for both adults and children, and a wide range of ales and wines. Booking advisable at weekends.

## Hobbs House Bakery

4 George St, Nailsworth, Gloucestershire, GL6 0AG
01453 839396
www.hobbshousebakery.co.uk
Mon-Fri 7.30am-6pm (5pm Sat)

WC ☒ 🔥

Unusual bakery-cum-café, an offshoot of the award-winning family-run bakery of the same name located in Chipping Sodbury. A variety of freshly baked bread, including an organic range, as well as cakes, pastries, sandwiches and drinks to take away or eat-in the small café upstairs. As you enter, you walk right past the busy kitchen and can see the bakers at work.

## Hunters Hall Inn

Kingscote, Tetbury, Gloucestershire, GL8 8XZ
01453 860393
www.huntershallinn.com
Mon-Sat 11am-11pm, Sun 12pm-10.30pm
Lunch 12pm-2pm (2.30pm sandwiches),
Eve meals 6.30pm-9.30pm (Sun 9pm)
2 miles west of A46 on the A4135 Tetbury-Dursley

P ☒ WC ☒ 🔥 CP ☗ 🖼

Creeper-clad 16th-century coaching inn with several bars, a restaurant, beamed ceilings and open fires. Large garden with lots of tables and a well-equipped children's play area. Convenient for lunch after the nearby Lasborough Park walk see pg 57. Booking advisable at weekends.

## The Priory Inn

London Road, Tetbury, GL8 8JJ
01666 502251
www.theprioryinn.co.uk
Mon-Sun 7am-10pm

P WC ☒ 🔥 ☗ 🔺 🖼 ♿

Friendly hotel/gastropub serving teas, coffees and cakes from 7am. Lunch served from 12pm using local produce cooked in wood-fired oven. Fantastic children's menu available. The landlord can recommend many buggy-friendly walks around Tetbury, or you can while away the afternoon by the fire!

## Woodruffs

24 High St, Stroud, Gloucestershire, GL5 1AJ
01454 759195
Mon-Sat 9am-5pm (no food service 11am-12pm)

WC ☒ 🔥 CP ☗ 🖼 ☒ 🖥

Award-winning organic café with a largely vegetarian menu, occasional fish dishes and vegan options. Additional seating upstairs, including a family room with small, partitioned toddler play area, toys and child safety gate preventing access to the stairs.

# SOUTH EAST OF BRISTOL

## SALTFORD & COMPTON DANDO

## Compton Inn

Court Hill, Compton Dando, BS39 4JZ
01761 490 321
Mon-Fri 4pm-11pm, Sat 12pm-12am,
Sun 12pm-10.30pm

P V WC ☗ 🔺 🔺 🖽 🖥

A small, unspoilt traditional pub with a large grassy garden. More suited to older children. Open all day at weekends

## The Crown

500 Bath Rd, Saltford, BS31 3HJ
01225 872117
Mon-Sat 11.30am-11pm, Sun 12pm-10.30pm
Food served Mon-Fri 12pm-3pm & 6pm-9pm,
Sat-Sun all day

P V ☒ WC ☒ 🔥 CP ☗ 🔺 🔺 🔺 ♿

Family-friendly pub on A4 between Bath and Bristol. There is a lounge bar with an open fire, a separate non smoking restaurant and a public bar, plus an outdoor children's play area. Food is served from a main menu and can be eaten anywhere in the pub and al fresco during the summer.

## The Riverside Inn

The Shallows, Saltford, BS31 3EZ
01225 873862
Open for food all day throughout summer.

Adjacent to Saltford river and lock. The upstairs pub and restaurant is smart and there is a conservatory for families and garden overlooking the weir. Very comfortable with an extensive menu.

## BATH

### The Boathouse

Newbridge Road, Bath, BA1 3NB
01225 482584
Mon-Sat 11am-11pm, Sun12pm-10.30pm

Located on the edge of Bath by the river, a great pub to round off a day out. Small play area outside, children can get access to the river, so be watchful! Open plan, modern styled bar restaurant where children are welcome throughout. New menu with good range of home-cooked meals, including a separate children's menu. No bookings necessary.

## BRADFORD-ON-AVON

### The Lock Inn Café

48 Frome Road, Bradford-on-Avon, BA15 1LE
01225 868068
www.thelockinn.co.uk
Mon-Sun 8.45am-6pm, Tue-Sat until 9.30pm

Situated on the popular Kennet & Avon Canal, a great stop-off on your cycle ride. Try the famous Boatman's Breakfast, alternatively enjoy a quick beer or leisurely coffee. Also hires out bikes, see Cycle Hire in Transport chapter.

## SOUTH OF BRISTOL

## CHEW MAGNA

### Carpenter's Arms

Stanton Wick, Nr Pensford, Somerset, BS39 4BX
01761 490202
www.the-carpenters-arms.co.uk
Food served Mon-Fri 12pm-2pm, 7pm-10pm
Sun 12pm-2.30pm, 7pm-9pm
Off the A368, about ¾ mile from Jct with A37

17th century miners' cottages converted into a pub with outdoor seating, low beams, log fires and two restaurants (booking advisable at w/e's). Overlooking the Chew Valley, this is a great place to relax after visiting the nearby Folly Farm. See Farms in Out & About in the West Country.

### Chew Valley Lake Tea Shop

Chew Valley Lake Picnic Area, Chew Stoke, BS40 8TF
01275 333345
www.bristolwater.co.uk
Mon-Sun 10.30am-4.30pm

Overlooking the lake, this friendly tea shop serves light snacks to main meals. Hot meals until 2.30pm. There are nature trails, one suitable for buggies, a landscaped picnic area, visitor centre and gift shop.

### The Blue Bowl

Bristol Rd, West Harptree, BS40 6HJ
01761 221269
Open all day, every day.
Food served Mon-Sat 12pm-2pm & 6.30pm-9.30pm,
Sun 12pm-9pm

Next to Chew Valley Lake, at the foot of the Mendips, this family-friendly pub offers a great menu. There is an enclosed children's play area with climbing frame.

# CLUTTON

## Hunter's Rest

King Lane, Clutton Hill, BS39 5QL
01761 452 303
Mon-Sat 11.30am-2.30pm, 6pm-11pm,
Sun 12pm-4pm, 6pm-10.30pm
Take A37 south from Bristol, follow brown signs

A real gem, this 18th century country inn with conservatory à la carte restaurant with children's menu is worth a visit. During the summer holidays, children eat free on a Wednesday night. Booking advisable, special offers available. Large family garden with famous miniature steam railway (third of a mile) summer w/e's, weather permitting.

## Warwick Arms

Upper Bristol Rd, Clutton, nr Shepton Mallet, BS39
01761 452256
Mon-Sat 11am-11pm, Sun 12pm-11pm

Busy pub offering good food with a popular playground and garden area. Gets busy at the weekend so advisable to book a table if eating there. Does have children's menu.

# COMPTON MARTIN

## Ring O'Bells

Main St, Compton Martin, BS40 6JE
01761 221284
Mon-Sat 11.30am-2.30pm, 6.30pm-9.30pm,
Sun 12pm-2.30pm

A cosy country pub with a comfortable no smoking family room. Excellent facilities including play equipment and tables in the garden. Does not take bookings.

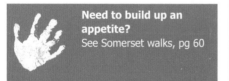

**Need to build up an appetite?**
See Somerset walks, pg 60

# WELLS

## Cloister Restaurant

West Cloister, Wells Cathedral, BA5 2PA
01749 676543
Mon-Sat 10am-5pm, Sun 12.30pm-5pm

A relaxed licensed restaurant in beautiful surroundings with homemade dishes and cakes. Ask for children's portions or spare plates. Central car park 10 mins.

## The Crown at Wells & Antons Bistro

Market Place, Wells, BA5 2RP
01749 673457
www.crownatwells.co.uk
Mon-Sun 12pm-2.30pm and 6pm-9.30pm

A medieval inn serving good food and fine wine in Wells marketplace, overlooking the Cathedral and Bishop's Palace. Has an outdoor café serving food all day throughout the summer. Free car park for residents only; central car park 10 mins.

## The Fountain Inn & Boxer's Restaurant

1 St Thomas Street, Wells, BA5 2UU
01749 672317
www.fountaininn.co.uk
Food Mon-Sun 12pm-2.30pm, 7pm-10.30pm

Award-winning, family friendly gastro-pub.

## The Good Earth Restaurant

4 Priory Rd, Wells, BA5 1SY
01749 678600
Mon-Sat 9am-5pm

Simple, quality whole-food restaurant and gift shop, with a wide range of vegetarian and vegan dishes. No children's menu as such, but happy to adapt to your requirements.

# GLASTONBURY

## Blue Note Café

2-4 High St, Glastonbury, BA6 9DU
01458 832907
Mon-Sun 9.30am-5pm

[V] [WC] [☒] [π] [♀] [λ]

An extremely busy, quick, casual and alternative licensed café serving wholesome vegetarian dishes throughout the day. Small portions and extra plates available. Car parking 5 mins away.

# SOUTH WEST OF BRISTOL

## LONG ASHTON

### The Angel Inn

172 Long Ashton Rd, Bristol, BS41 9LT
01275 392 244
Mon-Fri 12pm-11pm, Sun 12pm-10.30pm

[V] [WC] [☒] [π] [CP] [λ] [ᴘ]

Pleasant traditional village pub with good range of food available. Half portions and extra plates for children. Children are welcome until 8.30pm. Restaurant gets busy on Sundays for the roasts, best to book.

## AROUND BRISTOL AIRPORT

### Dundry Inn

Church Rd, Dundry, BS41 8LH
0117 964 1722
Mon-Thu 12pm-3pm, Fri-Sun All day

[P] [V] [WC] [☒] [π] [CP] [♀] [λ] [ᴘ]

Quiet local pub with garden. Friendly staff (paper and crayons on request) and an excellent menu. Open all day in the summer.

## Fox & Goose

Bridgwater Road, Barrow Gurney, BS48 3SI
01275 472202
Mon-Sat 11am-11pm, Sun 12pm-11pm

[P] [WC] [λ] [CP]

Child-friendly pub offering daily children's menu. Special Sunday menu including a roast. Best to book. No play area but large garden and deck.

## The Airport Tavern

Bridgewater Rd, Lulsgate, BS40 9XA
01275 472217
Mon-Sat 12pm-3pm, Sun 12pm-6pm

[P] [V] [WC] [☒] [π] [CP] [♀] [λ] [ᴘ] [▦] [⊞] [ᴘ]

A pleasant family-friendly pub. Nice patio and garden with play equipment and the added attraction of low flying aircraft!

# YATTON & CLEEVE

## Bridge Inn

North End Rd, Yatton, BS49 4AU
01934 839100
www.inlodge.com
Mon-Sun 12pm-11pm

[P] [✐] [WC] [☒] [π] [CP] [☺] [λ] [ᴘ] [▦] [ᴛ]

A Hungry Horse Pub with extensive pub menu served all day, does not take bookings. Children over 1 year can use the Indoor Action Zone for £2 per session, height restrictions apply.

## Full Quart

Hewish, Yatton, BS24 6RT
01934 833077
Food served 12pm-3pm & 6pm-9.30pm every day
About 3 miles outside WSM on A370

[P] [V] [✐] [WC] [☒] [π] [CP] [☺] [λ] [ᴘ] [▦] [⊞] [♿]

Popular pub with family room and large garden where there is an assault course. Good varied menu served in the dining room, carvery served on Sundays 12pm-6pm, advisable to reserve a table.

## The Lord Nelson

58 Main Rd, Cleeve, BS49 4NR
01934 832170
Mon-Thu 12pm-9.30pm, Fri & Sat 12pm-10pm,
Sun 12pm-9.30pm

[P] [V] [✐] [WC] [✄] [⊓] [CP] [⊙] [♟] [�↗] [↘] [△] [Ⓐ]

Busy, popular pub serving good value Hungry Horse menu with children's menu. Large screen TV showing key sporting events in main bar plus pool tables. Outdoor play area and a small indoor area, plus children's cinema showing films from 12pm-9pm. Private skittle alley can be booked for functions.

# CONGRESBURY

## Cromwells

2 Kent Rd, Congresbury, BS49 5BE
01934 833110
Mon-Fri 12pm-9pm

[P] [V] [WC] [✄] [⊓] [CP] [⊙] [♟] [↗] [↘] [△] [♿]

Formerly the Bell Inn, now an 80 seater bar/restaurant with separate family room serving food all day including a smaller eaters menu, carvery and fish. Large family garden.

## The Terrace Café

Cadbury Garden Centre, Smallway, BS49 5AA
01934 875 767
Mon-Sat 9.30am-5.30pm, Sun 10am-4.30pm
Hot food from 11am

[P] [V] [✐] [WC] [✄] [⊓] [CP] [↗] [↘]

Busy licensed restaurant based in popular garden centre serving teas, coffees all day. There are some tables outside where there is more space for toddlers.

# CHURCHILL

## Burrington Inn

Burrington Coombe, Burrington, Bristol, BS40 7AT
01761 462227
www.burrington.co.uk
Mon-Sun 10am-11pm
Next to garden centre, Burrington Coombe

[V] [✐] [WC] [⊓] [CP] [↗] [△]

Nestled at the foot of the Mendip Hills in picturesque Burrington Combe, open all year round serving coffee, afternoon teas, snacks or full meals plus ice cream parlour.

## Langford Inn

Lower Langford, Nr Churchill, BS40 5BL
01934 863059
Mon-Sun 12pm-11pm

[P] [V] [WC] [✄] [⊓] [CP] [⊙] [♟] [↗] [↘] [♿]

Charming, old restored coaching inn with a family room, patio area, walled garden and restaurant. Varied children's menu or small portions from adult's menu. Gets busy at the weekend, so advisable to book. Room available for baby changing on request.

# WESTON-SUPER-MARE

## Bucket and Spade Pub

Somerset Avenue, West Wick Island, Weston-super-Mare, BS22 8PD
01934 521 235
Mon-Sun 11am-11pm

[P] [V] [✐] [WC] [✄] [⊓] [CP] [⊙] [↗] [↘] [♿]

A Wacky Warehouse pub with soft play area costing £2.50 per child over one year, height or age restrictions apply. Food served all day from extensive pub menu.

## Hobbs Boat

Bridgwater Rd, Lympsham, Weston-s-Mare, BS24
01934 812 782
Mon-Sat 11.30am-11pm, Sun 12pm-10.30pm

[P] [V] [✐] [WC] [✄] [⊓] [CP] [♟] [↗] [↘] [△] [Ⓐ]

Part of the Brewers Fayre chain of pubs, extensive pub menu and separate children's menu. It has a small play area where children can play whilst parents dine.

## Seven VII

Seven Beach Road, Weston-super-Mare, BS23 1AS
01934 636969
www.viibar.com
Mon-Sun 12pm-8pm

Large beach front bar/restaurant with conservatory serving wide range of lunchtime snacks and evening meals. Children have a small playroom located at the back with range of toys from ELC. Great place for chilling with friends while children play!

## The Crown

The Batch, Skinners Lane, BS25 5PP
01225 314864
Mon-Sun 11am-11pm, food served 12pm-2.30pm
off A38 heading towards Weston-super-Mare

Close to the Mendips, this country pub serves farmhouse style food using local produce including casseroles, chillis, jacket potatoes and a great beef sandwich. Children allowed only in side rooms. No separate children's menu, but happy to adapt for kids.

## BURNHAM-ON-SEA

### Fortes Ice Cream Parlour

213 Pier Street, Burnham-on-Sea, TA8 1BT
01278 782 651
Mon-Sun 9am-6pm (Summer 9pm)
Located just off the seafront

Near to the Tourist Information Office. Extensive menu offering delicious home-made ice cream and other treats. Nothing more expensive than £5!

### The Goat House Restaurant

Bristol Road, Brent Knoll, Burnham-on-sea, TA9 4HJ
01278 760 995
Wed-Sun 11.30am-2.30pm, Sun 12pm-2.30pm

Open from Wednesday to Sunday serving a seasonal menu using locally-sourced produce at lunchtime and evenings. No separate children's menu, but will provide smaller portions from current menu. Fully licensed.

**Are your children learning to ride bikes?**
Try the beach between Brean and Burnham.

# WEST OF BRISTOL

## PILL

### Rudgeleigh Inn

Martcombe Rd, Easton-in-Gordano, BS20 0QD
01275 372363
Mon-Sat 12pm-11pm, Sun 12pm-10.30pm

Large country pub with a great outdoor play area, to suit pre-schoolers and above. Serves extensive pub menu all day. The Sunday carvery is very popular, so bookings advised.

### The Anchor

Ham Green, Pill, BS20 0HB
01275 372253
Mon-Sat 11am-11.30pm, Sun 11am-11pm

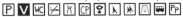

A village pub with a separate family room. There is a garden and play area. Snacks also available as well as main meals.

### The Priory

Station Road, Portbury, Bristol, BS20 7TN
01275 378 411
Mon-Sat 11.30am-11pm, Sun 11am-10.30pm

Family-friendly pub serving great food, with a selection of roasts on Sundays. Children's menu available. Loads of space for children to run about in the summer.

## NAILSEA

### The Old Farm House

Chelvey Rise, off Trendlewood Way, Nailsea, BS48
01275 851 889
Mon-Fri 11.30am-3pm, 5.30pm-11pm,
Sat-Sun 12pm-11pm

Nice traditional pub under new ownership using fresh produce in extensive menu. Very popular on Sundays when they serve a carvery alongside the full menu, bookings advisable. There is a family room complete with a toy box and a safe play area outside with climbing frames.

## The Star Inn

Stone Edge Batch, Clevedon Rd, Tickenham, BS21
01275 858836
Mon-Fri 12pm-2.30pm, 5.30pm-11pm,
Sat 12pm-3pm, 6pm-11pm, Sun 12pm-10.30pm

Large pub under new ownership, serving traditional food with an activity room and a large garden. Theme night held once a month in aid of local children's hospice. Call for details.

## PORTISHEAD

### Gordano Gate Brewer's Fayre

Wyndham Way, Portishead, BS20 7GA
01275 846 526
www.whitbread.co.uk
Mon-Thu & Sun 12pm-8pm, Fri & Sat 12pm-9pm
90 min play session £2 per child

A Whitbread Brewsters pub, completely family-oriented. Fun Factory supervised soft play for older children with face painting juggling and U3's Ball Swamp. Child tagging and CCTV for parental peace of mind!

## Marine Lake Café

Lake Grounds, Portishead, BS20
01275 842248

Friendly café, near children's play area and lake, serving snacks, fast food and ice creams. Makes a good afternoon out — feed the ducks, play in the park and retreat to the café.

## CLEVEDON

### The Little Harp Inn

Elton Rd, Clevedon, BS21
01275 343739
Mon-Sat 11am-11pm, Sun 12pm-10.30pm

Good restaurant pub on the seafront near the children's play area. In the summer there are lots of outside tables, or you can sit inside the large conservatory. Blackboard menu, with an added carvery option on Sundays.

### The Moon and Sixpence

15 The Beach, Clevedon, BS21 7QU
01275 872443
Food served Mon-Sat 12pm-9.30pm, Sun 12pm-4pm

Pleasant pub, set back off road near the pier, with a few tables in the car park. Upstairs is a family non-smoking area. A roast option on Sundays, can take bookings.

### The Old Inn

Walton Rd, Clevedon, BS21
01275 790052
Mon-Sat 7.30am-11pm, Sun 8am-11pm

Near Clevedon Court, popular pub offering traditional home cooked food. Open for breakfast from 7.30am and on Sundays bookings are advised for the roast lunch served from 12pm-2.30pm. There is also a big fenced garden full of play equipment.

# TRANSPORT

Diana Beavon

## CONTENTS

## INTRODUCTION

If you want to ditch the car for a special day out, or enjoy a slower pace of life (be it on the water, by bike or on the train), then this chapter has all the information that you will need. Where possible, we have included a web address so you can check the most up-to-date details before you set out.

Many of the listings link in with those in the Out and About and Eating Out chapters, so you may want to do some cross-referencing to make a real expedition of your day.

### Travel Information
www.travelbristol.org

This website, designed by Bristol City Council, provides a range of travel and transport information. It includes a trip planner whether you are on foot, public transport or bike, and real time information for selected bus services, as well as links to other travel information websites.

### Travel Bristol Centre

11 Colston Ave, Bristol, BS1 4UB
Mon-Fri: 10.30am-5.30pm, Sat: 10am-1pm

Self-serve terminal, booking hotline, leaflets and brochures

### Transport Direct

www.transportdirect.info

This useful website allows you to choose your destination and check out the most convenient form of transport to get to where you are going.

### Traveline — public transport information

0870 608 2608
www.traveline.org.uk

# AIRPORT

### Bristol International Airport

Lulsgate, BS19 3DY
0870 121 2747
www.bristolairport.co.uk

See Family Holidays & Weekends Away

# BUS & COACH

### First Buses

0845 602 0156
www.firstgroup.com

Operating 38 services throughout the Bristol area, with ticket offers for all day use:

- FirstFamily ticket: unlimited travel all day on First buses in Bristol, after 9am Mon-Fri and at any time on weekends and bank holidays. £6.50 for family up to 5, but no more than 2 adults.

- FirstDay South West ticket gives you unlimited travel all day on FirstGroup services in the West of England (some restrictions apply). £7 adult before 9am, £6 after, £5 child, £15 Family (2+2).

- FirstAttraction tickets are also available, combining your fare with your attraction

ticket, including Zoo Safari, Bus Skate Special, First Film Odeon and @Bristol.

Tickets can be purchased at the Travel Bristol Centre (Colston Street), Bristol Bus Station Booking Office and your local bus shop.

### Bristol Bus Station

Marlborough Street, BS1 3NU
0117 926 8843

Major redevelopment of the bus station is now complete, facilities include toilets, shops, café and ticket offices.

### South Gloucestershire Bus Co.

Timetable 0117 979 3311

### Bristol International Flyer

Daily 5.30am-10.30pm
Return fares: £7 adult, £6 child, £16 family (2+2)

Non-stop 30 minute bus service from Bristol Bus & Coach Station or Bristol Temple Meads direct to the airport. No prebooking necessary.

### National Express

Enquiries & reservations 08705 808080
8am-10pm
www.nationalexpress.com

Many economy fares available but many need to be booked in advance. Economy tickets exclude travel on Fridays and many Saturdays. On-line booking is available or buy tickets at Bristol Bus Station, some Bus Shops, travel agents and Tourist Information Centres. Family Coachcard allows children to travel for free, at £8 (1+1) or £16 (2+2). Coaches depart from Bristol Bus Station.

### Bristol City Sightseeing Tour

0870 4440654 information hotline
www.bristolvisitor.co.uk, www.city-sightseeing.com
Easter-Sep: 10am-5pm
Call for prices, U5's free, one child free per adult passenger

Tickets available on the bus or from Bristol Tourist Information Centre and the Travel Bristol Information Centre. This open-top, live guide sightseeing bus takes in all the major attractions: including at-Bristol, Bristol Zoo, ss Great Britain, Clifton Village and the British

Empire and Commonwealth Museum. Discount available on entry to a number of attractions on presentation of your bus ticket. You can hop on and off the bus at any of the 20 stops en route. Children fun packs available. See advertisement, pg 133.

# PARK & RIDE

0870 608 2608 (Traveline)

## Brislington Park and Ride

Located: off A4, Bristol-Bath Road
Mon-Fri 6.45am-7pm, every 10 mins, Thu last bus leaves the city centre at 8.03pm, Sat 7.40am-7pm.

The journey time is approx. 15 mins. Operates a circular route stopping at: Temple Gate, Old Market, Temple Way, Haymarket and Broad Quay.

## Long Ashton Park and Ride

0117 966 0399
Located: A370 towards the SW of the City. Mon-Fri 7am-7pm every 10-12 mins, Thu last bus leaves the city centre at 8pm, Sat 8am-6pm

The journey time is 10-15 mins. Operates a circular route stopping at: Harbourside, Augustine's Parade, Baldwin Street, Victoria Street and the Haymarket. Saturday service stops at: St Augustine's and St James Barton, outside House of Fraser. Up to three children travel free with a paying adult.

## Portway Park and Ride

Located: A4 Portway, Shirehampton
Mon-Fri 6.50am-7pm, every 15 mins, Sat 7.30am-7pm

Journey time into central Bristol approximately 30mins. Up to three children travel free with a paying adult.

## Tollgate (M32) Park and Ride

Located: multistories car park at bottom of M32
Mon-Fri 7am-6.40pm, every 10 mins

The journey time is 5-10 mins to Broadmead.

# RAIL

**National rail enquiries**
06457 48 49 50
www.nationalrail.co.uk

**First Great Western**
Customer service 0845 600 5604
Mobility impaired 08457 413775

**Wessex Trains**
www.wessextrains.co.uk
0870 900 2320

**Train Tracker**
0871 200 4950

Voice automated information about direct trains for that day

## Bristol Parkway

Stoke Gifford, Bristol, BS12 6TU
Ticket office Mon-Sat 5am-7pm, Sun 8am-7pm
Parking £4.50/day on weekdays, £2/day at weekends

This station has a number of facilities including lifts to platforms, disabled access, bicycle storage, self-service ticket machines, a shop and café on the first floor, and a regular bus service into Bristol city centre. Ticket office open Mon-Sat 5am-7pm, Sundays 8am-7pm. Ticket office, toilets and baby changing located near entrance.

## Temple Meads

Booking office open Mon-Sat 5.30am-9.30pm,
Sun 6.45am-9.30pm
Short-term parking on station forecourt (up to
20 mins free) longer-term parking £6.50/24hrs,
£9/24hrs undercover

Beautiful historic station. Lifts down to subway
then up to platforms. Main toilets in subway
with mother's room (baby changing) off the
Ladies'. Refreshment outlets to be found on
platforms 3 and 10, as well as in the subway.
WHSmith in main entrance. Shuttle bus
operates to the airport, as well as regular bus
services into and around Bristol.

## Bristol Severn Beach Line

www.wessextrains.co.uk
0870 900 2320
Day returns from only £2.30 (under 5's free), pay on
the train

The Bristol to Severn Beach railway line runs
from Temple Meads to the Avonmouth, from
here a bus service connects you to Severn
Beach.

## Friends of Suburban Bristol Railway (FOSBR)

www.fosbr.org.uk

A campaign group whose aim is to keep,
promote and improve the services and
facilities on the line.

# RAILWAYS FOR PLEASURE

## Ashton Court Estate Minature Steam Railway

0117 946 7110
www.bristolmodelengineers.co.uk
Apr-mid Oct: Occassional Suns & B/Hs 12pm-5.30pm
Enter through Clifton Lodge on A369, turn right,
then right again

Sit astride trains on track ½ mile long. Ramps
and footbridges for pushchairs are by the
ticket office. Toilets at the golf café. Santa
specials can be booked in advance. Phone or
see website for operating dates.

## Avon Valley Railway

Bitton Station, Willsbridge, BS15
0117 932 7296 talking timetable
0117 932 5538 general enquiries
www.avonvalleyrailway.co.uk
Easter-Oct: Sun, B/H's
Tue-Thu during school holidays
£5 adult, £3.50 child (U3's free), £13.50 family (2+2)

Fare allows unlimited travel on day of issue.
This line runs along the former Mangotsfield
to Bath Green Park branch of the old Midland
Railway. The line has now been extended to
a new platform at the Avon River side with
links to boat trips and the Avon Valley Country
Park, see Out & About in the West Country
chapter. Special events such as days out with
Thomas The Tank Engine and Santa Specials
require booking.

## Bristol Harbour Railway

See Out and About in Bristol

## Dean Forest Railway

Norchard Railway Centre, Lydney, Gloucestershire
01594 843423 information line
01594 845840 enquiries
www.deanforestrailway.co.uk
Apr-Oct: Sun, B/H's, some weekdays in the summer
£8 adult, £5 child, £24 family (2+2), U5's free
M4, M48 Chepstow, Norchard is on B4234 just north
of Lydney (Accessible by train and bus)

This line runs from Norchard to Lydney
Junction, then on to Parkend. Special
timetabled events throughout the summer
and Christmas include days out with Thomas
The Tank Engine, Diesel Days and Santa
Specials. Booking essential. Other attractions
include riverside walks, boating lake, park,
Railway Museum, café in classic restaurant
coach open on Steam Days. Pushchairs can
be stored in the station building, or put on the
train using disabled ramps provided.

## East Somerset Railway

Cranmore Railway Station, Shepton Mallet,
Somerset, BA4 4QP
01749 880417
www.eastsomersetrailway.com
Apr-Oct: w/e's & some weekdays in the summer
Nov-Easter: Sun only
£6 adult, £4 child (U3's free), £17 family (2+2)
A37, A361

🖉 ᴡᴄ 🚽 👶 🚃 💺 ♿ 🚻

A round trip of 35 minutes. Platform tickets include the train shed, signal box and museum. Special events include Days with Thomas and Santa Specials, booking essential. Restaurant and model shop (only open on Steam Days). The station is buggy friendly with storage space on the trains.

## Gloucestershire and Warwickshire Railway

The Railway Station, Toddington, Glos, GL54 5DT
01242 621405 (talking timetable when closed)
www.gwsr.com
£9.50 adult, £6 child, U5's free, £26 family (2+3)
M5 Jct 9, A46, B4077 junction with B4632

🅿 👶 ♿ 💺 🧺

Fare allows unlimited travel on day of issue. The railway operates a round trip of 20 miles from Toddington to Cheltenham Race Course station with a brief stop along the way at Winchcombe. The line passses through the beautiful Cotswold hills and you will have views over the Vale of Evesham to the Malvern Hills beyond. Special events take place throughout the season, most notably Days Out with Thomas and Santa Specials.

## Perrygrove Railway

Coleford, Forest of Dean, Glos, GL16 8QB
01594 834991
www.perrygrove.co.uk
Apr-Sep selected days & Oct half term
£4 adults, £3 child, Free U3's (no credit cards)
½ mile south of Coleford on B4228, nearest mainline railway station Lydney

🅿 🖉 ᴡᴄ 🚽 👶 🚼 ♿ 🚻 ♿

Fare allows unlimited travel on day of issue. Narrow gauge railway runs through farm and woodland for a 1½ mile return trip. Visitors also able to walk through the woods (with pushchairs), explore the indoor village and

secret passages, and take part in an optional treasure hunt (£1.80). Birthday parties welcome. Book to see Santa coming down the chimney.

## West Somerset Railway

The Railway Station, Minehead, Somerset, TA24 5BG
01643 707650 talking timetable
01643 704996 general enquiries
www.west-somerset-railway.co.uk
All year but not daily, phone for full timetable
£3.20-£12.40 depending on journey length, discount for children, free U5's
M5 Jct 25, follow brown tourist signs to Bishops Lydeard

🅿 🖉 ᴡᴄ 👶 🚼 💺 ♿

The train line runs for 20 miles between Bishop's Lydeard and Minehead along the coast and Quantock Hills. Ten restored stations along the line have a variety of signal boxes, museums, displays and steam and diesel engines to visit. Buffet on all regular, timetabled trains. Special events include Thomas The Tank Engine, Santa Specials and Steam Gala Days, booking is essential.

# CYCLING ORGANISATIONS

## Bristol Cycling Campaign

Box No. 60, Booty, 82 Colston St, BS1 5BB
www.bristolcyclingcampaign.org.uk
Membership £5, concessions available

Regular Sunday rides organised, some quite short and suitable for families. BCC members also campaign to improve accessibility and safety for cyclists. For further information either obtain a leaflet (distributed in cycle shops) or visit the website.

## CTC (Cyclist Touring Club)

Cotterell House, 69 Meadrow, Godalming, Surrey
01483 417217
www.ctc.org.uk

Campaigns for the rights of cyclists. Membership provides you with 3rd party insurance, legal aid, route information and bi-monthly magazines.

## Life Cycle UK

86 Colston Street, Bristol, BS1 5BB
0117 929 0440
www.lifecycleuk.org.uk

Provides information and advice on cycling with your children. Runs one-to-one parent training lessons costing £25, plus monthly bike maintenance workshops, see website for more details.

## Sustrans

2 Cathedral Square,, College Green, Bristol, BS1 5DD
Information line 0845 113 0065
Head office 0117 926 8893
www.sustrans.org.uk

This sustainable transport charity works on practical projects to encourage people to walk, cycle and use public transport in order to reduce motor traffic and its adverse effects. Their main project is the National Cycle Network which currently provides more than 10,000 miles of cycling and walking routes throughout the UK. Maps and free leaflets also available.

Sustrans is also involved in Safe Routes to School project, encouraging children to cycle and walk to school. Free information pack available.

# CYCLE HIRE COMPANIES

## Bristol Bicycle Hire

Smeaton Rd, adj to Bonded Warehouse,
Cycle Route 41, Hotwells
0117 965 5192, 0780 3651945 (mobile)
Easter-Oct: £10-£12 per day, £7-£9 half day, additional days half price

[P] [WC] [⅄]

Pre-booked bike hire. Children's trailers and seats.

## Forest of Dean Cycle Hire

Pedalabikeaway Cycle Centre, Colliery Offices,
Cannop Valley, near Coleford
01594 860065
www.pedalabikeaway.com
Jul, Aug & school holidays: every day
Apr-Oct: Tue-Sun 9am-6pm, Nov-Mar: Tue-Sun 9am-5pm
From £7 adult 2hrs, £4 child 2hrs

[P] [✎] [WC] [⚒]

This friendly shop is situated on the 10-mile circular family cycle trail, hiring out bikes, buggy and bike trailers. Helmets are free. Family rate discount available. Their motto is "bikes for everyone", particularly those those with special needs. Routes, maps, information, books, parts, accessories and repairs available. The Café is open winter w/e's and daily in summer — delicious chips!

## Lock Inn Cottage

48 Frome Road, Bradford-on-Avon, Wiltshire, BA15
01225 868068
www.thelockinn.co.uk
Daily 9am-6pm
From £7 adults, £5 child for 3hrs

[WC] [⚡] [⚒] [⚒]

Here you will find an extensive bike/hire shop and canal-side café, ideally situated on the Kennet and Avon canal towpath. You can hire (or buy!) all family biking equipment, helmets, seats, trailers etc. Canoes and boats also for hire, see below.

## The Bath and Dundas Canal Co.

Brass Knocker Basin, Monkton Combe, Bath
01225 722292
www.bathcanal.com
Open daily, but ring first between Nov-Mar
£14 adult, £7 child per day, hourly rates available, pre-booking recommended

Offers a range of family bikes and accessories to hire. Canoes and boats for hire, see below.

# CYCLE ROUTES

## Ashton Court

After passing through the entrance to Ashton Court by the suspension bridge, take the second track on the right (after the road for the golf course). There are numerous trails through the woods but it is very hilly and quite rough.

## Ashton to Pill Cycle Way

Starts from the Create Centre on Cumberland Road, or from Leigh Woods if you take the first right after the Clifton suspension bridge and follow the road for ¾ mile; it is signposted from there. Refreshments can be bought in Pill.

## Bristol and Bath Cycle Way

This is a 13-mile route which you can start either from Bristol Bridge or from St Phillips Road, Old Market. Bitton is an interesting place to stop, where there is a steam railway (or start your ride from here, as the route crosses the road). Pubs along the way include the Bird in Hand and the Jolly Sailor on the river at Saltford.

## Forest of Dean Cycle Trail

See Cycle Hire section

This is a beautiful area for cycling. There is a popular circular 12-mile family cycle route, with several access points (one being, Pedalabikeaway, listed above).

## Kennet and Avon Canal Towpath

This goes east out of Bath, starting behind Bath Spa railway station. Three easy access points are: Bradford-on-Avon (station car park); Hilperton Marina (car parking and toilets); and the visitor centre at Devizes Wharf (pay and display). A cycle route with plenty to look at on the canal and several

places to stop for food and drink. Besides the aquaducts at Avoncliff and Dundas, the other amazing feat of engineering is the flight locks at Caen, West of Devizes. Canal cycle tracks can be narrow in places, so not suitable for inexperienced cyclists, however they are flat so you may have a whinge-free day!

# FERRY & BOAT TRIPS

## Bristol Ferry Boat Company

See Dockside in Out & About in Bristol

## Bristol Queen

01934 613828
www.bristolqueen.com
Apr-Oct
£8 adult, £4 U14's

Sailings from Knightstone Harbour, Weston-super-Mare and occasionally from Portishead. Most popular cruises are 1hr trip from Weston along the Brean Down peninsula. Also 2hr cruises around both Holm Islands, and occasional trips to Cardiff Bay and Steep Holm. Facilities: small snack shop, high weather viewing deck, toilets, and commentary. For timetable and further information contact Bristol Queen or Weston-super-Mare Tourist Information Centre, see Out & About in the West Country chapter.

## Canal Boat Trips on MV Barbara McLellan

Wharf Cottage, 15 Frome Rd, Bradford-on-Avon, BA15 1LE
01225 868683
www.katrust.org
End Mar-Oct: w/e's & B/H's & Wed pm
From £4.50 adult, £3.50 child, £13 family, free U5's
[WC] [♿]

A relaxing way to see the canal is on this comfortable narrowboat. Three trips are offered: past the Tithe Barn to Meadows Bridge, 1hr; to Avoncliff Aquaduct, 1½hrs; east to Widbrook, 1hr. Advance bookings can be made at the Cottage Shop, except in Aug when tickets can only be bought on day of trip. Boat leaves from the cottage on Canal Wharf less than half a mile south of town centre. Wheelchair lift and toilet on board. See website for details of special trips including Santa Specials.

## Canal Narrow Boat Hire

If you've ever fancied taking a canal boat out yourself for a day or more, contact one of the following companies.

**Sally Boats**
01225 864923, www.sallyboats.ltd.uk
Operates out of Bradford-on-Avon.

**Anglo-Welsh Waterway Holidays**
0117 304 1122, www.anglo-welsh.co.uk
Have bases in Bath, Bristol and Monkton Combe.

**Wessex Narrow Boats**
www.wessexboats.co.uk, 01225 765243
Located 3 miles from Bradford-on-Avon, at Staverton Marina, day hire possible.

**Bath Narrow Boats**
Bathwick Hill, Bath
01225 447276, www.bath-narrowboats.co.uk
Mainly day hire.

## The Bath & Dundas Canal Co.

Brass Knocker Basin, Monkton Combe, Bath
01225 722292
www.bathcanal.com
Daily 8am-dusk, some seasonal variations
Electric boats from £59 per day,
Canadian canoes from £14 for 2hrs
Take A36 south of Bath, at Monkton Combe turn left at lights on to B3108

You can hire electric boats, canoes and even narrow boats for holidays or short breaks. There are no locks on the canal between Bradford-on-Avon and Bath. See Cycle Hire above.

## The Lock Inn

48 Frome Rd, Bradford-on-Avon, Wiltshire, BA15 1LE
01225 868068
www.thelockinn.co.uk
Daily 9am-6pm
Canoe Hire: £20 up to 3 hours, £30 up to 9 hours

You can hire canoes to paddle along the canal from this pleasant spot. It's easiest to go towards Bath as there are no locks to negotiate (canoes must be caried round) and there are plenty of pubs and tearooms along the way. Pre-booking is advisable as it gets very busy in the summer. Credit/debit card necessary for deposit. Also see Cycle Hire above.

## Waverley & Balmoral

Waverley Excursions Ltd, Waverley Terminal, Glasgow, G3 8HA
0845 1304 6467
www.waverleyexcursions.co.uk
May-Sep, from £14 adult, child half price, free U5's

Sailings from Clevedon Pier, Bristol and Weston-super-Mare (also from Minehead, Ilfracombe, Watchet, Sharpness and Bridgwater). Cruise in "Big Ship" style aboard the Waverley, the last sea-going paddle steamer in the world and the Balmoral, a traditional pleasure cruise ship. Cruises around Holm Islands and the coast of Wales. For full details and timetable contact Waverley Excursions Ltd directly or the Weston-super-Mare Tourist Information Centre. Facilities include a self-service restaurant, fully licensed bar, heated observation lounges, souvenir shops.

To land on Steep Holm and Flat Holm see Severn Adventures in Out & About in the West Country chapter. To land on Lundy island see Camping in Family Holidays & Weekends Away.

# ACTIVITIES

**Rachel Miller**

## CONTENTS

## INTRODUCTION

Watching your children develop confidence and skills through sports and activities is one of the joys of being a parent. Finding the right activity for your kids is not always straight-forward, however. Never fear! We've made it easy, with this comprehensive guide. There's a wide range of physical and artistic classes for pre-schoolers, as well as all the swimming pools and soft play venues that Bristol and the West Country have to offer. And whatever your school-age children are into — whether they are mad about sport, long to perform or want a challenge — there are plenty of clubs and classes to keep them busy. And there's more. We provide lots of contacts to help you organise good quality after-school and holiday care. And, of course, we've got masses of ideas for parties, with a whole host of wonderful entertainers and exciting venues.

# SPORTS DIRECTORY

When it comes to sport, you name it, Bristol's got it. Popular sports such as football and rugby are extremely well catered for but there's much more on offer, from archery to ice skating. And, if you like the great outdoors, there are opportunities to ski, climb, skateboard, horse ride, canoe, cycle, sail and even water ski, all close to home. In addition, Bristol has some impressive sporting facilities at the many leisure centres across the city, so check out the Sports Centre tables in the Colour Reference Section to find out more.

## ARCHERY

### Cleve Archers

Moorend, Nr Hambrook, Bristol
01454 852181
www.clevearchers.co.uk
clevearchers@uk2.net
Apr-Oct: Sat am
Membership £20 juniors

This archery club has a thriving Junior Club. There are beginners courses during May and June for 7-18's. There is an additional fee to shoot indoors during the winter months.

**For more places to do archery, see:** The Action Centre, Aardvark Endeavours, Mendip Outdoor Pursuits, Young Bristol Outdoor Activities and Black Rock Outdoor Education in Outdoor Pursuits.

## BADMINTON & BASKETBALL

See the Sport Centre tables in the Colour Reference Section.

## BOWLING

### Bowlplex

Unit 4, Aspect Leisure Pk, Longwell Green, BS30
0117 961 0000
www.bowlplex.co.uk
Off peak-peak, £2.95-£4.95 adult, £2.50-£4.65 child, free U4's prior to 7pm with full paying adult

### Hollywood Bowl

Avonmeads Retail Pk, St Philips Marsh, BS2 0SP
0117 977 1777
www.hollywoodbowl.co.uk
Open daily

### Hollywood Bowl at Cribbs Causeway

The Venue, Cribbs Causeway, Bristol, BS10 7TT
0117 959 2100
www.hollywoodbowl.co.uk
Open daily
Sun before 12pm: child goes free with full paying adult, free U4's with a full paying adult at anytime, call for further offers and prices. Special offers available after school

### Megabowl

Brunel Way, Ashton Gate, Bristol, BS3
0117 953 8538
www.megabowl.co.uk
Open daily
Family hour, up to 6 people £14.50,
Mon-Fri 12pm-6pm & w/e's 10am-1pm

The Time Out Club is available to youth or social groups who register with Megabowl and then can play for £2 per person per game.

# CLIMBING

## Bristol Climbing Centre

St Werburgh's Church, Mina Rd, St Werburgh's, BS2
0117 941 3489
www.undercover-rock.com
£10 taster sessions for beginners, Fri 5pm-6pm, 6-15yrs, pre-booking required

This dedicated indoor climbing centre features over 150 climbs up to 10 metres high, catering for all abilities from complete beginners to national champions.

## The Warehouse

Parliament St, Gloucester, GL1 1HY
01452 302351
www.the-warehouse.co.uk
Mon-Fri 12pm-10pm, Sat-Sun 10am-10pm

Impressive climbing venue with up to 180 routes. The main room has walls up to 13 metres. Rock Rats club for 8-16yrs. Taster sessions available. Also caters for children's parties.

# CRICKET

## Bristol Youth Cricket League

0117 330 6502
www.bristolycl.play-cricket.com
bycl@blueyonder.co.uk
Season runs: Apr-Aug
Facilities for indoor nets Feb-Apr

There are around 40 youth cricket teams in and around Bristol, with players ranging in age from 6-18yrs. Teams are organised by age, from the U9's up to U17's, playing in leagues and knockout cups. The Quick Cricket Festival for the U9's is held every summer. Whether you live in Bristol or outside, call to find your nearest team. Register before November to ensure you get a place.

## Damien Forder Cricket Academy

07771 560 338
www.dfca.co.uk

Cricket coaching for all ages and abilities, including groups and one to one. Focusing on batting, bowling and fielding, designed to improve basic skills. Classes are held at different venues and take place after school and at weekends. Parties also available.

## The Bristol YMCA CC

Golden Hill, Henleaze
www.ymcacricket.com
0117 940 9234

This is one of Bristol's oldest cricket clubs, founded in 1878. It has an excellent youth set-up that attracts junior cricketers from across the district. There are teams for all ages, from U11's up to U17's. During the winter it provides indoor net sessions and competes in the Bristol Indoor Cricket League. It hosts numerous social events, with a cricket theme, for all the family.

# CYCLING

## Cycle Paths

www.forestofavon.org.uk

There are some excellent cycle paths in Bristol, see pg 89.

**The Avon Timberland Trail, Ashton Court:** Built by mountain bikers for mountain bikers, suitable for all abilities.

**Bristol and Bath Railway Path:** 16 miles of flat cycling taking you through some beautiful countryside.

**Leigh Woods:** Special marked paths for cyclists.

**River Avon Trail:** This 23 mile route takes you from Pill Harbour to Bath.

## Bristol BMX Club

The Tumps, Waterside Drive, Coniston Rd, Patchway
07875 146489
harry.price@hotmail.com
Mar-Sep: Wed, 5pm onwards, weather permitting
Members £3; non-members £5 on the night
Membership £15 per year

The BMX Club is open to all ages. You need to bring your own BMX bike with padding, wear long sleeve tops and long trousers and gloves as well as a helmet. Stump pegs on bikes must be unscrewed. Races start at 6.30pm and you'll be entered according to age. The top two in any race go up into the next group. You can take part in regional and national events.

## Life Cycle UK

86 Colston St, Bristol, BS1 5BB
0117 929 0440
www.lifecycleuk.org.uk

Group cycling courses for 8-11yrs at venues in Bristol. Also courses for 11-18yrs with one instructor to two cyclists. Teaching road safety on and off roads. Free maps provided.

# FENCING

## Bristol Fencing Club

Redland High School for Girls, Redland Rd, Bristol
01934 843984
www.bristolfencingclub.com
Sat 10am-12am

Juniors from 8-14yrs.

# FOOTBALL

## Amateur Football Alliance

www.amateurfa.com

There are loads of football teams and leagues all over Bristol and this is the place to find them. Click on Find a Club and enter your age group and postcode to find a boys or girls' football club close to home.

## Avon Sports Academy

0117 904 6686
www.avonsportsacademy
info@avonsportsacademy.co.uk

A wide variety of opportunities for football fanatics, from holiday camps to after school clubs. Soccer schools in the holidays are aimed at 5-13yrs. Coaching is available in after-school clubs for up to 11yrs. There are opportunities for advanced players to attend the Football Development Centre, the only FA-sanctioned academy in the South West. All enquiries are dealt with by email, full details on the website.

**The Combe Dingle Crusaders FC**
Coombe Dingle Sports Complex
Sat: 9.30-11am, boys U7's
Sat: 10.30-12pm, boys 8-11yrs
Sat: 10.30-12pm, girls all ages
Wed: 5pm-6pm, girls 8-13yrs

## Bristol City Football Club

Ashton Gate Stadium, Bristol, BS3 2EJ
0117 963 0619
www.bcfc.co.uk

**Holiday soccer**
0117 963 0636 coaching enquiries

The club visits local schools to host football coaching and extra-curricular sessions. There are also coaching courses during the Easter and summer holidays.

**Free tickets**
0117 963 0636 Football in the Community Dept

This family-friendly club has its own Family Enclosure. Prices start at £5 for U16's. You can also apply for free tickets for U11's (when accompanied by an adult) under the Fans of the Future scheme.

## Bristol Rovers Football Club

Memorial Stadium, Filton Ave, Horfield BS7 0BF
0117 952 2581
www.bristolrovers.co.uk
brfccommunity@btconnect.com

**Free tickets**
U11's can watch some games for free (call to check availability) when accompanied by a full-paying adult. Tickets must be bought in advance, by 5pm the previous day.

**Holiday soccer**
Venues:
Gordano Sports Centre
The Grange School, Warmley
The Filton College W.I.S.E campus, Stoke Gifford

Holiday soccer schools for girls and boys aged 7-13yrs. Bristol Rovers also offers after school clubs and football training in schools, by arrangement with head teachers. Talented players can attend the Rovers' School of Excellence and may even end up playing for Bristol Rovers!

**Tour the ground**
Junior football teams can arrange to visit the Bristol Rovers ground on a match day to have

lunch, watch the game, meet the players and have their picture taken on the pitch.

## Gloucestershire Football Association

www.gloucestershirefa.com

Gloucestershire FA oversees all the youth football leagues in the Bristol area, of which there are many. The GFA website is a great place to find all the necessary contact details.

# GYMNASTICS

## Bristol Hawks Gymnastic Club

Gymnastics World, Roman Rd, Lower Easton, BS5
0117 935 5363/973 7481

**Open Gym (4-6yrs)**
Sat am, £3

**Open Gym (7-10yrs)**
Sat am, £3.50 ¾hr session

**Shaolin Martial Arts (5-7yrs)**
Thu evenings for older children, phone for details

Fun, challenging, stimulating and safe. All coaches qualified. BGA grades followed. Drinks & snacks available. Buggies left in changing rooms. Holiday schemes and advanced gymnastics for children aged 8 and over, available in the evenings. Structured classes for talented gymnasts. See also Pre-school Gym below.

## Bristol School of Gymnastics

Old Bishopston Methodist Church,
245 Gloucester Rd, Bristol, BS7 8NY
0117 942 9620

**Under 7's**
Mon evening

**Over 7's**
Wed/Thu evening

General gymnastics with apparatus, taught by qualified coaches. Aimed at all ages from 3-18yrs. School aged children encouraged to start on Saturdays and progress towards competitive gymnastics. See also Pre-school Gym below.

## Fromeside Gymnasti

Watleys End Rd, Winterbourne,
01454 776 873/777 749

All classes taken by qualifi
aged 4-6yrs take place after sche
on Saturday morning. BGA award scheme. Children progress to competition level by invitation. See also Pre-school Gyms below.

## Kingswood Gymnastic & Trampoline Centre

The Wesley Studios, Kingswood Foundation Estate, Britannia Rd, BS15 8DB
0117 947 6449

**Classes for U2's**
Wed 9.45am

**Structured classes for all ages up to 12**

Fun sessions by qualified & experienced staff. BGA award scheme. Offering a variety of activities including bar, beam and rhythmic gymnastics, trampolining, team games, group activities, parachute and ball games. Holiday fun sessions. See Parties section for party hire.

## City of Bristol Gymnastics Centre

c/o Hartcliffe Engineering Community College, Teyfant Rd, Hartcliffe, BS13 0RL
0117 377 3420
www.bristol-city.gov.uk/gymnastics

Recently opened, offering fully qualified coaching sessions for all ages.

# HOCKEY

## Redland Ladies Hockey Club

01454 898384
£30-90/yr depending on age and competition level

**Redmaids School, Westbury-on-Trym**
Sun 10am-12pm: Juniors (9-14yrs)

**Golden Hill, Kellaway Avenue**
Tue 6.30pm-8pm: Seniors (15+yrs)

All matches take place at Redmaids School as part of a league organised by Sports West.

## ...SE RIDING

### Gordano Valley Riding Centre

Moor Lane, Clapton in Gordano, Bristol, BS20 7RF
01275 843473

Lessons, rides and lead-outs for everyone from 5yrs+. Children's birthdays are catered for. There are regular holiday clubs offering a range of activities including riding and grooming.

### HorseWorld

Staunton Lane, Whitchurch, BS14 0QJ
01275 540173
www.horseworld.org.uk
visitor.centre@horseworld.org.uk

If your child is mad about horses, this is the place to come. See full entry in Out and About in Bristol pg 13.

### Kingsweston Stables

Lime Kiln Cottage, Kingsweston Rd, Lawrence Weston, BS11 0UX
0117 982 8929
Classes and hacking: £12 per ½ hour, £17 per hour

Riding lessons and hacking for over 4's to adult. Pre-booking required, call for details.

### Tynings Trekking Centre

Charterhouse, Blagdon, Bristol, BS40 7XU
01934 742501
www.tynings.halvor.co.uk

Rides, lead-ons and treks. Magical Mendip scenery, all rides off-road and lessons also available.

### Urchinwood Manor Equitation Centre

Urchinwood Manor, Congresbury, Bristol, BS49 5AP
01934 833248
www.urchinwoodmanor.co.uk

Teaching centre, offering lessons for all ages and stages, including working towards competitions and BHS exams for those that want to compete.

## ICE SKATING & SKIING

### Bristol Ice Rink

Frogmore St, Bristol, BS1 5NA
0117 929 2148
www.jnll.co.uk
Session times vary — call for details
From £5.50 including skate hire

P WC CP ✕ ⌴ ♿

General, family and disco sessions available for all abilities. Boots from child size 5. Long sleeves, trousers and gloves are recommended. Tuition available for all ages and abilities and courses run to the NISA fun skate programme.

Disabled skating sessions available although access to building is difficult but staff are happy to assist. Also ice karting for over 18's. Also see Party section

**Junior Ice Hockey (under 19yrs)**
Tuesdays, booking is advisable.

### Christmas Ice Rinks

There are usually ice rinks at Castle Park, City Centre and the Mall, Cribbs Causeway in December for a real Christmassy skating session.

### Gloucester Ski & Snowboard Centre

Robinswood Hill, Matson Lane, Gloucester, GL4 6EA
08702 400375
www.gloucesterski.com
Daily 10am-10pm, except Thu, Sat-Sun 10am-6pm
Call for prices & more details

P WC ↟ ✕ ♿

Kids Adventure Club, ages 6-16, for those that can ski recreationally. Includes a lesson and a drink.

Private & group lessons available from 6 yrs, snowboarding from 12yrs. Tubing sessions from 4yrs to adult, £5 a session. Adapted equipment available for disabled customers.

## The Action Centre

Lyncombe Drive, Churchill, N Somerset, BS25 5PQ
01934 852335
www.highaction.co.uk, info@highaction.co.uk
9.30am-10pm
Costs vary according to activity (Start at £4.50 for tobogganning)

Floodlit dry ski slope open all year. Any age permitted providing they can snowplough, stop, turn & use button drag lift, booking not necessary. Lessons available for all abilities from 4yrs. Snow Blading for skiers from 6yrs. Tobogganing (4-12yrs under parental supervision) and snowboarding from 7yrs (dependent on height). Activity days run by a qualified instructor, teaching skiing, archery and rifle shooting. Also quad biking, power kiting and mountain boarding. Booking essential for all activities except recreational skiing. Also see Parties section.

# KARTING AND DRIVING

## Castle Combe Skid Pan and Kart Track

Castle Combe Circuit, Chippenham, SN14 7BW
01249 783010
www.castlecombecircuit.co.uk

Junior kart racing for 10-15yrs (with a min. height of 4'8") on 1st & 3rd Sunday of every month. Pre-booking essential. Phone for possible summer school sessions.

## Jumicar Bristol

01454 250219
www.jumicarbristol.co.uk

Road safety instructions for children, aged 6-12 in real junior-sized cars. Currently run at ASDA WallMart car park, Cribbs Causeway.

## The Raceway

Avonmouth Way, Avonmouth, Bristol
0800 376 6111
www.theraceway.co.uk

Huge indoor racing track offering the chance to get behind the wheel for all ages. There's a youth club for ages 8-15yrs on a Sunday morning. Then there are opportunities for driving practice for anyone over 12yrs.

## West Country Karting

The Lake, Trench Lane, Winterbourne, BS36 1RY
01454 202666
www.westcountrykarting.com

350 metre outdoor karting circuit. Must be at least 5'1" for karting, shorter and you will not reach the pedals! Quad biking available for ages 6-12yrs. Open all year but closes on very quiet days, call for opening times and prices. Party bookings taken.

# MARTIAL ARTS

## Bedminster Judokwai

Ashton Park Sports Centre, Ashton Park School, Bower Ashton
07834 619437
www.bedminsterjudokwai.co.uk
pt007f5937@blueyonder.co.uk
Tue 6.15pm-7pm, U16's, beginners
Tue 7pm-8pm, Graded juniors
Fri 7.15pm-8.45pm, all ages

Judo for all ages from 5yrs to adults.

## Bristol Karate Club

Holy Nativity Church Hall, School Rd, Totterdown
0117 977 9029
www.bristolkarateclub.org.uk
enquiries@bristolkarateclub.org.uk
Thu 6.30pm, junior classes, £3 per session

New members are welcome anytime and there are no age limits.

## Bristol School of Tai Chi

0117 949 3955
taichi@bristoltaichi.com

Tai chi for children 7+yrs, at the following venues: Gloucester, Glastonbury, Yate, Thornbury, Bishopston, Nailsea, Weston-super-Mare and Clifton.

## Karate

Tim: 07980 863061
Bradley Stoke Community Centre
Tue 6.30pm-8pm

Karate for all ages and abilities. You can pay £5 to drop-in but there's membership for those that want to come regularly.

## KEBBA

07989 773950
www.kebba.co.uk, mail@kebba.co.uk
Tue/Wed, Staple Hill
Thu Keynesham
Sun Warmley

Martial arts classes for children aged 7+yrs. One month free trial available.

## Matt Fiddes Academy

0800 0354660
www.mattfiddes.com

National martial arts chain offering a mix of kick boxing, TaeKwonDo and Kung Fu. Call for further details of clubs in Bristol.

## ShotoRyu Karate

814 Filton Ave, Filton, Bristol, BS34 7HA
0117 969 5697
www.shotoryukarate.co.uk
Nick Moller: 0117 969 5697

Sessions are held throughout the week at Horfield, Easton & Henbury Sports Centres. See Sport Centres in Colour Reference Section.

Also at Greenway Centre and Kingswood 17th Bristol Scouts Hall. Ages 5+yrs. Parents can take classes with their children.

## Taekwon-Do

0845 6001967
www.puma-uk.com

Taekwon-Do is the Korean martial art of punching and kicking, offering improvements in strength, endurance, flexibility, stamina, self-control, confidence and relaxation. Sessions held at many venues across Bristol and the West.

# OUTDOOR PURSUITS

All good outdoor pursuits companies should be licensed by The Adventure Activities Licensing Authority. The AALA can be contacted on 02920 755715 or go to www.aala.org. Also see Outdoor Pursuits in The Forest of Dean & the Wye River pg 42.

## Aardvark Endeavours

Broadway House, Axbridge Rd, Cheddar, BS27 3DB
01934 744878
www.aardvarkendeavours.com
burt@bc1.net

Aardvark is a non-residential outdoor pursuits company but it's based at a caravan park if you do need somewhere to stay. It offers abseiling, gorge walking, rock climbing, archery, rifle shooting, caving, pot holing and kayaking. Most activites are suitable for anyone aged 7+yrs.

## Avon Kite Flyers

Paul Clark: 01454 320065
www.avonkiteflyers.org.uk
akf@subzero.plus.com
£10 per family per year, inc. 3rd party insurance cover

This kite flying club is popular with families. The club acts as a focal point and information source for local kite flyers of all abilities. There are regular fly-ins at Ashton Court on the first Sunday of the month. Membership benefits include 10% discount at local kite shops. The club is well known for its displays and regularly attends kite festivals.

## Black Rock Outdoor Education

16 St Andrews Rd, Cheddar, BS27 3NE
01934 744389
www.blackrockoutdoors.co.uk

Black Rock offers the full gamet of outdoor activities including: caving, abseiling and climbing, kayaking, archery, ropes, off-road biking and mountain weekends away. Most activities are suitable for everyone from 8yrs and Black Rock caters for all types of groups, from schools and clubs to families.

## Bristol Activities Centre

Avonquay, Cumberland Basin, Bristol, BS1 6XL
0117 353 2299
www.bristolactivities.org.uk
bac@bristol-city.gov.uk

Activities include: caving, climbing, kayaking, team building, hillcraft, abseiling, canoeing, orienteering and mountain biking. Sessions take place on weekdays as well as weekends and last 2½hrs. BAC caters for established groups such as schools and youth clubs, but you can put your own group together and they also do activity parties.

## Bristol Orienteering Klub

0117 975 6545
www.freenetpages.co.uk/hp/bristolklub

A family club for all ages, part of a national network of clubs. Orienteering involves walking or running around a designated area, visiting control points along the way. You can compete against your own age group.

## Mendip Outdoor Pursuits

Laurel Farmhouse, Summer Lane, Banwell
01934 820518
www.mendipoutdoorpursuits.co.uk

Caving, kayaking, abseiling, orienteering, archery, raft and bridge building, assault courses and hill walking — all in the beautiful Mendips. For ages 8yrs+.

## The Action Centre

Lyncombe Drive, Churchill, N Somerset, BS25 5PQ
01934 852335
www.highaction.co.uk, info@highaction.co.uk
9.30am-10pm
Costs vary according to activity (Start at £4.50 for tobogganing)

As well as its floodlit dry ski slope, the Action Centre offers activity days run by a qualified instructor, teaching skiing, archery and rifle shooting. Also quad biking, power kiting and mountain boarding. Booking essential for all activities except recreational skiing. Also see parties section.

## The Adventurous Activity Company

0117 925 3196
www.adventurousactivitycompany.co.uk

The Adventurous Activity Company works with schools, youth clubs or any groups to provide challenges and activity days, featuring everything from canoeing to rock climbing and abseiling. Available to groups of children aged from 8yrs.

## Young Bristol Outdoor Activities

0117 953 7921/07812 151131
www.youngbristol.com
rw@youngbristol.com

Half-day outdoor pursuits events in and around Bristol for groups of eight, including canoeing, kayaking, sailing, raft-building, abseiling, caving, climbing and rock sports, mountain biking and archery.

## RUGBY

### Bristol Saracens Rugby Club

Bakewell Memorial Ground, Station Rd, Cribbs Causeway
0117 950 0037
webmaster@bristolsaracensrfc.co.uk
Sun 10.30am, training for U12's and younger
Wed 6.30pm U14's to U17's

Young Saracens offers qualified coaches for teams starting from the U7/8's up to U17's.

### Bristol Shoguns Rugby Club

0117 952 6114
www.bristolshoguns.co.uk

The Shoguns have an active community programme in local schools and sports clubs, as well as holiday rugby camps.

### Clifton Rugby Club

Cribbs Causeway
0117 950 0445
www.cliftonrugby.co.uk
Sun 10am-12pm

Mini and junior rugby for all age groups from U7's up to 18. Touch rugby for U8's.

## SKATEBOARDING

### Motion Ramp Park

74-78 Avon St, St Phillips, Bristol, BS2 0PX
0117 972 3111
www.motionramppark.co.uk
Every day, 12pm-12am
£6 per rider per day

A competition-level indoor ramp complex for skateboards, bikes and blades. For beginners up to extreme, including mini ramps, vert walls, sub-boxes and the brand new Jersey Barrier. The Motion Shop offers board and bike repairs and upgrades as well as Motionwear urban clothing.

### Skate Parks In Bristol

www.sk8m8.com

The sk8m8 website provides details for hundreds of skate parks in the UK. In the Bristol area, there are plenty of venues to choose from, including: Dame Emily Smythe Park, Bedminster; St George's Park; Filwood Park, Hengrove; Withywood Skatepark; Southey Park, Kingswood; Keynesham Memorial Park; Emersons Green; Bradley Stoke; Patchway; Warmley and Portishead. Full details and directions are on the website.

## SWIMMING

Safety and confidence in the water is important for everyone. There are a wide variety of lessons available. Check out the region's swimming pools in the Colour Reference Section. Most pools have Leisure Sessions when any age can go along, but times do change, so it's best to ring first.

Babies should have their first triple vaccine before going swimming and most pools require babies to have a swim nappy. An adult must accompany every child under 8yrs. Each pool has different adult to child ratios, some 1:2 and others 1:1 for young children, so check first.

### Backwell Swimming Club

Backwell Leisure Centre, Farleigh Rd, Backwell, BS48
01275 463726
www.backwellswimmingclub.me.uk

Training and competitive swimming for ages 5-19yrs. Friendly galas and larger sponsored tournaments.

### Badminton Pool

0117 962 7972

Term-time swimming courses. Also, four-day intensive courses in diving, snorkelling and octopush (like underwater hockey!) run three times a year in April, July and December.

### Bristol Central Swimming Club

0117 968 1650
www.swimbristol.btinternet.co.uk
swimbristol@btinternet.com

Bristol Central Swimming Club runs sessions for swimmers at all skill levels, from learners to international level swimmers. The club

### Junior Lifesaving

Winterbourne Swimming Pool
0800 953 0059
Friday evenings
£25 for ten week course

Children aged 8-14yrs can become a Rookie Lifesaver. The programme has four components: water safety, rescue, self rescue and emergency response.

### Soundwell Swimming and Diving Club

0117 957 4042
www.soundwellswim.org.uk

This club offers the chance to learn to swim for all ages from 6-18yrs, as well as competitive swimming and diving. It meets at Kingswood Leisure Centre, most nights of the week.

### Splash Happy Swim School

0117 979 8266
splash_happy@hotmail.com

Swimming lessons with qualified teachers at Badminton Girls' School and Clifton High School for children up to 16yrs, of all abilities, including special needs. Classes held at weekends and some weekday evenings.

offers the chance to take part in swimming, synchronised swimming and water polo.

### Bristol Henleaze Swimming Club

www.bristolhenleazesc.org.uk
info@bristolhenleazesc.org.uk
0117 969 8276 Liz Richardson, Swim School
0117 935 5636 Judith Bush, Development & Competition Squads

This friendly and competitive swimming club offers swim schools as well as competition squads for all ages. Based at Clifton High School and the new Horfield Pool in Bristol.

### Clifton Swim School

0117 973 7245

Long established Easter and summer swim school. Courses for children from 5yrs. Beginners to ASA challenge awards, snorkelling and diving. Blocks of 10 lessons every morning over 2 weeks. Friendly tuition in small groups, held in warm pool in Clifton. Call for reservations and further information.

### Water Babies

0117 373 7959
www.waterbabies.co.uk, bristol@waterbabies.co.uk
£10 per ½hr session (blocks of 13)
Max 10 per group

Swimming lessons designed to introduce babies, under 1yr, to water. Word association, repetition, games and songs are used to encourage the development of natural swimming skills including the ability to swim underwater. All are taught without the use of armbands. Lessons take place at various pools in the Bristol and Bath area.

# Activities

## OPEN AIR POOLS

### Greenbank Outdoor Pool

Wilfrid Rd, Street, Somerset, BA16 0EU
01458 442468
www.greenbankpool.co.uk
May-mid Sept: Mon-Fri 12am-6.45pm termtime,
Sat-Sun 10am-6.45pm, summer hols 10am-6pm.
£4 adult, £3 child, U2's free. Ring or see website for
details of season tickets

This pleasant heated outdoor pool surrounded
by grass is less than five minutes' walk
from Clark's Village. There are two pools, a
separate children's area, a new Wet Play
Area and refreshments. Picnics welcomed.
Small car park.

### Portishead Open Air Pool

Esplanade Rd, Portishead, BS20 7HD
01275 843454
May-Sep

Heated open air swimming pool with separate
toddler pool. Indoor changing rooms, showers
and sunbathing terraces. U8's must be
accompanied by an adult. 1:1 ratio for U5's.
See the region's swimming pools in the Colour
Reference Section.

### Sandford Parks Lido

Keynsham Rd, Cheltenham, Gloucestershire, GL53
01242 524430
www.sandfordparkslido.org.uk
swim@sandfordlido.freeserve.co.uk
Mid Apr- Sep: Daily 11am-7.30pm
£3.50 adult, £5 (1+1) or £9 (2+2), U5's free, Various
season tickets available — ring for details
M5 J11, A40 to Cheltenham then follow tourist signs.
It's next door to Gen. Hospital.

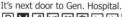

Large heated outdoor pool set in landscaped
gardens with spacious terraces for sunbathing
and a café. Separate children's pool for
U8's, paddling pool for toddlers and slides.
Two children's play areas, table tennis and
basketball. Lockers in the heated changing
rooms. Pay and display car park next door.

## Stratford Park Leisure Centre

Stratford Rd, Stroud, Gloucestershire, GL5 4AF
01453 766771
www.leisure-centre.com
Outdoor pool: end May-1st w/e Sept
Leisure Centre all year
£3.10 adult, £1.70 child, £5.60 family (2+2)
See Museum in the Park

Set in 32 acres of parkland this leisure
centre provides indoor and outdoor facilities
for a variety of sports. The outdoor pool is
particularly popular in summer, with grass and
terrace sunbathing areas. There are crèche
and party facilities available.

## WEST COUNTRY POOLS

### Bradford-on-Avon Swimming Pool

St. Margaret St, Bradford-on-Avon, Wiltshire, BA15
01225 862 970
www.bradfordswimmingpool.co.uk
enquiries@bradfordswimmingpool.co.uk
Daily, call for more details

Parent and toddler (U5's) swimming sessions
in warm smaller pool, £2.65. Adult-to-child
ratio of 1:2. Two elephant slides, rings, floats,
toys and balls available.

Sat 11am-12.30pm, fun swim for all ages
with floats and inflatables. Lessons from 1yr.
Sloped entrance at rear. Special activities in
school holidays, including life guard courses,
diving, canoeing and distance swims.

### Newport Centre

Kingsway, Newport, South Wales
01633 662 662
Daily

Public sessions seven days a week. Warm
leisure pool with splash area, wave machine,
slide and play equipment. Spacious changing
rooms. U5's 1:1 adult to child ratio, 5-7yrs
1:2. Swimming lessons and soft play also
available. Other activities include canoeing,
archery, trampolining and water polo. Holiday
activities for all age groups.

## Sedgemoor Splash

Mount St, Bridgwater, Somerset, TA6 3ER
01278 425 636
Open daily, please call for details.
adult, £3.85; child, £2.75; U4's free;
family tickets £10.50.

Excellent warm fun pool with two water flumes, river run, bubbles, water jets & wave machine. Gently sloping splash area and separate children's pool with bubbles. Adult to child ratios U5's 1:1, 5-8yrs 1:2.

# TENNIS

## Bristol Central Tennis Club

Derby Rd, St Andrew's Park, Bristol
07887 633 095
www.bctc.org.uk
admin@bctc.org.uk

There are regular coaching sessions on Saturday mornings and during school holidays. The junior squads train on week nights after school in term time.

## Bristol Lawn Tennis and Squash Club

Redland Green, Redland, Bristol
0117 973 1139
www.bltsc.co.uk

After school and holiday classes for all ages from 4yrs.

## Coombe Dingle Tennis Centre

Coombe Dingle Sports Complex, Coombe Lane, Stoke Bishop
0117 962 6718
www.peterbendall.org.uk
Peter Bendall: 07973 641132

Ten-week courses run after school every term for all ages and abilities. Youngsters showing promise will be invited to join Junior Select, a competitive squad that meets three times a week. Holiday courses are also available.

## Cotham Park Tennis Club

71 Redland Rd, Bristol
0117 974 1044
www.cothamtennis.net

Regular coaching in the holidays and during term time as well as junior squads.

## Henleaze Tennis Club

Tennessee Grove, off Springfield Grove, Henleaze
01275 543449

Coaching starts with mini tennis and goes on to a more structured programme for players leading up to performance level. There are courses after school, at weekends and during school holidays. During the winter months, coaching is offered at the indoor tennis centre at Coombe Dingle.

## Kings Tennis Club

Maplemeade, Kings Drive, Bishopston, Bristol
0117 942 7667
www.kings-tennis.net

Kings offers a fun programme throughout the week for all ages and abilities.

**Drop-in sessions**

Sat 9.30am-10.30am, 3-8yrs, £2
Sat 10.30am-11.30am, 9-12yrs, £2

To teach the FUNdamentals of tennis in a non-competitive environment.

**Mini Tennis**

After school throughout the week

For aspiring youngsters teaching not only the technical skills but also scoring and playing in team competitions.

## Knowle Tennis Club

Wells Rd, Knowle, Bristol
0117 977 3996
www.knowletennis.pwp.blueyonder.co.uk

Thriving junior coaching programme with sessions on Saturday mornings for all abilities, as well as ten-week courses during term time.

## Mini Tennis

Coombe Dingle Sports Complex, Combe Lane, Bristol, BS9 2BJ
0117 962 6723

Mini Tennis is available at these venues across the city:
Sat: St George's Park
Sat: Eastville Park Tennis Club
Sat: Horfield Park
Sat & Sun: Canford Park
Sun: Ashton Park
Wed/Thur/Sat: St Paul's Tennis Club

## Westbury Park Tennis Club

0117 962 2663
www.westburyparktennisclub.co.uk

Saturday morning coaching for all ages from 4yrs.

# WATER SPORTS

## Bristol Avon Sailing Club

Mead Lane, Saltford, BS31 3ER
01225 873472
www.bristol-avon-sailing.org.uk
enquiries@bristol-avon-sailing.org.uk

This family-friendly club offers reasonable membership rates for families and juniors and the chance to sail on a mile-long stretch of the River Avon. Royal Yacht Association accredited courses for beginners are run every spring.

## Bristol Sailing School

0117 926 0703
www.bristolsailingschool.co.uk

Sailing lessons for all ages in Bristol Harbour. Courses are usually held during school holidays and last from 1-3 days.

## Bristol Water Ski Club

0117 987 9575
www.bwsf.co.uk
Every other Sat
Winter: 8.30am-12.30pm summer: 9am-1pm
£20 per session

Water skiing in the harbour is available to all ages. Kids as young as four can have a go as long as they bring their own wetsuit. You don't even have to be a strong swimmer as you wear buoyancy aids. Bristol Water Ski Club is an Approved Ski Boat Driver Award Test Centre.

# SOFT PLAY & PRE-SCHOOL GYM

## PRE-SCHOOL GYM

### Baskerville's Gym

Englishcombe Court, Englishcombe Lane, Bath, BA2
01225 339991

Classes every day for all ages from 6 months to teenagers. Courses are made up of ten sessions per term with four terms a year. Enthusiastic gymnasts can work towards BGA awards.

**Pre-school soft play**
Sun 10am-11.30am.

### Bristol Hawks Gymnastic Club

Gymnastics World, Roman Rd, Lower Easton, BS5
0117 935 5363/973 7481

P ✏ WC 🚻 🚹 🚹 👜

**Parent & Toddler (18mths-4yrs)**
Tue/Wed/Thur am, £3.50 per session, £18/6 weeks

**Pre-School Gym Class (2-5yrs)**
Tue/Wed/Thu am, prices as above

**Young Beginners (4-6yrs)**
Wed pm, £3.50, £18 for 6 weeks

**Play Gym (under 5's)**
Sat am, 2 sessions, £2 ½hr session

**Open Gym (4-6yrs)**
Sat am, £3

Fun, challenging, stimulating and safe. All coaches qualified. BGA grades followed. Drinks & snacks available. Buggies left in changing rooms. See also Gymnastics above.

# Bristol School of Gymnastics

Old Bishopston Methodist Church,
245 Gloucester Rd, Bristol, BS7 8NY
0117 942 9620

### Under 3's
£26.40/8 weeks
Play based, including songs and juice/biscuit, parent stays

### Over 3's
£28.80/8 weeks
Parents encouraged to leave

### Open sessions 4-10yrs
Sat am, £3 per session

### Pre-school classes
Mon/Wed/Thu/Fri

General gymnastics with apparatus, taught by qualified coaches. See also Gymnastics above.

# Fromeside Gymnastics Club

Watleys End Rd, Winterbourne, Bristol, BS36 1QG
01454 776 873/777 749

All classes taken by qualified coaches. See also Gymnastics above.

### Jellies
Tue/Wed 9.15am-10am, £2.50
Drop in session for walking under 2's, parents stay

### Parent & Toddlers
2-3yrs with parents
Tue/Wed 10am, registration fee £15, £3.50 weekly charge, pre-booking required

### Gym Tots
3-4yrs without parents
Tue 11am, Mon/Fri 2pm, registration fee £15, £3.50 weekly charge, pre-booking required

# Jack in a Box

Waterford Hall, Waterford Rd,
0117 962 3758
www.jackinabox.info
katewrightjackbox@hotmail.

### Soft play for tinies (under 20 mths)
Tue/Wed/Fri 9.25am-10.15am, £3.50

Wide variety of equipment with free play and music. No pre-booking necessary.

### Mini-gym (20 months to 3 years)
Tue/Wed/Fri 2 sessions at 10.45am & 11.35pm, £3.80 per session, payable half-termly

Working with carer round circuits of apparatus. Pre-booking necessary.

### Pre-school gym (3 to 5 yrs)
Tue/Wed/Fri pm, £3.80 per session, payable half-termly.

Working independently in small groups and following BGA badge schemes. All classes supervised by qualified staff. Popular and friendly group.

# Star Jumpers Gym Club

0117 957 0009
£3.50-£4.50 per ¾hr session, payable termly
Venues: Emerson's Green, Staple Hill, Downend and Pucklechurch

A structured programme of pre-school gymnastics and physical play, designed by British gymnastics specifically for children under five years of age. Four types of class are available based on age and ability, 5mths-5yrs. Also are classes for 5-7yrs, held after school.

# Tumble Tots

0117 377 8884
www.tumbletots.com/bristol
tumbletotkelly@fsmail.net
Downend, Hanham, Stoke Gifford, and Long Ashton

Gym Babes, 6mths through to Tumble Tot, 5yrs. Free trial sessions available. Physical pre-school play programme with structured, fun activities designed to help children with agility, balance, co-ordination and communication skills. Uses bright and stimulating equipment with trained staff.

# PLAY

## 23 Jump

22 Concorde Rd, Bristol, BS34 5TB
0117 931 2733
www.123jump.co.uk, bristol@123jump.co.uk
Mon-Fri 10am-6.30pm, Sat 10am-7pm
Sun 10am-6.30pm
£1.50 adults, £6 4+yrs, £5 U4's, free U1's

Active safe play for children 0-12yrs. This new indoor play centre near Cribbs Causeway, run by friendly staff, has three large playframes, a toddler zone, trampolines, football pitch, café, ten-pin bowling and five themed party rooms all under one roof.

## Castaways Bourne Chapel

Waters Rd, Kingswood, Bristol, BS15 8BE
0117 961 5115
Tue-Sat 9am-5.30pm
General play 0-6mths free, 7-17mths £1.25, 18+mths £2.60

Two tiers of fun for U11's which includes small inflatable bouncy, climbing equipment, two ball pools, slides, soft play area, separate toddler/baby area based on under water theme. Also available as a party venue.

### Treasure Tots (pre-school)

Thur 10am-12pm, term time, £3.30

Activities, toys, drink, fruit & biscuits. Very popular with limited spaces.

## Elmgrove Centre Rumpus Room

Redland Rd, Cotham, Bristol, BS6 6AG
0117 924 3377
www.elmgrovecentre.org.uk
elmgrv.admin@elmgrovecentre.org.uk
Mon-Fri 9.30am-1.30pm
50p per child.

Drop-in soft play session for U7's, occasionally pre-booked for a party.

## Gordano Gate Fun Factory

Gordano Gate, Wyndham Way, Bristol, BS20 7GA
01275 846526
Mon/Wed/Fri: 10am-12pm, £2

Weekly drop-in parent and toddler sessions held in the Fun Factory, full use of all facilities for the U5's. Sessions last 1½hrs. Special VIP sessions with a helium balloon and face painting cost £4.

## Parent Play & Stay/Time Zone Kidz at The Mall

Time Zone Kidz, The Mall at Cribbs Causeway, Bristol, BS34 5UR
0117 915 5802
Mon/Wed/Fri 10am-12pm, Tue/Thu 10am-3.30pm, term time only, £2.50 for up to 2hrs

Parent Stay and Play: soft play with ball pit, trikes, construction toys, dolls, books etc and adventure play room. Buggy store available in reception.

Also crèche available, £1.90 per ½hr, max stay 2hrs.

## Planet Kids

Bristol Mega Bowl, Brunel Way, Ashton Gate, BS3
0117 953 8538
www.megabowl.co.uk
Wed-Fri 12pm-6pm, Sat-Sun 10am-6pm
Daily sch hols 10am-6pm
£3.50 or £12 for 4 children

Adventure play centre for U12's.

## Riverside Leisure Club

Station Rd, Little Stoke, Bristol, BS34 6HW
01454 888 666
Daily 10am-6pm
1½hr sessions, £2.70 U5's, £3.10 over 5's

Mayhem Soft Play: 3mths-10yrs (under 4'11"). Separate areas for toddlers and older children.

## The Alphabet Zoo Children's Playcentre

Old Bingo Hall, Winterstoke Rd, Bedminster, BS3
0117 966 3366
Daily 10am-7pm, inc. B/H's, last admission 5pm
2hr sessions, £2.75 U4's, £3.49 4+yrs Mon-Fri
£3.99 w/e's

Play centre for 1-11yrs. Large area filled with huge variety of interesting, colourful and challenging equipment, including the new Mega Slide, a 10ft inflatable slide. Good separate toddler area including junior bouncy castle. Equipment for over 5's available to toddlers when quiet during school hours if supervised. Wheelchair access available.

**Toddler mornings**
Tue/Thu, 10am-12pm, £1.99 including drink and snack

# ARTS & ENTERTAINMENT

## ARTS & CRAFTS

### Orchard Workshops
Kingswood Foundation, Britannia Rd, Kingswood, BS15 8DB
0117 967 0799

Saturday morning arts and crafts club. Each class is a self-contained session focusing on one craft, such as metalwork, woodwork, jewellery making, silversmithing, glass or photography. Fully-inclusive for both able and disabled children from 8-15yrs. Book in advance. Janet also runs summer holiday workshops.

### Recreating
01454 414915
elizabeth@vooght.com

Art and craft workshops held in the school holidays including half terms. Based in Thornbury and aimed at ages 8-14yrs. Based on small groups of children, so it gets booked up very quickly but Elizabeth can be booked for additional sessions.

### Ticky Tacky
Church of the Good Shepherd Hall, Bishop Rd, Bishopston, BS7 8NA
0117 951 6206
Fri 10-11.15am, 2-4yrs, £1 per person, term time

Painting, sticking, drawing, singing and baking activities on a Biblical theme. Friendly and involved leaders.

## UWE Bristol School of Art, Media and Design
Bower Ashton Campus, Kennel Lodge Rd, BS3 2JT
0117 328 4810
www.uwe.ac.uk/amd
amd.shortcourses@uwe.as.uk

Animation courses for 7-11yrs on Saturdays over six weeks. Also week-long summer courses in animation and drawing.

## CIRCUS SKILLS

### Circomedia
St Paul's Church, Portland Sq, Bristol
0117 935 3260
www.circomedia.com

Circomedia offer a range of learning opportunities for young people. Circus skills have been shown to engage young people that may feel alientated from mainstream education. Life skills are developed such as listening, communication and concentration. Workshops and weekly sessions are available.

### Circus Bugz & Circus Maniacs
Office 8A, The Kingswood Foundation, Britannia Rd, Kingswood, BS15 8DB
0117 947 7042
www.circusmaniacs.com
info@circusmaniacs.com
Sat sessions, term time only, 11wks
3-5yrs £30 (¾hr), 5-7 yrs £50 (1½hrs)
7+yrs £70 (2½hrs)
P WC ↥

Circus unites aspects of both sport and arts, providing the creative freedom to be original and unique.

**Circus Bugz (3-7yrs)**

A range of activities designed to enhance hand/eye co-ordination, posture, balance, movement and creativity. "Caterpillar Awards" for 3-5 yrs and "Butterfly Awards" for 5-7 yrs. Parents and carers are welcome to participate.

**Circus Maniacs (7+yrs)**

Opportunity to get physical by learning skills inc. trapeze, tight-wire, acrobatics, juggling, unicycling & stilt-walking. Taster sessions available. See website for further details.

## COOKERY

### Quartier Vert

85 Whiteladies Road, Bristol
0117 904 6679
www.quartiervert.co.uk

This creative cookery school offers workshops and summer holiday courses for young people from 7yrs.

## DANCE

### 344 Dance School

Alexandra Pk, Fishponds, Bristol, BS16 2BG
0117 965 5660
www.dancestation.org.uk
Branches at: Bradley Stoke, Long Ashton, Wick, Knowle and Fishponds

[P] [WC] [A] [🛒]

Ballet, modern jazz, tap, drama, singing, Irish dancing & shows for children of 2½yrs to adults, including classes for teenage beginners. Sessions weekdays after school and Sat. Also summer schools. Full-time dance college for 16+yrs. Dancewear and tuck shop.

### Annette Adams School of Dance

0117 968 4879
www.theannetteadamsschoolofdance.co.uk

Classes are held at Horfield Methodist Church and the Kelvin Players Drama Studio, both on Gloucester Road. Ballet from 3yrs and modern, jazz and tap from 5yrs. Classes held after school and Saturday mornings. Working towards RAD and ISTD exams.

### Ashley's Rise Morris Dancing

0117 940 1566
ashleyrisemorris@aol.com
Horfield United Reform Church
Tue 6.15pm-7.15pm

A performing English morris team for ages 8-16yrs. Mainly Border and some Cotswold dancing. And if that doesn't mean anything to you, don't worry, absolute beginners are positively encouraged. First session free and you can pay termly or weekly. There are

regular performances at fetes and fairs in the summer and at Seasonal Customs. All costumes provided, apart from black trousers.

### Bollywood Dance

0117 931 4443
www.bollywooddance.co.uk
info@bollywooddance.co.uk

Classes for all ages from 4yrs to adult. Classes are held in Hotwells, Easton and Bradley Stoke. Workshops can also be arranged. Call for further details.

### Bristol Community Dance Centre

Jacobs Wells Rd, Hotwells, Bristol, BS8 1DX
0117 929 2118
www.bristolcommunitydancecentre.co.uk

You'll find every type of dance class on offer at this fantastic centre, including flamenco, hip hop, breakdance, Bollywood and African dance. There are also classes in yoga, pilates and jitsu defence.

## Bristol School of Dancing

Lansdown Rd, Clifton, Bristol, BS8 3AB
01278 434 081
From £38 per term, dependent on age.

Classes in all stage dance and movement for ages 2-11yrs. 1 hour sessions held daily. Call for details.

## Chance to Dance

Southville Centre, Beaulieu Rd, Southville
07879 483106
Thu 10.30am-11.15am
&
St Bartholomews Parish Hall, Sommerville Rd, St Andrews
Thu 2pm-2.45pm
£2.50 one child, £4 for two

Informal drop-in, interactive session for 2-4yr olds to develop mobility and co-ordination skills. Parent participation required.

## Danceblast@the Tobacco Factory

Tobacco Factory, Raleigh Rd, Southville
0117 964 6195
anne@danceblast.co.uk
Sat 3-18 yrs, Sun 14-18yrs, £5 per 1½hr session

All types of dancing: ballet, jazz, lyrical and hip hop as well as some singing and acting included, working towards an annual show. Sessions are drop-in.

## Funk It Up Dance Company

07816 498774
www.funkitupdance.com
info@funkitupdance.com

Hip hop and street dance for all ages and abilities, every evening from Monday to Thursday, from 7yrs to adult.

## Henleaze School of Dancing

0117 962 3224
Mon-Fri
Venues:
St Peters' Church Hall, Henleaze
Stoke Bishop Village Hall

Ballet & tap for ages 5-11yrs. Also music and movement classes for ages 3-5yrs.

## Kuumba

0117 944 7504
www.kuumba.org.uk
7-11yrs: Thur 6pm-7pm

Weekly classes in all kinds of dance from R&B and dance hall to ragga, working towards performances. Summer courses available.

## Southville Centre

Beaulieu Rd, Southville, Bristol, BS3 1QG
0117 923 1039

### Bristol School of Dancing & Ballet Classes (3yrs+)

Mon 4.15pm-7pm, 45 min sessions.

### Music Magic

Thur 9.15am-10.15am
Sarah Sweeting: 0117 966 4170

## Stapleton School of Dancing

01453 844 430
From £23 per term
Venues:
Begbrook Primary School, Stapleton
Christ Church Hall, Quaker Rd, Downend
The Ridgewood Community Centre, Yate

Ballet, modern & tap for children 2+yrs. Summer School available for over 5's during the last week of July. Call for details.

## Stepping Out School of Dance

Baptist Church Hall, Station Rd, Shirehampton
01454 615463/07971 099706
Wed/Fri/Sat drop-in classes

Classes for all ages from 18 months to adult, including ballet, tap, jazz and pop. Regular performances, no set uniform.

## Street Vibes Dance

The Sanctuary Church, 55 High St, Staple Hill, BS16
07980 509461
streetvibesdance@blueyonder.co.uk

### Breakdancing classes for 'Boyz'

Wed 5.45pm.

### 'Girlz'

Thu 6.30pm

Drop-in sessions aimed at 7-18yrs. Learn everything from hip hop to street dance.

## The Big Act

0870 8810367
www.thebigact.com

Classes in acting, singing and dancing for children up to 18yrs. There are no auditions, places are offered on a first come first served basis. New students can come for a free trial lesson. Students regularly perform shows in Bristol. There are three venues in Bristol:

**The Tobacco Factory, Southville**
Sun 11.30am-1pm (4-7yrs)
Fri 5pm-7pm (8-18yrs)

**Gate C, Knorr Bremse Ind Park**
Douglas Rd, Kingswood, BS15 8NL
Sun 12.45pm-2.15pm (4-7yrs)
Sun 1.45pm-3.45pm (8-18yrs)

**Bradley Stoke**
New venue about to open, call for further details

## Westbury Park Dance Centre

St Albans Church Hall, Westbury Park, BS6
0117 968 3682
westburyparkdancecentre@hotmail.com
After school & Sat

Classes following RAD Ballet and ISTD Jazz/Modern/ Tab syllabuses. Children (all ages, from 3yrs) will work towards occasional shows.

## Wingfield School of Ballet

0117 950 3916
wingfieldschool@brentry.freeserve.co.uk
Venues: Patchway, Little Stoke, Thornbury, Almondsbury, Brislington & Bradley Stoke Leisure Centre
Ballet classes for 3+yrs. Tap and modern dance for 4½+yrs. Prepares children for RAD & ISTD examinations, shows & Eisteddfod.

## Youth Dance

Bristol Community Dance Centre, Jacobs Wells Road, Hotwells, BS8 1DX
0117 377 1063

Creative and contemporary dance classes for 5-7yrs, 7-11yrs and 11-15yrs. Summer schools also available.

# DRAMA & THEATRE SKILLS

## Bigfoot Drama Academy

0870 0114948
www.bigfoot-theatre.co.uk

New to Bristol, Bigfoot offers a special approach to drama. Starting with a topic, the work that is produced is child-led and is all about building confidence and improving empathy and communication. Currently offering Saturday morning sessions in Bath for ages 8-11yrs and 12-14yrs, with more classes opening soon in Bristol. Holiday workshops also available.

## Bristol Old Vic

King St, Bristol, BS1 4ED
0117 987 7877
www.bristol-old-vic.co.uk
Fri 11am-11.45am, call to check
£1.50 pp

Fun sessions for pre-school children with songs, stories, performing and a chance to meet some of the people who work at the theatre. No need to book but phone to check times and dates. Holiday workshops.

## Bristol Old Vic Youth Theatre

King St, Bristol, BS1 4ED
0117 949 3993 Ext 226
www.bristol-old-vic.co.uk

Offers young people, 7-21yrs, the chance to develop a wide range of practical theatre skills. It has over 400 members from across the South West. Sessions take place once a week on weekday evenings and Saturday mornings and cost £35 or £40 per term, depending on age. There is a long waiting list.

## Bristol School of Performing Arts

Elmgrove Centre, Redland Rd, Cotham, BS6 6AG
01278 434 081
Thu/Sat, 2hr sessions, term time
£95 for 10 weeks

Drama classes for 6-16 yrs. Holiday workshops available. Lamba examinations are available.

## Centre Stage

01454 851938
www.centrestage.bizland.com

Two-hour drama sessions with the emphasis on improving confidence. Including dance, drama, singing and movement, with all ages (7-18yrs) working together. No auditions, opportunities for all and regular workshops from professionals, on everything from stage fighting to African dance. Sessions take place on Saturday mornings at Winterbourne and on Monday evenings in Yate. Call for further details.

## Drama Queens

Southville Centre, Beaulieu Rd, BS3 1QG
07977 681954
Weds 5.30pm-6.30pm 8-11yrs,
6.30pm-7.30pm 11+yrs

Creating ideas, producing stories, learning stage and life skills, showing off, dressing up and having fun.

## Helen O'Grady Drama Academy

0117 924 4944
www.helenogrady.co.uk
alison.mazanec@btinternet.com
Venues: Frampton Cotterell, Keynesham, Bishopston, Portishead, Westbury-on-Trym, Almondsbury, Redland and Kingswood

Lower Primary (5-8yrs)

Upper Primary (9-12yrs)

Youth Theatre (13-17yrs)

The programme offered at the academy aims to provide on-going confidence and skills in verbal communication through drama. Working towards summer performances. Sessions after school and at weekends. Call for details of times and venues.

## ITV West Television Workshops

ITV West, Bath Rd, Bristol, BS4 3HG
0117 972 2497
www.itv.com, adam.fresco@itv.com
5-26yrs
Sessions at w/e's, after school and in holidays, according to age

ITV West offers drama and production workshops training young people in performance, presenting and production for

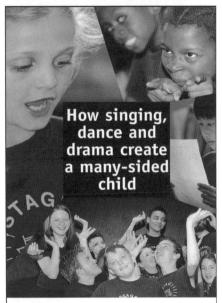

**How singing, dance and drama create a many-sided child**

I F YOUR CHILD is aged between 4 and 16 he or she is ready for Stagecoach. We teach the skills needed to act, sing & dance.

Soon they will grow more confident, speak more clearly, move more easily, act more naturally, become self-aware. These skills don't vanish as the curtain falls. They are learnt for life.

Weekly classes held out-of school hours.

Week long workshops are held in summer.

### To enrol phone your local Principal:

| | |
|---|---|
| ASHTON & PORTISHEAD | Heidi **0117 9532500** |
| COTHAM & WINTERBOURNE | Diana **0117 9593995** |
| KEYNSHAM & TOTTERDOWN | Nathalie **01225 484785** |
| WESTON-s-MARE | Caroline **01278 788744** |
| BATH | Carole **01225 359997** |

# STAGECOACH
## THEATRE ARTS SCHOOLS
www.stagecoach.co.uk

tv, theatre, radio and film. There are regular performances and you could get to make your own short films. Unsurprisingly, there is a waiting list but it's worth filling in an application form online to get your name down. The workshops also act as a casting resource for tv and film. Previous students have appeared in everything from Harry Potter to Casualty.

## Ivy Arts Theatre School

Torwood House, Durdham Pk, Redland, BS6 6XE
07748 983 436
Sat 10am-12pm & 12.30pm-2.30pm.
From £10 per session

P WC 人

Qualified teachers offer a broad range of theatre crafts, performing, singing, movement & dance for children 5-14yrs. Pre-booking essential. Children are split into age-related groups, but also spend some time integrated together. Working towards one major musical every summer. Workshops available during Easter and summer holidays.

## Kick Off Youth Theatre

The Hope Chapel, Hope Chapel Hill, Hotwells
0117 929 1883
Mon 5pm-6.30pm (7-11yrs) and
6.30pm-8pm (12-18yrs)
£3 per session £2 concessions, payable half termly

An opportunity for children, 7-18yrs, to learn skills such as acting, voice, mime, masks and perform shows. Members must be prepared to have a great time and show commitment to attendance and rehearsal. Qualified drama teacher.

## QEH Youth Theatre

QEH Theatre, Jacobs Wells Rd, Bristol, BS8 1JX
0117 914 5805
www.qehtheatre.co.uk
7-11yrs, Mon 4pm-5.30pm
£5.50 per session (max 16 children) payable in advance

Youth theatre with sessions for all ages from 7-16yrs. Movement, sound, art and craft, games, storymaking and telling, improvisation, role-play, mime and plays. New sessions for ages 11-13yrs and 14-16yrs being established, phone for more information.

## Stagecoach

0117 986 2500
www.stagecoachbristol.co.uk
info@stagecoachbristol.co.uk

Offers part-time training in drama, singing and dance to children and teenagers (4-16 yrs) of all abilities. There are no auditions. Their ethos concentrates on confidence and self-esteem. Visit their website, see advertisement, pg 111, or phone for further details.

Ashton/Portishead 0117 953 2500

Keynesham 0117 330 5953

Cotham 0117 953 2500

Winterbourne 0117 959 3995T

Totterdown 01225 484785

## Star 'um' Young

01275 544576, 07914 187737
£8 per hr, 2hr sessions (although shorter sessions for 3-4 yr olds) 6 wk term paid in advance
Venue: Backwell Playhouse

Arts and theatre school for the very young, 3-7 yrs. Activities include drama, dance, voice coaching, mime, stage crafts, theatre history and end of year and Christmas performances. Other venues planned for 2006/07.

# FILM

## Cinekids @ The Watershed

1 Canon's Rd, Harbourside, Bristol, BS1 5TX
0117 927 5100
www.watershed.co.uk, kids@watershed.co.uk
Adults £3.50, children £2

Cinekids is aimed at children aged 8-12yrs. It's a once a month event, with a film showing and workshop or talk afterwards. To get advance notice of the next events by email, call the box office or send an email.

**Planning a trip to the theatre?**
Check out our complete listings on page 11.

# PRE-SCHOOL MUSIC & MOVEMENT CLASSES

## Child's Play at the Crotchet Factory

1 Edward St, Eastville, BS5 6LW
0117 951 8015

Music workshops providing a fun, hands-on introduction to a mixture of music. Holiday and private sessions available, including tuition in piano, keyboard, guitar, flute, violin and recorder.

**Baby class**
Tue/Fri 9.45am-10.15am

**2-3yrs**
Tue/Fri 10.30am-11.00am

**Over 3's**
Tue/Fri 11.15am-12pm, Tue 2pm-2.45pm
Sat 10.45am-11.30am

**Workshops for 4-8yrs (12 children max)**
Percussion, recorder, keyboard, guitar and singing. Sessions last ¾-1hr.

## Hum and Drum

28 Dublin Crescent, Henleaze, Bristol, BS9 4NA
0117 962 1328/924 3159
Mon-Fri am & pm, Sat am
£45 per term for weekly ¾hr session

Introduction to basic musical concepts through playing a wide variety of instruments. Classes for 6mths-11yrs. Carers of younger children stay, but are encouraged to leave over 3's. Sat (4-11yrs) music workshop. Piano, violin & recorder lessons after school (up to 18 yrs). Holiday workshops for all ages to 11.

## Jo Jingles

01454 610553
www.jojingles.co.uk, pam.jojingles@tiscali.co.uk
Venues: Redland, Emersons Green, Warmley, Yate, Bradley Stoke, Portishead, Clevedon, Thornbury and Mothercare at Eastgate

Weekly classes for pre-school children. Introduction to music, singing and movement including percussion instruments, action songs, sound games and nursery rhymes.

## Jolly Babies/Music with Mummy

01454 619 773
30 min sessions, payable half termly

Jolly babies is a chance to share your baby's first musical experiences, for ages 0-12 months. Music with Mummy classes are for ages 1-4yrs with carers. Fun with music through movement, games and using simple instruments. Some sessions during school holidays. Both classes take place at various venues. Call for further details:

| | |
|---|---|
| Julie Thompson/Bradley Stoke | 01454 619 773 |
| Deb Denny/Downend | 0117 957 4443 |
| Anne-Marie Collier/Frampton Cottrell | 01454 773 267 |
| Maria Vise, Henleaze/Redland | 0117 940 5803 |
| Ruth Wong/Thornbury | 01454 413 905 |
| Kelly Allen/Hengrove | 0117 907 1422 |
| Katie Cox/Staple Hill | 0117 957 1382 |
| Sophie Lincoln/Henbury | 0117 950 4913 |
| Caz O'Doherty/St Andrews | 0117 908 9080 |
| Tara Sahni/St George | 0117 941 4573 |

## Lucy Time

Cotham Parish Church, Cotham Rd, Cotham, BS6
Lucy Livingstone: 0117 924 9455
Tue/Wed/Fri, 7 sessions per week
£4.50 ¾hr session payable half termly

Uses themes from nature to sing, dance, and celebrate the festivals. Children, aged 18mths-4yrs, are grouped according to age. Carers of younger children join in sessions but over 3's may stay on their own.

Also sessions for parents with young babies. These promise parents a chance to nourish

...elves as well as their babies, through an ...ity-based group, using music, movement ...d props. 1hr session, £6.

## Mini Musicians

01275 394344
sarah@4mmaw.freeserve.co.uk
Mon 9.45am & 10.40am, ages 18mths-4yrs
£3.50 per session, payable termly, second child £2
Venue: Long Ashton Village Hall Club Room, disabled access

Singing, rhythm, instruments, games, music and movement for pre-school children. Classes given by a qualified music teacher.

## Music Makers

33 Cornwall Rd, Bishopston, Bristol, BS7 8LJ
0117 924 1124
Tue am & pm
From £2 per session (term time)

Introduction to music & movement for under 5's using accordion, percussion and additional props. Children (18mths-4yrs) attend sessions, grouped according to age, lasting 30 or 45 mins. Carers of older children settle them in the group and can have a cuppa in the kitchen. Occasional children's parties. Pre-booking required.

## Rhymetime

Ebenezer Methodist Church, British Rd, Bedminster
0117 966 7028
Thu 10am-10.30am, toddlers from 18mths,
10.45am-11.15am, babies up to 18mths
£2 per family, payable on the day

Rhymetime is a lively music and action group, with separate sessions for babies and toddlers. Sit in a friendly circle on the floor and sing along with the guitar to many favourite nursery rhymes and songs. Babies join in with the action using the instruments provided. Just turn up to take part.

## Shake, Sing & Boogie

52 Harrington Rd, Stockwood, BS14 8LD
01275 891644
tanyabracey@blueyonder.co.uk
St Martin's Church Hall, Knowle
Wed 9.30am & 10.30am
Sturminster Community Association, Stockwood
Thu 9.30am
£2.50 per session, payable per half term

Music groups for U5's. Children learn a variety of nursery rhymes and action songs. They also get to play a selection of instruments. Classes last ¾hr, the first class is free. "The highlight of our week"

## Sing and Sign

0117 950 0017
Course of ten sessions (¾hr each) £50, term time
Venues: Westbury-on-Trym, Portishead, Westbury Park, Hanham, Knowle, Keynesham, Redland and Horfield

Sing and Sign is a programme of songs and rhymes for babies from 7-18+mths, teaching simple gestures (derived from sign language) which parents can use to enhance communication with their babies. This course is based on three levels which move into phonics, the alphabet and colours as children progress. Older children welcome.

## Tatty Bumpkin

0117 952 0070
www.tattybumpkin.co.uk
goldenbrown77@blueyonder.co.uk
Mon am and after school at Horfield Baptist Church

Movement and story classes, with animal adventures, inspired by yoga. For ages 18mths-5yrs. With great music and ends with a lovely relaxation! Ring for more details.

## Toddler Tunes

0117 962 2336
Newman Hall, Grange Court Rd, Westbury-on-Trym
Mon/Thu 10am & 11am
Horfield Baptist Church, Gloucester Rd
Tue/Weds 10am & 11am
£2.50 per child, £1.50 for siblings

Singing classes with action songs and rhymes, instruments and puppets. Informal and fun atmosphere, parents/carers expected to participate. No pre-booking required. Suitable for all pre-school children.

## MUSIC TUITION

Finding a good music teacher can be difficult, whether you play an instrument or are looking for singing lessons. A good place to start is on the website below or asking at musical instrument shop where they often keep details of teachers in the area.

### Incorporated Society of Musicians

10 Stratford Place, London, W1C 1AA
020 7629 4413
www.ism.org

This is an excellent website with private teachers listed by UK region. The teachers have been approved for their Register of Professional Private Music Teachers. Gaining approval entails careful scrutiny of qualifications, experience and achievement. This rigorous approach is applied to each instrument offered. A member of the Register will have passed a DfES List 99 or Criminal Records Bureau Disclosure check. They will also have to follow the ISM Code of Ethics and Practice.

### Child's Play at the Crotchet Factory

1 Edward St, Eastville, Bristol, BS5 6LW
0117 951 8015

Music workshops providing a fun, hands-on introduction to a mixture of music. Holiday and private sessions, including tuition in piano, keyboard, guitar, flute, violin and recorder.

Workshops for 4-8yrs (12 children max). Percussion, recorder, keyboard, guitar and singing. Sessions last ¾hr-1hr.

### Hum and Drum

28 Dublin Crescent, Henleaze, Bristol, BS9 4NA
0117 962 1328/924 3159
penraw@aol.com
Mon-Fri am & pm, Sat am
£45 per term for weekly 45 min session

Piano, violin & recorder lessons after school, up to 18yrs. Holiday workshops up to 11yrs.

### Opus Music

486 Wellsway, Bath, BA2 2UD
01225 460 209 ( 24 hr)

Individual and group piano tuition from 5-18yrs.

## MUSIC GROUPS & BANDS

### 37th Kingswood Drum and Bugle Corps

0117 961 4607
www.37th.co.uk, h.ian@btinternet.com
St Stevens School, Kingswood
Tue/Sun evenings: Seniors (12-25)
Fri evening: Cadet Corps (7-13yrs)
Subs are £2 a week

This award-winning Corps plays around the country and even further afield during the summer season. Complete beginnners are welcome, newcomers will be taught to read music and given the chance to try a range of instruments. Instruments and uniforms are provided.

### Christchurch Choir & Music Group

Christchurch, Clifton Down Rd, Clifton
0117 973 2011
Free — call for details.

Two weekly choirs, for ages 7-11yrs and 11-18yrs.

### City of Bristol Brass Band

07977 137646
www.cobbb.co.uk
steve@cobbb.co.uk
St Bonaventures School, Bishopston
Fri 6pm

This thriving youth band is primarily aimed at 7-12yr olds, and there are opportunities to join the main band. Regular performances include events such as the Harbour Festival. There is a subscription but newcomers can try for free for three months and instruments are provided.

## South Gloucestershire Music Service

01454 863147

Early years music groups for children in reception up to year 2.

Bands, orchestras and string groups for accomplished musicians. Phone for further details of times and places.

# GROUPS

## ACTION GROUPS

### The Boys' Brigade

01442 231 681 (UK Headquarters)
www.boys-brigade.org.uk

The Boys' Brigade is one of the largest Christian Youth Organisations in the United Kingdom with 60,000 members in over 1500 locations. It provides a programme of activities for children and young people from 5-18yrs, which is underpinned by the Christian Faith. For more information on your local group, contact the Boys' Brigade's UK Headquarters.

### Fun Factory

Bristol Community Church, Bourne Chapel, Waters Rd, Kingswood, BS15 8BE
0117 947 8441
Mon, 6.30pm-8pm

P WC 🕮 🖼 📖

Fun-filled club for children (7-10yrs), activities include outings, theme nights, crafts, games & cooking.

### The Girls' Brigade

01235 510425
www.girlsbrigadeew.org.uk
Venues: Bath, Henbury, Southmead, Kingswood, Bishopston, Staple Hill, Bedminster, St Anne's St George, Wedmore Vale, Fishponds, Hanham, Keynsham, Nailsea, Street, Weston-super-Mare, Yate

Christian charity operating in 60 countries offering girls the chance to develop in confidence, ability and friendship, for all ages from 4yrs.

### Woodcraft Folk

13 Ritherdon Road, London, SW17 8QE
020 8672 6031
0845 458 0169 South West Organiser
www.woodcraft.org.uk
info@woodcraft.org.uk

National progressive educational organisation designed to build self-confidence and increase awareness of issues such as the environment. Aimed at all ages from 4yrs, Woodcraft Folk meet weekly for drama, discussion, games, crafts, singing and dancing. Also opportunities for camping and hostelling weekends. For details of the nearest group, call the South West organiser.

## SCOUTING MOVEMENT

### The Scout Association UK

Gilwell Pk, Chingford, Essex, E4 7QW
0845 300 1818
www.scouts.org.uk

Scouting has been around for nearly a century and over that time has evolved into an international organisation offering young people adventurous activities, social awareness and the chance to grow in confidence and independence. It is hugely popular with both boys and girls, making waiting lists long. Some forward planning may be needed if you want your child to take part.

The Scouting Association is constantly looking for potential new leaders, helpers and fundraisers. Contact Avon Scouts, below, if you have a few hours to spare. "It's a lot of fun."

**Looking for some action?**
See Out Door Pursuits on pg 98.

## Avon Scouts

Woodhouse Park, Almonsbury, South
Gloucestershire, BS32 4LX
01454 613 006
www.avonscouts.org.uk
office@avonscouts.org.uk

## Beavers

6-8yrs
1 hr per week
Contact Avon Scouts for your nearest colony

Fun, friendship, games and activities with badge rewards.

## Cubs

8-10½yrs
1½ hours per week
Contact Avon Scouts for your nearest pack

Fun, activities, games, challenges and badges. Outdoors is emphasised with camps which can be for a weekend or longer if planned during the holidays.

Following on from Cubs your child can progress through to the Scout Troop followed by the Explorer Unit. At each level, the responsibility and team work increase as does the level of adventure. To find out more contact Avon Scouts or see the national Scout website.

# GIRLGUIDING

## Girlguiding UK

0800 169 5901
www.girlguiding.org.uk

An offspring of Scouting, initiated at the beginning of the last century by Baden-Powell's sister. It too has developed into a worldwide movement. It offers young people the chance to make friends outside school, learning teamwork and an awareness of the community they live in. There are opportunities for new experiences and adventure. And like Scouting, it's about developing confidence, self awareness and respect. Below is an overview of the various stages in Girlguiding, however if you want more information, visit their excellent website or call the number above.

## Rainbows & Brownies

### Rainbows 5-7yrs

"Rainbows have fun!" They take part in indoor and outdoor activities as part of a programme called the Rainbow Jigsaw. The meetings are full of games and activities.

### Brownies 7-10yrs

Belong to a Pack and work in small groups called Sixes. These small groups nurture friendships and team spirit. They take part in indoor and outdoor activities that challenge them. Meetings are full of games and activities. Packs often go away on holiday, to camp or an overnight sleepover.

Following on from Brownies are Guides and the Senior Section, see their website for more details.

# AFTER SCHOOL CARE

There are many nurseries, child minders and schools that provide breakfast clubs and after school care. They are run by play workers who help children learn, play and relax with their friends. Our readers have recommended the following schemes to us but there are many more and we recognise that location is a crucial factor. It's best to contact BAND and CIS (below) to get a comprehensive list of all the facilities in your area.

## BAND

The Centre for Creative Play, Sevier St, St Werburghs, BS2 9LB
0117 954 2128
www.bandltd.org.uk
admin@band.org.uk

Bristol Association for Neighbourhood Daycare Ltd provides lists of after school clubs, play/holiday schemes, and other daycare facilities. BAND can help groups apply for funding to set up childcare facilities locally.

## Children's Information Service

The Proving House, Sevier St, St Werburghs, BS2
0845 129 7217
www.cisbristol.co.uk
enquiries@cisbristol.co.uk
Mon & Fri: 8am-4pm, Tue-Thu: 8am-8pm

Provides free, impartial and confidential information/guidance on a full range of childcare, children's services and resources in Bristol.

## CKC Holiday Play Scheme

Easton Christian Family Centre, Beaufort St, BS5 0SQ
0117 955 5877
After sch: Mon-Fri until 6pm, £5 per session
Sch hols: Mon-Fri 8.30am-5.30pm, £12 per day

A variety of activities offered for 4-11yrs both after school and during the holidays. Activities aim to be fun, stimulating, educating and challenging. A homework room is available. Pre-booking essential.

## Clevedon Montessori School

34 Albert Road, Clevedon, BS21 7RR
01275 877743
clevedonmontessorisc@blueyonder.co.uk
Mon-Thu: 3pm-5pm
£4 pp per hour, inc tea

P 😊 🔦 🏠 🏫 🚌 🖊

After school club run during term time for 3-8yrs.

## Ecole Francaise de Bristol

c/o Henbury Village Hall, Church Lane, Henbury, BS10 7QG
0117 959 3311
www.ecolefrancaisebristol.co.uk

After school classes and holiday activity weeks and workshops for 4-10yrs. Also provides pre-school activities, see Early Education.

## Southmead Adventure Playground

Doncaster Rd, Southmead, BS10 5PP
0117 950 3607
Tue-Fri 3.30pm-6.45pm in winter, 3.30pm-7.45pm in summer
Sats & sch hols 10am-12.45pm & 2pm-5.45pm
Free

A variety of activities for under 16's including sport and craft. Facilities include an all-weather pitch, play area for U8's, a large soft play room for U8's and a climbing area. U6's must be accompanied by an adult.

## The Red House Children's Centre

1 Cossins Rd, Westbury Park, BS6 7LY
0117 942 8293
www.redhouse-nursery.org.uk
info@redhouse-nursery.org.uk

P WC 👁 🏠 🏫

Provides before and after school care for U11's along with holiday play scheme schemes. See advertisement.

## Tiny Tots Day Nursery

130 High St, Hanham, BS15 3EJ
0117 947 5436

Pre and after school care available, phone for details.

# HOLIDAY CLUBS

## Sport & leisure centres

Many offer additional sessions in the holidays along with courses and fun-filled days for older children. See Sport Centre listings in the Colour Reference Section.

# CLUBS

## BHP Childcare Magic

The Whitehouse Centre, Fulford Rd, Hartcliffe, BS13
0117 954 1884
bhp@blueyonder.co.uk

32-place holiday play scheme for ages 5-14yrs. Activities include cooking, crafts and sports plus trips.

## Chat-a-Box

Redland Parish Church, Redland Green, Redland, BS6
0117 946 4690
www.redland.org.uk, info@redland.org.uk
From £25 for a week, additional costs apply for trips

Activity week for children aged 7-11yrs, held in the first full week of the summer holidays. Themed programme with various fun groups and lively Christian teaching. Also available, Café Culture for those in school years 7 and 8, with an activity-based week with Christian teaching and sports such as tennis, swimming and climbing.

## Clifton College Holiday Activities

Clifton College Services Ltd, 2 Percival Rd, BS8 3LE
0117 315 7666
www.cliftoncollegeuk.com
From £23 per day, £13 half day

A range of holiday activities suitable for 4-16yrs which include a mix of football, tennis, water sports, cookery, drama, arts and crafts. They also run a programme of weekly courses suitable for 12-16yrs. These cover tennis coaching, horse riding, sailing, hockey and drama. The courses have become very popular, so advance booking is necessary.

## King's Camp, Bristol

King's Camp, Badminton School, Westbury-on-Trym
0870 345 0781
www.kingscamp.org
From £85 (4 days)

Part of a national scheme of activity day camps in the Easter and summer holidays for 5-17yrs. Activities have a sports emphasis but there are also art and crafts, games and team building excercises. The camps are registered with Ofsted.

## Kingswood Foundation

20 Old School House, Britannia Rd, Kingswood, BS15
0117 947 7948
www.kfl.org.uk

A charity focussing on innovative arts-based youth work for 8-19yr olds. Its regular summer school, in early August, offers street dance, circus skills and instant music (made with old tins and cardboard) culminating in an impressive show on the Saturday after a week of activities. There are other regular holiday schools throughout the year.

## Torwood House

Durdham Park, Redland, BS6 6XE
0117 973 5620
Open 8am-6pm
£24 per day, £14 ½ day for ages 5-11yrs

Holiday care for children up to 11yrs. Activities include PE, games, drama, music, cookery, arts and crafts, trips and outings.

# PARTY IDEAS

Birthday parties provide great excitement for children but organising them can leave you with a splitting headache. Well now you can relax. We have researched a wide variety of venues and entertainers so there's something to suit everyone, to ensure that the big day goes smoothly and that your nerves don't get too frazzled.

# CHILDREN'S ENTERTAINERS

## Avon Sports Academy — Football Parties

0117 904 6686
www.avonsportsacademy.co.uk
info@avonsportsacademy.co.uk
£40

One hour of qualified football instruction at a venue of your choice, 20 children max. Includes balls, bibs, cones and goals. Enquiries are dealt with by email.

## Away with the Fairies!

07766 670940

Magical fairy parties with dressing-up, face painting, dance, stories and games. Suitable for 4-7yrs. Parties run at a venue of your choice anywhere in the Bristol and Bath area. Max 20 children, group of 15 recommended.

## Cassandra, Storyteller

38a Paultow Rd, Bristol, BS3 4PS
0117 966 3864, 0797 107 7774
www.storiesinmotion.co.uk
cassandrawye@yahoo.co.uk

An internationally-acclaimed storyteller, she creates an exuberant and vividly expressive performance, involving the audience in every twist and turn of the story. "Children and adults' imaginations are totally engaged by her unique and participative style of storytelling." See advertisement.

## Cats Whiskers

15 The Ridge, Coalpit Heath, Bristol, BS36 2PR
01454 853454
www.catswhiskers.biz
helen@catswhiskers.biz
From £60

Face painting, body art, temporary tattoos for parties, events and promotions. Strict code of practice regarding hygiene and use of safe professional paints (for sensitive skin). A maximum of 24 children for a two-hour party session.

# Mr Browns Pig
# Puppeteer and Entertainer

**Enchanting Puppet Shows**
Pirate Parties
Music, Magic & Mayhem

**Shows for all ages and events**
0117 963 4929
www.puppetsonline.co.uk

## Fancy Faces

98 St Werburghs Pk, BS2 9YU
0117 955 4166
freabuckler@hotmail.com
From £40

Professional and friendly artist creates delightful results with face painting. Happy to do fêtes and larger events as well as parties.

## Jack Stephens Magician

42 Netherstreet, Bromham, Chippenham, SN15 2DW
01380 850453
www.jackstephens.co.uk
jackstephens@abra-cadabra.co.uk
£90

Jack's fun show features magic, puppets, singing with a guitar, games, balloon modelling and "above all lots of audience participation". Gears the performances for all venues and occasions.

## Mad Science

Unit 13, Kenn Court, Roman Farm Rd, BS4 1UL
0845 3008400
www.madscience-sw.com
enquiries@madscience-sw.com

A Mad Scientist will arrive at your child's party and entertain them with things like indoor fireworks, lively chemical magic and gooey slime! Add-ons include Hover Craft Ride, rocket launches, laser light shows rides and cotton candy making. "Interactive and surprisingly mess-free activities that will amaze your guests". See advertisment in the Colour Reference Section, pg 133.

## Magical Mandy

37 Newbridge Hill, BA1 3PR
01225 429876
www.magicalmandy.co.uk & www.rentawizard.com
magic@rentawizard.com
From £95

Wonderful magic shows with a choice of themes. Mandy organises games, prizes, balloon modelling as well as the magic show. Fancy dress competition optional. Mandy is a member of the Magic Circle.

## Mr Brown's Pig – Puppet Shows and Pirate Pantomine

15 Vicarage Road, Southville, Bristol, BS3 1PD
0117 963 4929
www.puppetsonline.co.uk
chris@puppetsonline.co.uk
From £85.00

These excellent puppet shows are for children aged 3+yrs, featuring an elaborate puppet booth with lights and music. The shows have lots of audience participation and humour. The Pirate Pantomine features puppets, comedy, music and magic. See advertisement.

## Pizzazz

Top Floor Flat, 6 Charlotte St, Bath, BA1 2NE
01225 333093, 07721 831263
gamesagogo@hotmail.com
From: £90

Circus skills parties/workshops with balloon modelling, face painting, caricatures, giant bubbles and parachute games. "Steve manages to include all children (and adults) with patience and humour!"

## Punch & Judy

6 Portland Place, Staple Hill, BS16 4PX
0117 965 7761
www.punchandjudy4u.co.uk
jhpunch@aol.com

Traditional English Punch and Judy for 3+yrs. Entertainment can also include magic and/or balloons depending upon the individuals requirements. Shows last up to 1hr and the costs vary.

## Tallulah Swirls

22 Cleave St, St Werburghs, Bristol, BS2 9UD
0117 377 4543
www.tallulahswirls.co.uk

Amy's beautifully hand-crafted puppets perform to all ages. "Lots of audience participation, singing and laughing followed by a chance for everyone to see how the show operates." Face painting and workshops also offered. See advertisement on pg 23.

## Tatty Bumpkin

0117 952 0070
www.tattybumpkin.co.uk
goldenbrown77@blueyonder.co.uk

Children's parties based on music and movement for ages 18mths-5yrs. Can be tailored to your child, incorporating favourite places, people and a theme into an animal adventure, with certificates and stickers and a party game.

## The Pink Strawberry Puppet Co.

46 Weston Rd, Long Ashton, N Somerset, BS41 9HH
01275 544576, 07914 187737
www.strawberrygallery.com
From £98

Anthony Churchill is a puppeteer who both teaches and performs. Performances can be geared to audience age and size. Workshops and puppet clubs teach puppet making, performing and its history.

## Wastenot Workshops

0117 941 4447
from £70 within Bristol area

Children can create their own masterpieces from recycled materials, anything from puppets to costumes and masks. Themes include mermaids, pirates, dragons and princesses. Face painting can also be included.

## Wizzo the Wizard

0117 950 8312
www.wizzothewizard.com
enquiries@wizzothewizard.com

Magic for children of all ages; there are puppets, balloon modelling and prizes for all. Wizzo also does Educational Road Safety Shows.

# PARTY GOODS

## A Swell Party

37a Princess Victoria St, Clifton Village, BS8 4BX
0117 923 7644
aswellparty@aol.com
Mon-Sat 10am-5pm

All types of party goods and complete balloon decoration service.

## Bib & Tucker

34 Thingwall Park, Fishponds, BS16 2AE
0117 965 7387
www.bibandtuckerfoods.co.uk
rachael.symons@btinternet.com

Home-cooked party food and celebration cakes. (Also does a range of children's frozen foods, using free range and organic ingredients, see website for details)

## Bristol Bouncy Castles

34 Green Dragon Rd, Winterbourne, BS36 1HF
07796 775522
From £45

Hires out assorted bouncy castles, slides, ball ponds, gladiators for indoor and outdoor parties and events. Delivery (within 25 miles of Bristol) and set-up are free.

## Cakes by Alison

01454 315742
www.cakesbyalison.co.uk
achomette@cakesbyalison.freeserve.co.uk
From £25

Cakes for all occasions: birthdays, christenings, weddings. Personalised to your requirements, will deliver free within 20 miles of Bristol.

## Parties2do

7 Thomas Avenue, Emersons Green, BS16 7TB
0117 957 3448
www.parties2do.co.uk

Party organiser offering as little or as much help as you need. Starting with party bags and boxes (tablewear, invitations, decorations) to organising the whole event with entertainer, food and venue. For older girls, there is The model experience — outfits, make-up and photo shoot.

## Party Pieces

Unit 1, Childs Court Farm, Ashampstead Common, RG8 8QT
01635 201844
www.partypieces.co.uk
sales@partypieces.co.uk
Mon-Fri 8.30am-6pm, Sat 9am-5pm

Mail order service for unusual plates, invitations and prizes.

## Time to Bounce   12'x14'  £50

39 Shortwood Road, Pucklechurch, Bristol, BS16 9PL
0117 937 4424
www.timetobounce.co.uk
sales@timetobounce.co.uk

Family-run & friendly service. Delivery and set up in Bristol area free.

# PARTY VENUES

## Sport & leisure centres

Many offer excellent facilities for children's parties. See the Sport & Leisure Centre listings in the Colour Reference Section. Call for details or visit their websites.

## Arty Party Ceramics

Wells Emporium, 18 Priory Rd, Wells, BA5 1SY
01749 671509
www.artypartyceramics.co.uk
artypartyceramics@yahoo.co.uk

Paint your own pottery at this café in Wells or at a venue of your choice (in the south west) for a birthday party. Suitable for all ages.

## B Delicious

2 Triangle South, Clifton, Bristol
0117 929 1789
Mon-Sat 10am-6pm

Small party groups can have creative fun with beads and feathers. No need for party bags, everyone gets to take home their creations.

## Bowling

**Hollywood Bowl**
Avonmeads Retail Park, St Philips Marsh, BS2 0SP
0117 977 1777

&
The Venue, Cribbs Causeway, Bristol, BS10 7TT
0117 959 2100
www.hollywoodbowl.co.uk

Bowling parties available for all ages. Call for details.

**Bowlplex**
Unit 4, Aspect Leisure Park, Longwell Green, BS30
0117 961 0000
www.bowlplex.co.uk

Parties available for all ages.

**Megabowl**
Brunel Way, Ashton Gate, Bristol, BS3
0117 953 8538
www.megabowl.co.uk
Parties available on Wed and Fri evenings & at w/e's
£9 per child, 2hrs

Bowling parties for groups of six or more. Includes two games, shoe hire, unlimited drinks, birthday tea, balloons, party bags and birthday cake for up to 12 children. Also includes a choice of activities, either balloon modelling or face painting.

# Activities

## Bristol Climbing Centre

St Werburgh's Church, Mina Road, BS2 9YH
0117 908 3491
www.undercover-rock.com

Climbing parties are very popular at this dedicated indoor climbing centre, which features over 150 climbs up to 10 metres high, catering for all abilities. The birthday child must be turning 7 or older and the youngest guest must be at least 6. Groups of up to 9 climbers for a flat rate of £90, including invitations and a t-shirt. The session lasts 1½hrs. There is a café serving drinks and snacks. You can bring your own food and eat in the large gallery area. It's necessary to book 4-6 weeks in advance.

## Bristol Ice Rink

Frogmore St, Bristol, BS1 5NA
0117 929 2148
www.jnll.co.uk
£9.50 per child, 5-12yrs

[P] [WC] [CP] [X] [🚌] [♿]

Ice skating birthday parties from £9.75 per person. Price includes ½hr private tuition, skating on public session, skate hire, two adults free skating, meal in party area and gift for birthday child. Disco skating sessions also available.

## Bristol Old Vic

King St, Bristol, BS1 4ED
0117 949 3993
www.bristol-old-vic.co.uk
From: £4 (not inclusive of ticket price)

[P] [V] [✎] [WC] [✄] [🍴] [CP] [♿] [X] [🚌] [♿]

Any performance can be combined with a party, in your own private area, before or after the show (max 30). You can bring your own cake.

## Bristol Zoo Gardens

Clifton, Bristol, BS8 3HA
0117 974 7307
www.bristolzoo.org.uk
£10 pp (min 8) includes zoo admission

Parties are available at weekends and during school holidays. The package includes hire of the Rainforest Room, picnic food boxes, animal masks and magic screen gift for each child along with free admission for three adults.

## Circus Bugz & Circus Maniacs

Office 8A, The Kingswood Foundation, Britannia Rd, Kingswood, BS15 8DB
0117 947 7042
www.circusmaniacs.com, info@circusmaniacs.com

[P] [WC] [♿]

Circus skills parties are mostly held on Sundays but other times are available. You can book up to 2hrs in the space and children will try everything from juggling to trapeze. You can have a picnic, or hire a room for a birthday tea. Ratio's of 1:8, adult to children. Call for further details.

## Coombe Dingle Tennis Centre

Coombe Dingle Sports Complex, Coombe Lane, Stoke Bishop
0117 962 6718
www.peterbendall.org.uk

Tennis parties are available with games and prizes.

## HorseWorld

Staunton Lane, Whitchurch, BS14 0QJ
01275 540173
www.horseworld.org.uk
visitor.centre@horseworld.org.uk
£9.50 pp (min 10)

If your child is mad about horses this is the place to party. Price includes entry, sandwiches and goodie bag. See entry in Out and About in Bristol pg 13.

## Jumicar Bristol

01454 250219
www.jumicarbristol.co.uk

Road safety instructions for children (0-12 yrs) in real junior-sized cars. Currently run at ASDA WallMart car park, Cribbs Causeway. Party bookings taken.

## SOFT PLAY & GYM PARTY VENUES

### 123 Jump

22 Concorde Rd, Cribbs Causeway, Bristol, BS34 5TB
0117 931 2733
www.123jump.co.uk
£13 per child

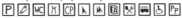

This new indoor play centre, run by a friendly crew, has five themed party rooms — disco, space, shark, enchanted castle and pirates. Unlimited play for every child along with an activity such as balloon modeling, disco, football or party games. The party pack includes invitations, hats, balloons, birthday cake, freshly prepared food, a party helper and a gift for the birthday child.

### Bristol Hawks Gymnastic Club

Gymnastics World, Roman Rd, Lower Easton, BS5
0117 973 7481/935 5363
From £80, 2-11yrs
Fri and Sat pm

1 hr in the gym and ¾hr in the party room. Bring your own food. Very popular venue, so book well in advance.

### Bristol School of Gymnastics

Old Bishopston Methodist Church, 245 Gloucester Rd, BS7 8NY
0117 942 9620
Parties available Sat & Sun pm
From £55 for 1½hrs, up to 20 children

Gym parties supervised by two coaches, includes trampolining. For girls up to 9yrs and boys up to 7yrs. Bring your own food.

### Castaways Bourne Chapel

Waters Rd, Kingswood, Bristol, BS15 8BE
0117 961 5115
£6.95 per child, up to 10yrs

A 2hr party of indoor adventure play. 1¼hr play, ¾hr in the party room for the birthday meal. Invitation cards and a party bag for

### Laserquest Bristol

The Old Firestation, Silver St, BS1 2PY
0117 949 6688
www.laserquest.co.uk
Mon-Fri 12pm-10pm, Sat 10am-10pm
Sun 10am-8pm
£7.95 pp, min 6 in a group, max 20

Two interactive laser games, each lasting 20 minutes plus free drinks, party bags and a gift for the birthday child and vouchers. No food, but 20% off your bill at the nearby Deep Pan Pizza, if you eat there after the party.

### Windmill Hill City Farm

Philip St, Bedminster, BS3 4EA
0117 963 3252
www.windmillhillcityfarm.org.uk
Times, availability and cost varies, call for details

Party room including tables, chairs and kitchen, available for hire. There is a café or bring your own food. Free access to the farm park.

each child are provided, along with a gift and a photo for the birthday child. The play area is not for the sole use of the party. Minimum number of children 12.

## Elmgrove Centre Rumpus Room

Redland Rd, Cotham, Bristol, BS6 6AG
0117 924 3377
Rumpus room: £30 for 2hrs
Large hall: £25 per hr (over 6 yrs)

WC 人

The Rumpus Room (soft play suitable for U7's) and an adjoining room for a tea party. The large hall can accommodate bouncy castles, which must be hired independently by the party organiser. Bring your own food.

## Fromeside Gymnastics Club

Watleys End Rd, Winterbourne, Bristol, BS36 1QG
01454 776 873/777749
Sat pm
£55-£60, 15-20 children

P 人 WC 人 人 人

1hr in gym (supervised by qualified coaches) followed by ½hr in coffee bar area (bring your own food).

## Kingswood Gymnastic Centre

The Wesley Studios, Kingswood Foundation Estate, Britannia Rd, BS15 8DB
0117 947 6449
£65 for exclusive use of gym, £10 use of tea room

P 人 WC 人

Sporty parties based on supervised activities (gym, trampolining, football, parachute & softplay games) with qualified instructor, suitable for 0-11yrs. Gym and disco parties available for 5-12yrs.

## Planet Kids

Bristol Mega Bowl, Brunel Way, Ashton Gate, BS3
0117 953 8538
www.megabowl.co.uk
£9 pp, 1hr in play area, 1hr in party room, up to 11yrs, min 6 children

P 人 WC 人 CP 人 人 人 人

A Party Captain is there to help, but parents must stay. Includes: invites, party bags, food, balloons, gift for every child. A cake which feeds 12 is included, extra cakes cost £5 each.

## Mayhem at Riverside Leisure Club

Station Rd, Little Stoke, BS34 6HW
01454 888 666
www.riversideleisure.com
From £40-£52.50 for 15-20 children

P V 人 WC 人 人 人 人 人 人 人 人 Pp

Soft play parties. Party room available, food provided for £2.50 per head, or BYO. Suitable for 0-10yrs, height restriction of 4'11".

## The Alphabet Zoo Playcentre

Old Bingo Hall, Winterstoke Rd, BS3 2NW
0117 966 3366
After school, any day in the holidays & w/e's
Variety of party packages: Bronze, £6.99 pp, Silver, £7.99 pp, Gold, £8.99 pp

P 人 WC 人 人 人 人 人 人 人 人

Parties for up to 11yrs, 1hr play and 1hr food and games in the party gallery. Minimum of 10 children.

## Time Zone Kidz

At the Mall's "Parent Play and Stay", Cribbs Causeway, BS34 5UR
0117 915 5802
Pre-booking required
Mon-Thu £60, Fri-Sun £65, for 2hrs

P 人 WC 人 人 人 人 人 人 人 人 人 人 人 人 人

Soft play parties up to 9yrs, max 24 children. BYO or use nearby fast food outlets. Parents must stay with party.

# PARTY VENUES OUTSIDE BRISTOL

## Bay Island Voyages

Pierhead Building, Cardiff Bay, Cardiff
029 2048 4110/01446 420692 out of hours
www.bayisland.co.uk
Run all year dependent on weather and demand
Fast Bay Cruise: £6 adult, £3 child U14's. Bristol Channel: £18.50 adult, £10 child

Thrill seekers need look no further than a high speed trip on the Celtic Ranger powered by two 225hp engines and travelling at up to 60mph! This is going to appeal more to older children, although babies and toddlers can be taken. The most popular option with younger children (from about 6yrs) is the half hour Fast Bay Cruise which tends to be calmer. For those with stronger sea-legs there are tours lasting between 1 and 2 hours which go up the coast or around Flat Holm and Steep Holm. The boat carries 12 passengers, waterproofs and life jackets are provided. Pre-booking advisable.

## Baskerville's Gym

Englishcombe Court, Englishcombe Lane, Bath, BA2
01225 339991
£80 for 1½hrs

Birthday parties available at weekends. Coaching for up to 18 children, bring your own food.

## Boomerang

Bowerhill, Melksham, Wiltshire, SN12 6TJ
01225 702000
www.boomeranguk.co.uk
M4 J17, A350 to Melksham then follow signs for Bowerhill & Sports Centre

Huge area of soft play equipment for U11's or 1.5m. A variety of party packages, see website for details. Also party equipment for hire, bouncy castles, sumo wrestling kit etc.

## Castle Combe Kart Track

Castle Combe Circuit, Chippenham, SN14
01249 783010
www.castlecombecircuit.co.uk

Junior kart racing for 10-15yrs (with a min. height of 4'8") on 1st & 3rd Sunday of every month. Pre-booking essential.

## Perrygrove Birthday Parties

Perrygrove Railway, Coleford, GL16 8QB
01594 834991
www.perrygrove.co.uk

A party with a difference. Time on the steam train, then picnic in their Stable Room or party food boxes can be supplied.

## Play Centre

Pier St, Burnham on Sea
01278 784693
Parties for 10-20 children, 2 hrs

Small indoor play centre. Sandwiches or hot food can be provided or you can BYO.

### Electric Car Racing

Small groups from 7yrs

The Play Centre also offers electric car racing parties with its 70-foot long car race track. Drinks are provided. Six cars can race at a time and races last 15 minutes.

## The Action Centre

Lyncombe Drive, Churchill, N. Somerset, BS25 5PQ
01934 852 335
www.highaction.co.uk

Parties can be based on a variety of different activities, including skiing, tobogganing and archery. Party food provided. Phone for more information.

## Togas & Tunnels

The Pump Room, Stall St, Bath, BA1 1LZ
01225 477785
www.romanbaths.co.uk
Children 6-11yrs, 1hr, w/e's only
11am-12pm, 3pm-4pm

The Roman Baths provide an unusual party venue. Children can explore secret tunnels, act as archaeologists and dress as Romans. They even learn how to sing Happy Birthday in Latin! Party bags and invitations included.

## West Country Karting

The Lake, Trench Lane, Winterbourne, BS36 1RY
01454 202666
www.westcountrykarting.com

Karting (5'1") and quad bike (6-12yrs) parties. Age and height restrictions apply.

## CAR GAME

When your passengers are bored on long journeys, try this game — it can keep them occupied for hours.

### PIP POP

Look out on the side of the road for the following things. One point each for calling out the right word...

| | |
|---|---|
| Phone box | "PIP" |
| Post box | "POP" |
| Pub | "PUB" |
| Parking sign (white P on blue sign) | "PARK" |
| Church | "PRAY" |
| Petrol station | "PUMP" |
| A "P" in a number plate | "PLATE" |
| Airport sign (picture of a plane) | "PLANE" |
| Public toilets | "PLOP" |

Invented by Harry, aged 7!

Send in your favourite car games or tips for keeping young travellers happy: www.titchhikers.co.uk

## PLAY DOUGH RECIPES

When all the bought playdough has gone hard, try making your own.

### Play dough (long life)

You will need:

1 cup of flour, half a cup of salt, 2 teaspoons cream of tartar, 1 tablespoon cooking oil, 1 cup of water with food colouring added.

Mix all ingredients together in a saucepan and cook over a medium heat stirring all the time. As it becomes lumpy, continue to stir until it forms a ball. Leave to cool then knead until smooth. It is now ready to use. Store in an airtight container for a long life.

### Modelling dough

Why not try this recipe for children who want to keep their masterpieces!

You will need:

2 cups flour, 1 cup salt, 1 tablespoon cooking oil, 1 cup water with food colouring if required.

Mix together flour, salt and oil. Add water until mixture forms a ball. Knead. Make your model or roll out and use cutters to make hanging decorations. Bake at 180°c for approx. 35-40 minutes. Cool, paint and varnish if required.

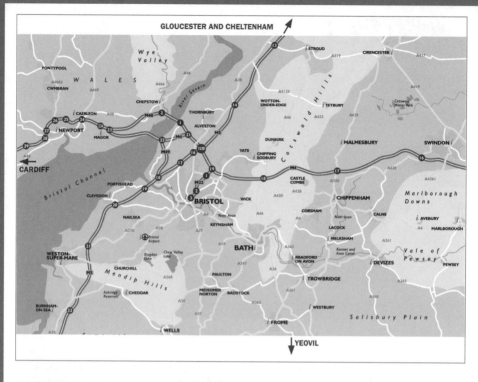

## BRISTOL DAYS OUT

One of the biggest challenges facing many families is how to get out of the house before lunchtime! But not every day out needs lots of forward planning. This at-a-glance guide should help you to make quick decisions about where to go and what to do with minimum fuss.

### Centre
At-Bristol, pg 9
Arnolfini cafe, pg 64
Central library, pg 15
IMAX cinema, pg 12

### Harbourside
ss Great Britain, pg 8
Brunel Buttery for lunch, pg 64
Industrial Museum, pg 9
Ferry ride, pg 8

### Clifton and the Downs
Bristol zoo, pg 7
Clifton Observatory and caves, 11
Downs Tea Room, pg 70
The Suspension Bridge, pg 6

### Ashton Court
Cycle paths, pg 89
Pitch and Putt, pg 22
Stables café, pg 73
Festivals and events, pg 24

### Blaise castle
Blaise House Museum, pg 9
Blaise Tearooms, pg 68
Castle Folly, pg 23
Playground, pg 20

### Park Street
Brandon Hill play area, pg 20
Cabot Tower, pg 6
Boston Tea Party for lunch, pg 66
Bristol City Museum and Art Gallery, pg 9

# Reference Section

| Icon | meaning |
|------|---------|
| **General** | |
| P | parking |
| WC | toilets |
| lift | lift |
| disabled | disabled facilities |
| buggy | buggy friendly |
| double buggy | double buggy friendly |
| no smoking | no smoking |
| nappy | nappy changing |
| feeding | feeding room |
| crèche | crèche |
| indoor | indoor play area |
| outdoor | outdoor play area |
| garden | garden |
| picnic | picnic area |
| dogs | dogs allowed |
| transport | nearby public transport |
| café | café |
| shop | shop |

| Icon | meaning |
|------|---------|
| **Pre-School** | |
| PP | parent participation |
| waiting list | waiting list |
| **Eating Out** | |
| high chair | high chair |
| toys/crayons | toys/crayons |
| V | vegetarian option |
| CP | children's portions/meals |

## SEASONAL DAYS OUT

Some activities are strictly seasonal, such as a walk through a wood full of bluebells or a ride on a Santa Special. We hope this guide will ensure you don't miss out on these lovely ideas. And, during the summer, don't forget you can always enjoy the sunshine after school. Why not visit Portishead Marina for an ice-cream or have a picnic supper on the Downs?

## SPRING

Visit Bowood in April/May to see rhododendrons and bluebells, pg 49
Walk through Lower Lodge Woods, pg 57
Folly farm, pg 59

## SUMMER

Bristol parks summer events, pg 19
St Pauls Carnival, pg 24
Ashton Court Festival, pg 24
Bristol Harbour festival, pg 24
Balloon Fiesta, pg 24
Portishead and the Marine Lake Café, pg 82
Bristol open top bus tours, pg 6
Open air pools, pg 102
Megamaze, pg 37
Bay Island Voyages, pg 44

## AUTUMN

Doors Open Day, pg 7
Westonbirt Arboretum, pg 36
Kite Festival, pg 24

## WINTER

Fireworks on the Downs, pg 24
Lasborough Park, Cotswolds, pg 57
Somerset carnivals, pg 24
Clearwell Caves at Christmas, pg 40
Clevedon Pier, lit up at Christmas, pg 27
Bristol Zoo carol concerts, pg 7
Santa Specials on steam trains, pg 86
Outdoor skating, pg 96

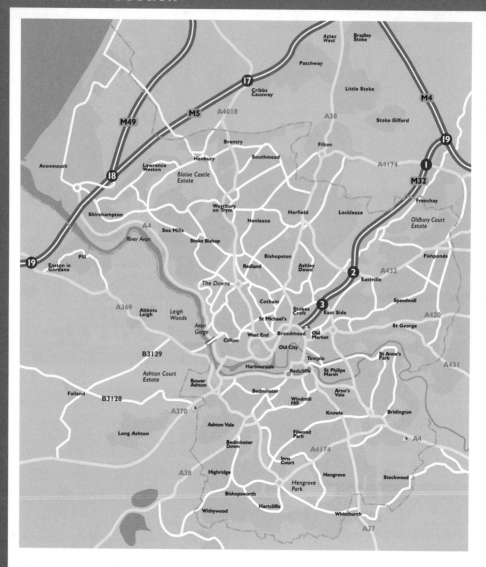

Maps courtesy of Destination Bristol
www.visitbristol.co.uk

## MORE GREAT SOURCES OF INFORMATION

### www.titchhikers.co.uk
See our website for seasonal events, new or changed listings.

### Destination Bristol
www.visitbristol.co.uk

### Venue Magazine
www.venue.co.uk
The What's-on Guide covering Bristol and Bath, for sale at newsagents throughout the region. Has regular Family sections with information on days out and activities for children.

### Primary Times (in Avon)
Distrubuted, free, throughout primary schools in and around Bristol. Lots of seasonal information on services and activities for children aged 4-11yrs.

Local papers and their websites will also help you keep your finger on the pulse.

### Bristol Evening Post
www.thisisbristol.co.uk

### Bath Evening Chronicle
www.thisisbath.co.uk

## FUN FOR FREE

This guide is packed with great ideas and lots of them are absolutely free. We've highlighted all the free stuff below, so you can have fun with your family without burning a hole in your pocket. Some of the museums run regular events for children, so check their websites for more details

### Amazing views

Cabot Tower, pg 6
Coaley Peak, Stroud, pg 34
The Suspension Bridge, pg 6

### Animal magic

Apex Leisure and Wildlife Park, pg 28
Hartcliffe Community Farms, pg 13
Lawrence Weston Community Farm, pg 13
St Werburgh's City farm, pg 13
Windmill Hill City Farm, pg 14

### Art galleries

Arnolfini, pg 8
Bristol City Museum & Art Gallery, pg 9
Cheltenham Art gallery and Museum, pg 39
National Museum and Gallery, Cardiff, pg 43
Royal West of England Academy (children go free), pg 10
Victoria Art Gallery, Bath, pg 30

### By the sea

Beaches, pg 61
The Goleulong 2000 Lightship, Cardiff, pg 43
Portishead Marina and Lake grounds, pg 26

### Craft centres

Clevedon Craft Centre, pg 26
Craft in the Bay, Cardiff, pg 45
The Shoe Museum, Street, pg 29

### Free food for kids!

Le Monde, pg 66
Henry Africa's Hot House, pg 67

## The great outdoors

## Libraries

## Museums and attractions

## Picnic spots

## Step back in time

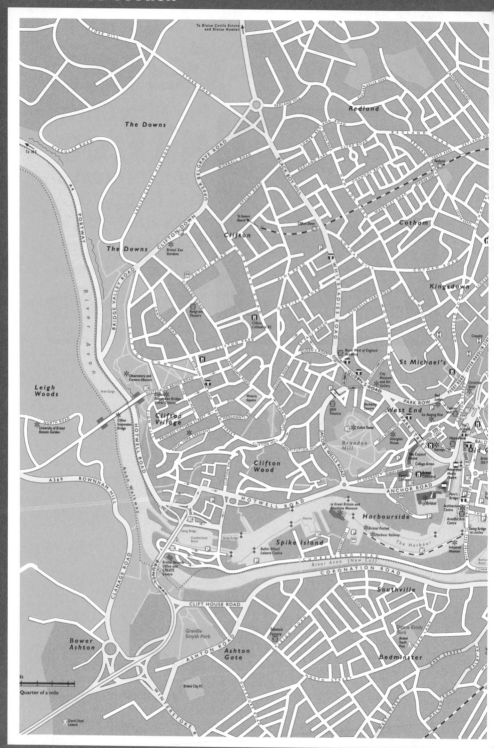

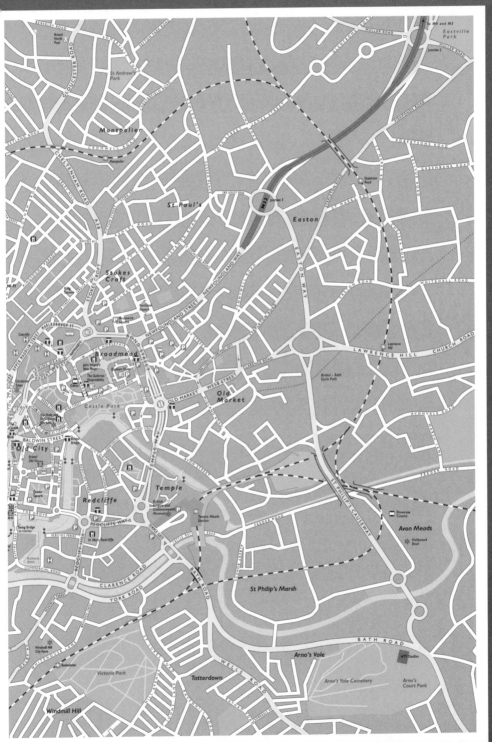

# Reference Section

## BRISTOL LEISURE CENTRES

For more details see: www.bristol-city.gov.uk/sport or www.filton-town-council.co.uk — centres may not necessarily provide courses or instruction in each sport listed

Leisure Centres
Open daily
♿ P ♿ apply to all centres

| Leisure Centre / Address | Aerobics | Badminton | Basketball for U12's | Boxercise | Crèche | Cricket Nets | Dance Classes | Football for U12's | Gymnastics | Gymnasium | Holiday Timetable | Martial Arts | Netball | Outdoor Facilities | Parties | Softplay | Squash courts | Swimming | Tennis | Trampolining | Volley Ball | Yoga |
|---|---|---|---|---|---|---|---|---|---|---|---|---|---|---|---|---|---|---|---|---|---|---|
| Ashton Park Sports Centre, 0117 377 3300 — Ashton Park School, Blackmoor's Lane, Bower Ashton | ✓ | ✓ |  |  |  | ✓ | ✓ | ✓ |  | ✓ | ✓ | ✓ | ✓ | ✓ | ✓ | ✓ |  |  | ✓ | ✓ |  | ✓ |
| Easton Leisure Centre, 0117 955 8840 — Thrissell Street, Easton | ✓ | ✓ | ✓ |  |  |  |  |  |  |  | ✓ | ✓ |  |  | ✓ | ✓ |  | ✓ |  |  |  | ✓ |
| Filton Sports & Leisure Centre, 01454 866686 — Elm Park, Filton |  | ✓ |  |  | ✓ |  |  |  |  |  | ✓ | ✓ |  |  | ✓ | ✓ | ✓ | ✓ | ✓ |  |  |  |
| Henbury Leisure Centre, 0117 353 2555 — Avonmouth Way, Henbury | ✓ | ✓ |  |  |  |  |  | ✓ | ✓ |  | ✓ | ✓ | ✓ | ✓ | ✓ |  |  | ✓ | ✓ |  | ✓ | ✓ |
| Horfield Sports Centre, 0117 903 1643 — Dorian Road, Horfield |  | ✓ |  | ✓ | ✓ | ✓ | ✓ | ✓ | ✓ |  | ✓ | ✓ |  | ✓ | ✓ |  |  |  |  | ✓ | ✓ | ✓ |
| Kingsdown Sports Centre, 0117 942 6582 — Portland St, Kingsdown | ✓ | ✓ |  |  | ✓ |  | ✓ |  | ✓ |  | ✓ | ✓ |  |  | ✓ |  | ✓ | ✓ |  | ✓ |  |  |
| St Paul's Community Sports Academy, 0117 377 3405 — Newfoundland Road, St Paul's | ✓ | ✓ | ✓ |  |  |  | ✓ | ✓ | ✓ |  | ✓ | ✓ | ✓ | ✓ | ✓ |  | ✓ |  |  |  |  | ✓ |
| Whitchurch Sports Centre, 01275 833911 — Bamfield, Whitchurch | ✓ | ✓ | ✓ |  |  | ✓ |  | ✓ |  |  | ✓ | ✓ | ✓ | ✓ | ✓ |  | ✓ |  | ✓ | ✓ | ✓ | ✓ |
| Withywood Sport Centre, 0117 377 22294 — Withywood Community School, Molesworth Drive | ✓ | ✓ |  |  |  |  | ✓ |  |  | ✓ | ✓ | ✓ | ✓ | ✓ | ✓ |  |  |  |  | ✓ | ✓ |  |

# BRISTOL SWIMMING POOLS

For more details see: www.bristol-city.gov.uk/sport except Filton Sports and Leisure see: www.filton-town-council.co.uk

Leisure Centres
Open daily
♿ P ☕ apply to all centres

| Address | Pool Size | Aquafit Classes | Swimming Sessions for U5's | Lessons | Swimming Club | Learner Pool | Off Poolside Changing Rooms | Spa Facilities | Playpen and Baby Changing | Disabled Facilities | Parking | Public Transport | Sub-aqua | Water Slide | Parties, floats & inflatables | Other Swimming Activities |
|---|---|---|---|---|---|---|---|---|---|---|---|---|---|---|---|---|
| **Bishopworth** 0117 964 0258 Whitchurch Lane, Bishopworth | 25m | ✓ | | ✓ | ✓ | | ✓ | | ✓ | ✓ | ✓ | ✓ | ✓ | | ✓ | |
| **Bristol South** 0117 966 3131 Dean Lane, Bedminster | 30m | | ✓ | ✓ | ✓ | | | | ✓ | ✓ | | ✓ | ✓ | | ✓ | water polo, canoeing |
| **Easton Leisure Centre** 0117 955 8840 Thrissell St, Easton | 25m | | ✓ | ✓ | ✓ | ✓ | ✓ | | ✓ | ✓ | ✓ | ✓ | | | ✓ | |
| **Filton Sports and Leisure Centre** 01454 866686 Elm Park, Filton | 25m | | ✓ | ✓ | ✓ | ✓ | ✓ | | ✓ | ✓ | ✓ | ✓ | | ✓ | ✓ | |
| **Henbury** 0117 353 2555 Avonmouth Way, Henbury | 25m | | ✓ | ✓ | ✓ | ✓ | ✓ | ✓ | ✓ | ✓ | ✓ | ✓ | ✓ | | | |
| **Horfield Sports Centre** 0117 903 1643 Dorian Rd, Horfield | 25m | | ✓ | ✓ | ✓ | ✓ | ✓ | | ✓ | ✓ | ✓ | ✓ | | | ✓ | |
| **Jubilee** 0117 977 7900 Jubilee Rd, Knowle | 25m | | ✓ | ✓ | ✓ | | ✓ | | ✓ | ✓ | | ✓ | | | ✓ | |

# SOUTH GLOUCESTERSHIRE LEISURE CENTRES

For more details see: www.southglos.gov.uk — centres may not necessarily provide courses or instruction in each sport listed

Leisure Centres
Open daily
♿ P 🚻 apply to all centres

| Leisure Centre | Address | Aerobics | Badminton | Basketball for U12's | Boxercise | Crèche | Cricket Nets | Dance Classes | Football for U12's | Gymnastics | Gymnasium | Holiday Timetable | Martial Arts | Netball |
|---|---|---|---|---|---|---|---|---|---|---|---|---|---|---|
| Bradley Stoke Leisure Centre 01454 867050 | Fiddlers Wood Lane, Bradley Stoke | ✓ | ✓ | ✓ | | ✓ | | ✓ | ✓ | ✓ | ✓ | ✓ | ✓ | ✓ |
| Downend Sports Centre 01454 862221 | Garnett Place, Downend | | ✓ | ✓ | | | ✓ | | ✓ | | | ✓ | ✓ | ✓ |
| Kingswood Leisure Centre 01454 865700 | Church Rd, Staple Hill | ✓ | ✓ | | | ✓ | | | ✓ | | ✓ | ✓ | ✓ | ✓ |
| Patchway Sports Centre 01454 865890 | Patchway Community College, Hempton Lane, Almondsbury | | ✓ | ✓ | | | | | ✓ | | ✓ | ✓ | ✓ | ✓ |
| Thornbury Leisure Centre 01454 865777 | Alveston Hill, Thornbury | ✓ | ✓ | ✓ | | | | ✓ | ✓ | ✓ | ✓ | ✓ | ✓ | ✓ |
| Yate Leisure Centre 01454 865800 | Kennedy Way, Yate | ✓ | ✓ | ✓ | | ✓ | ✓ | ✓ | ✓ | ✓ | ✓ | ✓ | ✓ | ✓ |
| Yate Outdoor Sports Complex 01454 865820 | behind Brinsham Green School, Yate | | | | | | | | ✓ | | | ✓ | | ✓ |

142

# NORTH SOMERSET LEISURE CENTRES

For more details see: www.n-somerset.gov.uk

| Leisure Centres Open daily | Address | Aerobics | Badminton | Basketball for U12's | Boxercise | Crèche | Cricket Nets | Dance Classes | Football for U12's | Gymnastics | Gymnasium | Holiday Timetable | Martial Arts | Netball | Outdoor Facilities | Parties | Softplay | Squash Courts | Swimming | Tennis | Trampolining | Volley Ball | Yoga |
|---|---|---|---|---|---|---|---|---|---|---|---|---|---|---|---|---|---|---|---|---|---|---|---|
| Backwell Leisure Centre 01275 463726 | Farleigh Rd, Backwell | ✓ | | | | | | | | | | | | | | ✓ | | ✓ | ✓ | | | | |
| Churchill Sports Centre 01934 852303 | Churchill Green, Weston-super-Mare | ✓ | ✓ | | | ✓ | | ✓ | | | | | | ✓ | | ✓ | | ✓ | ✓ | ✓ | ✓ | | |
| Gordano Sports Centre * 01275 843942 | Gordano School, St Mary's Rd, Portishead | ✓ | ✓ | ✓ | | ✓ | | ✓ | | ✓ | | | | ✓ | | ✓ | | ✓ | | ✓ | ✓ | | |
| Hutton Moor Leisure Centre 01934 425900 | Hutton Moor Rd, Weston-super-Mare | ✓ | ✓ | ✓ | | ✓ | ✓ | ✓ | ✓ | | ✓ | ✓ | ✓ | ✓ | ✓ | ✓ | ✓ | ✓ | ✓ | ✓ | ✓ | ✓ | ✓ |
| Parish Wharf Leisure Centre 01275 848494 | Harbour Road, Portishead | ✓ | ✓ | ✓ | | ✓ | ✓ | | ✓ | | ✓ | ✓ | ✓ | | ✓ | ✓ | ✓ | | ✓ | | | ✓ | ✓ |
| Scotch Horn Leisure Centre 01275 856965 | Brockway, Nailsea | ✓ | ✓ | ✓ | ✓ | | | ✓ | ✓ | | ✓ | ✓ | ✓ | ✓ | ✓ | ✓ | ✓ | | | | | | ✓ |
| Strode Leisure Centre 01275 879242 | Strode Way, Clevedon | ✓ | ✓ | ✓ | | | ✓ | | ✓ | | | ✓ | | | | ✓ | ✓ | | | ✓ | | | ✓ |
| Swiss Valley Sport Centre * 01275 877 182 | Clevedon School, Clevedon | | ✓ | ✓ | | | ✓ | ✓ | ✓ | | ✓ | ✓ | | ✓ | ✓ | ✓ | | ✓ | ✓ | ✓ | ✓ | | |
| Wyvern Sports Centre * 01934 642426 | Marchfields Way, Weston-super-Mare | | ✓ | ✓ | | | | ✓ | ✓ | | ✓ | ✓ | | ✓ | | ✓ | | | | ✓ | ✓ | ✓ | |

*Leisure centre attached to a school so restricted opening times during school hours

# Reference Section

## BATH AND NORTH EAST SOMERSET LEISURE CENTRES

For more details see: www.aquaterra.org — centres may not necessarily provide courses or instruction in each sport listed

Leisure Centres
Open daily
♿ P 🚰 apply to all centres

| Centre | Address | Aerobics | Badminton | Basketball for U12's | Boxercise | Crèche | Cricket Nets | Dance Classes | Football for U12's | Gymnastics | Gymnasium | Holiday Timetable | Martial Arts | Netball | Outdoor Facilities | Parties | Softplay | Squash Courts | Swimming | Tennis | Trampolining | Volley Ball | Yoga |
|---|---|---|---|---|---|---|---|---|---|---|---|---|---|---|---|---|---|---|---|---|---|---|---|
| Bath Sports and Leisure Centre 01225 462565 | North Parade Road, Bath | ✓ | ✓ | ✓ | ✓ | ✓ | | ✓ | ✓ | ✓ | ✓ | ✓ | ✓ | ✓ | ✓ | ✓ | ✓ | ✓ | ✓ | ✓ | ✓ | ✓ | ✓ |
| Chew Valley Leisure Centre * 01275 333375 | Chew Lane, Chew Magna www.cvleisure.com | ✓ | ✓ | ✓ | | | ✓ | | ✓ | ✓ | ✓ | ✓ | ✓ | ✓ | ✓ | | | | | ✓ | | ✓ | ✓ |
| Culverhay Sports Centre * 01225 486902 Mon-Fri 01225 480882 Eve/WE's | Rush Hill, Bath | ✓ | ✓ | ✓ | | | | | ✓ | | ✓ | | ✓ | ✓ | ✓ | ✓ | | ✓ | ✓ | | | ✓ | |
| Keynsham Leisure Centre 01225 395161 | Temple St, Keynsham | ✓ | ✓ | ✓ | | ✓ | | ✓ | ✓ | ✓ | ✓ | ✓ | ✓ | | | ✓ | ✓ | ✓ | ✓ | | | ✓ | ✓ |
| South Wansdyke Sports Centre 01761 4015522 | Rackvernal Rd, Midsomer Norton | ✓ | | | | ✓ | | | ✓ | | ✓ | ✓ | ✓ | | ✓ | ✓ | ✓ | ✓ | | ✓ | ✓ | | ✓ |
| Writhlington Sports Centre 01761 438559 | Radstock, Knobsbury Lane www.writhlingtonsportscentre.co.uk | ✓ | ✓ | ✓ | | | ✓ | ✓ | ✓ | ✓ | ✓ | ✓ | ✓ | ✓ | ✓ | ✓ | | | | ✓ | ✓ | ✓ | ✓ |

*Leisure centre attached to a school so restricted opening times during school hours

# FAMILY HOLIDAYS & WEEKENDS AWAY

**Lucy Saunders**

## CONTENTS

## INTRODUCTION

Getting away for a family break can be great fun, although the planning and packing is often hard work. However, with a bit of forethought and the right place to stay to meet your needs, family holidays can be a success!

This chapter tries to take some of the stress out of planning your holiday by catering for a wide range of budgets and types of holidays. These range from campsites and YHAs to self-catering cottages and luxury family hotels. Bristol is well placed as a starting point for a wide variety of holiday destinations within a 2-3 hour car journey. We've divided up this chapter into regions and according to types of accommodation so you can find something to suit your preferences and budget. And you can book in confidence, knowing that all our listings have been highly recommended by parents.

## Family Holiday Association

16 Mortimer St, London, W1T 3JL
020 7436 3304
www.fhaonline.org.uk

The Family Holiday Association helps provide holidays for families in need. Applications are accepted from referring agencies (social workers, health visitors) on behalf of families. Families have to be on a low income, have at least one child of 3+yrs and have not had a holiday in the last four years.

# HOTELS

Staying in hotels, though it may not come cheap, has never been better for parents and children. The choice, from basic to luxury, is increasing, the facilities for children improving, and the possibility to rest and relax inviting. Things to ask:

- Lift and pram access to rooms
- Baby listening and babysitting
- The size of rooms and the availability of cots/extra beds
- Children's menu/portions and prices

All the hotels we feature in this guide have many facilities that make your stay, not to mention your packing, easier but they are also truly welcoming of children and there will be lots for your children to do once you are there. As with all types of accommodation, however, if you need something specific for your stay, make sure that you confirm it is available prior to booking.

# SELF-CATERING

Self-catering in this country ranges from cottages in remote locations to chalets and lodges in holiday parks. Self-catering is arguably the most home-from-home situation that you will get with a holiday, which may be a blessing or a curse depending on your situation. If you self-cater, you can cook for the varied diets and keep to a budget. There

are also often washing facilities and usually there is more privacy than other holiday options.

Many of the places that we mention allow you to have the flexibility of self-catering with the convenience of onsite restaurants and facilities, which may including babysitting services.

## Helpful Holidays

01647 433593
www.helpfulholidays.co.uk

Over 500 self-catering holiday cottages across the South West from Dorset to Cornwall. Established in 1982, this company comes well recommended. Quality accommodation.

## NCT Houseswap

01626 360689
www.bristolnct.co.uk
Annual: £25.85

The houseswap register is a list of over 257 families who are willing to swap houses with each other in order to have free accommodation. The Register is a list by county of members' homes, so you can match up with someone whose home is suitable for your age of children, where there will be similar equipment and toys. At least one child must be under 13yrs.

# B&Bs

Unlike hotels, B&Bs generally do not offer evening meals, snacks for hungry toddlers at 5am or babysitting services. There is also the added concern that your child may wake the house. However, those we have listed warmly welcome young children.

## Alistair Sawday's Special Places to Stay: British Bed & Breakfast

01275 464891
www.specialplacestostay.com
Guides from £12.99

This is one of the many guides produced by this local publisher. The B&B guide is specially recommended although the guide on British hotels, inns and other places is also excellent. There is a clear key in all guides indicating whether children are welcome.

# YOUTH HOSTELLING ASSOCIATION

0870 770 8868
www.yha.org.uk

One of the leading budget accommodation providers in the UK. Its name suggests it is only for the young, free and single traveller but this is no longer the case. It attracts travellers of all ages and many hostels welcome families with both young and growing children. There are more than 200 YHAs all over the UK in some stunning locations. There are a further 4000 in 90 overseas destinations. It is no longer necessary to be a member of the YHA, however annual family membership is £25 which is good value. **All prices listed in this chapter apply to YHA members. Add on a per night supplement of £3 per adult, £1.50 per child if you are a non-member.**

# CAMPING

Camping with children of all ages can be enormous fun and an affordable way to get away from it all. Camping no longer needs to equate to roughing it either as many campsites have excellent facilities — should you want them! The many benefits include lots of freedom for children to run around and you can cook your own food.

Possible disadvantages include no babysitting services, the noise of the other campers, worries about the noise of your own children and of course ... the rain!

# SOUTH WALES

Stunning countryside from the mountains near Brecon to the unspoilt and sweeping beaches of the Gower and Pembrokeshire.

## B&Bs

### Four Seasons Guest House

62 Gwscwm Rd, Pembrey, Carmarthenshire, SA16
01554 833367
Open all year
£25pp 2 sharing, £6 child sharing the room

A small, friendly guest house set very close to Pembrey country park and Burry Port Harbour. It makes an excellent touring base to visit the Gower Peninsula, Pembrokshire and the magnificient beach at Pembrey.

## YHAs

### Brecon YHA

Groesffordd, Brecon, Powys, LD3 7SW
0870 7705718
www.yha.org.uk
Feb-Nov Open daily
Nov-Feb w/e's only
£30.90 2-bed, £54.50 4-bed, £59.50 5-bed, £5 for ensuite

A Victorian family house built 175 years ago which lies 2 miles from Brecon. Standing in ample grounds, the hostel has cots, high chairs and baby baths available, and a washing machine. For older children, there is a games room and TV.

## Broad Haven YHA

Haverford West, Pembrokeshire, SA62 3JH
0870 770 5728
www.yha.org.uk
Mar-Oct
Group bookings in winter
£27 2-bed, £48 4-bed

Single storey hostel overlooking St Brides Bay, close to the beach just 100yrds away. Cots, high chairs and baby baths available. All rooms are ensuite with shower. Games room, TV, washing facilities and garden for children to play in. Restaurant for breakfast and evening meals.

## Penycwm YHA & YMCA

Whitehouse, Penycwn, Haverfordwest, Pembrokeshire, SA62 6LA
0870 770 5988
www.yha.org.uk
Open all year
£45.50 3-bed, £54.50 4-bed, £74.95 6-bed

This 5 star hostel has all ensuite bedrooms with TVs. There are large grounds, games room, washing facilities and towel hire. At the time of going to press, the hostel is changing to a YMCA hostel but will be run on the same lines.

## Poppit Sands YHA

Seaview, Poppit, Pembrokeshire, SA43 3LP
0870 7705996
www.yha.org.uk
Open all year, closed Sun/Mon except Jul & Aug
£31.95 2-bed, £49.50 4-bed, £69.95 6-bed

A charming hostel that was formerly an inn. YHA Poppit Sands sits in 5 acres of grounds with lots of outdoor space for children. The grounds reach down to the sea and overlook a blue flag sandy beach. Although the hostel welcomes children under three, it should be noted that there are steps down from the car park.

## Port Eynon YHA

Old lifeboat house, Port Eynon, Swansea, SA3 1NN
0870 770 5998
www.yha.org
Easter-Nov open daily
Winter group bookings only
£26 2-bed, £45 4-bed,

Port Eynon YHA was originally a lifeboat station and it is located right on the beach on the beautiful Gower Peninsula near Swansea. It offers fantastic views from the lounge right across the bay. The hostel is ideal for water sports enthusiasts, bird watchers, walkers or families that just want to play on the beach.

# CAMPSITES

## Llanmadoc Caravan & Campsite

Llagadranta Farm, Gower, Swansea, SA3 1DE
01792 386202
www.caravancampingsites.co.uk (link from here)
Apr-Oct

This is a great campsite located on one of the Gower's beautiful beaches. The site is basic but very peaceful. Plenty of walking and stunning views. Owners are very friendly. The site accepts tents, caravans and motor homes and has 50 pitches available.

## Pembrey

Pembrey Country Park, Pembrey, Carmarthan, SA16
01554 833913
www.sirgaer.com (link from this site)
Mar-Oct
Caravans £5-10, tents £1.60-£2.50 pp, U5's free
Only takes groups of 6 units or more

A very basic campsite, no showers but it is a short walk from a world-class beach, sandy with surf. Within this beautiful forested park, there are some great facilities, dry ski slope, toboggan run, horse riding, cycling, playground, pitch and putt and crazy golf.

## Pencelli Caravan and Camping

Pencelli, Brecon, Powys, Wales, LD3 7LX
01874 665451
www.pencelli-castle.co.uk
Closed Nov-Dec
Caravan £16 2 adults, tents £8 per adult, £4.50 per child, free U5's

Pencelli Castle campsite is highly recommended as having the "cleanest and best equipped campsite toilet block'" It won the national tourism award for Wales 2003, "best place to stay". Very family-friendly, with well-run facilities and a children's play area. Gas available and electric hook-ups for caravans.

## Porthclais Farm

St Davids, Pembrokeshire, Wales, SA62 6RR
01437 720 256
www.porthclais-campsite.co.uk
Easter-Oct open daily
£5 adult, £2 child pppn

Set within the Pembrokeshire National Park Porthclais Farm is a small, family-run campsite, with acres of space. The site has basic but adequate facilities (toilets, wash basins, showers, washing up area, and drinking water). Located right on the sea front. Caerfai, Porthsele and Whitesands beaches are nearby, as is St David's, the smallest city in the UK.

# GLOUCESTERSHIRE

A very pretty county which includes the Cotswolds, with beautiful stone villages. There are many fantastic family activities to enjoy.

## B&Bs

### Calcot Manor Hotel

Nr Tetbury, Gloucestershire, GL8 8YJ
01666 890391
www.calcotmanor.co.uk
Open all year
£235-£370 for B&B, £25 child supplement 0-12yrs, £30 12+yrs

A charming Cotswold farmhouse, elegantly converted into a stylish hotel with a luxury spa. It offers many facilities for families and children. There are family rooms, playzone (Mez for older children), cots, babysitting/listening and high tea for children at 5pm. "So geared up for children you don't notice they're there!"

# SELF-CATERING

### Hoburne Cotswold Water Park

Broadway Lane, South Cerney, Cirencester, Glos
01285 860 216
www.hoburne.com
Please contact the park for pricing

Accommodation includes caravans, lodges and chalets, in addition to touring pitches, surrounds four lakes teeming with wildlife. There is a huge range of facilities in and around the Lakeside Club. There are indoor and outdoor pools, family restaurants and bars, 10-pin mini bowling, a soft play area, adventure playground, and pool, table tennis, tennis, canoes and an amusement arcade for older children and teenagers. There is also the Sammy Seahorse Club for children aged 4-11yrs, but please note that a responsible adult must stay with the children at all times. Cots are provided at an additional charge.

## YHAs

### Slimbridge YHA

Shepherds Patch, Slimbridge, Glos, GL2 7BP
0870 7706036
www.yha.org.uk
Feb-Oct daily during sch hols, w/e's only term time
£25.50 2-bed, £43.50 4-bed, £52.95 5-bed
£62.50 6-bed,

A large brick-built building close to the famous WWT Wildfowl and Wetlands centre, not far from Bristol. Children can watch birds on the duck pond in the observation lounge. Children under 3yrs are welcome and older children will enjoy the grounds and games room.

### Stow-on-the-Wold YHA

The Square, Stow-on-the-Wold, Glos, GL54 1AF
0870 7706050
www.yha.org.uk
Feb-Oct daily
Nov-Jan w/e's only
£50 4-bed, £65 6-bed, £5 supp for ensuite

A listed 16th century townhouse right in the main square of this charming Cotswold market town. It has been comfortably refurbished but has managed to retain its original exposed beams and 17th century staircase. Baby equipment and washing machine are available. There is also a restaurant serving breakfast and supper.

### Welsh Bicknor YHA

Welsh Bicknor YHA, Nr Goodrich, Ross-on-Wye, HR9
0870 7706086
www.yha.org.uk
Easter-Oct open
Oct-Easter open w/e's only
From £31.95-£69.95, 2-6-bed

This is a charming YHA in a pretty former Victorian rectory set in the Wye Valley with a river running through the grounds. It enjoys beautiful views of the Forest of Dean and Symonds Yat rock. Facilities include a games room, TV, washing machine and a restaurant serving breakfast and evening meals.

## CAMPSITES

### Christchurch Caravaning and Camping Site

Bracelands Drive, Christchurch, Coleford, GL16 7NN
0131 314 6505
www.forestholidays.co.uk
End Mar-early Nov
£6.90-£16.20 per pitch per night

Excellent for families, this site is on a gentle slope high above the beautiful Wye Valley, with waymarked walking routes down to the river through the surrounding woodland. Nearby are the Clearwell Caves ancient iron mines. Hot showers/water.

### Croft Farm Leisure & Waterpark

Bredons Hardwick, Tewkesbury, Glos, GL20 7EE
01684 772 321
www.croftfarmleisure.co.uk
1st Mar-31st Oct
Closed for water sports.
Please call for more information.

Lakeside camping and caravan park with sailing, windsurfing and canoeing — tuition and equipment hire.

### Hoburne Cotswold Water Park

Broadway Lane, South Cerney, Cirencester, Glos, GL7 5UQ
01285 860 216
www.hoburne.com
Caravans: from £225- £550 per week. Chalets and lodges: from £246 per week. (Dependent on season)

For full description, see Self-Catering.

# WILTSHIRE

A great touring base to see some World Heritage tourist sites and other attractions: Stonehenge, Avebury, Bath and Longleat.

# DORSET & HAMPSHIRE

The coastline offers lovely coves and a variety of pebble and sandy family beaches, keep your eyes open for fossils!

## SELF-CATERING

### Center Parcs

Longleat Forest, Warminster, Wiltshire, BA12 7PU
08705 200 300
www.centerparcs.co.uk
Open all year.

With nature on your doorstep and over 100 activities to choose from, it's the perfect place to take a short break. You can choose to do as much or as little as you like. Cots are provided, there is babysitting and activities for children. Covered swimming pool with outdoor heated rapids, slides and wave machine.

## CAMPSITES

### Brokerswood Country Park

Brokerswood, Westbury, Wiltshire, BA13 4EH
01373 822 238
www.brokerswood.co.uk
£8-£23 per pitch per night depending on season and type

A Gold Conservation Award winning site, Brokerswood is well located for visiting Bath, Salisbury, Stonehenge, Longleat and beyond. The site offers generous size pitches on a flat, open field. There is a centrally-heated shower block ensuring a comfortable stay all year round. There is no additional charge for awnings or showers, and pitch prices, which include access into the Country Park, are based on 2 adults and up to 2 children.

## HOTELS & B&Bs

### Moonfleet Manor

Fleet, Nr Weymouth, Dorset, DT3 4ED
01305 786948
www.luxuryfamilyhotels.com
Open all year
£160-£200 double, B&B

Moonfleet manor is beautifully set lying at the end of a winding 2 mile lane. It overlooks Chesil Beach and the Fleet lagoon. The manor is Georgian and has a colonial feel with planters chairs and parquet floors. Children are well catered for with a crèche, outdoor play area, games, swimming pool (in need of some refurbishment) and a huge indoor play area.

### The Sandbanks Hotel

Sandbanks, Poole, BH13 7PS
01202 707377
www.sandbankshotel.co.uk
Open all year.
From £83.50 B&B pppn, £88.50 DB&B, £35 8-12yrs, £19 3-8yrs, £10 2-3yrs, £6 U2's

Located on a Blue Flag award beach, most bedrooms at The Sandbanks Hotel have a sea or harbour view and a balcony. The hotel has an AA red rosette for the beachside brasserie, a large car park, and many leisure facilities. For the children there is a restaurant, fully Ofsted-registered crèche on site (extra), many activities for all ages (holiday club, soft play, games, discos, karaoke), and indoor pool with fun flume. There are many family rooms with cots provided and baby listening. Babysitting is available on request. Newly opened spa and treatment rooms.

## SELF-CATERING

### Sandy Balls Holiday Centre

Godshill, Fordingbridge, Hampshire, SP6 2JY
01425 653042
www.sandy-balls.co.uk

For full description, see Camping in this section.

## YHAs

### Swanage YHA

Swanage, Dorset
0870 7706058
www.yha.org.uk
Open Feb-Nov, w/e's only during term-time
Closed Dec-Jan
£34.50 2-bed, £55 3-bed, £69 4-bed,

This is a large elegant Victorian manor house just a few minutes walk from the town centre of Swanage and its safe, sandy beaches. The hostel welcomes families of all ages, from babies to teenagers. The TV and games room are popular with children, and there is a washing machine and baby equipment available. It is closed on weekdays during term-time due to school groups.

## CAMPSITES

### Sandy Balls Holiday Centre

Godshill, Fordingbridge, Hampshire, SP6 2JY
01425 653042
www.sandy-balls.co.uk
Open all year
Accommodation per week from £93-£1113, many variations. Touring/camping from: £14 pn

Sandy Balls is situated in the New Forest, bordered by the river Avon and set in 120 acres of woods and parklands. The holiday centre consists of forest lodges, luxurious holiday homes, touring and camping. There are first class facilities including a swimming pool, riding stables, children's acitivities, bar and restaurant. Cots are provided.

### Tom's Field Camping

Tom's Field Rd, Langton Matravers, Swanage
01929427110
www.tomsfieldcamping.co.uk
Open March-Oct
£3.75 pp per night, family tent £9.50, U5's free.
Walkers barn £8.50 per night

Tom's Field is a lovely, peaceful campsite. It is right in the middle of the beautiful Dorset coastline, ideal for walking, climbing and family holidays. It is near Swanage with its lovely sandy beach and 20 minutes' walk from the Dorset coastal footpath. Tom's Field also has a walkers barn, available all year with three bunk rooms, bathroom and kitchenette.

## SOMERSET

Beautiful and varied scenery from the tranquil countryside around Bath and Wells to the rugged landscape of Exmoor National Park.

## HOTELS

### Woolley Grange

Woolley Green, Bradford on Avon, BA15 1TX
01225 864705
www.woolleygrange.com
From £135 per room pn

Jacobean Manor House set in open countryside on the outskirts of Bradford on Avon, eight miles from Bath. Facilities include the Woolley Bears' Den, an outdoor play area, children's croquet, bikes, football, play stations and an outdoor heated swimming pool. Cots are provided and there is a baby listening/sitting service. Nappy buckets, nappy sacks and changing mats are available. Bottles and food items for babies can also be stored, and there is a steriliser and microwave in the Den.

## SELF-CATERING

### Butlins

Minehead, Somerset, TA24 5SH
0870 242 1999 general, 01643 703331 Minehead
www.butlinsonline.co.uk
Open all year
Costs vary

Good quality self-catering and half-board accommodation. Apartments are airy with 4 different grades dependent on position and equipment. Indoor and outdoor activities from high rope courses and horse riding to fairground rides and a water park. There is evening entertainment and kids clubs.

### Pitcot Farm Cottages

Pitcot Lane, Stratton on Fosse, Bath, BA3 4SX
01761 233108
www.pitcotfarm.co.uk
Open all year
From £300-£630 pw high season

Surrounded by open farmland these newly converted cottages in a single storey barn are well equipped with log burners, TV/video, cots and highchairs. There is an indoor tennis court housed in a large barn.

### YHAs

### Minehead YHA

Alcombe Combe, Minehead, Somerset, TA24 6EW
0870 770 5968
www.yha.org.uk
Daily Jul-Aug
Flexible winter openings
£41 3-bed, £44 4-bed, £63 6-bed

Attractive country house high on Exmoor hills just 2 miles from beaches. Plenty of easy walking routes from the back door. Exciting trails for mountain bikes. Meal service for breakfast and dinner. Cots available and laundry facilities. Limited parking.

## CAMPSITES

### Newton Mill Camping

Newton Road, Bath, BA2 9JF
01225 333909
www.campinginbath.co.uk
Open all year.
Tent & car: £13 caravans/motorhomes: £15, free U3's, £2.50 3-16yrs family rate, £2.50 hook-up

Newton Mill Camping is located in a hidden valley close to the centre of Bath. There is a children's playground, free fishing, nearby café, bar and restaurant, and hot showers/water. There is also the level, traffic-free Bath-Bristol cycle path and frequent bus services.

## DEVON

A family favourite with our readers. It has a wonderful coastline and dramatic scenery across the Dartmoor National Park.

## HOTELS & B&Bs

### Cheriton Guest House

Vicarage Rd, Sidmouth, Devon, EX10 8UQ
01395 513810
www.smoothhound.co.uk/hotels/cheritong
Open all year
£27 pp B&B, children over 3yrs half price

A large town house backing onto the river Sid with parkland beyond. Half mile walk to sea front. All bedrooms are ensuite with TV and tea/coffee facilities. Cots and baby listening. Large rear garden. Evening meals and packed lunches available on request.

**Looking for sand and surf?** See our favourite family beaches in Out & About in the West Country pg 61.

## Dodbrooke Farm

Michelcombe, Holne, Devon, TQ13 7SP
01364 631461
www.dodbrookefarm.com
£27 pp B&B, half price U5's, free U2's

Judy runs this beautiful 17th century longhouse. Lovely family atmosphere. Fabulous garden, swing, sandpit and cobbled yard with goats and hens. Well-equipped with cot and high chairs. There is also a converted barn available for self catering.

## Fingals Hotel

Dittishaw, Dartmouth, TQ6 0JA
01803 722 398
www.fingals.co.uk

This is a fabulous, individual, quirky hotel run with much energy and imagination by Richard and Sheila. Richard has restored the original run-down farmhouse into an informal yet stylish hotel. This is particularly suitable for older children with a range of activities including swimming, snooker and tennis, and even houses a mini-cinema.The hotel also has a self-catering family barn available for hire which is perfect for a family of four. A barn is attached to the hotel and all hotel facilities are available for use.

## Saunton Sands Hotel

Braunton, Devon, EX33 1LQ
01271 890 212
www.sauntonsands.co.uk
From £77 pn, please call for rates and special offers

Saunton Sands has a range of hotel rooms and self-catering apartments to suit the particular needs of your family. The special facilities for children include a children's pool, games room, junior putting green, adventure area, nursery with toys, babysitting and baby listening. There is also a full programme of children's activities during school holidays. Other facilities include indoor and outdoor heated swimming pools, table tennis, pool tables, tennis, squash, gym, sauna, solarium, and beauty treatments. Cots are provided.

## The Cottage Hotel

Hope Cove, Kingsbridge, South Devon, TQ7 3HJ
01548 561555
www.hopecove.com
From £48 pppn DB&B low season, includes children sharing parents room, £2 U1's, £7.50 1-3yrs, £12 4-8yrs, £16.50 9-12yrs

A traditional family hotel, set in 2½ acres leading via sloping footpaths to two beautiful beaches and the pretty village of Hope Cove. There is a relaxed atmosphere in the hotel, where children are made welcome with an unsupervised play area, high tea menu, cots and baby listening service. A classic seaside holiday.

## Thurlestone Hotel

Thurlestone, Nr Kingsbridge, Devon, TQ7 3NN
01548 560382
www.thurlestone.co.uk
From £79 pppn DB&B for a min of 2 nights (low season)

A lovely family-friendly hotel set very close to the beautiful blue flag Thurlestone Sands beach. There is a games room, play room and toddler paddling pool for younger children. Older children can swim in the indoor and outdoor pools or try sailing or riding. The hotel has been awarded the Henry Duck award by the Egon Ronay guide for children. There is a spa, sauna, tennis, squash, badminton, snooker, table tennis and a 9-hole golf course.

## Woolacombe Bay Hotel

Woolacombe, Devon, EX34 7BN
01271 870388
www.woolacombe-bay-hotel.co.uk
Feb-Dec
Low season/peak season - £150/£250 double per person, £10/£50 child sharing, Prices vary throughout the year, 'phone for more details

This grand Victorian hotel overlooking the stunning beach of Woolacombe is a well-equipped, with indoor and outdoor pools, an adventure playground and a playhouse crèche for U5's. Older children can join the beach

club with organised activities, from quad biking to surf lessons. There are beautiful views from the hotel.

# SELF-CATERING

## Gabriel's Loft

2 Dartmouth Rd, East Allington, Nr Totnes, Devon
01548 853089
www.toadhallcottages.com
May-Sept
From £260-£671

Lovely little cottage, 4½ miles from the beach, 200yrds from the pub. Sleeps 4-6 people. Enclosed rear garden. Virtual tour of the house on the website.

## Hall House

Cornworthy, Nr Totnes, Devon
01548 853089
www.toadhallcottages.com
Open all year
£427-£1099

Stunning house with beautiful decorations throughout, in the pretty village of Cornworthy, near the river Dart. Sleeps 8. Beach 7 miles, pub opposite, shops 2 miles. Take a virtual tour of the house on the website. Dogs allowed by arrangement.

## Lundy Island

Bristol Channel, North Devon, EX39 2LY
01271 863636
www.lundyisland.co.uk
Contact Lundy Island Shore Office for prices.

Lundy offers visitors a wide range of buildings in which to stay, including a castle, lighthouse and gentleman's villa. There are 23 self-catering properties. For more details on Lundy itself, see entry under Camping.

## Ruda Holiday Park

Croyde Bay, North Devon, EX33 1NY
0870 220 4600
www.parkdeanholiday.com
Mar-Nov
Please phone for accommodation prices

Ruda Holiday Park is only a short walk from a blue flag beach. Activities include surf lessons, mountain boarding, tennis courts, fishing, horse riding, cascades tropical adventure pool and 3 children's clubs. There is also an entertainment lounge, bar, café and take away, supermarket and gift shop. Highchairs and cots £10 per week.

## Salcombe Holiday Homes

Orchard Court, Island St, Salcombe, TQ8 8QE
01548 843485
www.salcombe.com
Rents vary

Set in this idyllic Devon seaside town. There are a wide range of holiday homes available, sleeping 2-18 people. Excellent website with virtual tours. Friendly staff to help you find the right property to meet your family's needs.

## Saunton Sands Hotel

Braunton, Devon, EX33 1LQ
01271 890 212
www.sauntonsands.com

Fully equipped 2-4 bed apartments. Hotel facilities included.

## Torridge House Cottages

Little Torrington, North Devon, EX38 8PS
01805 622542
www.torridgehouse.co.uk
www.southwoodcottage.co.uk
Open all year

Family farm holidays, U7's especially welcome. Join us on the farm, help feed the animals. Pigs, lambs, chickens, rabbits, and ducklings. Outdoor heated pool. Ten lovely cottages, truly child-friendly. Cots provided and babysitting available.

## Westermill Farm Cottages

Exford, Exmoor, Somerset, TA24 7NJ
01643 831238
www.westermill.com
From £160-£490 pw

Share the beautiful 500 acre sheep and beef farm. Delightful Scandinavian-style accommodation set in beautiful, grassy paddocks. Seven cottages sleeping 2-8 people. Stabling for horses available.

# YHAs

## Beer YHA

Towns End, Bovey Combe, Beer, EX12 3LL
0870 7705690
www.yha.org.uk
Mar-Oct open daily
Oct-Mar closed Tue-Wed, occasionally rented out as a complete hostel, phone for availability
£49.50 4-bed, £59.50 5-bed, £69.95 6-bed

This is a lovely YHA on the edge of Beer, set in a light and airy country house. It has a large lawned garden, fantastic for children to play in. There is a cot, baby bath and high chair available, and towels can be hired. Breakfast and evening meals available.

## Okehampton YHA

Klondyke Rd, Oakhampton, Dartmoor, EX20 1EW
0870 770 5978
www.yha.org.uk
Open Jan-Nov, but phone to check availability
Closed Dec-Jan
£34.95-£77.50, 2-6-bed

This hostel is fantastic for family-based activity holidays, set in 3 acres of grounds. It offers multi-activity breaks with a variety of activities, from kayaking to rock climbing for 5+yrs. On the edge of Dartmoor National Park, YHA Okehampton is based in a uniquely preserved Victorian railway goods shed offering modern two to six bed family rooms. Cots and high chairs are available on request. It has a TV, games room and washing machine.

# CAMPSITES

## Lundy Island Camp Site

Bristol Channel, North Devon, EX39 2LY
01271 863636
www.lundyisland.co.uk
From £6 pppn
2hr boat crossing from Bideford or Ilfracombe or winter helicopter service from Hartland Point

For a get away from it all short holiday or a weekend break, a trip to Lundy Island is a must. After a short boat trip from Ilfracombe on the MS Oldenburg, visitors can camp or stay in one of the many Landmark Trust properties on the island. Booking in advance is essential. Campsite facilities include washroom facilities and showers. A haven for birdwatchers, climbers, canoeists and divers, Lundy is a favourite for people with a love of the great outdoors. Described as a child's 1000-acre playground, there is something for everyone.

## Ruda Holiday Park

Croyde Bay, North Devon, EX33 1NY
01271 890477
www.ruda.co.uk
From £7 per pitch per night.

For full details see entry under self-catering.

# CORNWALL

When the sun shines there is nowhere quite like Cornwall. Stunning beaches, coves, coastal walks and pretty fishing ports make it another family favourite.

## HOTELS & B&Bs

### Bedruthan Steps Hotel

Mawgan Porth, Cornwall, TR8 4BU
01637 860860
www.bedruthan.com
Open all year
Low season/peak season £75pp/£116pp double DBB, discounted rates for children

Wonderfully welcoming to families, set above a beautiful beach. There are footpaths in both directions along the stunning North Cornish coast. The hotel has fabulous facilities for children of all ages with indoor and outdoor swimming pools and play areas. For older children, there is a cyber café and a surf school, and also a spa for adults. Recent winner of Cornwall Hotel of the Year 2005.

### Fowey Hall Hotel

Hanson Drive, Fowey, Cornwall, PL23 1ET
01726 833866
www.luxuryfamilyhotels.com
Open all year
From £195 double

Fowey Hall is set in 5 acres of gardens overlooking the charming Cornish port of Fowey. It is family-friendly with 12 family suites and 4 pairs of interconnecting rooms. Children are very well catered for, with a kids club, swimming pool and nursery teas, and for older children there is a pool table and Nintendo, TV and video. There are also plenty of outdoor games and BBQs in the summer.

### Stoke Barton Farm

Stoke, Hartland, Bideford, Devon, EX39 6DU
01237 441 238
Open Easter until October
£4.50 adult, £2 child pppn, free U5's, £2 hook-up

Stoke Farm is a beautiful spot on the North Devon Coast. There is ample space for camping and for children to run around safely, dogs are allowed. There are basic but adequate facilities, the campsite commands wonderful views down to Hartland Quay. The tea rooms have variable opening times. "Stoke Barton farm is quite simply a wonderful, peaceful place to stay. A welcome change from busy, commercial campsites."

### The Bulstone

Higher Bulstone, Branscombe, EX12 3BL
01297 680446
www.childfriendlyhotels.com
Room rate from £85 low, £100 high season B&B for family 2+2 (children U11yrs)

The Bulstone is set in the heart of the countryside and has been designed with children in mind. A home from home without all the hard work. All rooms are child friendly, with changing mats, cots, nappy buckets and baby listening devices. There is a kitchen for your use, with bottle steriliser, fridge, milk, microwave, ironing equipment. There's a laundry service and laundrette. Other facilities include a large playroom, an outdoor play area with tractors, swings, slides, climbing frames, cars and guinea pigs! Children's tea is served at 5pm. Babysitting can be arranged.

### Westermill Farm

Exford, Exmoor, Somerset, TA24 7NJ
01643 831238
www.westermill.com
Open all year
£4 adult, £2 child, £2 vehicle, £1 dog

Set in a beautiful, secluded valley in the centre of Exmoor on the river Exe, suitable for fishing and bathing. Waymarked trails from campsite. Laundry, dish washing and seasonal shop. Stabling for horses available.

## Higher Lank Farm

St Breward, Bodmin, Cornwall, PL30 4NB
01208 850716
www.higherlankfarm.co.uk
Nov-Feb closed for maintenance

This is a very special place to stay for pre-school children. It's a working farm with animal feeding after breakfast. There is a wonderful outdoor play area and a selection of indoor toys. Lucy has everything that you could need when it comes to equipment, facilities and toys, so you can travel light. Home-cooked suppers, toddler meals, and babysitting available. Restaurant and pub 1½ miles.

## St Enodoc Hotel

Rock, Cornwall, PL27 6LA
01208 863394
www.enodoc-hotel.co.uk
Open Mid Feb-Mid Jan
Low season/peak season £155/£215 double pp BB, £10 extra child (in same room)

St Enodocs is in a lovely location set against Cornwall's rugged north coast overlooking Rock. The views sweep across the Camel estuary towards Padstow. The hotel is bright and modern with 15 double bedrooms and five spacious family suites. Children of all ages welcomed, and facilities include a children's play room and an outdoor swimming pool.

## SELF-CATERING

### Higher Lank Farm

St Breward, Bodmin, Cornwall, PL30 4NB
01208 850716
www.higherlankfarm.co.uk
Closed Nov-Feb for maintenance
From £475-£1200 per week

Lucy specialises in meeting the needs of families with pre-school children and babies. Older siblings are welcome but for children over 6yrs, the barn accommodation may suit your needs better. These are 17th century newly-converted listed barns with young families in mind. Daily chamber maid.

## Polruan Cottages

Cornwall
01726 870 582
www.polruancottages.co.uk
Open all year
Cottages priced individually

There are over 50 holiday cottages to hire from this excellent company. The website gives full details for each cottage, including tariffs and availability. This family run business selects individually owned homes, most of which overlook Fowey harbour or the sea.

## The Olde House

Chapel Ample, Wadebridge, Cornwall, PL27 6EN
01208 813 219
www.theoldehouse.co.uk
Open all year
From £325 low season to £1265 peak season, per cottage

The Olde House comes highly recommended. Each cottage is well equipped for children with cots and high chair included. There is a farm trail as well as the beaches of Daymer Bay and Polzeath nearby. The leisure centre has an adventure playground, tennis courts, indoor pets corner, snooker table, play barn, heated indoor swimming pool and jacuzzi. Prices include all facilities.

## YHAs

### Golant YHA

Penguite House, Golant, Nr Fowey, PL23 1LA
0870 770 5832
www.yha.org.uk
Mar-Oct
Group bookings winter

Set in 3 acres of beautiful grounds with a further 14 acres of woodland behind to explore. It overlooks the lovely Fowey estuary, just 4 miles from the sea. Welcomes children under 3yrs and provides lots of space with TV, games room and traffic free grounds for older children. Restaurant serves breakfast and supper with table licence. Washing machine, cots and self-catering kitchen also available.

## Treyarnon Bay YHA

Treyarnon Bay, Padstow, Cornwall, PL28 8JR
0870 770 6076
www.yha.org.uk
Open all year
£45 3-bed (£50 ensuite), £55 4-bed, £66 5-bed

P V ☑ ♟ ☒ ⊞ ☒

A fabulous location set on the wild Cornish coastline. YHA Treyarnon is right on the beach in the bay of Treyarnon. It was formerly a 1930s summer residence and has been recently updated. The hostel's location makes it a popular family base. It is excellent for teenagers and runs surf courses, and has a surf board store. Not recommended for U3's.

## YHA Lizard

Lizard Point, TR12 7NT
0870 770 6120
www.yha.org.uk
Mar-Oct, flexible during winter mths
£46 3-bed, £49 4-bed, £60 5-bed, £70 6-bed

P WC ☑ ⌂ CP ♟ ⬜ ⊞ ⬛ ☒

Formerly a Victorian hotel. Acquired by the National Trust, it opened as a hostel in 2003 and has stunning views of Lizard Point. This 5 Star YHA is family-friendly with cots, 3 ensuite rooms, BBQ area and bike store.

# CAMPSITES

## Lower Treave Caravan Park

Crows-An-Wra, Penzance, Cornwall, TR19 6HZ
01736 810 559
www.lowertreave.demon.co.uk
Apr-Nov open
Low season/peak season £4/£5pp, £2 child, free U4's, caravan hire £215-£315 per week

P WC ⬜ ☺ ⊞

Lower Treave is a very well run campsite close to the beautiful beaches of Sennen and Porthcurno. The site covers 4½ acres and has been well landscaped to provide 80 spacious touring pitches on 4 terraced levels with views across the surrounding countryside.

## Old MacDonalds Farm

Porthcothan Bay, Padstow, Cornwall, PL28 8LW
01841 540829
www.oldmacdonalds.co.uk
Mar-Nov
£5.50 adult, £4.50 child peak season, £3 hook-up

P ⬜ ☒ ☺ ⊞

A small family campsite with trampolines, slides and other play equipment as well as a whole farm of animals where children are encouraged to hold and feed rabbits, lambs, calves and ponies. Pony and train rides. 5mins walk from Porthcothan Bay.

## Trevedra Farm Caravan & Campsite

Sennen, Penzance, Cornwall, TR19 7BE
01736 871818 summer, 871835 winter
Easter or 1st Apr-31st Oct
£4 adult, £1 5-10yrs, £2 11-15yrs, free U5's, £3 hook-up, £1 pitch only

P WC ☒ ☺ ⊞

Run by the same family for 65yrs. A working farm where you can watch cows being milked. Located close to the beautiful Sennen Cove and coastal footpath. There is a separate camping field with its own toilet/shower facilities. The shop has daily deliveries, bread, cakes, take-away breakfast, lunch and evening meals in peak season. Launderette & utility room. Booking essential in peak season.

## Treyarnon Bay Campsite

Treyarnon Bay, Padstow, Cornwall, PL28 8JR
01841 520681
www.treyarnonbay.co.uk
Apr-Sep
£11 per unit peak, £7 per unit off-peak

Sea views from site, only 200yrds from a family beach and cliff walks. The site has toilet blocks shower and laundry room. The hotel next door with bar and evening entertainment welcomes campers.

# LONDON

Showing your children the sites of London can make a great weekend. The museums, interactive exhibitions, historical palaces, theatres and parks will keep you busy!

# HOTELS

## Express By Holiday Inn

295 North End Rd, West Kensington, W14 9NS
020 7384 5151
www.exhiearlscourt.co.uk
£80 family room (2+2)

There are 15 London hotels in this chain offering good value accommodation. This hotel is particularly close to public transport and easy access to central London. The rooms are clean but on the small size, all are ensuite and have tea and coffee making facilities. Cots need to be pre-booked and staff can refrigerate infant food. Self-serve continental breakfast. 24-hour drinks bar. Parking available at a charge. Visit their website for low season offers.

# YHAs

## Hampstead Heath YHA

4 Wellgarth Rd, Golders Green, London, NW11
0870 770 5846
www.yha.org.uk
Open all year
£39 2-bed, £61 3-bed, £78 4-bed, £96.30 6-bed

This hostel is set in the suburb of Hampstead Heath in North West London. It is a busy hostel but popular with families as it has an enclosed garden with a pond and picnic tables. The hostel welcomes U3's with its child and baby equipment, while older children will enjoy the games room, TV and internet access.

## St Pancras YHA

79-81 Euston Rd, London, NW1 2QE
0870 7706044
www.yha.org.uk
Open daily all year
From £44-£130 B&B

This is a modern hostel opposite St Pancras and a short walk from Euston and Kings Cross stations. It offers comfortable, basic accommodation in family rooms close to central London transport links. The hostel provides baby equipment including cots and high chairs but these need to be pre-booked.

# BRISTOL

The new arrival of children in the family often means lots of visitors. If they need to stay overnight and you are limited for space, there is plenty of accommodation in Bristol to choose from.

## HOTELS

### Henbury Lodge

Station Rd, Henbury, BS10 7QQ
0117 950 2615
www.henburylodge.com
From £94 per room, £15 per child 2-14yrs

A luxury Georgian country hotel in Bristol, Henbury lodge is extremely welcoming to children. It has very large family rooms which accommodate up to 5 individuals (for example, one double, 2 singles and a cot). The hotel chefs are more than willing to accommodate children's varying diets in the restaurant, with half portions of adult meals also available. Cots are provided and babysitting can be arranged. There are also toys and books for children provided in the hotel lounge. Ground floor rooms are available and there is assistance up the two front steps to the hotel. And for those of you planning large family celebrations, parties can also be catered for (the dining room seats 34).

### Westbury Park Hotel

37 Westbury Rd, Bristol, BS9 3AU
0117 962 0465
www.westburypark-hotel.co.uk
Doubles from £60. Family rooms from £75, no charge for babies

The Westbury Park Hotel is a detached Victorian house on the edge of Bristol's famous Durdham Downs. It is an AA four diamond rated hotel and also has the English Tourist Board Silver Award. There are two large rooms accommodating two adults and two children, and also a large twin interconnecting with a large double. Two cots (and bedding) are available (please check availability at time of booking). Bottles can be heated and baby food stored in a refrigerator.

## SELF-CATERING

### Bristol YHA

14 Narrow Quay, Bristol, BS1 4QA
0870 770 5726
www.yha.org.uk
Open all year
£40 2-bed, £62 4-bed, £66 ensuite 4-bed, prices include breakfast

This is a great base for visiting families or relatives as it is set down on the quayside with views over the waterways. The hostel has been sympathetically restored to create a relaxing place to stay, with games room, TV area, washing machines, self catering kitchen and the café has a table licence. There is a cot and highchair available and towels can be hired.

### Days Serviced Apartments

30-38 St Thomas St, Redcliffe, Bristol, BS1 6JZ
0117 954 4800
www.premgroup.com
From £70 per unit per night

These centrally-based, luxury, one or two bedroom serviced apartments are located a minute's walk from St Mary Redcliffe Church. Each apartment has a fully equipped kitchen with cooker, refrigerator, freezer, dishwasher, washing machine and microwave. There is also secure car parking on request (chargable at a daily rate). Bed linen and towels are provided, as are cots. However high chairs are not provided. There is an on-call manager, and a shopping service is also available.

## CAMPSITES

### Brook Lodge Farm Camping & Caravan Park

Cowslip Green, Bristol, Somerset, BS40 5RB
01934 862 311
www.brooklodgefarm.com
Telephone for pricing and further information.

P ⚐

Brook Lodge Farm is a family-run country touring park, based in the private grounds of a small farm. It is situated ten miles from Bristol city centre, making it an ideal place to stay if you want to camp when you visit family and friends in Bristol. Among its many charms, there is an abundance of wildlife, a stream, and natural play areas for children. There is an outdoor swimming pool. Parents must supervise their children in all areas.

# HOLIDAYS FURTHER AFIELD

## AIR TRAVEL

Bristol and the West Country are well served for travelling further afield, with Bristol International Airport (BIA), which has scheduled flights to many destinations.

### Bristol International Airport

Bristol, BS48 3DY
0870 1212 747
www.bristolairport.co.uk

Being a relatively small airport, everything is within easy walking distance for parents with children in tow. Facilities include baby changing on all floors, lifts, shops and restaurants (all have high chairs).

### Bristol Airport tips

The shops sell nappies and baby food, and the restaurant will warm bottles if needed. If your flight is seriously delayed and you have a young child, the airport has travel cots, bottles and nappies on stand-by.

If travelling with small children on your own, or if you need extra assistance, there are always BIA hosts available to help you to and from the plane.

### Airportcarz

Bristol Int Airport, Lulsgate Bottom, BS48 3DY
01275 474888
www.airportcarz.com
Located on the way to Pick-up Car Park via covered walkway

Private hire taxis based at UK airports. They have people carriers suitable for larger families and minibuses for disabled travellers. You can use your own child seats which they can store while you are away, although their Galaxies can take children from 6 months. We have had some reader feedback on their service, the message is make sure you specify your requirements clearly.

## SEA TRAVEL

Travelling by ferry can be one of the least stressful ways to do long journeys, particularly with young children (although there may be a long journey from your arrival port).

Many ferry companies now have play areas, and for the older children, there are often cinemas or televisions. Booking a cabin on longer crossings can also have its advantages.

### Brittany Ferries
08703 665 333, www.brittany-ferries.co.uk
Plymouth to Roscoff and Santander
Poole to Cherbourg

### Condor Ferries Limited
0845 345 2000, www.condorferries.co.uk
Weymouth & Poole to Guernsey, Jersey & St Malo

### Irish Ferries
08705 17 17 17, www.irishferries.com
Pembroke to Rosslare

### Stena Line
08705 707 070, www.stenaline.co.uk
Fishguard to Rosslare

### Swansea Cork Ferries
01792 456 116, www.swansea-cork.ie
Swansea and Cork

# TIME OUT FOR ADULTS

**Paula Brown**

## CONTENTS

## INTRODUCTION

Finding time for yourself when you have a family is no mean feat. In this chapter we list hobbies, sports, relaxation facilities, new skills and retraining that you can undertake while your children are cared for (and a couple where they're not but worth mentioning). We've also tried to include listings of things you can do from home. We hope they will give you some ideas when time, money and often energy is limited! If you think of more, let us know.

Crèche information is given in several sections within this chapter. They are intended as temporary care and you are generally required to stay on the premises.

Most crèches need to be booked in advance, some with long waiting lists.

## Before You Start

These chapters are also well worth looking at:

**Family Holidays & Weekends Away**

Many of us need time out on holiday but children can be at their most demanding away from home. You will find loads of tips and ideas for family breaks.

**Advice & Support**

There are many support groups giving advice and respite care. Some offering crèche facilities, whilst you learn a skill, see Families & Individuals page xxx

# HOBBIES AND DEVELOPING SKILLS

It can be very liberating to gain a new qualification, retrain or take up a new hobby. Many colleges have crèche facilities or courses that can be taken in the evenings. There are also numerous correspondence courses.

The larger educational centres are listed first, then the rest are alphabetical followed by a section on distance learning.

**The Adult Learners' Framework**
0800 923 0323

Enables you to accrue credits and certificates for courses taken across a range of education providers.

# ADULT & COMMUNITY EDUCATION

## City of Bristol

College Green Centre, St George Rd, BS1 5UA
0117 312 5000
www.cityofbristol.ac.uk
enquiries@cityofbristol.ac.uk

City of Bristol College, Bristol City Council and a number of community organisations have formed a partnership to offer over 1000 vocational, leisure and accredited courses in over 30 venues across the city. They are of a high quality and are designed to be interesting and rewarding.

It is one of the UK's largest colleges with 10 main college centres. These are Bedminster, Ashley Down, Hartcliffe, Lawrence Weston, Soundwell, Downend, Parkway, College Green, Monarch House and Folly Lane. The first five have have day care nurseries and crèche facilities. However other centres can put students in touch with local childcare providers, ask for details.

Their website is comprehensive and broadband users can download their Community Learning Course Guide. Prospectuses are also available in supermarkets, libraries, job centres and community centres.

## Filton College

Filton Avenue, Filton, BS34 7AT
0117 931 2121
www.filton-college.ac.uk

Comprehensive range of courses.

**Filton College Nursery**
0117 969 3990
Mon-Fri 7am-6pm, 0-5yrs

Crèche and after school play scheme during holidays and an overnight facility 0-11yrs.

## University of Bristol

8-10 Berkeley Square, BS8 1HH
0117 928 9000
www.bris.ac.uk

Range of under/postgraduate courses and evening classes open to the public.

**University of Bristol Nursery**
0117 928 6077
Mon-Fri 8.30am-5.30pm, 3mths-5yrs

A long waiting list, giving priority to students and staff.

## University of the West of England

Coldharbour Lane, Frenchay, BS16 1QY
0117 965 6261
www.uwe.ac.uk

Range of under/post graduate courses and courses open to the public.

### Halley Nursery at St Matthias Campus

College Road, Fishponds, BS16 2JP
0117 328 4452
Mon-Fri 8.30am-5.30pm, term time only
6mths-5yrs, £13-15.75 1/2 day

Availability varies, book prior to course, priority to students.

## Barton Hill Workshop

43 Ducie Road, Barton Hill, BS5 0AX
0117 955 6971
www.bartonhillsettlement.org.uk

Courses include English, maths, computing, teaching, counselling and hobbies.

**Crèche**
9.30am-11.45am, 12.30pm-3.30pm, 8wks-5yrs
£5 deposit, £2 1st child, £1.50 additional siblings

## Folk House Adult Education Centre

40A Park Street, Bristol, BS1 5JG
0117 926 2987

Languages, dance,music, fitness, arts and personal development. No crèche but many of the courses are in the evening or at weekends.

## Hartcliffe Health & Environmental Action Group

The Gate House Centre, Hareclive Road, BS13 9JN
0117 946 5285

Cooking and nutrition projects for pregnant women and families with children under 5yrs from the BS13 area, with a free crèche. Contact them direct or via your health visitor.

## Knowle West Health Association

Filwood Community Centre, Barnstaple Road, Knowle, BS4 1JP
0117 963 9569

Classes cover health, cooking and childcare.

**Crèche**
0117 963 6475
0-8yrs, 50p per session

Run to coincide with classes, times vary according to which projects are running.

## Silai For Skills

176-178 Easton Rd, Easton, Bristol, BS5 0ES
0117 941 5180
www.silai.org.uk
Mon-Fri 10am-3pm, term-time only

Provides courses in creative textiles for women. Crèche available.

## St Paul's Learning and Family Centre

94 Grosvenor Road, St Pauls's, BS2 8XJ
0117 914 5470

IT, basic skills, English as a second language, crafts, languages, healthy living.

**Crèche**
Mon-Fri 9.30am-12pm & 12pm-3pm
6 mths-4yrs, free

## The Park Centre

Daventry Road, Knowle, BS4 1QD
0117 903 9770

Basic skills, language, childcare and crafts.

**Crèche**
Mon & Wed 10am-12pm, Tue & Wed 1pm-3pm
0-4yrs, free if attending course, can be flexible

## Workers Educational Association

7 York Court, Wilder Street, BS2 8QH
0117 916 6500
www.wea.org.uk

Basic skills, arts and crafts, teaching qualifications, history, literature and creative writing. Limited childcare facilities but can arrange crèches for courses run for women's or community groups.

## DISTANCE LEARNING

Distance learning can work well with family life. The following are distance learning institutions which offer a variety of courses.

### Learn Direct

0800 101 901

www.learndirect.co.uk

An online learning network offering over 450 courses in Business, English and Maths, many of which are free or subsidised, paced to suit. Courses available online and through Alexandra Park, Fishponds and Greenway Centre, Southmead.

### Learn Direct Helpline

0800 100 900

Impartial advice to help you choose from over a million courses (many online) including Learn Direct courses UK-wide.

### Open University

0870 9000 310

Well-respected undergraduate and postgraduate courses.

## FITNESS

When you are physically exhausted from childcare, the thought of exercise may be the furthest thing from your mind. Exercise can increase your stamina and release endorphins! Across the city and the West Country are local leisure centres, many providing crèche facilities. Look out for swimming pools offering free swims in pregnancy.

View the Leisure Centre tables in our Reference Section to see what is on offer and where there are crèche facilities. Some classes allow babies in their car seats/prams.

Alternatively if you have childcare support in the evening, there is often a good choice of classes at this time. Failing all of this there are always exercise and relaxation videos but they require more motivation!

## PRIVATE HEALTH CLUBS

Joining fees and monthly membership (often with minimum terms) can be very motivating! Those listed here have a variety of facilities. Most have gym and spas, some have pools. A few are open to non-member off peak but unless stated otherwise, assume the clubs are members only. Those listed below provide crèches, most require pre-booking.

### Better Bodies

94 High St, Portishead, BS20 6AJ
01275 845353

**Crèche**
Mon, Wed, Fri 9am-11am
0-5 yrs, £2 per session

Gym facilities only, non-members can use gym and crèche.

### David Lloyd Club

Ashton Road, Ashton, BS3 2HB
0117 953 1010
www.davidlloydleisure.co.uk

**Crèche**
Mon-Fri 9am-5pm (closed 12.30pm-1.30pm)
Sat: 9.30am-3.30pm, Sun: 10am-2pm
3mths-5yrs, £3.25/hr

You may need to book well in advance.

### En Forma Health Club

Bath Hill, Keynsham, BS31 1EB
0117 987 3262
www.enforma.co.uk

**Crèche**
Mon-Fri 10am-12noon
from 6wks, £5 non-members, £3 members

Fitness classes, sauna and crèche are open to non-members during crèche hours. Crèche runs on a first-come basis.

### Esporta Health and Fitness Club

Hunts Ground Road, Stoke Gifford, BS34 8HN
0117 974 9740
www.esporta.com

### Crèche

Mon-Fri: 9am-3pm exc Weds 9am-12.30pm,
Fri: 5pm-7pm, Sat-Sun 9.30am-12.30pm
6wks-5yrs, £3.60/hr 2hrs max

Holiday activities and sports for children aged 5-11yrs.

## Fitness Factory

17 Broad Road, Kingswood, BS15 1HZ
0117 935 2060
www.fitnessfactoryltd.co.uk

### Crèche

0117 949 7748
Mon-Fri 9am-11am
6wks-4yrs, £1.50/hr members, £2/hr non-members

Non-members may use spa and crèche.

## Livingwell Health & Leisure Club

Cotham Gardens, 80 Redland Road, BS6 6AG
0117 942 5805
www.livingwell.com

### Crèche

Mon-Fri: 9.30am-2.30pm, 0-5 yrs, £3/hr

## Next Generation Club

Greystoke Avenue, Westbury-on-Trym, BS10 6AZ
0117 959 7140
www.ngclubs.co.uk

### Crèche

017 950 2550
Mon-Fri 9am-5pm (closed 12pm-1pm)
3mths-5yrs, £4/hr, pre-booking required

Non-members can use the privately run crèche but not the facilities.

## Redwood Lodge

Beggar Bush Lane, Failand, BS8 3TG
01275 395888, 01275 395829 crèche

### Crèche

Mon-Fri: 9.15am-3pm, Sat-Sun: 9.45-1pm
6mths-5yrs, £3.50/hr

## Riverside Leisure Club

Station Road, Little Stoke, BS34 6HW
01454 888 666

### Crèche

Mon-Fri 9.30am-11.25am
3mths-5yrs, £1.75/hr, £2.30 2hrs

## PERSONAL TRAINERS

If you are looking for pregnancy and postnatal exercise classes please refer to the Pilates and yoga instructors listed in Healthcare pg xxx

### Blooming Fit

www.bloomingfit.com
£19.99 annual membership

Here is something new. A virtual personal trainer! Online advice for keeping fit during and after your pregnancy.

### Fit for Life

07817 809734
From £30/hr pp

Pregnancy and postnatal exercise programmes designed to each individual. Covers Bristol area and can cater for groups.

### Get Fitter

0779 289 6230
www.getfitter.net
From £35/hr

Vikki has two young children and is aware of the needs of parents. She is a fully qualified nutrition consultant, personal trainer, fitness coach, yoga and Pilates instructor.

### Karen Hutchinson

07960 950858
£25/hr pp

Personal training, fitness plans, slimming, sports injuries, postnatal issues, working with groups or individuals in their homes. Flexible hours in west Bristol area.

## RELAXATION

If going back to college or treadmills aren't your idea of relaxation, you might want to try a massage in the comfort of your own home or a sauna while the children are in a crèche.

Some of the private gyms listed above offer spa, relaxation facilities and crèche to non-members. Some offer one-off day rates. Student practitioners often give free treatments.

Contact: Filton College Health & Beauty Department on 0117 909 2319.

## RELAXATION CENTRES

### Relaxation Centre

9 All Saints Road, Clifton, BS8 2JG
0117 970 6616
www.relaxationcentre.co.uk
Mon-Thu 11am-10pm, Fri-Sun 9am-10pm

Offers a range of holistic treatments, spa facilities and gift vouchers; no membership required. No crèche.

### The Massage Centre at Kingsdown Sports Centre

Portland Street, Kingsdown, BS2 8HL
0117 942 6582
www.bristol-city.gov.uk/sport

**Crèche**
Mon & Fri 9.30am-11.30am, Tue-Thu 10am-12pm
8 wks-4yrs £1.40 per child, £1 for extra child

A variety of treatments and spa.

## MOBILE THERAPY

**Ashram 4 Body Harmony**
07740 245890
Bharti will do various massage techniques, reflexology, beauty treatments, food intolerance test and reiki.

**Essential Health**
01225 478900
£18-30
Jo does reflexology, aromatherapy and Indian head massage and will travel within Bath area, working evenings and weekends.

**Helen Dix**
0117 935 2564
£20-30
Practices shiatsu and will travel across the Bristol area.

**Sole Relief**
01454 615315 or 0781 479 2530
Rebecca practices reflexology or Indian head massage in the north Bristol area.

**Stan Patrzalek**
0117 952 2071
Thai yoga massage, Stan covers the wider Bristol area with flexible working hours.

## MOBILE HAIRDRESSERS & NAIL TECHNICIANS

**Heidi Mobile Hairdresser**
07770 234804 or 0117 961 5925
Mon-Fri, Wed & Thu eve, Sat am
From £15
Will colour, perm and cut adults and children's hair. Covers greater Bristol area.

**Kreative Cuts**
0117 983 8657 or 07762 014470
From £15
Jane will do a variety of hair treatments and cuts for men, women and children.

**Mobile Nail Technician**
0117 377 8317 or 07779 877024
From £30
Ann does nail extensions, flexble working hours.

**Stacy Graham**
0117 987 1987
Mon-Fri school hours, Tue & Thu eves
From £15 adult, £4 child
Experienced hair stylist. Cuts for the whole family.

## ALLOTMENTS

Bristol City Council Allotments Dept
0117 922 3737

As quirky as this may sound, allotments give reward and relaxation to people nationally. Many of our readers recommend having an allotment as a good way to unwind, get fit and keep the kids entertained.

### Windmill Hill City Farm

Philip Street, Bedminster, BS3 4EA
0117 963 3299
www.windmillcityfarm.org.uk

**Crèche**
Tue,Thu, Fri: 9.30am-11.30pm & 12.45pm-2.45pm
Fri: 12.30pm-2.30pm
1-5 yrs, £3 members, £4 non-members

Allotments available and crèche if you'd rather not have your children dissecting worms while you dig!

## ART CLASSES

www.cityofbristol.ac.uk/course/community

Classes tailored to your creative abilities are available across the city, see the course finder at the City of Bristol website or investigate those classes advertised at your local library. There are also some great arts trails across the West check out one at:

www.southbank-bristol.co.uk.

### Art Coach

07939 001123
laurel.smart@blueyonder.co.uk

For practicing artists and beginners. 1:1 tutoring or 'a critical friend' to help you progress with your work. Laurel is an experienced artist and painting and drawing tutor. Support, advice and encouragement. Free initial meeting in your own home.

### Stitch and Bitch

www.stitchnbitch.co.uk

Another version of this is Knit and Natter! Get creative and meet others who enjoy the fun and benefits of this hobby. Use the website to find a local network. "Research proves that your pulse rate slows and your blood pressure lowers when you knit," Good luck!

## MUSIC CLASSES

If you have played a musical instrument in the past or have always wanted to, now might be the time to re-engage or start afresh.

Many music shops have lists of tutors, see those listed in Shopping pg xxx

### Incorporated Society of Musicians

10 Stratford Place, London, W1C 1AA
020 7629 4413
www.ism.org

This is an excellent website with private teachers listed by UK region. The teachers have been approved for their Register of Professional Private Music Teachers.

Browse some of Bristol's art and music shops, see Shopping chapter pgs 257 & 258

## SHOP IN YOUR HOME

### Home Party Agent

If you like retail therapy why not combine shopping with a party in your own home. These are becoming increasingly popular. From cosmetics to children's books, agents of these companies will bring the products to your home, give you and your friends a short presentation and let you browse. As the host, you will get free products.

Some local agents are listed below but you may need to use the main websites to find an agent in your area. If you really like this idea, becoming an agent is a good way to earn money and work around the kids. Schools, toddler groups, pre-schools and gyms may find this list useful for stalls at school fares or other events.

### Barefoot Books

0117 952 0070 or 01225 322400
www.barefootbooks.co.uk
barefoot-paula@blueyonder.co.uk

Local children's books publisher. Beautifully produced books great for standby presents or special occasion gifts.

### Body Shop

0845 9050607
www.uk.thebodyshop.com
ukcustomer.relations@the-body-shop.com

Ethically sourced cosmetics.

### Mini IQ

0845 652044
www.mini-iq.co.uk
enquiries@mini-iq.co.uk

Educational toys, books & games for babies & children.

### Padme Pashminas & Accessories

01458 833 553
www.padmecollection.com
pashminas@padmeclothing.com

Fair trade pashminas, bags and clothes from Nepal.

### Pampered Chef

01753 211020
www.pamperedchef.com

Sells quality kitchen utensils, oven-wear and time-saving gadgets.

### Phoenix Trading
0208 875 9944
www.phoenix-trading.co.uk
info@phoenix-trading.co.uk
Greetings cards, gift wrap & stationery

### Usborne Books at Home
079841 32563
www.usbornebooksathome.co.uk
allison.scaduto@bigfoot.com
Books for babies through to teenagers. From touchy feely books to information books with internet links. Good range of fiction for older children. Allison covers Bristol & Bath area.

### Virgin Vie
0845 300 8022
www.virgincosmetic.com
Jewellery and cosmetics.

# ENTERTAINMENT

## Theatre & Arts

It is easy to forget how much is on offer at art galleries, theatres and cinemas across the West. Many of them are listed in our Out and About Chapters, see pages xxx.

### Venue Magazine
www.venue.co.uk

### Evening Post
www.visitbristol.com

Both these publications are excellent at keeping your finger on the pulse. An evening out without children can be recharging, as long as it isn't too late...!

## CINEMA
These two cinemas specifically welcome parents and carers with young children so you can catch the latest film with your little one in tow.

### Curzon Cinema
Old Church Road, Clevedon, BS21 6NN
01225 871000
baby@curszon.org.uk for membership information
Wed: 10am

Members of this cinema can take babies up to 1yr (and older children if the certificate is U, PG or 12A) and watch a film in (relative!) peace. The auditorium is slightly lighter and the soundtrack a little quieter than normal. Buggies can be looked after and there are changing facilities.

### The Cube
4 Princess Row, Kingsdown, Bristol, BS2 8NQ
0117 907 4190

For parents and carers with babies under 1yrs. A bi-weekly programme with lowered movie volume and extra lighting in the auditorium. Pram area and baby changing facilities.

## STAYING IN
### 20th Century Flicks in Clifton
0117 974 2570
www.20thcenturyflicks.co.uk
Enormous stock of arty and epic films to hire on video and DVD from independents to blockbusters.

### DVD Hire by Post
www.amazon.co.uk
www.blockbuster.co.uk
www.sainsburysdvdrental.co.uk
A bit of forward planning required but it can all be done without leaving the house!

# FAMILY HEALTHCARE

**Elspeth Ponitn**

## CONTENTS

## INTRODUCTION

Caring for our children's physical and mental health is one of parenting's most important roles. From the moment that we find out that we are going to have a baby, we take on this huge responsibility for another life, while at the same time needing to take care of ourselves.

In this chapter, we provide all the information you need about antenatal classes, home and hospital births and postnatal support. We also cover child development.

We are very fortunate to have many healthcare services available to us in and around Bristol but it can be hard to know where to turn. This directory can help, giving a comprehensive list of recommended clinics and practitioners. It also lists the full range of NHS services to access in an emergency.

# GENERAL HEALTH CARE

## HEALTHCARE SERVICES

### Avonweb
www.avon.nhs.uk

Contact and online site providing information about local NHS services, such as GPs, dentists, hospitals and opticians.

### Maternity and Health Links
Charlotte Keel Health Centre, Seymour Road, Eastonl
0117 902 7100

Information videos and bilingual scripts in many languages. Also interpreting and advocacy services available.

### NHS Direct
0845 46 47
www.nhsdirect.nhs.uk

A confidential advice line, staffed by nurses, offering healthcare advice 24 hours a day. They will assess your needs and either give advice or refer you to your out of hours GP or hospital. They also give information about local NHS services, such as GPs and dentists.

## PRIMARY CARE TRUSTS (PCTS)

### Bath and North East Somerset PCT
St Martin's Hospital, Midford Rd, Bath, BA2 5RP
01225 831800
www.banes-pct.nhs.uk

### Bristol North PCT
King Square House, King Square, Bristol, BS2 8EE
0117 976 6600
www.bristolnorthpct.nhs.uk

### Bristol South and West PCT
King Square House, King Square, Bristol, BS2 8EE
0117 976 6600
www.bristolswpct.nhs.uk

### North Somerset PCT
Waverley House, Old Church Rd, Clevedon, BS21
01275 546 770
www.northsomerset.nhs.uk

### South Gloucestershire PCT
1 Monarch Court, Emerald Park, Emerson's Green, BS16 7FH
0117 330 2468
www.sglos-pct.nhs.uk

## GPs & NURSES

### Family Doctor (GP)

If you or a member of your family are have any health concerns, your first point of contact will probably be your family doctor (GP). If your problem occurs out of surgery hours, you can contact NHS Direct (see above). If you are not registered with a GP, you can find the telephone number of the nearest surgery in the yellow pages under Doctors, from NHS Direct, Avonweb or your local Primary Care Trust, see above.

### Practice Nurses

Registered nurses, usually based in health centres or surgeries, work closely with GPs and often run clinics in specialised areas, such as family planning, diabetes and asthma.

## WALK-IN CENTRES

NHS walk-in centres provide treatment for minor injuries and illnesses seven days a week. You don't need an appointment and will be seen by an experienced NHS nurse.

### Bristol (City Gate) NHS Walk-in Centre
33 Broad Street, BS1 2EZ
0117 906 9600
www.nhs.uk
Daily 8am-8pm

### South Bristol NHS Walk-in Centre
5 Knowle West Health Park, Downton Road, Knowle West, BS4 1WH
0117 903 0003
www.nhs.uk
Daily 9am-9pm

Nurses here also offer blood tests and ear syringing services.

**Need an out of hours pharmacy?**
See our listing in Shopping & Services, pg 268.

## HOSPITALS & MENTAL HEALTH

### A&Es

The following hospitals all have accident and emergency departments.

**Frenchay Hospital**
Frenchay Park Road
0117 970 1212 (ext 3887)

**Royal United Hospital, Minor Injuries**
Combe Park, Bath, BS1 3NG
01225 428331

For emergency but not immediate life threatening illnesses or injuries:

**The Bristol Royal Hospital for Children**
Upper Maudlin Street
0117 927 6998

**The Bristol Royal Infirmary**
Marlborough Street
0117 923 0000

### Avon and Wiltshire Mental Health Partnership NHS Trust

Bath NHS House, Newbridge Hill, Bath, BA1 3QE
01225 731732
www.awp.nhs.uk

Information regarding mental health needs for both service users and carers.

## LATE NIGHT PHARMACIES

In all chemist shops (or pharmacies) there is a pharmacist on duty who is able to give advice on the treatment of many health problems. There will always be a pharmacy in your area open outside normal shop hours. A list of these is published daily in the Bristol Evening Post or can be obtained by telephoning NHS Direct. For more details see Shopping and Services pg 268.

## ADVICE & COMPLAINTS

### Complaints

If you are not happy with the care that you have received from any aspect of the NHS, you have every right to complain. For information about how to make a complaint, see www.nhs.uk or contact your local PCT, see above.

### Healthcare Advice

For further advice when using NHS services:

**United Bristol Healthcare Trust**
0117 928 3571/2917

**Bristol Royal Hospital for Children**
0117 342 8065

**Bristol South and West PCT**
0117 900 2289

**Bristol North PCT**
0117 900 3433

**North Bristol NHS Trust:**
Frenchay Hospital
0117 918 6646
Southmead Hospital
0117 959 6285

## COMPLEMENTARY HEALTHCARE

This section puts several branches of western medicine under the same umbrella as those medicines which are traditionally thought of as complementary. Some of these services can be received within the NHS but many are private; some offer reduced rates.

Most of the clinics, practitioners, and complementary therapy governing associations listed below offer their services to non-specific age groups or clients. If your needs are more specific, see the relevant sub chapters below.

**Institute of Complementary Medicine**
PO Box 194, London, SE16 7QZ
0207 237 5165
www.icmedicine.co.uk

The Institute is a charity providing information on all complementary medicines.

## Bristol Natural Health Service

407 Gloucester Rd, Horfield, BS7 8TJ
0117 944 4448

Wide range of treatments.

## Clinic of Natural Medicine

126 Whiteladies Road (above Neal's Yard Remedies),
Clifton, BS8 2RP
0117 946 6035

Offers a wide range of therapies and a free
initial 15 minute consultation to select a
suitable treatment. Reduced rates for children.
No access for buggies.

## Clover House Children's Complementary Therapy Centre

447 Bath Road, Saltford, Bristol, BS31 3AZ
01225 344047
www.cloverhouse.org
info@cloverhouse.org

An appointment includes seeing 3 therapists
covering aromatherapy, nutrition & imagery
to help with fears surrounding illness. Ring for
appointment. Payment by donation, £10 min.

## Kingswood Natural Health Centre

355-359 Two Mile Hill Rd, Kingswood, BS15 1Af
0117 914 5590
www.kingswoodnaturalhealth.co.uk

Provides a range of complementary and
holistic therapies in a professional and
relaxing environment.

## Natural Health Clinic

39 Cotham Hill, Cotham, BS6 6JY
0117 974 1199
www.thenaturalhealthclinic.com

Wide selection of practitioners including
homeopathy and cranial osteopathy.
Concessions offered.

## The Centre for Whole Health

12 Victoria Place, Bedminster, BS3 3BP
0117 923 1138

Offers acupuncture, Chinese herbal medicine,
counselling, homeopathy, massage and
osteopathy.

## The Chandos Clinic

21 Chandos Rd, Redland, BS6 6PG
0117 974 5084
www.chandosclinic.co.uk

Practitioners offering osteopathy, homeopathy,
reflexology, shiatsu, health kinesiology, allergy
therapy, osteopathy for babies and growing
children, medical herbalist, physiotherapy,
massage and acupuncture.

## The Clifton Practice

8-10 Whiteladies Rd, Clifton, BS8 1PD
0117 946 6070
www.thecliftonpractice.co.uk

Offers all the main complementary and
alternative therapies.

## The Fishponds Practice

834 Fishponds Rd, Fishponds, Bristol, BS16 3XA
0117 949 1290
enquiries@fishpondspractice.co.uk

Offers osteopathy for pregnancy, children and
babies. It is also home to a range of other
therapies offered by a team of qualified and
accredited practitioners.

# ACUPUNCTURE

Used in traditional Chinese medicine for
around 4,000 years. It involves the painless
insertion of fine needles into specific points on
the body. Treatment is sometimes available on
the NHS.

### British Acupuncture Council

63 Jeddo Road, London, W12 9HQ
0208 735 0400
www.acupuncture.org.uk

Free information and lists of local
practitioners. Look for letters such as MBAcC,
after a practitioner's name.

# AROMATHERAPY

Aromatherapy is the holistic application
of essential oils, often involving massage.
Aromatherapy can be used on small children
and can be beneficial during pregnancy,
labour and postnatally.

**The International Federation of Aromatherapists**
61-63 Churchfield Rd, London, W3 6AY
0208 992 9605
www.ifaroma.org

Provides lists of local practitioners. Look out for MIFA after a practitioner's name.

**The Register of Qualified Aromatherapists**
PO Box 3431, Danbury, Chelmsford, Essex
01245 227 957

Professional association of aromatherapy practitioners who have undergone training of the highest standards. Write with SAE or phone to find an aromatherapist in your area.

For listings of aromatherapists and those qualified to do baby massage, see Ante/Postnatal sub chapters below.

# CHINESE MEDICINE

## AcuMedic Chinese Medical Centre
Manvers Chambers, Manvers Street, Bath, BA1 1PE
01225 483 393
www.acumedic.com

Treatments for babies from (6+mths) and children with skin conditions such as eczema and psoriasis. Reduced rates available. Staff help with buggies over the steps at entrance.

## Chinese Medicine & Skin Centre
51 Sandy Park Rd, Brislington, Bristol, BS4 3PG
0117 972 4716

Qualified and registered consultant of Herbal Medicine and Acupuncture. Treatments offered can help most common and chronic disorders including baby and children's eczema, impetigo, scabies, flu, coughs, poor appetite and constipation.

## Oriental Medicine Practice
35 North View, Westbury Park, BS6 7PY
0117 907 8890
www.orientalmedicine.co.uk

Offers acupuncture, shiatsu, Chinese herbs, nutritional consultation and allergy testing for babies and children. Has practitioners who will support women in pregnancy and during labour, both in hospital and for home births.

# CHIROPRACTORS

Chiropractors diagnose and treat conditions rising from the mechanical dysfunction of the joints and their effects on the nervous system. Chiropractors use their hands to adjust the joints of your spine and extremities where signs of restriction in movement are found.

**The British Chiropractic Association**
Blagrave House, 17 Blagrave St, Reading, RG1 1QB
0118 950 5950
www.chiropractic-uk.co.uk

Make sure your pracitioner is registered with the General Chiropractic Council (GCC).

## Vital Health Clinic
8 North View, Westbury Park, BS6 7QB
0117 973 0878

Chiropractors and osteopaths with a particular interest in treating women pre-conceptually and throughout pregnancy. They also treat babies and children for infantile colic, growing pains and headaches.

# COUNSELLING

## The British Association of Counselling and Psychotherapy
BACP House, 35-37 Albert St, Rugby, CV21 2SG
0870 4435252
www.bacp.co.uk

Lists of local therapists are available online or by sending a SAE. Look for BACP, UKCP, UKRC, BCP after a counsellor's name.

**Dominique Ker**
0117 968 6030
sakoilsky@msn.com

Counsellor (also in practice with Relate) offering women and couples the chance to go through their birth experience, particularly if it was difficult or having a negative impact on their relationship or that with their baby.

## CRANIAL OSTEOPATHS

Cranial osteopathy is a delicate form of manipulation to the skull and facial bones. Treatment can be helpful in pregnancy and for babies and young children with feeding difficulties, colic, sleep disturbances, behavioural problems, learning difficulties, asthma and ear infections. It can be available on the NHS. Also see Osteopaths below.

**International Cranial Association**
478 Baker St, Enfield, Middlesex, EN1 3QS
0208 367 5561
kbs07@dial.pipex.com

Publishes a directory of practitioners.

**The Craniosacral Therapy Association of the UK**
Monomark House, 27 Old Gloucester Street, London, WC1N 3XX
07000 784735
www.craniosacral.co.uk
info@craniosacral.co.uk

Practitioner listing and information on craniosacral therapy.

## Bristol Centre for Craniosacral Therapy

26 Cairns Rd, Bristol, BS6 7TY
0117 942 8647
www.bristolcraniosacral.co.uk

Craniosacral therapy for pregnancy, babies and children. A very gentle whole body therapy addressing structural problems and restrictions, arising from the birth process. Also helpful with colic, digestive, respiratory, anxiety and stress difficulties. Mums encouraged to take sessions too. Young children with problems from glue ear and hyperactivity to dyslexia and cerebral palsy are treated. Children's rates.

## Bristol Children's Osteopathic Clinic

Chandos Clinic, 21 Chandos Road, Redland, BS6 6PG
0117 974 5084
Mon-Fri 9am-5pm

Cranial osteopathy treatment from 0-16yrs, conditions including glue ear, colic, feeding difficulties & asthma.

## HOMEOPATHY

Homeopathic medicines are derived from a variety of plants, animal materials and minerals.

**The British Homeopathic Association**
Hahnemann House, 29 Park St West, Luton, LU1 3BE
0870 444 3950
www.trusthomeopathy.org

Details of medically qualified homeopaths. Look for the letters MF Hom, FF Hom.

**The Society of Homeopaths**
11 Brookfield, Duncan Close, Moulton Park, Northampton, NN3 6WL
0845 4506611
www.homeopathy-soh.org

Information about homeopathy, and register of qualified homeopaths in your area.

## Children's Homeopathic Clinic

St Werburghs City Farm, Watercress Rd, St Werburghs, BS2 9YJ
0117 914 1694
www.bristol-natural-health-service.co.uk
jomorgan.rshom@blueonder.co.uk

Low cost homeopathic treatment for 0-18 yrs.

## Individual Practitioners

**Chris Wilkinson DSH RSHom**
24 Dunkerry Rd, Windmill Hill, Bristol
0117 963 2306

**Claire Long, DSH RSHom**
82 Richmond Road, Montpelier, BS6 5EW
0117 942 9744

**Diane Murray, RSHom**
The Centre for Whole Health, 12 Victoria Place, Bedminster, BS3 3BP
0117 946 6035

**Gordon Adam, DSH RSHom**
0117 942 6810

**Lesley Harris, DSH RSHom**
30 Thingwall Park, Fishponds, BS16 2AE
0117 902 8484

**Maddhu Anhes, DSH PCH RSHom**
St Andrews and Totterdown.
0117 977 8737

**Penny Stirling, DSH RSHom**
The Centre for Whole Health, 12 Victoria Place, Bedminster, BS3 3BP
0117 923 1138

# MASSAGE
**The Massage Therapy Institute**
Lower Ground Floor, 20 Enford St, London, W1H 1DG
www.cmhmassage.co.uk

An educational and professional organisation for massage therapists and others interested in the health sciences. Lists registered therapists in your area.

**Anne Badger, MGCP**
0117 963 6557
annebadger@madasafish.com

# NUTRITION

## Pre-conception Nutrition
Audrey Kalsi BSc (Hons) Dip ION
01225 789513, 07734 839496
optnutclinic@aol.com

Specialises in fertility problems treating many couples with unexplained infertility, whether you are trying for a natural pregnancy or trying to conceive through IUI or IVF. Clinics in Bath and Bristol.

## Catherine Turner BSc (Hons) Msc
Clare Collins & Associates, 16B Chandos Road, Redland, BS6 6PE
0117 330 8672
hst@blueyonder.co.uk
[WC] [♿] [♿]

A state-registered dietitian for children and adults. Advice given on allergies, food refusal, weight problems and fussy eating. Individual appointment or group sessions.

## Children's Nutrition Clinic
01225 789513, 07734 839496
optnutclinic@aol.com

Natural treatments for children's health problems including asthma, colic, eczema, learning and behavioural problems, digestive complaints, lack of energy, poor weight gain, and recurrent colds/infections. Clinics in Bath and Bristol.

# OSTEOPATHY
Osteopathy treats faults which occur in the musculo-skeletal system due to stress, injury and sometimes disease. It can be beneficial during pregnancy and for small children. Osteopathy can be available on the NHS.

**General Osteopathic Council**
Osteopathy House, 176 Tower Bridge Road, London, SE1 3LU
0207 357 6655
www.osteopathy.org.uk

List of registered osteopaths and fact sheets. Under the Osteopaths Act 1993, all qualified Osteopaths have to be listed with the General Osteopathic Council.

## The Fishponds Practice
834 Fishponds Rd, Fishponds, Bristol, BS16 3XA
0117 949 1290
enquiries@fishpondspractice.co.uk

Offers osteopathy for pregnancy, children and babies. It is also home to a range of other therapies offered by a team of qualified and accredited practitioners.

## Sneyd Park Osteopaths
4 Rockleaze Rd, Sneyd Park, Bristol, BS9 1NF
0117 968 5107
www.bristolosteopaths.com

Treats a range of complaints from aches and pains, to headaches and period pains to name but a few. Specialising in mechanical, visceral and cranial approaches.

# REFLEXOLOGY
Working on reflex points on the feet to treat imbalances in the whole body. It is drug free and can be used to treat many conditions. It can be beneficial during pregnancy, aiding sleep and reducing aches and pains. Some women find it makes labour shorter and less painful. It can also help with fertility problems.

**Association of Reflexologists**
27 Old Gloucester St, London, WC1 3XX
0870 5673320
www.aor.org.uk, info@aor.org.uk

Lists of registered reflexologists.

### British Reflexology Association
Monks Orchard, Whitbourne, Worcester, WR6 5RB
01886 821 207
www.britreflex.co.uk
Lists registered reflexologists.

### Alison Burlingham MAR
01275 394493
Alison holds the practioners certificate in reflexology and is a full member of the AOR. One of her specialisations is antenatal and postnatal reflexology.

### Henrietta Gibbs Dip BSR MIFR
0117 942 2769 mob. 07812 187730
henriettagibbs@onetel.com
Mon-Fri 9am-3pm
Runs clinics in Redland and Westbury Park. Treats adults and children with various conditions, many hormonal. Works to leave the body healed, balanced and healthy.

### Ruth Bolgar MIFR
0117 924 1252
Offers reflexology for pregnancy and for mums at any time. Ring for a friendly and confidential chat. Ruth sees people in a peaceful treatment room in her own home.

## SHIATSU

Practitioners use fingers, palms, elbows, knees and feet to apply pressure to the energy lines, to stimulate the body's energy flow. Treatment can be particularly helpful to pregnant women and children.

### The Shiatsu Society UK
Eastlands Court, St Peters Road, Rugby, CV21 3QP
0845 130 4560
www.shiatsu.org

The governing body for all Shiatsu practioners. Look for the letters MRSS after the name. Provides practitioner listings.

### Bristol School of Shiatsu
4 Brecknock Road, Knowle, BS4 2DD
0117 977 2809
www.shiatsubristol.co.uk
shiatsubss@blueyonder.co.uk

Contact for details of practitioners in the area, registered with the Shiatsu Society UK.

## ANTENATAL HEALTHCARE

Bristol has many services available to women during their pregnancy. The aim of this part of the chapter is to give information on pregnancy rights as well as services. For details of home and hospital births see the Birth subchapter below. For pre-conception advice see our Advice and Support Directory at the back of the book, pg 278.

### Health in Pregnancy

There are many books available about health in pregnancy, which you can find at your local library or book shop. Your midwife and GP will also give you advice on foods to avoid in pregnancy, exercise etc.

Taking regular and appropriate exercise is recommended while pregnant and Bristol has many opportunities for exercise to suit any budgets. See also Time Out for Adults.

Many women will be apprehensive about the birth itself and especially the pain of labour. Parentcraft classes provide a chance to discuss concerns, see Parentcraft below.

**Antenatal Depression:** Experienced by about 10% of women some who will never have been depressed before. The symptoms to look out for are similar to those for postnatal depression (see Postnatal below). If you think you are suffering from antenatal depression, do seek medical advice. It is not only mothers-to-be that suffer from depression but also fathers-to-be.

## MATERNITY RIGHTS

For details about maternity rights, please refer to the Department of Trade and Industry, or the Advisory Conciliation and Arbitration Service (ACAS).

### ACAS
0117 946 9500
www.acas.org.uk

An independent and impartial service to prevent and resolve disputes and to build harmonious relationships at work.

**Department of Trade and Industry**
0870 1502500
www.dti.gov.uk

Information about parental leave and maternity rights. Parental leave is available to employees who have, or expect to have, parental responsibility for a child, and have worked for their current employer for a year.

**Maternity Alliance**
Third Floor West, 2-6 Northburgh Street, London, EC1V 0AY
020 7490 7638
www.maternityalliance.org.uk
info@maternityalliance.org.uk

Supports pregnant women and parents-to-be, working to ensure that all babies have the best possible start in life.

## MIDWIVES

Antenatal care has been designed to help ensure that expectant mothers and their babies remain healthy throughout the duration of the pregnancy. This is most commonly shared between your GP and midwife. In Bristol, there is the opportunity to go with a community or independent midwife for your antenatal care.

Your first midwife appointment is usually between the 8th and 12th weeks of pregnancy. Some women, because of health problems or difficulties with previous pregnancies, may need to see an obstetrician. Your midwife or GP will be able to advise you.

### Community Midwives

Working for the NHS and usually based at your local surgery or clinic. They provide care and advice during pregnancy and for the first ten days after birth. If you are planning a home birth, they will also deliver your baby. Community midwives in Bristol work in teams so you will probably see more than one midwife during your pregnancy.

### Independent Midwives

Qualified, regulated midwives who have chosen to work outside the NHS in a self-employed capacity, whilst still supporting

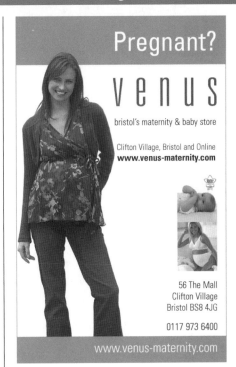

its aims and ideals. They care for women during pregnancy, birth and afterwards and liaise with other healthcare professionals if necessary. In Bristol, bookings are only taken for planned homebirths although, if necessary, midwives can accompany their client into all hospitals. Contact practices for costs.

**Bristol Birth Practice**
0117 9090475; 0117 9245375
www.bristolbirth.co.uk
sally@magic-tree.com, jomtaylor@tiscali.co.uk

Offering a home birth service which includes your own midwife for pregnancy, birth and a month afterwards; informed support and 24 hour emergency contact. Covering Bristol, Bath and surrounding area.

**Sue Learner**
58 Bellevue Crescent, Cliftonwood, BS8 4TF
0117 927 6131
Covering central Bristol and occasionally further out, offering home-based ante-natal birth preparation, intra partum and post natal midwifery care. She has an information leaflet and sometimes gives advice by telephone.

## SCANS & TESTS

In Bristol, any antenatal scans and tests are carried out at St Michael's hospital, Southmead hospital, or the private BUPA hospital (the nuchal translucency scan is only available privately). Your midwife or GP will give you details of the various scans and tests that you may have. At 18-20 weeks an ultrasound scan checks your baby's growth and development and how many babies you are carrying! You may also wish to also ask the sex of the baby. For a small fee you can purchase ultrasound pictures.

### ARC (Antenatal Results and Choices)
020 7631 0285
www.arc-uk.org

Offers information and support throughout antenatal testing and when serious abnormalities are diagnosed.

### BUPA
The Glen, Redland Hill, Durdham Down, Bristol
0117 973 2562

### Southmead Hospital
Southmead Road, Westbury-On-Trym, Bristol
0117 950 5050

### St. Michael's Hospital
St. Michael's Hill, Southwell Street, Bristol
0117 923 0000

## PARENTCRAFT

Antenatal classes are designed to prepare parents for the experience of birth and the task of looking after their new baby. They cover health in pregnancy, coping with labour, birth choices, pre- and postnatal exercises, relaxation techniques, and how to care for and feed your new baby.

These classes provide a chance to meet other parents. Classes may be provided by your midwife or independent practitioners and the NCT. If this is not your first pregnancy, there are refresher courses.

**Need maternity clothes?**
See maternity shops and mail order in Shopping and Services, pg 249

## BIRTH PREPARATION

### NCT antenatal classes
Sarah Baker: 0117 902 3811
www.bristolnct.ik.com
nb007f0808@blueyonder.co.uk

Antenatal classes for all parents-to-be run by the National Childbirth Trust (NCT), a charity that aims to help all parents have a life-enriching experience of pregnancy, birth and early parenting.

### NCT Maternity Sales
www.nctms.co.uk

Sells a range of books for pregnancy, birth, early days and parenthood. Keep an eye out for the well-advertised nearly new NCT sales, where a great deal of good value recyling goes on!

### Independent classes

### Birth-Wise
0117 927 6818
Fri am: Windmill Hill area
Gentle Active Birth yoga, relaxation, tea and discussions. Also offers birth companion/doula and 1:1 birth preparation/postnatal sessions.

### Chris Fielder
Avon Cottage, White Hart Steps, BS8 4TQ
0117 929 4894
Runs a series of birth preparation sessions for women and their partners, see Yoga, below.

### Dominique Ker
0117 968 6030
sakoilsky@msn.com
Offers active birth workshops on Saturdays over 6 weeks. These are for the pregnant woman and her birth attendant or partner, and are based on the work of Janet Balaskas.

### Birthing Awareness
0117 973 3965
www.birthingfromwithin.com
Birth and parenting preparation workshops offering expectant parents and birth partners a holistic and individual approach to pregnancy, birth and parenthood. The workshops offer practice in proven pain-coping strategies, practical information on birth choices, exploration with birth art to

meet your beliefs, fears and hopes, what to expect from parenthood, and a resource and reference pack.

### Vivien Tallis
0117 924 8610
vivientallisyogaplus@fsmail.net
Active birth classes. Held in the Redland area.

### Well Mother
24 Dunkerry Road, Windmill Hill, BS3 4LB
0117 963 2306
www.wellmother.org
suzanneyates@btinternet.com
1:1 sessions of massage and shiatsu for pregnancy and birth. Birth preparation.

## AROMATHERAPY

### Anne Badger, MGCP
0117 963 6557
annebadger@madasafish.com

Offers aromatherapy pregnancy massages and aromatherapy blends for use in labour.

## BIRTHING POOLS & MATERNITY EQUIPMENT

### BORN in water
Born, 64 Gloucester Rd, Bristol, BS7 8BH
0845 130 2676
www.bornshop.org
siu-ming@borndirect.com

All the equipment that you could need to set up your water birth, including pool, floor padding, stool for use in the pool, floatation pillow, birthing ball, and a breastfeeding pillow.

### Natural Babies
11 Bartletts Road, Bedminster, Bristol, BS3 3PL
0117 966 7311
info@naturalbabies.co.uk

A long established company that hires heated pools for birth and relaxation. Prices from £45 per week.

### The Good Birth Company
18 Beauley Rd, Southville, BS3 1PY
0117 966 9119, 07940 874370
www.thegoodbirth.co.uk

An independent agent covering the West Country. Choose from a range of equipment, then delivered to your home. Informative brochure available and friendly service.

### NCT Electric Breast Pump Hire
Fiona Hunter: 0117 962 1176
Helen Gardhouse: 0117 924 8528
NCT helpline: 0870 4448708

The NCT in Bristol have hospital standard, electric breast pumps for hire.

### NCT Valley Cushion Hire
Alison White 966 4148
Liz Moreland 907 6798

The NCT (www.bristolnct.ik.com) have agents who hire valley cushions for use in the first few weeks after birth.

## ObTENS

53 Linden Rd, Westbury Park, BS6 7RW
0117 924 1982
www.obtens.co.uk, obtens@btinternet.com

ObTENS hire out TENS machines for drug-free pain relief during labour. Hire for a six week period around the baby's due date costs £19.

## HYPNOTHERAPY

### Acorn Hypnotherapy

58 The Glebe, Wrington, BS40 5LX
01934 262091
www.acornhypnotherapy.co.uk
lisbet@acornhypnotherapy.co.uk

For pregnancy and birth. Using a holistic approach to address many physical and psychological antenatal and postnatal conditions and experiences, helping both mum and baby. Free initial consultation. Clinics in central Bristol and north Somerset.

### Braybrooke Hypnotherapy

0117 939 3999
www.braybrookehypnosis.co.uk

For natural childbirth, stress, anxiety and depression. Free 20 minute consultation.

### Bristol Hypnotherapy Clinic

The Courtyard, 11A Canford Lane, BS9 3DE
0117 968 6886
www.childbirth-bristol.co.uk
info@childbirth-bristol.co.uk

Using hypnosis in childbirth can allow you to be in control of your mind and body, reducing fear, anxiety and discomfort. During pregnancy, back pain, nausea, hypertension can be reduced. Phobias, ante and postnatal depression are specialties.

## SWIMMING

### Free swimming for pregnant women

Bristol Community Sport
www.bristol-city.gov.uk/sport

To qualify for free swims during pregnancy, you will need to purchase a SportsCard, available from various sports centres. Bring with you your credit card sized NHS Prescription Charge Maternity Exemption Certificate (available via your GP).

## YOGA & PILATES

### Antenatal Yoga Classes with Sally

Summerhill Methodist Church, Air Balloon Rd, St George, Bristol
0780 389 6268
Thu 5.30pm-6.45pm
£36 6 week course

A gentle class for all stages of pregnancy that combines relaxation, stretching and breathing.

### Chris Fielder

Avon Cottage, White Hart Steps, BS8 4TQ
0117 929 4894

Day and evening classes from her home. Birth preparation sessions also available, see above.

### Dominique Ker

c/o Relaxation Centre, All Saints Rd, Clifton
0117 968 6030
sakoilsky@msn.com
£7 per class.

Evening antenatal yoga classes. Advance booking essential.

### Simply Pilates

0117 942 6809, 07980 236948
www.simply-pilates.co.uk
info@simply-pilates.co.uk

Bristol's first fully equipped and dedicated Pilates studio offering equipment and mat classes. Pilates works on the deep core muscles which support the spine and the joints, improving posture and realigning muscles. Helpful during and after pregnancy.

### Vivien Tallis

0117 924 8610
vivientallisyogaplus@fsmail.net

Pregnancy yoga. Held in the Redland area.

# BIRTH HEALTHCARE

Choosing where you give birth should be about what is best for you and your family.

In Bristol, you have the choice of giving birth at home or in hospital. In both instances you will be attended by a midwife. Although birthing in a hospital is still the more common option there have been many moves by the Government to take birth back into the home. This is based on the premise that home birth is as safe as hospital birth for most women.

If you choose to give birth in hospital, there is now the option of either the midwife-led or the consultant-led units at both St. Michael's and Southmead hospitals. If you opt for the midwife-led birthing suite, there is the option of a water birth (although use of it cannot be guaranteed due to demand on the day).

Choices for Bristol should increase in the future, with plans for community birthing centres, see www.birthcentrebristol.org.uk

## HOME BIRTHS

### Bristol Home Birth Group

www.bristolhomebirth.org.uk
Alison White: 0117 966 4148

Offering encouragement, information and support for parents and parents-to-be who would like their children born at home. A range of topics are discussed at meetings, with an experienced midwife and occasional guests to share specific expertise.

## HOSPITAL BIRTHS

### Southmead Hospital
0117 950 5050

### St. Michael's Hospital
St. Michael's Hill, BS2 8EG
0117 923 0000

Both have neonatal intensive care units.

# REGISTERING THE BIRTH

**Registration District: Bristol**
Quakers Friars, BS1 3AR
0117 903 8888
MonTue/Thu/Fri 9am-5pm, Wed 10am-4pm, late nights & Sat by appt only

**Southmead Hospital**
Monks Park Lodge, BS10 5NB
0117 903 8888
Ring for an appt

# POSTNATAL HEALTHCARE

Some women are fortunate, having straightforward births with bodies that bounce back very quickly. However, for some, things are not that straightforward. A difficult birth can leave mothers feeling drained and in discomfort. A new baby, particularly for first time parents, can also induce anxieties. Sometimes just getting out and involved with local parent groups, see Playgroups & Early Education, or taking some time out for yourself, see Time Out for Adults, can help.

**Postnatal Depression:** Affects 10% of women. Symptoms include anxiety/panic attacks, fatigue, feeling low, sleeplessness, and irritability, aches and pains and fears of unknown cause. Your health visitor will use a questionnaire/scale after the birth to detect signs of postnatal depression, but it can occur at any time. It can also occur in fathers. See Advice & Support Directory.

This part of the chapter lists people and places that you can contact for postnatal support, relaxation or other therapy.

# HELP & SUPPORT

### Health visitors

These are nurses, based at local clinics, with training in child development, health education and the social aspects of health. They visit you at home after your baby is ten days' old and stay in touch with you until your child starts school. They advise on all aspects of childcare including feeding, sleeping, crying and behaviour problems. Your health visitor performs your child's developmental checks.

## Breastfeeding Counsellors

If you have difficulties breastfeeding, you can contact your midwife, health visitor or NCT breastfeeding counsellor for help and support.

### NCT Breastfeeding Counsellors

0870 444 8708
www.bristolnct.ik.com,
www.nctpregnancyandbabycare.com

Contact details for local breastfeeding counsellors. Also, see the NCT newsletter (available to members and in Bristol libraries).

## NCT Postnatal Support

08704 448 707
www.bristolnct.ik.com, www.nctpregnancyandbabycare.com

If you are a member of the NCT, a local member will contact you before or soon after your baby is born. It will be mother who knows what is happening locally and will be happy to chat.

# COMPLEMENTARY THERAPIES

## Jill Glover

Alma Vale Centre, 30 Alma Vale Road, Clifton
0117 377 1186

Acupuncture and Chinese herbs for postnatal depression, exhaustion and menstrual difficulties.

# BABY MASSAGE

There are many benefits of baby massage for the baby and the mother, including: strengthening and regulating the digestive, respiratory and circulatory systems; helping to relieve symptoms of colic and gas; relaxation for both carer and baby; encouraging nurturing skills which may help alleviate postnatal depression.

### Anne Badger, MGCP

0117 963 6557
annebadger@madasafish.com
Baby massage classes in Southville and other venues which are open to all including babies with special needs. Anne also offers postnatal aromatherapy massage to mothers.

### Jayne Moffat, CIMI

014546 14390
Baby massage classes in outer NW Bristol: Pill, Almondsbury, Bradley Stoke.

### Katie May, Health Visitor

Woodbine Cottage, Pye Corner, Hambrook, BS16 1SE
01454 776 831
Katie has made a self-instructing baby massage video. Send a cheque for £10 made payable to Katie May.

### Melissa Carter-Taylor, CIMI

01225 859 890
Baby massage covering Bath and Glastonbury.

### Teresa Bultitude, CIMI

0117 949 8428
tbultitude@blueyonder.co.uk
Baby massage in Kingswood, Fishponds, Hanham and outer North East Bristol.

### Victoria Kubiak, CIMI

164 Old Church Rd, Clevedon, BS21 7TU
01275 876688
Baby massage instruction in Bristol areas.

### Well Mother

24 Dunkerry Road, Windmill Hill, BS3 4LB
0117 963 2306
www.wellmother.org
suzanneyates@btinternet.com
Teaching baby massage techniques and/or working directly on your baby as well as baby exercise classes to support development.

# YOGA & RELAXATION

### Dominique Ker

0117 968 6030
sakoilsky@msn.com
Fortnightly yoga for mother and baby.

### Leonie de Mearns

0117 966 3145
babyyoga@gmail.com
Various locations across Bristol, 6 week courses
Gentle postnatal stretches, meditation, baby games, singing and shiatsu massage. A class for both mother and baby (1-6mths).

**Suzanne Yates**
24 Dunkerry Road, Windmill Hill, BS3
0117 963 2306
www.wellmother.org
suzanneyates@btinternet.com
1:1 postnatal yoga, massage and shiatsu.

**Vivien Tallis**
0117 924 8610
vivientallisyogaplus@fsmail.net
Postnatal yoga in Redland.

# CHILD HEALTHCARE

The following section gives a choice of Bristol services, national helplines and charities that are commonly used. It also gives some brief editorial about aspects that cause the most concern and confusion. For any queries not addressed here, please consult the chapter on Advice and Support or your health visitor.

# DEVELOPMENT

For the first five years of your child's life, developmental reviews are held at your local clinic. They focus on your child's growth and development, checking their vision, hearing, speech and movement.

You will be given a Personal Child Health Record, which contains charts used to monitor your child's progress and information about immunisations. This record should be taken to all your child's clinic and hospital visits.

# EYES

Eye checks are carried out during your child's developmental reviews. If there are any problems, they may be referred to an optician or a hospital clinic. Children are eligible for free eye tests at an optician from the ages of 1-16yrs. A list of opticians can be found in the Yellow Pages, from Avonweb or your local PCT (see the start of this chapter).

**Bristol Eye Hospital**
Lower Maudlin Street, BS1 2LY
0117 923 0060
http://www.ubht.nhs.uk/eye

# TEETH

Dentists advise that you should begin brushing your child's teeth as soon as they come through and you should also take them to the dentist regularly for check-ups. All children are entitled to free dental treatment at any NHS dentist, a list can be found in the Yellow Pages (listed under Dental Surgeons), from Avonweb or your local PCT.

**Dental Emergencies:** You should call your own dentist if you need emergency dental care, as they should have an out-of-hours service. If you do not have a dentist, call NHS Direct on 0845 46 47.

**British Dental Association**
www.bda-dentistry.org.uk

**Dental Helpline**
0870 333 1188

**Dentists**
0117 976 6600
www.avon.nhs.uk

# ACCIDENTS

Accidents are the most common cause of death in children. There are many ways to prevent accidents and you can discuss these with your health visitor, or see our list of contacts below.

**Child Accident Prevention Trust**
18-20 Farringdon Lane, London EC1R 3HA
020 7608 3828
www.capt.org.uk

This is a national charity committed to reducing the number of children and young people killed, disabled and seriously injured as a result of accidents.

**St. John's Ambulance**
The Harry Crook Centre, Raleigh Road, Bedminster, Bristol, BS3 1AP
0117 953 3880
www.avon.sja.org.uk
courses@avon.sja.org.uk

St John Ambulance run baby and small

children first aid courses, for groups of 6 to 12 people. They can be run in your own home, place of work or other suitable venue.

**The Royal Society for the Prevention of Accidents**
Birmingham, B5 7ST
0121 248 2000
www.rospa.co.uk

## CHILDREN'S WARDS

If your child needs to go into hospital, they will be admitted to a separate children's ward where they will be looked after by specially trained nurses, doctors and support staff in bright and friendly surroundings. You will be encouraged to stay with your child and take an active part in his or her care and if you wish, to sleep overnight with them.

Each of the hospitals also has play specialists who help to make hospital life as normal as possible, by encouraging children to play as they would at home. They also have specific toys and games, designed to help children understand the treatments they are being given and distractions for some of the more unpleasant procedures that may be carried out such as blood taking.

Older children, who are staying in hospital for long periods, may be disappointed to learn that the hospitals also have school teachers to help them with their studies!

**Bristol Royal Hospital For Children**
Upper Maudlin Street, BS2 8HW
0117 923 0000

**Frenchay Hospital**
Frenchay, BS16 1LE
0117 970 1212

**Southmead Hospital**
Westbury-on-Trym, BS10 5NB
0117 950 5050

## AILMENTS & CONDITIONS

There are many agencies offering information and support on medical conditions, see Advice & Support Directory.

## COT DEATH & MENINGITIS

See Advice & Support for information on both these conditions.

## IMMUNISATION

Immunisation may protect your child against dangerous infectious diseases. They are given at your local clinic. Full details of which immunisations are given and when are written in your Personal Child Health Record. If you have any questions about immunisations, you can discuss them with your health visitor.

## COMPLEMENTARY HEALTHCARE

There are many complementary therapies available to babies and children. See the Complementary Healthcare section at the beginning of this chapter.

## ALLERGY THERAPY

Allergy therapy looks specifically at food and chemicals in relation to health and the development of disease and symptoms. It can help to control and sometimes cure a very large range of common allergic ailments. A few examples include asthma and hyperactivity in children.

### Allergy UK

3 White Oak Sq, London Rd, Swanley, BR8 7AG
Helpline 01322 619 898
Mon-Fri 9am-5pm
www.allergyuk.org
Membership £20

Aims to increase understanding and awareness of allergy. Information, advice and support helping sufferers manage allergies.

### Victoria Kubiak APNT Di ONC

164 Old Church Rd, Clevedon, BS21 7TU
01275 876688

A qualified allergy therapist and nutritional counsellor. Works from Sneyd Park Osteopaths, see above.

# CHILDCARE 0-4 YEARS

**Diana Beavon**

## CONTENTS

## INTRODUCTION

This chapter aims to highlight what paid-for childcare facilities are available for children from just six weeks old up to the time they start their primary education at five years old.

Before considering your options, think carefully about the personality of your child, then chat to other parents for recommendations, do take up references yourself including calling Ofsted and ask lots of questions along the way.

As a mother of two young children, I chose a big, busy nursery for my confident daughter who was rising two, but when it came to my son, I felt he needed more one-to-one care and opted for a childminder.

## Children's Information Service

The Proving House, Servier St, St Werburghs,
Bristol BS2 9LB
0845 129 7217
www.cisbristol.co.uk
enquiries@cisbristol.co.uk
Mon & Fri: 8am-4pm, Tue-Thu: 8am-8pm

This is a good starting point to find out what childcare is offered in your area, including which child minders have vacancies. They are a mine of information, visit their website or give them a call. See advertisement.

### Bath & North East Somerset Family Information Service

Keynsham Town Hall, BS31 1NL
0800 0731214
www.bathnes.gov.uk/fis
fis@bathnes.gov.uk

### CIS North Somerset

Early Years & Childcare Team North Somerset
P.O. Box 51, Town Hall, Weston-super-Mare,
Somerset, BS23 1ZZ
01275 888 778
cis@n-somerset.gov.uk

### CIS South Gloucestershire

Riverside Court, Bowling Hill, Chipping Sodbury,
BS37 6JX
01454 868 666
cis@southglos.gov.uk

## USEFUL WEBSITES

### Daycare Trust

www.daycaretrust.org.uk
This charity website includes helpful information on choosing the right childcare.

### National Day Nurseries Association

www.ndna.org.uk
Charity aiming to enhance the development and education of children in their early years

### Parents Centre

www.parentscentre.gov.uk
Information and support for parents about children's learning, their schooling and childcare options.

### HM Revenue & Customs

www.hmrc.gov.uk
Check your eligibility for receiving Tax Credits and Child Benefits.

## Office for Standards in Education (Ofsted)

www.ofsted.gov.uk
0845 601 4772, Early Years Regional Centre

All nurseries, playgroups, pre-schools, crèches, out-of-school care clubs and childminders come under the jurisdiction of Ofsted who register and inspect facilities. Recent reports can be downloaded from their website, although for security, childminders' names and addresses are withheld, so you will need to ask them for their unique reference. Alternatively contact the CIS or your Ofsted Early Years Regional Centre.

Ofsted will also investigate complaints about the providers and take action to close facilities down if necessary.

# DAY NURSERIES

Open all year round, Monday to Friday, day nurseries provide full-time day care for children from as young as six weeks old up to five years old. They are inspected by Ofsted and must meet national daycare standards and adhere to specific staff-to-child ratios and numbers of qualified staff.

When visiting, find out what a typical day entails and how many other children will be in the room with your child. Also ask what the carer to child ratio is.

Some of the benefits of nurseries is that your child will mix with peers and learn social skills; they will learn to cope with being looked after by different carers with a variety of personalities; they will have access to a wide variety of equipment.

Many day nurseries take children on a part-time basis, some for just a morning a week, which may be useful for those of you looking for some time to yourself. Friday is often a day that part-time working parents don't use their nursery. So you may find a space then.

## CHILDREN'S INFORMATION SERVICE FOR BRISTOL

Registered Charity No: 1053854

Are you looking for childcare?

Would you like to know about different types of childcare and what to look for when choosing childcare?

Would you like information on the Nursery Education Grant or Tax Credits?

### THEN WE CAN HELP!

**We have the answers to all these questions PLUS lots more......**

Call our friendly helpline on 0845 129 7217
8am-4pm Monday & Friday
8am-8pm Tuesday-Thursday

enquiries@cisbristol.co.uk
www.cisbristol.co.uk

# CENTRAL BRISTOL NURSERIES

## BEDMINSTER

### Little Friends Nursery

City of Bristol College, Marksbury Rd, BS3 5JL
0117 312 5419
Mon-Fri: 8am-5.30pm

Accepts children aged 18mths-5yrs.

### South Street Family Unit

British Road, Bedminster, BS3 3AU
0117 903 9941

Part of social services facilities, all children are referred by health visitors. Places allocated by a panel.

## CITY CENTRE

### Buffer Bear Nursery

Clock Tower Yard, Temple Meads, Bristol, BS1 6QH
0117 907 9935
bristol@bufferbear.co.uk
Mon-Fri: 8am-6pm
Underneath British Empire Museum

Friendly nursery providing care and education for children aged 3mths-5yrs. Can offer a short 'school day' from 9.30am-3.30pm and term time only places on a limited basis.

### Redcliffe Early Years Centre

Spencer House, Ship Lane, Redcliffe, BS1 6RR
0117 903 0334
redcliffe_n@bristol-city.gov.uk
Mon-Fri: 8am-6pm

Designated children's centre operating a neighbourhood nursery caring for children, from 6mths-4yrs. Call for an application form.

## CLIFTON

### Amberley Hall

21 Richmond Dale, Clifton, BS8 2UB
0117 974 1550
Mon-Fri: 8am-6pm

Accepts children aged 3mths-5yrs. Qualified teacher, plus teachers for dancing.

### Clifton Tots

8 St Paul's Road, Clifton, Bristol, BS8 1LT
0117 923 7416
Mon-Fri: 8am-6pm

Accepts children aged 3mths up to school age.

### Mornington House Day Nursery

Mornington Road, Clifton, BS8 2UU
0117 973 3414
Mon-Fri: 8am-6pm

Accepts children aged 6wks-5yrs.

## COTHAM

### Archfield House Nursery

2 Archfield Road, Cotham, BS6 6BE
0117 942 2120
www.archfieldhousenursery.co.uk
sue@archfieldnursery.wanadoo.co.uk
Mon-Fri: 8am-6pm

Cares for children from birth-5yrs. Wonderful large garden with pets and summer house. Qualified teacher and visiting french teacher. See advertisement.

### Bristol University Day Nursery

34 St Michael's Park, Kingsdown, Bristol, BS2 8BN
0117 927 6077
www.bris.ac.uk/Depts/Nursery
Mon-Fri: 8.30am-5.30pm

Accepts children aged 3mths-5yrs. Priority given to students and staff of the University.

## ST PAULS

### St Pauls Day Nursery

Little Bishop St, St Pauls, BS2 9JF
0117 377 2278
www.education.bcc.lan/
st_pauls_day_n@bristol-city.gov.uk
Mon-Thu: 9.30am-4pm

State nursery providing sessional daycare for 2-5yr olds. Children referred to a panel through health visitors or social worker.

## SOUTHVILLE

### First Steps Day Nursery

Southville Centre, Beaulieu Road, Bristol, BS3 1QG
0117 953 3043
Mon-Fri: 8am-6pm

Small, friendly relaxed nursery based in a large room at the Southville Centre, with a private outside play area. Flexible session times offered for 1-5yr olds.

# NORTH WEST BRISTOL NURSERIES

## CLEVEDON

### Folly Farm Day Nursery

Clevedon Road, Tickenham, BS21 6RY
01275 854597
Mon-Fri: 8am-6pm

Quality care and pre-school education for 2-5yr olds in a rural setting. Provision for special needs.

**Nursery Head: Mrs Sue Chadwick**
2 ARCHFIELD ROAD, COTHAM, BRISTOL, BS6 6BE
TELEPHONE: 0117 942 2120
www.archfieldhousenursery.co.uk

## WE WELCOME TO OUR NURSERY
### children from 3 months to 5 years

**Our activities include:**
Qualified Teacher for 3-5 year olds; Large Garden; Adventure Playground; Summer House;
Sand Pit; Cooking; Clay; Woodwork; Sand; Painting; Craft; Gardening; Creative Play;
Music; Drama; Stories; Preparation for 'Big School'

### COME AND SEE FOR YOURSELF

---

## HENBURY

### Acorns Nursery

Henbury Hill House, College Park Drive, BS10 7AN
0117 950 5885
www.acornsnurseries.co.uk
Mon-Fri 8am-6pm

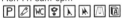

Full and part-time care offered for children,
aged 6wks-5yrs. Located in large house, U1's
are upstairs, while U2's rotate between six
different rooms downstairs.

---

## LAWRENCE WESTON

### Step Ahead Day Nursery

City of Bristol College, Broadlands Drive, BS11 0NT
0117 312 5695
Mon-Thu: 8am-5.00pm, Fri: 8-4.30pm

Takes children aged 2-5yrs from parents
attending college or in local community.

---

## Sansway House Day Nursery

89A Saltmarsh Drive, Lawrence Weston, BS11 0NL
0117 982 9609
kellyclark5@blueyonder.co.uk
Mon-Fri: 7.30am-6.30pm

Affordable and flexible childcare. Can offer
full-time and even occasional care for
children, aged 3mths-11yrs. Separate rooms
for different ages, plus an out-of-school room
for older children. Large garden and indoor
soft play room. See advertisement, pg 193.

---

## SHIREHAMPTON

### Mama Bear's Day Nursery

112-116 Grove Leaze, Shirehampton, BS11 9QU
0117 982 3345
www.mamabear.co.uk
mamabearshire@btconnect.com
Mon-Fri: 7.30am-7pm
Off the A4 Portway, near the Park & Ride

Cares for children aged 3mths-5yrs in a fun, friendly and safe environment where children enjoy learning and make new friends. Nursery school available for 3-4yr olds.

# NORTH BRISTOL NURSERIES

## ASHLEY DOWN

### Ashgrove Park Day Nursey

60 Ashgrove Rd, Ashley Down, BS7 9LQ
0117 951 3123
Mon-Fri: 8.15am-5.45pm

WC ☎ 👶 👶 🔲 📧

Open for children aged 6wks-5yrs, been established since Jan 1990.

### Brunel Nursery

City of Bristol College, Ashley Down, BS7 9BU
0117 312 5126 / 07977 926346
Mon-Fri: 8am-6pm

✎ WC ☎ 👶 👶 🔲 📺 🚌 ♿ 📧

Students on low income or benefit with children aged 3mths-5yrs can apply to the Learner Support Fund. Nursery also has an after school collection from Sefton Park and runs a playscheme in the holidays.

## BISHOPSTON

### Clyde House Day Nursery

1 Nevil Rd, Bishopston, BS7 9EG
0117 924 7488
Mon-Fri: 8.15am-5.45pm

✎ WC ☎ 👶 👶 🔲 📧

Accepts children aged 6wks-5yrs. Established 1988.

## FILTON

### Abbeywood Tots Day Nursery

97 Station Rd, Filton, Bristol
0117 969 3990
Mon-Fri: 7.45am-6pm

P ✎ WC ☎ 👶 👶 🔲 🚌 📧

Accepts children aged 0-5yrs.

### Priory Day Nursery

99 Gloucester Rd North, Bristol, BS34 7PT
0117 969 2503
Mon-Fri: 7.30am-6pm

P ✎ WC ☎ 👶 👶 🔲 📺 🚌

Friendly, safe nursery with caring staff offering learning through play. Takes children aged 6wks-5yrs.

## HENLEAZE

### Toybox

11 The Drive, Henleaze, Bristol, BS9 4LD
0117 962 3010
Mon-Fri: 8am-6pm

👶 👶 🔲 📺 🚌

Homely environment, caring for children aged 3mths-5yrs.

## REDLAND

### Art Raft Piglets Nursery

St Saviours Hall, Woodfield Rd, Redland, BS6 6JQ
0117 904 6358
www.artraft.com
pigletsnursery@artraft.com
Mon-Fri: 8-6pm

👶 👶 📺 🚌 📧

Self-contained day nursery with a strong arts focus for children aged 12mths-5yrs. See adverisment, inside the front cover.

### Hampton Road Day Nursery

118-120 Hampton Rd, Redland, Bristol, BS6 6JD
0117 946 7054
Mon-Fri: 8am-6pm

👶 👶 🔲 📺 🚌

Home from home for babies and children aged 0-5yrs.

## Pooh Corner Day Nursery

46 Lower Redland Rd, Redland, BS6 6ST
0117 946 6178
www.poohcornernursery.co.uk
poohcorner.redland@virgin.net
Mon-Fri: 8am-6pm

Friendly caring environment for 3 mths-5yr olds. Separate floors for under and over 2s. Excellent facilities.

## The Green Door Day Nursery

35 Belvoir Rd, Redland, BS6 5DQ
0117 985 3267
www.greendoornursery.co.uk
greendoornursery@blueyonder.co.uk
Mon-Fri: 8am-5.45pm.

Accepts from birth to 5yrs. Children learn through guided play sessions.

## The Rocking Horse Day Nursery

34 Northumberland Rd, Redland, BS6 7BD
0117 924 0431
www.rockinghorsebristol.co.uk
Mon-Fri: 8am-6pm

Cares from birth to 5yrs. All qualified staff. See advertisement.

## Tin Drum Nursery

32 Redland Grove, Redland, Bristol, BS6 6PR
0117 924 7175
tindrumnur@aol.com
Mon-Fri: 8am-6pm

Warm, caring and happy environment for 0-4yr olds, with separate rooms and activities for different age groups. Helpful staff keen to stimulate and care for the children, always ready to answer questions and give full reports of daily activities. Frequent outings.

## Torwood Lodge Nursery

27-29 Durdham Park, Redland, BS6 6XE
0117 923 8889
www.torwoodhouse.bristol.sch.uk
emailus@torwoodhouse.bristol.sch.uk
Mon-Fri: 8am-6pm

Caring and efficient nursery providing a stimulating environment for children from birth to 2yrs. Older children may continue their care at the adjoining Torwood House School Nursery.

## ST ANDREWS

## Zebedees Day Nursery

26-28 Walsingham Road, St Andrews, BS6 5BT
0117 985 3389
Mon-Fri: 8am-6pm

Friendly nursery open 52 weeks of the year for 3mths-4yr olds, with excellent facilities including soft play and a security system.

Nursery nurses and early years' teacher employed.

# HORFIELD

## Peter Pan Nursery

1 Churchways Crescent, Horfield, BS7 8SW
0117 935 5410
ellen@ppan.fsbusiness.co.uk
Mon-Fri: 8am-6pm

Experienced staff with years of service offering full-time care for children from birth to 5 yrs.

## The Honeytree Day Nursery

c/o Monks Park School, Filton Rd, Horfield, BS7 0XZ
0117 931 4650
Mon-Fri: 8am-6pm

Accepts children from 6wks-5yrs.

# SOUTHMEAD

## Southmead Day Nursery

Doncaster Road, Southmead, Bristol, BS10 5PW
0117 377 2343
southmead_day_n@bristol-city.gov.uk
Mon-Fri: 8am-6pm

Cares for children aged 6mths-4yrs.

# WESTBURY-ON-TRYM

## Lake House Day Nursery

2 Lake Road, Westbury-on-Trym, BS10 5DL
0117 962 2948
Mon-Fri: 8am-5.45pm

Offers full-time care from birth to 5yrs, with Montessori practical life section, French and pre-school group.

## Little Bears at St Ursula's

St Ursula's High School, Brecon Rd, Westbury on Trym, BS9 4DT
0117 962 8812
hglynn@blueyonder.co.uk
Mon-Fri: 8am-6pm

State of the art centre offering pre-school education for children aged 3-4yrs, offering a wide range of actitivities, plus a separate art and design area. Can provide care from 8am until 6pm if required.

## Manor House Day Nursery

145 Southmead Rd, Westbury on Trym, BS10 5DW
0117 962 9620
www.themanorhousenursery.co.uk
Mon-Fri: 8am-6pm

Housed in a large manor house with lots of space, it aims to meet needs of individual children. Facilities include sensory garden and separate craft rooms.

## Once Upon a Time Day Nursery

2&4 Downs Cote Drive, Westbury-on-Trym, BS9 3TP
0117 962 5203
Mon-Fri: 8am-6pm

Cares from 6wks to 5yrs in a home environment with separate room for babies. Each child has their own key worker who stays with them during all activities.

## We Care For Children
### Aged 3 Months - 5 Years
### 8am - 6pm
### Monday to Friday

### Information
### Mary Regan or Sarah Bradley
### 46 Lower Redland Road, Bristol

### 0117 946 6178
### www.poohcornernursery.co.uk

---

### Primary Steps Day Nursery

C/O Next Generation Health Club, Greystoke Avenue,
Bristol, BS10 6AZ
0117 950 2550
www.primarysteps.com
Mon-Fri: 8am- 6pm

Attached to Next Generation Health Club,
offering full-time care from 3mths-5yrs in
three separate rooms. Also acts as club
crèche.

## WESTBURY PARK

### Daisychain Children's Day Nursery

Vining Hall, Etloe Road, Westbury Park, BS6 7PB
0117 970 6828
Mon-Fri: 8am-6pm

For children aged 2-5yrs offering a bright,
cheerful and well-equipped nursery close to
Durdham Downs. Friendly, dedicated, qualified
staff with full-time qualified teacher.

---

### Downs Park Day Nursery

46 Downs Park West, Westbury Park, BS6 7QL
0117 962 8526
Mon-Fri: 8.00am-5.45pm

Cares from birth to 5yrs.

### The Red House Children's Centre

1 Cossins Rd, Westbury Park, BS6 7LY
0117 942 8293
www.redhouse-nursery.org.uk
Mon-Fri: 8am-6pm

Friendly and welcoming. Cares for children
aged 2-5yrs. See advertment.

**Need an afternoon outing?**
There are some great
storytime sessions at your
local library, pg 14

195

# NORTH EAST BRISTOL NURSERIES

## DOWNEND

### Bambinos Day Nursery

63 Downend Rd, Downend, BS16 5UF
0117 330 5300
bambinosdaynursery@hotmail.com
Mon-Fr:i 8.00am-6pm

🅿️ ✏️ 🆆🅲 ♿ 🔲 📖

Accepts children from birth to 5yrs.

## FISHPONDS

### Fledglings Day Nursery

25 Oldbury Court Rd, Fishponds, BS16 2HH
0117 939 3398
Mon-Fri: 8am-5.30pm

✏️ 🆆🅲 ♿ 🔲 📖

Accepts children from birth-5yrs.

### Stepping Stones Day Nursery

1 Hawkesbury Rd, Fishponds, BS16 2AP
0117 965 7269
Mon-Fri: 8am-6pm

✏️ 🆆🅲 ♿ 🔲 📖

Est. 1975 for children 2-5yrs. Stimulating but very cosy environment.

### UWE Students' Union Halley Nursery

St Matthias Campus, College Rd, Fishponds, BS16
0117 328 4452
nursery@uwe.ac.uk
Mon-Fri: 8.30am-5.30pm

🅿️ ✏️ 🆆🅲 ♿ 🔲 📖

Accepts children from 6mths-5yrs, priority given to students of UWE, can accept children from the community.

## HAMBROOK

### Barn Owl Nursery

Old Gloucester Rd, Hambrook, BS16 1RS
0117 956 2222
Mon-Fri: 8am-6pm

🅿️ ♿ 🔲 📖

Small village nursery, with experienced staff, catering for children aged 2-5yrs.

# EAST BRISTOL NURSERIES

## EASTON

### Easton Community Children's Centre

Russell Town Ave, Bristol, BS5 9JF
0117 939 2550
easton_childrens_centre@yahoo.co.uk
Mon-Fri: 8am-6pm

Centre offers day care facility for children 6mths-5yrs.

### Little Haven Day Nursery

261 Crews Hole Rd, St George, Bristol, BS5 8BE
0117 941 4484
Mon- Fri: 8am-6pm

🅿️ ✏️ 🆆🅲 ♿ 🔲 📖

Friendly pre-school nursery with baby unit. Excellent facilities with full-day and half-day sessions.

### Redroofs Nursery

227 Kingsway, St George, BS5 8AH
0117 949 2600
www.redroofsnursery.co.uk
Mon-Fri: 8am-5.30pm

✏️ 🆆🅲 ♿ 🔲 📖

Personal profiles are kept by key workers who are all nursery nurses. During summer months children, have access to swimming pool.

## EMERSONS GREEN

### Leapfrog Day Nursery

St Lukes Close, Emersons Green, BS16 7AL
0117 956 8222
www.leapfrogdaynurseries.co.uk
Mon-Fri: 7am-7pm

Accepts children aged 0-5yrs.

## HANHAM

### Tiny Tots Day Nursery

130 High St, Hanham, BS15 3EJ
0117 947 5436
Mon-Fri: 7.30am-6pm

Full and part-time day care for 0-8yr olds, including holiday club and before and after school care.

## KINGSWOOD

### Hillside Day Nursery

Potterswood, Britannia Rd, Kingswood, BS15 8DB
0117 960 4330
www.hillsidedaynursery.co.uk
Mon-Fri: 8am-6pm

Family-run nursery caring for 0-5yrs, 10% discount for siblings.

### Kingswood Foundation Nursery

43 Britannia Rd, Kingswood, Bristol, BS15 8DB
0117 935 2222
www.kfdn.co.uk, info@kfdn.co.uk
Mon-Fri: 8am-5.30pm (6pm on request)

Day nursery accepts children aged 6wks-5yrs. Part of Kingswood Gymnastics and Trampolining Centre, giving children access to all facilities. Staff will also take children on walks or swimming lessons, with parental authority.

## STOKE GIFFORD

### Leapfrog Day Nursery

Hunts Ground Rd, Stoke Gifford, BS34 8HN
0117 979 9977
Mon-Fri: 7.30am-6pm

Accepts children aged 3mths-5yrs.

## WARMLEY

### Redroofs Nursery

24 Poplar Rd, North Common, Warmley, BS30 5JU
0117 949 2700
Mon-Fri: 8am-5.30pm

Accepts children from 0-5yrs. During summer months, children can enjoy swimming lessons.

## The Rocking Horse Day Nursery

Grange School, Tower Rd North, Warmley, BS30 8XQ
0117 947 6218
www.rockinghorsebristol.co.uk
Mon-Fri: 7.30am-6pm.

Cares for children aged 6wks-5yrs. All qualified staff. See advertisement.

# SOUTH EAST BRISTOL NURSERIES

## BRISLINGTON

### Abacus Day Nursery

6-8 Emery Rd, Brislington, BS4 5PF
0117 977 2868
Mon-Fri: 8am-6pm

Accepts children aged 3mths-5yrs.

### Mama Bear's Day Nursery

216 Allison Rd, Brislington, BS4 4NZ
0117 972 8234
www.mamabear.co.uk
mamabearbriz@btconnect.com
Mon-Fri: 7.30am-7.00pm

Cares for children aged 3 mths-5yrs in a fun, friendly and safe environment where children enjoy learning and make new friends. Nursery school available for 3-4yr olds.

## KNOWLE

### Busy Bee Day Nursery

268 Wells Rd, Knowle, BS4 2PN
0117 977 5357
busy-bee@btconnect.com
Mon-Fri: 8am-5.30pm

Accepts children aged 6mths-5yrs with a separate pre-school section. Access to pets, creative activities, plus visits to library and themed activities.

### Court House Day Nursey

270 Wells Rd, Knowle, BS4 2PU
0117 977 2210
Mon-Fri: 7.30am-6pm

Cheerful nursery for 6wks-5yrs with a high staff ratio & well planned curriculum.

### Knowle West Early Years Centre

Leinster Avenue, Knowle, Bristol, BS4 1NN
0117 903 0214

Full-time day care offered by referal for children, aged 2-3yrs.

# SOUTH BRISTOL NURSERIES

## Four Acres Children's Centre

c/o Four Acres Primary School, Withywood, BS13
0117 903 0460
four_acres_day_n@bristol-city.gov.uk
Mon-Fri: 8am-6pm

Full day care facilities for children from birth to 3yrs.

## DAY NURSERY SCHOOL

### *Providing excellent care and early education*

Our philosophy at The Rocking Horse Day Nursery is to enhance each child's curiosity, motivation and independence through sensitive support of qualified and experienced early years practitioners and to ensure all children feel included, secure and valued. We embrace active learning through play both indoors and outdoors.

Each nursery has received very good grades during OFSTED inspections. Please view the OFSTED website at www.ofsted.gov.uk/reports

For further information please ring the nearest nursery and arrange a visit.

We are at:

- **34 Northumberland Road, Redland, Bristol, BS6 7BD ☎ 0117 9240431**
- **C/O The Grange School, Tower Road North, Warmley, BS30 8XQ ☎ 0117 9476218**

## Mama Bear's Day Nursery

Hengrove Community Arts College, Petherton Rd,
Hengrove, BS14 9BU
01275 891 316
www.mamabear.co.uk
mamabearhengrove@btconnect.com
Mon-Fri: 7.30am-7pm

Cares for children aged 3mths-5yrs in a fun, friendly and safe environment where children enjoy learning and make new friends. Nursery school available for 3-4yr olds.

## SOUTH WEST BRISTOL

### Asquith Court Nursery

C/O David Lloyd Tennis Club, Ashton Rd, BS3 2HB
0117 953 2830
Mon-Fri: 8am-6pm

Full day care offered for children aged 3mths-5yrs in a safe, stimulating environment. Also able to offer a pre-school curriculum.

### Teddies Nursery

Clanage Road, Bower Ashton, Bristol, BS3 2JX
0117 953 1246
www.teddiesnurseries.co.uk
Mon-Fri: 8am-6pm

Part of the BUPA Group, Teddies accepts children from 3mths-5yrs, offering nurtured play and learning activities to help develop confidence and social skills.

## CHILDMINDERS

A childminder is someone who is not a relative of the child and is registered by Social Services to look after children in their home. Registration includes a criminal records check of all persons involved (and anyone else living with them) and inspection of the premises to look at health and safety and educational welfare issues. Following registration, childminders are inspected by Ofsted.

Contracts are usually signed setting out the hours, fees, food costs and so on. Ensure you check their references.

**Advantages:**

- Your child sees the same carer each time in a relaxed home-from-home setting
- Often the most economical form of childcare at £3-5/hr per child with no tax and national insurance to pay
- May accommodate irregular, part-time or unsociable hours
- May pick up children from school or pre-school.

**Disadvantages:**

- Alternative cover will need to be arranged if your child or the childminder is ill or on holiday
- Your child's routine is determined by the childminder
- Your child may be the only one there at times

### National Childminding Association

Royal Court, 81 Tweedie Road, Bromley, BR1 1TG
020 8290 2410/ 0800 1694486
www.ncma.org.uk
info@ncma.org.uk

The NCMA offers a free guide called Choosing a Home Childcarer, quote CHC1, with a SAE.

## NANNIES

A nanny is someone who cares for your child in your home with their undivided attention. Most hold an appropriate childcare qualification, such as an NNEB, B-Tec or NVQ3. The best way to find a good nanny is to use one of the agencies listed.

You may find that it is possible to share a nanny if you only want a limited number of days. Nannies cannot be self employed so you will need to sort out your Nanny's tax and national insurance; there are some companies that can do this for you for a fee.

**Advantages:**

- They come to you, providing care when you need it to suit your needs
- Children are still cared for when ill
- Constant individual care provided in the comfort of your own home
- Nannies should do everything to do with the children e.g. sort out laundry, prepare meals, clean and tidy their bedroom
- Cost effective if care required for more than one child.

**Disadvantages:**

- They are not subject to the requirements of The Children Act 1989 so are not registered or police checked. Nanny agencies will vet candidates although it is the parent's responsibility to research and check a nanny's background and references
- Can be quite expensive at £6.50-8.50 per hr+ if required full-time for one child
- You will pay 4 weeks holiday and some parents make up wages on top of statutory sick pay.

# Alphabet Childcare

For the very best Permanent or Temporary Nannies, Nursery Nurses and Babysitters. Providing the quality care children deserve.

0117 9591161 - www.alphabet-childcare.co.uk
Email: alphabet@btconnect.com

## MOTHERS' HELPS

Usually assisting parents at home, they are not normally trained in childcare although they may have lots of experience and have completed relevant courses/first aid. Costs range from £5-£7.50/hr, they can work full or part-time, living in or out.

**Advantages:**

- Flexible helping hand with children and light housework
- Ideal part-time option if children at school
- Most nanny agencies have mother's helps on their books.

**Disadvantages:**

- Often unqualified therefore should not be left in sole charge of young children
- As an employer you will have to sort out their tax and NI contributions

### City of Bristol College

Room 5E5, College Green Centre, Saint Georges Rd, Bristol, BS1 5UA
0117 312 5278

Family placements needed for students on childcare courses. Families need to have a baby under 1yrs and students must be supervised. Families need public liability insurance. Police checks will be carried out.

## CHILDCARE AGENCIES

### Alphabet Childcare

46b High St, Westbury-on-Trym, BS9 3DZ
0117 959 1161
alphabet-childcare.co.uk
alphabet@btconnect.com

Long-established agency with a register of nannies, nursery nurses and babysitters. See advertisement above.

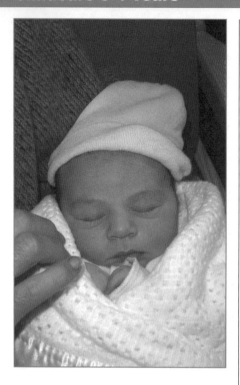

## Bristol Nannies

29 Royal Victoria Park, Bristol, BS10 6TD
0117 950 5526
dina.hartnolll@btopenworld.com

Specialists in finding the most appropriate, quality childcare.

## Clifton Nannies

Saville Place, Saville Court, Clifton, Bristol, BS8 4EJ
0845 0039495
www.cliftonnannies.co.uk
enquiries@cliftonnannies.co.uk

Able to find experienced childcare for temporary or permanent positions, including after school cover and babysitting.

## Park Lane Nannies

51 Knowleworth Crescent, Bristol, BS16 6RZ
0117 373 0003
www.parklanenannies.com
jo@parklanenannies.com

Established 1988, able to provide a variety of help from nannies to housekeepers and maternity nurses.

## Star Nannies

67 Sheldons Court, Winchcombe St, Cheltenham, GL52 2NN
01242 512 636
www.starnannies.co.uk
tracey@starnannies.co.uk

Agency placing nannies and maternity nurses throughout the UK and overseas.

## MATERNITY NURSES

Usually employed just before and immediately after you have a baby to care exclusively for the newborn. May be a qualified nanny with experience with young babies, a qualified nurse, midwife or health visitor. Usually working on a short-term contract (from 2wks-6mths) living with the family. Maternity nurses are frequently in short supply therefore start looking early to book them up.

**Advantages:**

- On call 24 hours a day up to 6 days a week

- Help with all aspects of baby's care, even during the night

- Sleeping and feeding routines encouraged

- They are self-employed so you don't need to arrange their tax and national insurance.

**Doulas**

Doula, pronounced doola, is a Greek word meaning "woman servant or caregiver". They will come before the birth and can even be on hand to give moral support at the birth if you need it. They are often just experienced women who will look after the whole family including doing household duties and caring for any children. Most doulas are self-employed and will offer a few hours a day as is needed, for between £9-10 per hour.

### Agencies Providing Maternity Nurses

**Alphabet Childcare**
46b High Street, Westbury-on-Trym, BS9 3DZ
0117 959 1161
www.alphabet-childcare.co.uk

**Park Lane Nannies**
51 Knowleworth Crescent, Bristol, BS15 6RZ
0117 373 0003
www.parklanenannies.com

# EMERGENCY COVER

What happens when your carefully arranged childcare provision falls apart due to the illness of your child, or perhaps the nanny or childminder?

Employment agencies for nannies and nursery nurses can provide temporary carers at short notice. A good agency will be able to provide you with details of their background, training, experiences and references at short notice. See details of agencies above or try the local telephone directory.

# NANNY TAX AND NI

### Nannytax

PO Box 988, Brighton, BN1 1NT
0845 2262203
www.nannytax.co.uk

Nannytax is the original and inexpensive countrywide payroll service, designed to look after your nanny's tax and national insurance contributions.

### The Alphabet Childcare Tax & NI

46b High Street, Westbury on Trym, Bristol, BS9 3DZ
0117 959 1161
alphabet@btconnect.com

Free advice to nannies, service can also set up pay and deduction records for employers for an annual fee.

# AU PAIRS

Aged 18-27yrs, an au pair is not qualified to look after children since they have come to study in this country. They should help around the house and assist with children for up to 5hrs a day over five days, for an allowance (average £50 pw), plus two evening's babysitting.

You should expect to enrol them in a class and will need to negotiate whether you will pay for their study. There are regulations laid down by the Home Office about appointing an au pair. Those from the EU do not need a work permit and have no time limit whilst restrictions apply to those outside the EU and they have to be formally invited by the host family.

**Advantages:**

- Helping hand with children and light housework

- Flexible hours to suit you such as after school and evenings

- Older children enjoy learning about the au pair's language and culture.

**Disadvantages:**

- Unlikely to meet them beforehand

- Unqualified therefore should not have sole charge of young children

- May not be able to speak good English or have a driver's licence

- Living with you as part of the family may encroach on your space.

### International Placement Agency (IPA)

10 Marlborough St, Bath, BA1 2TX
01225 481973
www.ipa-aupairs.co.uk
enquiries@ipa-aupairs.co.uk

Established and managed by Sandrine Picquart who has 11yrs of expertise with au pair and nanny placements.

## The Au Pair Answer

27 Oakfield Road, Clifton, BS8 2AT
0117 974 4779
www.languageproject.co.uk
aupuair@languageproject.co.uk

Specialists in au pairs placed throughout the UK both long and short term (from 2+mths).

# BABYSITTERS

Having time to yourself in the evenings is important, but it can be difficult finding someone you can trust to look after your children. Expect to pay from £5 per hour for their services. Ideally a babysitter should be over 15yrs old and you should check what experience they have with children, or if they have any childcare training. Also check references. The agencies below can help or try advertising at local colleges for student nannies or at local nurseries for nursery nurses.

## Alphabet Childcare

46b High Street, Westbury-on-Trym, BS9 3DZ
0117 959 1161
alphabet-childcare.co.uk

## Bristol Babysitting Agency

2 Medway Court, Thornbury, BS35 2hl
01454 853523

Evening babysitting within Bristol and surrounding areas on an ad hoc basis.

## Featherbed Homecare Ltd

Buckingham Lodge, Station Rd, Keynsham, BS31
0117 986 0710

Able to provide ad hoc babysitting services.

## Time to Share

Unit 55, Easton Business Centre, Felix Rd, BS5 0HE
0117 941 5868
www.time2share.org.uk
info@time2share.org.uk

For children with learning difficulties, this organisation provides sitters and caters for individual needs. Families are matched on a one-to-one basis with a volunteer.

# CRÈCHES

Crèches are available all over the region in shopping centres, colleges and leisure centres. See Shopping, Time Out for Adults and Leisure Centre tables to find a crèche near you. Most will require you to be on the premises.

# MOBILE CRÈCHES

Crèches with qualified staff and appropriate equipment can be hired for short periods of time to look after a set number of children during a special occasion such as a wedding or company fun day.

The following listings provide a mobile creche facility.

## Easton Community Children's Centre

Russell Town Ave, Bristol, BS5 9JF
0117 939 2550
easton_childrens_centre@yahoo.co.uk

Centre can provide an on-site crèche facility for individuals or organisations, alternatively, carers can be sought for a mobile crèche at any location, day or night. Call to confirm costings.

## ABC Childcare Crew

46b High Street, Westbury-on-Trym, BS9 3DZ
0117 959 1161
www.abcchildcarecrew.co.uk
info@abcchildcarecrew.co.uk

# PLAYGROUPS & EARLY EDUCATION 0-4 YEARS

**Alex Reed**

## CONTENTS

## INTRODUCTION

Attending toddler groups and pre-schools is a great way to meet other parents, but it's also a vital part of your child's social development and education. This chapter looks at weekly groups held specifically for children prior to pre-school. It then highlights the various options available before your child heads off to primary school at five. For other pre-school advice and ideas, contact the excellent organisations below or see our chapter on Activities 0-12 Years.

### Children's Information Service

Unit 40, Easton Business Centre, Felix Rd, Easton, BS5 0HE
0845 129 7217
www.cisbristol.co.uk
enquiries@cisbristol.co.uk

Provides free, impartial and confidential information or guidance on a full range of childcare, children's services and resources in Bristol. "A font of all knowledge!"

### CIS North Somerset

Early Years & Childcare Team North Somerset
P.O. Box 51, Town Hall, Weston-Super-Mare,
Somerset, BS23 1ZZ
01275 888 778
cis@n-somerset.gov.uk

### CIS South Gloucestershire

Riverside Court, Bowling Hill, Chipping Sodbury,
BS37 6JX
01454 868 666
cis@southglos.gov.uk

## Sure Start

www.surestart.gov.uk

Sure Start is a government initiative working with parents and children to promote the development of pre-schoolers, particularly those disadvantaged, to ensure they are ready to thrive when they get to school. Over the coming years, the original Sure Start local programmes will be replaced by Childrens Centre's with the broader premise of offering day care and focusing on health and education needs.

There are currently four main centres in Bristol, all of which were formally Sure Start programmes.

### Footprints Children's Centre

0117 903 9781

### Seamills Children's Centre

0117 968 8970

### Four Acres Children's Centre

0117 903 0460

### Children's Centre at Bannerman Rd School

0117 377 2080

The aim is to open more centres, in many different areas of Bristol, over the next 10 years. As this is an evolving scheme, it is worth checking the details on their website or contacting The Children's Information Service above.

**Are you working part-time and need childcare at home?**
Find out about the alternatives on pgs 200-204.

## GROUPS FOR BABIES

For a new mum, it can be really helpful to discuss the highs and lows of having a baby with others in the same situation. Most health visitors run postnatal groups where you can go and chat to other mums, get your baby weighed and air any concerns.

### NCT Open Houses

31 Walsingham Rd, St Andrews, Bristol
0117 942 2067
janet.bremner@btinternet.com

The National Childbirth Trust (NCT) offers a way of meeting other parents and their children through open houses. Parents open their house (providing a drink and biscuit) for parents and their babies/children. Details are published in the quarterly NCT Bristol newsletter.

Open houses are a useful way of meeting other parents, especially if you are new to the area and can provide social contact through the baby and pre-school years. You do not have to be a member of the NCT to attend.

## TODDLER GROUPS

We have listed all the toddler groups by the day the group meets each week. A quick glance at their name or address will let you know if it is local to you. If you are unable to find a group in your area, keep an eye on noticeboards in libraries, churches and doctors surgeries where they might be advertised, or call the CIS, see above. Let us know if you find one that should be listed here.

Toddler groups are held during school terms and are for children under 4yrs. They are a good way for parents to meet up informally and for your child to socialise and try new skills under your supervision.

There is usually a quiet area for baby siblings. Most groups charge a small fee for a drink and a biscuit.

# DAILY PLAYGROUPS

## Bristol Children's Playhouse

Berkeley Green Rd, Eastville, BS5 6LU
Jackie Cutmore: 0117 951 0037
Mon-Fri 9am-3.15pm
£15 membership per year

Informal drop-in for parents/carers open to all, every day, with extensive play equipment and playgrounds outside. Friendly, qualified, welcoming staff. Summer trips organised.

## Rowan Tree Kindergarten Parent and Toddler Group

12d Cotham Rd, Cotham, BS6 6DR
Winny Mossman: 0117 933 9990
Mon-Fri 9.30-12.15
£4 per session paid half-termly in advance

Part of Bristol Steiner Waldorf School's Kindergarten, sessions are held for parents and toddlers in homely surroundings with natural play materials. Sessions include crafts, break time and circle time.

## Sydenham Road Under Fives Toddlers

Totterdown Baptist Church, Syndenham Rd, Totterdown, BS4 3DF
Wendy McCarthy: 0117 977 3246
Mon-Fri 9.45am-11.30am
£2.20, additional siblings £1

Toddle Up for children aged 2-3yrs. Refreshments included. Parent pack available.

# MONDAY

## Ashton Vale Toddlers

Ashton Vale Community Centre, Risdale Rd, BS3 2QY
Lindsey Hickery: 0117 963 9283
Mon 9.30am-11.30am
£2 per family, includes refreshments

Drop-in session for children aged 0-4yrs. Spacious, friendly environment, lots of toys to enjoy and a different craft activity each week.

## Barton Hill Family Playcentre

Barton Hill Settlement, 43 Ducie Road, BS5 0AX
Vadna Chauhan: 0117 955 6971
Mon 9.15-11.45am, £1

Structured group for pre-school children with art activity, construction toys, home/fantasy corner, sand & water play. Separate soft play area for babies. Dads welcome.

## Cairns Rd Café with toddler zone

Cairns Rd Baptist Church, Cairns Rd, BS6 7TH
0117 9425 669 (Church Office)
Mon/Wed/Fri 9am-2pm, reduced hours in holidays

Free, fun soft play in large hall. Plenty of toys and a café with drinks and food, excellent toddler lunches for £1. Can be crowded but no booking required.

## Cotham Drop-in Playcentre

Cotham Parish Church, Cotham Road, BS6 6DP
Drew Esam: 0117 974 1152
Mon 1.30-3.30pm
£1 per family

Suitable from birth up to pre-school. Two halls, one for older and more mobile children. Sing song to finish. Refreshments included.

## Filton Avenue Nursery School

Blakeney Road, Horfield, Bristol, BS7 0DL
Maureen Clifford: 0117 377 2680
Mon 9am-11.30am

Free drop-in sessions for parents/carers with strong walkers up to 3yrs.

## Fulford Family Centre

237-239 Gatehouse Ave, Withywood, BS13 9AQ
Jenny Lewis: 0117 978 2441
Mon 9.30am-11.30am

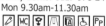

Free drop-in sessions for U5's for parents/carers living in the Hartcliffe, Bishopworth and Withywood areas. Crèche also provided.

## Gay Elms Sure Start

Gay Elms Primary School, Withywood Rd, BS13 9AX
0117 377 2818
Mon 1pm-2.45pm
30p, includes refreshments

Tiny Tots informal drop-in for 0-2yr olds.

## Highridge Sure Start

Lakemead Grove, Highridge, Bristol, BS13 8EA
Faye Morgan: 0117 978 1028
Mon 9.30am-11.30
50p, includes breakfast

Informal baby breakfast run for 0-2yr olds.

## Mothercare Toddler Art & Craft Group

Mothercare World, Eastgate Centre, BS5 6X2
Stephanie Jordan: 07753 270 089
Mon 10am-11.30am
£1 per child

Art and craft session so an opportunity to make a mess away from home! Meeting in the café where mums can relax with a drink. Toddlers are provided with juice and biscuit.

## Parkway Parent and Child Project

Parkway Methodist Church, Conduit Place, St Werburghs, BS2 9RU
Sue Dowd: 0117 935 0205
Mon 9.30am-12pm
£1 per family

Drop-in sessions run throughout the year. Safe and stimulating environment with separate area for older children to ride bikes.

## Rainbow Tots

Kensington Baptist Church Hall, Seymour Rd, Easton
Amanda Pearce: 0117 955 7768
Mon 10am -12pm, 60p

Friendly church-run group meets three times a week for 0-4yr olds. Offers a craft activity every week, lots of toys plus baby area.

## Southmead Day Nursery

Doncaster Road, Southmead, Bristol, BS10 5PW
Liz Harper: 0117 377 2343
Mon 9.15am-11.15am

Free, informal drop-in sessions for children aged 0-4yrs. Parents can use the library or attend family learning activities, while children use the Sensory Room and outdoor play area.

## St Josephs Toddlers

St Josephs Church Hall, Forest Rd, Fishponds, BS16
Cathy Williamson: 0117 914 7173
Mon 1.45pm-3.15pm
£1 (second child 50p), annual sub £2

Variety of toys and activities, including baby area for children up to 4yrs.

## St Mary's Mother & Toddler Group

St Mary's Magdalene Church Hall, Mariners Drive Stoke Bishop, Bristol
Jenny Williams: 0117 968 3892
Mon 1.30pm-3.30pm
£1.50 per family

Informal drop-in group aimed at toddlers. Welcomes 0-4yr olds. Creative activity, lots of toys and separate baby play area.

## St Peter's Parent & Toddler Group

St Peter's Church Hall, The Drive, Henleaze, BS9 4LD
Parish Office: 0117 962 3196
Mon 10am-12pm
50p per family per session

P ✐ WC ♨ ⟨ ⟩ Pp

Children from bumps to nursery age, meets twice a week. Parents, grandparents, nannies are welcome to join. Action songs at the end.

## Stepping Stones Toddlers

Salem Chapel, Trafalger Terrace, Bedminster Down
Karen Davis: 0117 985 4819
Mon 9.30-11.00am
£1 per family
Entrance to Chapel on Hardy Road

P ✐ WC ⟨ ⟩ Pp

A chance to meet other mums and toddlers. Lots of toys with soft play area. All welcome.

## Tots Time, Brislington

St Christopher's Hall, Hampstead Rd, BS4 3H
Alison Paginton: 0117 977 2016
Mon 9.30am-11.30am

P ✐ WC ⟨ ⟩ 🖼

Popular group for children aged 0-3yrs. Lots of craft activity tables, dressing-up and books. Refreshments served mid-morning, followed by singing and then ride-on toys, trucks and parachute fun. Please ring for place.

## Trinity Tots ABC Club

Holy Trinity Church, Hotwells Rd, BS8 4ST
Sally Forster: 0117 929 3951
Mon 9.30-11.30am
£1 per child with max of £2 for family

✐ WC ⟨ ⟩ 🖼 Pp

Drop-in friendly group for pre-school children offering variety of toys and music for all ages. Healthy snacks for children and adults.

## Tyndale Baptist Church Baby & Toddler Group

Tyndale Baptist Church, Whiteladies Rd, Clifton, BS8
Denise Lewis: 0117 968 6752
Mon 2-3.30pm (term time only), £1

P ✐ WC ⟨

Caters for children aged 0-4yrs.

## Victoria Park Toddlers

Victoria Park Baptist Church, St Johns Lane, Bedminster
Brendan Bassett: 0117 373 0477
Mon 9.30-11.30am
£1 for one child, £1.50 for two or more

✐ WC 🕐 ⟨ Pp

Drop-in group for 0-4yr olds, with U1's area. Variety of toys, craft activities and sand. Fathers regularly attend.

# TUESDAY

## Bib Club

Clifton Health Clinic, Mortimer Road, BS8 4EX
0117 973 5425
Tue 10.30am-12pm

✐ WC ⟨ Pp

Free drop-in facility for first time mums with babies under 6mths to meet for a chat. Organised by clinic health visitors.

## Counterslip Baptist Church

648 Wells Road, Whitchurch, Bristol, BS14 9HT
Jane Wood: 01275 833 377
Tue 10am-11.30am
£1, additional child 50p

P ✐ WC ⟨ 🏠 ⟨ 🖼 Pp

Parent and toddler group held in a large carpeted area with wide variety of toys appropriate to age range. Small waiting list, please phone before coming.

## Downend Baptist Church Toddlers

Salisbury Road, Downend, Bristol, BS16
Rachel Baker: 0117 956 1374
Tue/Wed/Thu 10-11.30am & Wed 1.30-3pm
£10 per term and £3 for siblings over 6mths

✐ WC ⟨ ⟩ 🖼 Pp

Sessions for 0-5yr olds. Large variety of toys, weekly activity for older children, plus song time and refreshments. Phone before attending.

## Ebenezer Parent, Baby & Toddler Group

Ebenezer Methodist Church Hall, British Rd,
Bedminster, BS3 3BW
Patricia Jorgensen: 0117 975 5518
Tue 1.30pm-3.30pm
£1.20 per family, includes refreshments

P ✐ WC 👤 👣 ♿

A long-established, very friendly group for parents with children aged 2wks-3yrs. There are plenty of toys and jigsaws along with an activity table for drawing, play dough and collage. Fathers and grandparents regularly attend. Summer outing and Christmas tea.

## Emmanuel Toddler Group

Emmanuel Chapel, Satchfield Cres, Henbury, BS10
Jayne Crocker: 0117 950 1951
Tue 9.15am-11.15am, £1.50

P ✐ WC 👤 👣 🅰 🚼 Pp

Meets once a week. Large range of toys including ball pool tent, book corner, play kitchen area, bikes, trikes and baby toys. Regular craft and singing. Quiet space in one room. Newcomers welcomed.

## Horfield Methodist Church Toddler Group

Horfield Methodist Church, Churchways Ave, BS7
Lyn Hughes: 0117 985 3940
Tue 9.30am-11.30am
£1, £1.50 2+ children
At entrance press 5 on entry panel

✐ WC 👤 👣 ♿

Informal drop-in for parents and carers with children aged 0-3yrs. Free play and singing.

## Jumping Beans

St Francis Church, North Street (opposite Aldi)
Sue Bryant: 0117 963 5053
Tue 9.15am-11.15am
£2 per session

P ✐ WC 👶 👤 👣 Pp

Weekly group for childminders and their children.

## Little Angels Parents & Toddler Group

6 Ashley Road, St Pauls, BS6 5NL
Tracey Mountsford: 0117 942 4607
Tue 9.30am-12pm, 50p

✐ WC 👤 👣

Small group meets three times a week, with space for 12-15 children, offering a variety of educational toys, trikes, tunnel, slide, dolls and prams. Fathers welcome.

## Long Ashton Toddler Group

Long Ashton Village Hall, Keedwell Hill, Long Ashton
Sarah Leong: sarah@4mmaw.freeserve.co.uk
Tue 1.30pm-3.30pm
£1, additional child 60p

✐ WC 👤 👣 🅰 🚼

Informal group held in Village Hall. Separate baby section and craft tables for toddlers. Entry includes light refreshments.

## Noah's Ark Stay & Play

Cairns Rd Baptist Church, Cairns Road, BS6 7TH
Carol de-Beger: 0117 944 6229
Tue 9.45am-11.45am (except 1st Tue of month)
£1 per session

P WC 🖽 Pp

Group for children aged 2-3yrs, plus their carer. Offers a Bible story craft activity and story. Numbers limited, please call for a place.

## Philip Street Chapel Toddlers

Philip Street, Bedminster, BS3 4EA
Debbie Loosley: 0117 953 9530
Tue 10am-11.30am
£1.30 per family
Entrance on Clarke St

P ✐ WC 👤 👣

Well-equipped friendly group in large carpeted hall. Welcoming to newcomers.

## Queen's Road Methodist Baby & Toddler Group

Queen's Road, Keynsham, BS31 2NN
Mrs Meath: 0117 987 7753
Tue 1.15pm-2.45pm
75p for one child, £1 for two

P ✐ WC 👶 👤 👣 🔔 🅰 Pp

Organised group for children aged 0-5yrs and their carers. Craft activity and lots of toys. Please call for a place.

## Rainbow Tots

Kensington Baptist Church Hall, Seymour Rd, Easton
Amanda Pearce: 0117 955 7768
Tue 10am-12 noon, 60p
⟦✐⟧⟦WC⟧⟦🚹⟧⟦🅰⟧⟦Pp⟧

Friendly church-run group meets three times a week for 0-4yr olds. Offers a craft activity every week, lots of toys plus baby area.

## Redland Toddlers

Redland Parish Church Hall, Redland Green Rd, BS6
Church Secretary: 0117 946 4690
Tue 10am-11.30am, £1
⟦✐⟧⟦WC⟧⟦🚹⟧⟦🚼⟧

Spacious hall with good variety of toys and separate carpeted room for babies. Weekly craft activity and singing. Friendly and welcoming group. Dads, Mums and carers attend. Refreshments included.

## St Mathews Church Toddler Group

Clare Road, Cotham, BS6 5TB
Sue Last: 0117 944 1598
Tue 10am-11.30am
⟦P⟧⟦✐⟧⟦WC⟧⟦⟧⟦Pp⟧

Enjoyable group with good facilities, runs twice a week.

## St. Michael All Angels Church Piglets Toddler Group

St Michael All Angels Church Centre
160a Gloucester Road, BS7 8NT
Kay Crawford: 0117 924 1187
Tue 9.45am-11.15am
£1.30 per family
⟦✐⟧⟦WC⟧⟦🚹⟧⟦🚼⟧⟦⟧⟦Pp⟧

Popular group for 0-4yr olds, plenty of toys, separate baby area. Three sessions a week.

**Do you know a good toddler group?**
Tell us at:
www.titchhikers.co.uk

## Stockwood Free Church Toddler Group

Ladman Road, Stockwood, Bristol
Margaret Nash: 01275834 896
Tue 1.15pm-3pm, £1
⟦P⟧⟦✐⟧⟦WC⟧⟦🚹⟧⟦🚼⟧⟦🅰⟧⟦Pp⟧

Toddler and baby group held in church hall. Climbing frame, carpeted area for babies. Activity table for jigsaws, duplo or play dough.

## Sunbeams

St Oswalds Church Village Hall, Cheddar Grove, Bedminster Down, BS13 7EN
John Lewis: 0117 964 2649
Tue 9.30am-11am, £1
⟦P⟧⟦✐⟧⟦WC⟧⟦⟧⟦🚹⟧⟦🚼⟧⟦🅰⟧⟦⟧⟦⟧⟦⟧⟦Pp⟧

For parents and carers of toddlers. Creative sessions with toys, art and a sing-song.

## White Tree Parent and Toddler Group

Westbury Park Methodist Church, 4 North View, BS6
0117 962 5425
Tue 10am-11.30am, £1
⟦✐⟧⟦WC⟧⟦🚹⟧⟦🚼⟧⟦Pp⟧

Group held in 3 rooms with activities, slide & ride on toys, plus area for U1's.

## Windmill Hill Children Family Centre

Philip Street, Bedminster, Bristol, BS3 4EA
Mary Radley: 0117 963 3299
Tue 9.45am-11.45 am
£1.50 members, £2.50 non-members
⟦P⟧⟦✐⟧⟦WC⟧⟦⟧⟦🚹⟧⟦🚼⟧⟦⟧⟦🅰⟧⟦⟧⟦⟧⟦⟧

Held twice a week for children aged 0-4yrs. Separate baby area, with indoor and outdoor toys for older children inlcuding art activities.

# WEDNESDAY

## Barton Hill Family Playcentre

Barton Hill Settlement, 43 Ducie Road, BS5 0AX
Vadna Chauhan: 0117 955 6971
Wed 1pm-3pm, £1

Young mums group, for mums up to 22yrs, with children under 5yrs.

## Broomhill Playgroup

St Peter's Church, Allison Road, Brislington, Bristol
Pat Ashmead: 0117 977 8138
Wed & Thu 9am-11am, £3.50

Organised for children 3yrs+. Big indoor play area for trikes while art activities take place in a small side room.

## Cairns Rd Café with toddler zone

Cairns Rd Baptist Church, Cairns Rd, BS6 7TH
0117 9425 669 (Church Office)
Mon/Wed/Fri 9am-2pm, reduced hours in holidays

Free, fun soft play in large hall. Plenty of toys and a café with drinks and food, excellent toddler lunches for £1. Can be crowded but no booking required.

## Chatter Clatter Club

Bethesda Church, 29 Alma Road, BS8 2ES
Karen: 0117 914 0368
Wed 10am-11.30am
£1, additional child 50p

Friendly group, for 0-3yr olds, with loads of toys, craft and singing. Welcomes newcomers.

## Child's Play Toddler Group

Easton Christian Family Centre, Beaufort Street,
Easton, BS5 0SQ
Gill Miles: 0117 955 5877
Wed 10am-12 noon
£1 to stay & £1.50 to leave child

Structured play session runs twice a week for U4's giving parents a chance to have a break.

Parenting courses, family support & English classes run alongside this play session.

## Coffee Pot Parent and Toddler Group

St Peters Church Hall, Church Rd, Bristol, BS13 8JU
Michelle Owen: 0117 963 9584
Wed 9.30am-11.30am

Well-organised group with craft activities every week, cooking, a puzzle area and plenty of bikes, prams and slides. Sing-song and refreshments available to buy.

## Counterslip Baptist Church

Counterslip Baptist Church, 648 Wells Road,
Whitchurch, BS14 9HT
Jane Wood: 01275 833377
Wed 10am-11.30am
£1, additional child 50p (for both groups)

Large space with mats and cushions for tiny babies as well as a good variety of floor toys, books and ride-on toys. All welcome.

Wed 1.30pm-3pm

Held in a large carpeted area with wide variety of toys. Please call before attending.

## Downend Baptist Church Toddlers

Salisbury Road, Downend, Bristol, BS16
Rachel Baker: 0117 956 1374
Tue/Wed/Thu 10-11.30am & Wed 1.30-3pm
£10 per term and £3 for siblings over 6mths

Sessions for 0-5yr olds, with lots of toys and weekly activities. Song time and refreshments. Phone before attending.

## Elmgrove Centre Mums & Tots

Redland Road, Cotham, BS6 6AG
0117 924 3377
Wed 10am-12pm, £1

Drop-in group offering a variety of toys and activities including painting and games. Refreshments available. Use the side door which has no steps. Rumpus Room is often open at this time, costing 50p per hour.

## Filton Avenue Nursery School

Blakeney Road, Horfield, Bristol, BS7 0DL
Maureen Clifford: 0117 377 2680

Wed 9am-11am, free drop-in sessions for parents/carers with strong walkers up to 3yrs.

Wed 1.15pm-3.15pm, free drop-in sessions for parents/carers with non-walking babies.

## Four Acres Sure Start

Four Acres Primary School, Four Acres, Withywood
0117 903 0460
Wed 9.30am-11.30am

Free informal drop-in for parents/carers with children aged 0-4yrs to stay and play.

## Highridge Sure Start

Lakemead Grove, Highridge, Bristol, BS13 8EA
Faye Morgan: 0117 978 1028
Wed 1pm-3pm
30p, including refreshments

Informal stay and play run for 0-4yr olds.

## Hanham Folk Centre Parent & Toddler Group

High Street, Hanham
Donna Stockham 0117 967 4439 (Folk Centre)
Wed 9.15am-11.15am
£1.50 one adult + child, 25p per extra child, plus £10.50 annual membership for folk centre

Group runs throughout holidays with organised trips in summer. Run by volunteers. Toys taken outside in good weather, plus weekly activities, refreshments included.

## Horfield United Reformed Church

139 Muller Road, Horfield, Bristol
Alison Kinnersley: 0117 951 3321
Wed 9.30am-11.30am

Informal group for 0-3yr olds, with craft activities, lots of toys and singing at the end.

## Imps

Henleaze & Westbury Community Church,
Eastfield Rd, Westbury-on-Trym, BS9 4AD
Jo Grover: 0117 962 3816
Wed 9.45am-11.30am, £1.50

Friendly welcoming group for 0-3yr olds with separate play areas, weekly craft activities and songs. Please phone before attending.

## Mums and Tots

Leonard Hall, United Reformed Church,
Waterford Rd, Henleaze
Sue Wright: 0117 962 4196
Wed 1.30pm-3.30pm, 50p

Small, friendly and welcoming group with good range of toys.

## Parent and Toddler Group

St George Baptist Church, Summerhill Rd, St George
Mary Weeks: 0117 955 0512
Wed 1.45pm-3.15pm
50p including refreshments

Drop-in friendly group for 0-4yr olds. Large hall to run around in. Everyone welcome.

## Parkway Parent and Child Project

Parkway Methodist Church, Conduit Place,
St Werburghs, BS2 9RU
Sue Dowd: 0117 935 0205
Wed 9.30am-12pm
£1 per family

Sessions run throughout the year in a safe, stimulating and supportive environment with separate area for older children to ride bikes.

## Redcliffe Early Years Centre

Spencer House, Ship Lane, Redcliffe, BS1 6RR
Mrs FM Blight: 0117 903 0334
Wed 1pm-3pm

Free informal group for toddlers.

## Rosemary Nursery School and Family Unit Stay & Play

Haviland House, St Jude's Flats, Bristol, BS2 0DT
Mrs Sarah Burns: 0117 377 3297
Wed 1.30pm-3pm

Free informal stay and play for parents/carers with children up to 5yrs.

## South Street Family Unit

British Road, Bedminster, BS3 3AU
Jo/Lisa: 0117 903 9941
Tue 9.30pm-12pm
50p per child

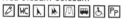

Play and stay arranged for the U5's.

## Southmead Day Nursery

Doncaster Road, Southmead, Bristol, BS10 5PW
Liz Harper: 0117 377 2343
Wed 9.15am-11.15am

Free informal drop-in sessions held for children aged 0-4yrs. Parents can use the resource library or attend family learning activities while children enjoy the Sensory Room and outdoor play area.

## St Bonaventures Toddler Group

St Bonaventures Church, 7 Egerton Road, Bishopston
Sinead: 0117 904 4806
Wed 1pm-3.00pm
£1 per family

Plenty of space for children aged 0-4yrs. A good variety of toys, weekly crafts and singing. Very friendly group, ideal place to meet locals, organic refreshments served.

## St Francis Toddlers

St Francis Church, North Street (opposite Aldi)
Sue Bryant: 0117 963 5053
Wed 9.15am-11.30am
£2 per session

Held in church hall, with art, craft and singing.

## St Patrick's Toddler Group

St Patrick's Community Centre, Blackswarth Rd, St George
Mrs Hawkins: 0117 940 0482
Wed 8.30am-11am, £1
Adjacent to St Patrick's School

Toys suitable for children up to 5yrs. Includes painting, trains, bricks, play dough and jigsaws. Sometimes runs in half term holidays.

## St. Michael All Angels Church Piglets Toddler Group

St. Michael All Angels Church Centre
160a Gloucester Road, Bristol, BS7 8NT
Kay Crawford: 0117 924 1187
Wed 9.30am-11am
£1.30 per family

This popular group for 0-4yr olds, runs three times a week. Plenty of toys with separate area for babies.

## The Salvation Army Candle Project Parent and Toddlers

6 Ashley Road, St Pauls, Bristol, BS6 5NL
Tracey Mountsford: 0117 942 4607
Wed 10am-12 pm, 50p

Small group meets three times a week, with space for 12-15 children, offering a variety of educational toys, trikes, tunnel, slide, dolls and prams. Fathers welcome.

## The Zoo mother and toddler

Bristol Zoo Gardens, Clifton Bristol, Bristol, BS8 3HA
0117 974 7384
Wed 9.30am-11am

Special package price for adult and children's refreshments. Non-members pay zoo entry, free entry for members. Held in a sectioned-off area of the Pelican Restaurant. Low-key atmosphere with toddler toys, puzzles and rugs out for babies. Chance for adults to relax while their charges play in a fun environment.

## Wessex Flyer Fun Factory

Hengrove Leisure Park, Hengrove Way, BS14 0HR
01275 834340
Wed 10.30am-11.30am, £2

Parents and toddlers have full use of all facilities for the U5's. Price includes light refreshments. Free child meals with adult main meals. Open during school holidays.

## W-O-T Toddlers

Westbury on Trym Methodist Church
Kerry Smith: 0117 959 3930
Wed 9.30-11.30am
50p per child, 25p additional children

Popular group for 0-4yr olds held in Church Hall. Large play area for older children with separate baby area. Weekly sing-song.

## Zetland Toddlers

Zetland Evangelical Church, 4&6 North Rd,
St Andrews, BS6 5AE
Eirene Carey-Jones: 0117 982 4796
Wed 9.45am-11.15am
50p per family

Small and friendly church-based group for 0-4yr olds. Lots of toys, weekly craft activities and circle time.

# THURSDAY

## Ashton Vale Toddlers

Ashton Vale Community Centre, Risdale Rd, BS3 2QY
Lindsey Hickery 0117 963 9283
Thu 9.30am-11.30am
£2 per family, includes refreshments

Drop-in session in spacious, friendly environment for children aged 0-4yrs. Lots of toys, singing and various craft activities.

## Barton Hill Family Playcentre

Barton Hill Settlement, 43 Ducie Road, BS5 0AX
Vadna Chauhan: 0117 955 6971
Thu 9.15am-11.45am, £1

Playing Together, a structured group for pre-school children, with art activity, construction toys, home/fantasy corner, sand and water play. Soft play area for babies. Dads welcome.

## Chatterbox (Toddler Group)

Horfield Baptist Church, 279 Gloucester Road,
Bristol, BS7 8NY
Valerie Harwood: 0117 924 3608
Thu 1.00pm-3.00pm, £1.50
Brynland Road entrance

Church based group for 0-4 yr olds, running twice a week. Varied toys, craft table, climbing equipment and ride-ons finishing with a story.

## Chelsea Tots

Chelsea Gospel Hall, Devon Road, BS5 6ED
Jane Cox: 01275 830 059
Thu 10am-11.30am, £1

Happy, friendly and caring environment for 0-4yr olds, with 10mins singing each session. Occasional crafts. Open to all.

## Christchurch Toddlers

Christ Church Crypt, Clifton, BS8 4EE
Parish Office: 0117 973 6524
Thu 10am-11.30pm, £1

Friendly environment for 0-3yr olds, with blanket and toys for babies, wendy house and bikes for toddlers. Different weekly craft activity and singalongs. Please phone, as there are restricted numbers.

## Counterslip Baptist Church

648 Wells Road, Whitchurch, Bristol, BS14 9HT
Jane Wood: 01275 833377
Thu 10am-11.30am
£1, additional child 50p

Held in a large carpeted area with wide

variety of toys appropriate to age range. Small waiting list, please phone for availability.

## Dinky Dolphins

Filton Sports & Leisure Centre, Elm Park, BS34 7PS
Gareth Hughes: 01454 866 686
Thu 10am-11am, £2.60 per session

Lively music, singing and play session with inflatables in the kiddies pool. From 6mths-5yrs, party packages available.

## Downend Baptist Church Toddlers

Salisbury Road, Downend, Bristol, BS16
Rachel Baker: 0117 956 1374
Tue/Wed/Thu 10-11.30am & Wed 1.30-3pm
£10 per term and £3 for siblings over 6mths

[P] [WC] [⚲] [⚹] [🚌] [📖] [Pp]

Sessions for 0-5yr olds. Large variety of toys, weekly activity for older children, song time and drinks. Please phone before attending.

## Filton Avenue Nursery School

Blakeney Road, Horfield, Bristol, BS7 0DL
Maureen Clifford: 0117 377 2680
Thu 1.15pm-3.15pm

Free drop-in sessions for parents/carers with strong walkers up to 3 years.

## Gay Elms Sure Start

Gay Elms Primary School, Withywood Rd, BS13 9AX
07900 497740
Thu 1pm-3pm, 30p

[P] [⚲] [⚹] [🔢] [📖] [🚌] [♿]

Toddler Time, a weekly informal drop-in for children aged 2-4yrs.

## Highgrove Parents and Toddlers

High Grove Church, Highgrove, Sea Mills, BS9 2NL
Debrah Marsh: 0117 968 5668
Thu 9.30am-11.15am
80p per family

[⚲] [WC] [⚹] [⚹] [🔢] [🚌]

Coffee & chat for parent/carers with children aged 0-4yrs. Good play equipment, craft activity, singing and storytime.

## Horfield Methodist Church Thursday Morning Group

Horfield Methodist Church, Churchways Ave, BS7
Lynne Richards: 0117 979 1010
Thu 9am-11.30am

[P] [⚲] [WC] [☺] [♿]

Free informal Church led fellowship group for adults with provision for children U4 to play.

## Horfield United Reformed Church

139 Muller Road, Horfield, Bristol
Alison Kinnersley: 0117 951 3321
Thu 9.30am-11.30am

[P] [⚲] [WC] [⚲] [⚹] [♿] [Pp]

Informal toddler group for 0-3yr olds, loads of toys, craft activity finishing with singing.

## Imps

Henleaze & Westbury Community Church,
Eastfield Road, Westbury-on-Trym, BS9 4AD
Jo Grover: Jo Grover 0117 962 3816
Thu 9.45-11.30am, £1.50

[⚲] [WC] [⚲] [⚹] [🔢] [📖] [Pp]

Friendly welcoming group for 0-3yr olds, with separate play areas, weekly craft activities and songs. Phone for spaces.

## Jelly Beans

St Oswalds Church, Cheddar Grove,
Bedminster Down, BS13 7EN
John Lewis: 0117 964 2649
Thu 9.30am-11am, £1

[P] [⚲] [WC] [⚷] [⚲] [⚹] [🔢] [🚌] [♿] [📖] [Pp]

For parents and carers of toddlers, creative session with toys, art and singing.

## Noah's Ark Playtime

Cairns Road Baptist Church, Cairns Road, BS6 7TQ
Carol de Beger: 0117 944 6229
Thu 10am-11.30am
Voluntary donations

[P] [⚲] [WC] [🔢] [Pp]

For 0-3yr olds, held in two rooms offering a variety of activities and toys: play dough, books, slide, trampoline, singing and instruments. Quieter carpeted area for babies.

Do you know a good toddler group?
Then tell us at:
www.titchhikers.co.uk

## Parent and Baby Group

Knowle Clinic, Broadfield Rd, BS4 2UH
0117 919 0200
Thu 10.30am-12 noon

Free group (20p refreshments). Mats with toys for babies. Occasional speakers on health issues. Health visitor available.

## Rainbow Opportunity Parent and Toddler Group

The Community Room, Proctor House,
Somerset Square, Redcliffe
Nicky Owen: 0117 9300 301
Thu 11am-1.30pm
Voluntary donation of £1

Playgroup for toddlers with delayed development or learning disabilities and their parents. Playtime with toys, craft and singing. Parents have an opportunity to chat and get the support they need. Makaton sign language is used.

## Rainbow Tots

Kensington Baptist Church Hall, Seymour Rd, Easton
Amanda Pearce: 0117 955 7768
Thu 10am-12pm, 60p

Friendly Church-run group meeting three times a week for 0-4 yr olds. Offers a craft activity with many toys and baby area.

## Redcliffe Early Years Centre

Spencer House, Ship Lane, Redcliffe, BS1 6RR
Mrs FM Blight: 0117 903 0334
Thu 1pm-3pm

Free Tums to Tots session with access to a health visitor.

## Redland Park Church Baby & Toddler Group

Redland Park Church, 1 Redland Park, BS6 6SA
Viv Hayden: 01275 847 692
Thu 10am-11.30am

Small friendly group for 0-4yr olds. Money raised from the group supports orphans overseas.

## Scramblers

St Francis Church, North Street, Bristol
Margaret Bishop: 0117 966 7670
Thu 11am-12.30pm
£1 per family, includes drinks

Suitable for 0-3yr olds. Access to church garden, good selection of toys and ride-ons. Mothers/carers help run this friendly group and organise evening get-togethers. About 40 children attend. The Vicar runs a short Play and Pray session with songs once a month.

## St. Michael All Angels Church Piglets Toddler Group

St. Michael All Angels Church Centre,
160a Gloucester Road, Bristol, BS7 8NT
Kay Crawford: 0117 924 1187
Thu 9.45am-11.15am
£1.30 per family

Popular group for 0-4yr olds, plenty of toys and area for babies. Three sessions a week.

## Stackpool Road and Methodist Church Parent and Toddlers

Stackpool Road Methodist Church, Southville, Bristol
Margaret Baber: 0117 963 7607
Thu 10am-12pm, £1.15
Corner of Stackpool Road and Howard Road

Popular and well-attended group with a caring and warm atmosphere for children aged 0-3yrs. Usually 60+ children, so can be quite boisterous, held in two halls. Fathers welcomed.

## Sticky Fingers

All Saints Church Hall, Grove Road, BS16
Jenny Emmett: 0117 907 9064
Thu 9.30am-11.30am
£2, additional child £1

Friendly, lively group for toddlers aged 1-3yrs. Wide range of activities, including sand and crafts along with construction toys. Small waiting list, regular attendance expected.

## Stockwood Free Church Toddler Group

Ladman Road, Stockwood, Bristol
Margaret Nash: 01275 834 896
Thu 1.15pm-2.45pm, £1

Held in church hall with climbing frame and carpeted area for babies. Activity table for jigsaws, duplo, play dough, sticking or painting.

## Under One's Group

Charlotte Keel Health Centre, Seymour Rd, Easton,
Chloe Bodard-Williams: 0117 951 2244
Thu 12pm-1pm (runs through holidays), 20p

Small informal drop-in group for U1's in restricted area with stimulating toys. Good for a chat with new mothers. Open to local parents and carers.

## Victoria Park Toddlers

Victoria Park Baptist Church,
St John Lane, Bedminster
Brendan Bassett: 0117 373 0477
Thu 9.30am-11.30am
£1 for one child, £1.50 for two or more

Drop-in group for 0-4yr olds held twice a week, with baby area and toys for U1's. Variety of toys, craft activities and sand. Fathers regularly attend. Outdoor area used.

## Wessex Flyer Fun Factory

Hengrove Leisure Park, Hengrove Way, BS14 0HR
01275 834340
Thu 10.30am-11.30am, £2 (open in sch hols)

Parent and toddler have full use of all facilities for the U5's. Price includes light refreshments. Free child meals with adult main meals.

# FRIDAY

## Baby Comes Too

Key Centre, Charlton Road, Keynsham
Mrs Heath: 0117 987 7753
www.babycomestoo.ik.com
Fri 9.45am-11.45am
£1 per family

For parents and carers of children aged 0-4yrs. Lots of toys, activities and singing session.Refreshments provided.

## Cairns Rd Café with toddler zone

Cairns Rd Baptist Church, Cairns Rd, BS6 7TH
0117 9425 669 (Church Office)
Mon/Wed/Fri 9am-2pm, reduced hours in holidays

Free, fun soft play in large hall. Plenty of toys and a café with drinks and food, excellent toddler lunches for £1. Can be crowded but no booking required.

## Chatterbox (Toddler Group)

Horfield Baptist Church (Brynland Road entrance),
279 Gloucester Road, Bristol, BS7 8NY
Valerie Harwood: 0117 924 3608
Fri 1pm-3pm, £1.50

Church-based group for 0-4 yr olds, running twice a week. Varied toys, craft table, climbing equipment and ride-ons, finishing with a story.

## Child's Play Toddler Group

Easton Christian Family Centre, Beaufort St, Easton,
Gill Miles: 0117 955 5877
Fri 10am-12pm
£1 to stay, £1.50 to leave child

Structured play session runs twice a week for U4's giving parents a chance to have a break.

## Fulford Family Centre

237-239 Gatehouse Ave, Withywood, BS13 9AQ
Jenny Lewis: 0117 978 2441
Fri 1pm-2.30pm

Free drop-in sessions for 0-5yr olds and their parents/carers living in the Hartcliffe, Bishopworth and Withywood areas.

## Gay Elms Sure Start

Gay Elms Primary School, Withywood Rd, BS13 9AX
07900 497740
Fri 10am-12.30pm
£1, older siblings 50p

Weekly baby café run for parents/carers to meet up and chat over lunch.

## Highridge Sure Start

Lakemead Grove, Highridge, Bristol, BS13 8EA
Faye Morgan: 0117 978 1028
Fri 9.30am-11.30 am
30p, includes refreshments

Informal stay and play for 0-4yr olds

## Kings Tots Parent and Toddlers

Bristol Community Church, Bourne Chapel, Waters Road, BS15 8BE
Fran Puckett: 0117 947 8441
Fri 10am-11.30am
£1, includes refreshments

Children aged 0-3yrs can play in a safe environment. Possible waiting lists.

## Little Angels Parents & Toddler Group

6 Ashley Road, St Pauls, Bristol, BS6 5NL
Tracey Mountsford: 0117 942 4607
Fri 9.30am-12pm, 50p

Small group meets three times a week, with space for 12-15 children, offering a variety of educational toys, trikes, tunnel, slide, dolls and prams. Fathers welcome.

## Mum's the Word!

Horfield Baptist Church, 279 Gloucester Rd, BS7 8NY
Katie Wilkinson: 0117 924 3608
Fri 2pm-3.30pm, 50p
Brynland Road entrance

Weekly small club for new mums with babies 0-6mths, lots of toys and a chance to chat.

## Redland Toddlers

Redland Parish Church Hall, Redland Green Rd, Bristol, BS6 7HE
Church Secretary: 0117 946 4690
Fri 10am-11.30am
£1, includes refreshments

Spacious hall with good variety of toys and separate carpeted room for babies. Weekly craft activity and singing. Friendly and welcoming group. Dads, Mums and carers attend. Refreshments included.

## South Street Family Unit

British Road, Bedminster, Bristol, BS3 3AU
Jo/Lisa: 0117 903 9941
Fri 1.30-3pm
50p per child

Play and stay for 0-5yr olds.

## Southmead Day Nursery

Doncaster Road, Southmead, Bristol, BS10 5PW
Liz Harper: 0117 377 2343
Fri 9.15-11.15am

Free, informal drop-in sessions for children aged 0-4yrs. Parents can use the resource library or attend family learning activities while children use the Sensory Room and outdoor play area. Lunch provided on Fridays.

## St Mathews Church Toddler Group

Clare Road, Cotham, BS6 5TB
0117 944 1598
Fri 1.30pm-3.30pm

Enjoyable group with good facilities, runs twice a week.

## St Pauls Day Nursery

Little Bishop St, St Pauls, Bristol, BS2 9JF
0117 377 2278
stpaulsdayn@bristol-city.gov.uk
Fri 9.30am-12.30pm

Free informal stay and play time for children aged 0-5yrs and their parents/carers.

## St Peter's Parent & Toddler Group

St Peter's Church Hall, The Drive, Henleaze, BS9 4LD
Parish Office: 0117 962 3196
Fri 10.30am-12.15pm
50p per family, Plus £1 per family per term

Children from bumps to nursery age, meets twice a week. Parents, grandparents, nannies are welcome to join. Action songs at the end.

## Stay and Play

Filwood Community Centre, Barnstaple Rd,
Knowle West, BS4 1JT
Jane Yeoman: 0117 963 6475
Fri 10am-12pm, 50p

Group for parents and toddlers from the local area. Emphasis on parents playing with their children. Painting room, craft activities and toys. Snack served half way through.

## Tots R-Us

Abingdon Church, Abingdon Rd, Fishponds
Catherine Williams: 0117 909 0423
Fri 10am-11.30am
50p per family, includes refreshments

Toddler group for families in the local area. New craft activity every week and puzzles and kitchen equipment. Move to new room refreshments, singing and a story. Finish with fun on the big toys, cars and trikes!

## Tots Time

St Christophers Hall, Hampstead Rd, Brislington
Alison Pagington: 0117 977 2016
Fri 9.30am-11.30am
£1.50, includes refreshments

Popular group for 0-3yr oldS. Craft activity

tables, dressing-up, books and much more. Refreshments served, followed by singing and then ride-on toys, trucks and parachute fun. Waiting list, so ring for places.

## United Parents Toddler Group

All Saints Church Hall, Grove Rd, Fishponds, BS16
Elaine Seretny: 0117 902 5257
Fri 10am-11.30am, £1.50

Friendly, well-established drop-in toddler group, originally set up to support mothers. Informal atmosphere with plenty of toys, cars, art activities and play dough.

## White Tree Parent and Toddler Group

Westbury Park Methodist Church, 4 North View, Bristol, BS6 7QB
0117 962 5425
Fri 10am-11.30am, £1

Group held in 3 rooms with activities, slide & ride-on toys, plus area for U1's.

## Windmill Hill Children & Family Centre

Philip Street, Bedminster, Bristol, BS3 4EA
Mary Radley: 0117 963 3299
Fri 9.45am-11.45am
£1.50 members, £2.50 non members

Held twice a week for children aged 0-4yrs. Separate baby area, with indoor and outdoor toys for older children inlcuding art activities.

# EARLY EDUCATION IN BRISTOL

## What is pre-school education?

The period from age three to the end of the reception year is described as the foundation stage. Children work through this initial stage of the national curriculum at a pre-school, playgroup or in a nursery class attached to a primary school, nursery school or day nursery. Most children transfer to the reception year in a primary school in the September following their fourth birthday.

This pre-school learning is a distinct stage and important both in its own right and in preparing children for later schooling. The early learning goals set out six areas of learning which form the basis of the foundation stage curriculum. These areas are:

- Personal, social and emotional development
- Communication, language and literacy
- Mathematical development
- Knowledge and understanding of the world
- Physical development
- Creative development

## Choosing the right pre-school facility

Only you as a parent can decide what is best for your child so we recommend that you visit as many places as you need to. There are many pre-school groups held in Church Halls often called playgroups, whilst some primary schools also offer pre-school education in a nursery class. Whatever you choose, your child will normally spend a morning or afternoon on their own there for about 2½ hours up to five times a week. Most will follow the same term dates as a school.

All pre-schools, playgroups and nurseries, where children attend sessions of less than four hours, are now inspected by Ofsted (Office for Standards in Education) to ensure that they meet national standards. When visiting, you can request a copy of their Ofsted report, or call your Ofsted Early Years Regional centre on 0845 601 4771.

For a comprehensive list of pre-schools, within your area, you can contact the:

**Children's Information Service**
0845 129 7217

**Pre-school Learning Alliance**
0117 907 7073

## Nursery education grants

All parents are entitled to claim assistance for the cost of pre-school education for their children once their child has reached 2yrs and 10mths, providing they attend a registered provider. This applies to children at bursery schools, playgroups, pre-schools or day nurseries.

Grants are claimed in the term following the child's third birthday up until the child reaches five years old. To access the grant parents will be asked by the provider to sign a Parental Registration form so that the pre-school can claim back the money and deduct it from the termly cost. In cases where the grant does not cover the entire cost of the pre-school session, parents will need to top up the fee.

The following two subchapters separates those pre-school establishments that are funded i.e. Local Authority Nursery Schools and those that are fee paying (although nursery education grants may apply).

# LOCAL AUTHORITY NURSERY SCHOOLS

The Local Education Authority funds a number of early education places to allow children to spend a year in nursery provision before starting school. Places are available at some infant schools which have a nursery class attached to the school or at council run nursery schools. If parents have applied for a nursery education grant, they cannot get a free early education place.

Parents who wish to apply for a place should contact the school directly. Attending the nursery attached to a primary school does not guarantee your child a place at the school. To find out if there is an LEA nursery class or school in your area contact your local Children's Information Service the start of the chapter.

# CENTRAL BRISTOL

## Cashmore Nursery School

Cashmore House, Barton Hill, Bristol, BS5 9PR
Ms Hannah Hill: 0117 903 0253
Mon-Fri 9am-3pm

Wide range of learning opportunities for 3-4yr olds. Shortly amalgamating with two local schools, creating a 60-place nursery class. This will another of Bristol's Children Centres, name to be confirmed.

## Cheddar Grove Primary School

Cheddar Grove, Bedminster Down, Bristol, BS13 7EN
Miss Abbott: 0117 903 0418
Mon-Fri 9am-11.30am, 12.45pm-3.15pm

LEA-funded nursery class for 3-5yr olds. Morning or afternoon sessions available.

## Redcliffe Early Years Centre

Spencer House, Ship Lane, Redcliffe, BS1 6RR
Mrs FM Blight: 0117 903 0334
Mon-Fri 9am-11.30am & 12pm-3.30pm

Foundation stage offered for 3-5yr olds living within the catchment area. Parents must call for an application form. Also Breakfast Club 8am-9am and Tea Club 3pm-6pm, £3p/h.

## Rosemary Nursery School & Family Unit

Haviland House, St Jude's Flats, Bristol, BS2 0DT
Mrs Sarah Burns: 0117 903 1467
Mon-Fri 9am-3pm

Local authority nursery school for children aged 3-4yrs.

## St James' & St Agnes' Nursery School

Halston Drive, St Paul's, Bristol, BS2 9JE
Ms L Driver: 0117 903 0337
Mon-Fri, term time only

Full and part-time education places available for 3-4yr olds.

## St Phillip's Marsh Nursery School

Albert Crescent, St Phillip's Marsh, Bristol, BS2 0SU
Mrs P S Willmott: 0117 977 6171
Mon-Fri 9am-3pm

Accepts children aged 3-4yrs, providing a range of activities to promote and encourage children's independence and learning.

## St Werburgh's Park Nursery School

Glenfrome Road, St Werburgh's Park, BS2 9UX
Mrs E Jenkins: 0117 903 0323
Mon-Fri 9am-3pm

Maintained nursery school offering nursery education and care.

# NORTH WEST BRISTOL

## Bluebell Valley Nursery School

Long Cross, Lawrence Weston, Bristol, BS11 0LP
Mrs Christine Menzies: 0117 903 1472

Early education for children 3-5yrs old. In addition, the school has inclusive places for children aged 3-7yrs who have complex and severe learning difficulties. Contact the school for further information.

## Henbury Court Primary School

Trevelyan Walk, Henbury, Bristol, BS10 7NY
Mr Tingle: 0117 377 2196
Mon-Fri 8.50am-11.30am, 12.40pm-3.20pm

Nursery class for 3yr olds, part-time and full-time places, phone for application procedure.

# NORTH BRISTOL

### Filton Avenue Nursery School
Blakeney Road, Horfield, Bristol, BS7 0DL
Mrs Rachel Edwards: 0117 377 2680
Mon-Fri 9am-11.30am, or 12.45pm-3.15pm (term time only)

Free pre-school education, from 3yrs for families in the North Bristol City Council area. Waiting list places for those attending either five mornings or five afternoons a week.

# NORTH EAST BRISTOL

### Blaise Primary School
Clavel Road, Henbury, Bristol, BS10 7EJ
Mrs Yvonne Roberts: 0117 377 2424
Mon-Fri 8.55am-11.30am, 1pm-3.30pm

Nursery class attached to the school offering pre-school education for those rising 4yrs, ideal for those wishing to go to the school.

### Little Hayes Nursery School
Symington Road, Fishponds, Bristol, BS16 2LL
Mrs S Rolfe: 0117 903 0405
Mon-Fri 9am-11.30am, 12.30pm-3pm

LEA run pre-school for 3-5yr olds, please phone for a place.

# EAST BRISTOL

### Speedwell Nursery School
Speedwell Road, Speedwell, Bristol, BS5 7SY
Mrs Gillian Lowe: 0117 903 0329
Mon-Fri 9.30am-12pm, 1pm-3.30pm

Local authority nursery school for children aged 3-4yrs.

Children's Information Service provides loads of great advice on early years childcare and education, see pg 205

# SOUTH EAST BRISTOL

### Burnbush Primary School
Whitox Road, Stockwood, Bristol, BS14 8DQ
Mr N Williams: 01275 832961
Mon-Fri 9am-11.30am, 12.45pm-3.15pm

LEA-funded nursery class attached to the school with pre-school places for 3-4yr olds.

### Waycroft Primary School
Selden Road, Stockwood, Bristol, BS14 8PS
Simon Rowe: 0117 377 2198
Mon-Fri 9am-11.30am, 12.45am-3.10pm

LEA-funded nursery school, attached to the school, offers pre-school education for 3-5yr olds.

# SOUTH BRISTOL

### Fairfurlong Primary School
Vowell Close, Withywood, Bristol, BS13 9HX
Peter Overton: 0117 377 2181
Mon-Fri 9am-11.15am, 1pm-3.15pm

Nursery class attached to the school offering pre-school education for 3-5yr olds.

### Four Acres Sure Start
Four Acres Primary School, Four Acres, Withywood, BS13 8RB
Dawn Butler: 0117 903 0460
Mon/Thu/Fri 9.30am-12pm, Wed 12.30pm-3pm

Free pre-school education from 2½-4yrs olds, registered with Sure Start.

### Gay Elms Primary School
Withywood Road, Withywood, Bristol, BS13 9AX
Annette Osbourne: 0117 903 0311
Mon-Fri 8.55am-11.30am, 12.40pm-3.15pm

Pre-school education offered for 3-5yr olds. Attached to the school.

## Gay Elms Sure Start

Gay Elms Primary School, Withywood Rd, BS13 9AX
07900 497740
Mon/Tue 9.30am-12 noon

Free pre-school education for 2½-4yr olds, registered with Sure Start.

## Highridge Infant School

Ellfield Close, Bishopworth, Bristol, BS13 8EF
Jill Spiteri: 0117 377 2366
Mon-Fri 8.45am-11.15am, 12.45am-3.15pm
Free

Nursery class for children rising 3yrs.

## Highridge Sure Start

Lakemead Grove, Highridge, Bristol, BS13 8EA
Faye Morgan: 0117 978 1028
Wed/Thu 9.30am-12pm

Free pre-school education for 2½-5yr olds, registered with Sure Start.

## Teyfant Community School

Teyfant Road, Hartcliffe, Bristol, BS13 ORG
Mr G Grimshaw: 0117 903 0356
Mon-Fri 8.30am-11.30am, 12.30pm-3pm

LEA-funded pre-school for 3-5yr olds. Attached to primary school.

# SOUTH WEST BRISTOL

## Ashton Gate Primary School

Ashton Gate Road, Ashton Gate, Bristol, BS3 1SZ
Mrs S Willson: 0117 903 0236
Mon-Fri 9am-11.30am, 1pm-3.30pm

LEA-funded pre-school for 3-5yr olds. Attached to school. Must be 3yrs old by 31 August. Please call to apply for a place.

# FEE PAYING PRE-SCHOOLS, NURSERIES AND PLAYGROUPS

Most pre-school groups are privately run, non-profit making organisations providing a fun learning environment through play, for children 2½-5yrs. Under the Ofsted guidelines, they must adhere to correct adult to child ratios, have a first aider on site and all members must be police checked. Sessions last 2-3hrs, costing £5-£10. Each child normally attends 2-5 sessions a week. Popular pre-schools have waiting lists, so get your child's name down at least a year before they are due to start. Opportunity Playgroups are set up for children with special needs, usually with trained staff. If your child has special needs, a Statement of Needs is required; your local education authority should be able to help you obtain this and advise you of local groups.

### Advantages:

• Good first step encouraging your child's learning and independence

• Local therefore your child will meet peers going on to the same school.

### Disadvantages:

• Parent participation is sometimes required on a rota basis

• Term time, short sessions, therefore usually not suitable for working parents.

## CENTRAL BRISTOL

### Windmill Hill Children & Family Centre

Philip Street, Bedminster, Bristol, BS3 4EA
Mary Radley: 0117 963 3299
Mon-Fri 8am-6pm

P V 🖊 WC ✂ 🎨 CP 🍼 🧸 ✈ 🎪 🅰
🧺 🖼 🎵 🤸 🚌 ♿ 📖

Nursery sessions for children aged
3mths-5yrs.

### Clifton High School Nursery Department

1 Clifton Park, Clifton, BS8 3BS
Heather Thomas: 0117 973 0201
www.cliftonhigh.bristol.sch.uk
8.30am-12pm mornings, 8.30am-3.30pm all day
3.30pm-6pm after school club for lower school

WC 🍼 🎪

Happy, lively and informal atmosphere for children rising 3yrs. Stimulating curriculum offered in a spacious building and gardens.

## NORTH BRISTOL

### Bluebells Pre-School

Shield Road School, Shields Av, Northville, BS7 0RR
Jacquline Thinnock: 01454 867 189
secretary@bluebellspre-school.co.uk
Mon-Fri 9am-12.30pm (£7) 12.30pm-3pm (£5.50)
9am-3pm (£12.50)

P 🧸 ✈ 🎪 🅰 📖

Pre-school education offered for children aged 2½-5yrs.

### Busy Bees Pre-School

St Peters Church, The Drive, Henleaze, BS9 4LD
Sian Jones: 07949 225350
Tue/Wed/Thu 9.15-11.45am,
Mon & Fri 12.30-2.45pm
£6 a session

P WC 🧸 ✈ 🎪 📖 Pp

Warm, caring and happy environment for 2½-5yr olds, "where each child feels valued".

### Candle Project Pre-School

Salvation Army, 6 Ashley Rd, BS6 5NL
Christine Jones: 0117 942 4607
Mon-Fri 9.30am-12pm
£3.50 a session

WC 🎪 🅰 🚌 📖

Sessions for children aged 2½+yrs, held in large hall upstairs with spacious carpeted area and wet play area. Courtyard for outside play.

### Eden Grove Playgroup

Eden Grove Methodist Church Hall, Eden Grove, Horfield, BS7 0PQ
Hazel/Sandy: 07765 204751
Mon-Fri 9.30am-12pm
£4.25 a session

WC 🧸 ✈ 🎪 📖

For children aged 2½-4+yrs. Friendly welcoming staff.

## Fallodon Playgroup

The Scout Hut, Fallodon Way, Henleaze, BS9 4HR
Jenny Aulds: 0117 942 7413, 07717 615070 mobile
Mon-Fri 9.15am-12pm
£6 a session, max 24 children

Privately-run playgroup, Ofsted inspected.
Children, aged 2½-5yrs, enjoy supervised
free play in a large hall and outside, weather
permitting.

## Harcourt Pre-School

Wells Room, St Albans Church, Bayswater Ave, BS6
Mrs Christine Williams: 0117 942 5128
Mon-Fri 9am-12pm
£9 a session

Established in 1956, for children aged
2½-5yrs. It is a happy, caring environment
ensuring children build up confidence.

## Horfield Methodist Playgroup

Horfield Methodist Church, Churchways Ave, BS7
Cherry Arnal: 07977 348850
Mon-Fri 9am-11.30am
£3.50 a session

Church sponsored pre-school, offering
foundation stage education for 2½-5yr olds.

## Horfield Welly Playgroup

Wellington Hill West, Horfield, Bristol, BS7 8GT
Mrs L Seymour: 07837 133 925
Tue-Fri 9.30am-12pm
£5.50 a session

Following Early Years guidelines, for children
aged 2½-4yrs.

## Jack and Jill Pre-School

Northcote, Great Brockeridge, Westbury on Trym,
Bristol, BS9 3TY
Julie Claridge: 0117 962 3382
Julie@jackandjillpre-school.co.uk
Mon-Fri 9am-12pm, 1pm-3pm
£4.20 per hour

Established 25 yrs ago. This small, friendly
pre-school in a quiet location, accepts children

from 2½yrs for afternoon sessions. Children
3+yrs stay five mornings a week.

## Little Bears at St Ursula's

St Ursula's School, Brecon Road, Westbury-on-Trym
Helen Glynn: 0117 962 8812
rupprechts@st-ursulas.bristol.sch.uk
Mon-Fri 8am-6pm

State of the art centre offering pre-school
education for children aged 3-4yrs. Offers a
wide range of actitivities, plus a separate art
and design area. Can provide care from 8am
until 6pm if required.

## Magic Dragon Pre-school

Church of the Good Shepherd Hall, Bishop Road,
Bishopston, BS7 8NA
Miriam Lord: 0117 924 3446
Mon-Thu 9.30am-11.45am, term time
£7 a session or nursery grant if applicable

Children aged 3-5yrs looked after in a friendly
atmosphere, with stimulating activities and
resources.

## Noah's Ark Pre-School

Cairns Rd Baptist Church, Cairns Road, BS6 7TH
Carol de Beger: 0117 944 6229
www.noahsarkps.org.uk
Mon-Fri 9.15am-11.45am, or 12.45pm-3.15pm
£6 a session, Lunch Club £3

Open to children of all faiths aged 2½-5yrs.
Christianity taught. Also an optional lunch club
Mon-Fri 11.45-12.45, so that children can stay
an extra hour or all day if desired.

## Pied Piper Playgroup

Bishopston Methodist Church, 245 Gloucester Rd,
Bristol, BS7 8NY
Mrs Jenny McCaren: 0117 942 5104
Mon/Tue/Wed/Fri 9.15am-12pm
£6 a session

Playgroup for children aged 2yrs/10mths-5yrs,
parent participation required twice a term.

## Redland High Nursery Class

1 Grove Park, Bristol, BS6 6PP
Judith Ashill: 0117 924 4404
admissions@redland.bristol.sch.uk
Mon-Fri 8.30am-3.45pm

Accepts girls aged 3-5yrs. Also offers after
school facilities until 6pm and a holiday club
for 3-11yr olds.

## Redland Pre-school

Friends Meeting House, 126 Hampton Road,
Redland, Bristol, BS6 6JE
Louise Douglas: 0117 908 0455
Mon-Fri 9.15am-1.15pm, term time
£11-15

Well-established friendly pre-school run by
an elected committee of parents. Places for
children aged 2-5yrs. Also offers lunchtime
sessions for older ones at an additional cost.

## Silverhill School Nursery

Swan Lane, Winterbourne, BS36 1RL
Ian Philipson-Masters: 01454 772 156
www.silverhill_school.co.uk
Mon-Fri 8am-6pm

Independent nursery and prep school for
children aged 2½-11yrs. Holiday scheme
available to pupils.

## St Bonaventures Pre-School

The Parish Hall, Priory Lane, Bishopston, BS7 8HN
Louise Stutt: 07840 796 993
Mon-Fri 9am-11.30am
£7.50 a session

Pre-school education for 3-4 yr olds.

**Redland Pre-school
Friend's Meeting House
126 Hampton Road
Redland, BS6 6JE**

Our friendly well established pre-school aims to provide children with skills which will prepare them for their reception year at school. We achieve this through play, in a safe and caring environment.

Opening hours

Sessions run from 9.15am - 12.00 pm
Extended sessions from 9.15am  1.15pm
Government funding available for 3 and 4 year olds

Tel: 0117 9080455
During opening hours to arrange a visit

Affiliated to the Pre-school Learning Alliance

## St Matthews Church Playgroup

Clare Road, Cotham, Bristol, BS6 5TB
Sue Last: 0117 944 1598
Mon/Wed/Thu/Fri 9.15am-11.45am,
Mon/Wed 12.30pm-3pm
£6.75 a session

Community playgroup offering pre-school fun
for 2½-4yr olds in a caring, supportive and
lively learning environment. Phone for a place.

## The Lantern Playschool

Redland Parish Hall, Redland Green Road, BS6 7HE
Monica Smith: 0117 9464 6992
Mon/Tue/Thu/Fri 9.15am-12.15pm
£148 per term (approx £12 per session)

A Christian school aimed at 3-5yr olds,
offering a high quality pre-school education.

## The Red House Children's Centre

1 Cossins Rd, Westbury Park, BS6 7LY
Jo Kirby: 0117 942 8293

Converted Redland house provides a home-from-home atmosphere for this friendly pre-school, taking children aged 2-5yrs, with a variety of sessions. See advertisement.

## Torwood House School

27-29 Durdham Park, Redland, BS6 6XE
Samantha Packer: 0117 973 5620
www.torwoodhouse.bristol.sch.uk
emailus@torwoodhouse.bristol.sch.uk
Mon-Fri 8am-6pm, continues through holidays

Friendly, independent nursery and preparatory school from 2-11yrs. Great location next to the Downs. Runs popular holiday club, see Activities pg 119.

## Westbury Baptist Pre-school

Reedley Road, Westbury on Trym, Bristol, BS9 3TD
Mary Hughes: 0117 962 9990
www.westburybaptist.org.uk
wbcoffice@fish.co.uk
Mon-Fri 9am-12pm or 1pm
9am-12pm £9, 12pm-1pm £4

Caring pre-school run with a Christian ethos.

## White Tree Pre-school

Westbury Park Methodist Church Hall, 4 North View, Bristol, BS6 7QB
Alwyn Leverton: 0117 962 5425
www.geocities.com/whitetreepre-school
white_tree_group@hotmail.com
Mon-Fri 9.15am-12pm, Thu 12.30pm -3pm
£6.50 per session

Pre-school education for 2½-5yr olds, within the context of the Christian faith. Warm, caring environment. Variety of activities provided in a large, airy, carpeted hall encouraging all areas of child development. Close to the Downs for walks.

## Windsor Playgroup

Sefton Park Youth Centre, Ashley Down Rd, BS7
Maureen Walford: 0117 947 0979
Tue/Wed/Thu 9.15-11.45am
£6 a session

Children start in the term they turn 2½yrs.

# NORTH EAST BRISTOL

## Bristol Children's Playhouse

Berkeley Green Rd, Eastville, BS5 6LU
Jackie Cutmore: 0117 951 0037
bristolchildrensplayhouse@yahoo.co.uk
Mon-Fri 9am-12.45pm term time
Small fee to be introduced

Pre-school nursery for children aged 2½-5yrs. Parent support required.

## St Josephs Pre-School

St Josephs Church Hall, Forest Rd, Fishponds, BS16
Cathy Williamson: 0117 914 7173
Mon-Fri 9am-11.30am, Tue/Wed/Fri 1pm-3.30pm
£4 a session

From 2yrs/10mths-4½yrs. Community-based group encouraging parent participation.

## Sticky Fish Pre-School

Fishponds Baptist Church, Downend Rd, BS16 5AS
Rachel Betts: 0117 904 2768
Mon-Fri 9.30am-12pm, Mon & Wed 12.30pm-3pm
£5 (pre-schoolers) £6.50 (2-3yrs)

Preparation for school, learning through play.
Takes children aged 2½-5yrs.

## EAST BRISTOL

### Barton Hill Family Playcentre

Barton Hill Settlement, 43 Ducie Rd, BS5 0AX
Vadna Chauhan: 0117 955 6971
Thu & Fri 1pm-3pm
£2 a session

Two's Group has a stimulating and social
environment, for children 2-3yrs. Preparing
them for the pre-school group.

### Barton Hill Family Playcentre Pre-school

Barton Hill Settlement, 43 Ducie Rd, BS5 0AX
Vadna Chauhan: 0117 955 6971
Mon 12.30pm-3pm,
Tue/Wed/Fri 9.15am-11.45am, term time
£2.50 a session

Pre-school runs four times a week for
2½-5yr olds.

### Crossways Pre-School

Blackhorse Centre, Blackhorse Rd, Mangotsfield
0117 957 3923
Mon-Fri 9.30am-2.45pm

Sessional or full day care for children aged
2½-5yrs. Very friendly, well-established school
with qualified staff.

### Fishponds Pre-School

St Johns Parish Hall, Lodge Causeway, Fishponds,
Bristol, BS16 2NW
07947 231 086
Tue-Fri 9am-11.30am, Tues 1pm-3.30pm, term time
£4 a session, plus one-off £5 admin fee

Charity pre-school run by a committee of
parents and friends, for children aged
3-5yrs. One large hall divided up for
different activities.

### Kingswood Methodist Church Playgroup

Grantham Rd, Kingswood, BS15 1JR
Laura Wood: 0117 961 3488
Mon/Tue/Wed & Fri 9.30am-12pm &
Thu 12.30pm-3.00pm
£5 a session

Offers a safe, stimulating environment for
2½-5yr olds with trained staff.

### St George Pre-school Group

The Baptist Church, Cherry Orchard Lane
Mrs Sharon Carstairs: 0117 935 4534
Mon-Fri 9am-11.30am
£3.55 a session

Accepts children aged 2½-4yrs.

## Tiny Happy People Nursery

Easton Christian Family Centre, Beaufort St, BS5 0SQ
Modupa Kefentse: 0117 955 5877
Mon-Fri 9.30am-12pm, 12.30pm-3pm, term time
£2.50 a session

A stimulating learning enviroment where children are supported to discover and learn through the foundation stage. Both inside and outside classrooms and lunches available.

# SOUTH EAST BRISTOL

## Christ Church Playgroup

Church Hall, Petherton Road, Hengrove, BS14 9BP
Heather Wayborn: 0117 975 4616
Mon/Tue/Thu 9am-11.30am. Also, at busy times Mon & Thu 12.30pm-3pm
£3 a session

Pre-school for children aged 2yrs/10mths-5yrs. Occasional parent participation required.

## Counterslip Baptist Church

648 Wells Road, Whitchurch, Bristol, BS14 9HT
Jane Wood: 01275 833377
worship@counterslip.co.uk
Mon-Fri 9.30am-12pm, Tues 12.30pm-2.45pm
£5 a session (nursery ed. grant from 3+yrs)

Pre-school for children aged 3-5yrs with a wide range of foundation stage activities.

## Hamilton Playgroup

Wick Road, Brislington, Bristol, BS4 4HB
0117 914 4471
Mon-Fri 9am-11.30am, 12.30pm-3pm
£4 a session

Friendly atmosphere with stimulating activities.

## Knowle West Play Centre

Filwood Broadway, Knowle, Bristol, BS4 1JC
Nicola Sherborne: 0117 963 1737
Mon-Fri 9.30am-12pm
£3.50 a session

Play sessions run for 2-5yr olds where parents can leave their children. Book in advance, minimum three sessions a week.

## Sunshine Under Fives Pre-school

St Gerard Majella Church Hall, Buller Road, BS4 2LN
Karon Nichol: 0117 977 4170
Mon-Fri 9.15am-11.45am or 12.15pm-2.45pm
£5 a session

A friendly, well-organised group with lots of activities for children aged 2yrs/10mths-5yrs. Members of Pre-school Learning Alliance.

## Queen's Road Methodist Church Pre-School

Queen's Road Methodist Church, Queen's Rd, Keynsham, BS31 2NN
Ginny Ireland: 0117 987 7753
Mon-Fri 9.30am-12pm,
Mon-Fri (excl Tue) 12.30pm-3pm
£4 a session

Accepts children aged 2yrs/9mths-5yrs, offering quality care and education.

## Sydenham Road Under Fives Playgroup

Totterdown Baptist Church, Sydenham Rd, BS4 3DF
Wendy McCarthy: 0117 977 3246
Mon-Fri 9am-11.45am
£6.75 a session

Stimulating, community-based group for 3-5yr olds. Lots of craft activities. Bikes used indoors and out (weather permitting). Run by voluntary committee.

## The Village Pre-school

St Lukes Church Hall, Church Parade, BS4 5AZ
0117 971 5222
Mon-Fri 9.15am-11.45am
£3.50 a session

Friendly, caring environment for 3-4yr olds.
Very good Ofsted inspection. Long-serving
experienced staff.

## Waycroft Primary School

Seldon Road, Stockwood, Bristol, BS14 8PS
Simon Rowe: 0117 377 2198
waycroft_p@bristol-city.gov.uk
Mon 9am-10.30am, Wed 1.30pm-3.00pm
£2 a session

Play to Learn session held at the school with
qualified play leader for 2-3yr olds. Must book
into a morning or afternoon session.

# SOUTH WEST BRISTOL

## Ashton Vale Pre-school

Ashton Vale Church, Risdale Rd, Ashton Vale, BS3
Lynne Branson: 07980 065 799
Mon-Fri 9am-11.30am for nursery age or
Mon-Fri 12.30pm-3pm for pre-nursery age
Nursery age free, pre-nursery age £3.50 a session

Pre-school focusing on early learning goals of
foundation stage, for children aged 3-5yrs.

# MONTESSORI NURSERY SCHOOLS

## Clevedon Montessori School

34 Albert Road, Clevedon, BS21 7RR
Maureen Burgoyne: 01275 877743
clevedonmontessorisc@blueyonder.co.uk
Mon-Fri 9am-3pm, term time
Morning Session £13, Full Day £26.20 (inc lunch)

Accepts children aged 2½-5yrs. In their
first year, children do a minimum of three
mornings, pre-schoolers do three full days.

## Stoke Bishop Montessori School

70 Parrys Lane, Stoke Bishop, Bristol
Sandra Harris: 0117 968 6960
stokebishopmontessori@hotmail.com
Mon-Fri 8am-6.15pm

Full and part-time places for 2-5yr olds.

## The Clifton Children's House

2 York Gardens, Clifton, BS8 4LL
Mrs Rosamund Payne: 0117 923 7578
www.bristolmontessori.co.uk
rjp@ygardens.demon.co.uk
Mon-Fri 9.15am-12pm or 1pm-3.15pm, term time

Well-established traditional Montessori
Nursery School accepting children aged 2½-
4½yrs. Younger children start in afternoons,
in a small group, progressing to mornings in
their pre-school year. See advertisement.

## STEINER EDUCATION NURSERY SCHOOLS

### Bristol Steiner Waldorf School

Rudolf Steiner Education, Redhill House, Redland
0117 933 9990
Mon-Fri 8.55am-3.30pm various sessions available
for early years

Provides alternative, quality education for
3-14yr olds.

### The Rowan Tree Kindergarten

12d Cotham Rd, Cotham, BS6 6DR
Janet Parsons: 0117 933 9990

Children from 3½-6yrs can learn in a homely
environment and develop at their own pace.

## DIFFERENT LANGUAGE GROUPS

### Clwb y Ddraig Goch (Welsh Club)

50 Richmond Street, Totterdown, Bristol, BS3 4TJ
Sioned Alexander: 0117 971 6478
sioned@alexanderthomas.co.uk

Structured sessions for 0-9yr olds on the
Welsh language and culture using games and
songs. Held at Windmill Hill City Farm every
third or fourth Sat of month. Phone for further
details.

### Deutsche Spielgruppe

The Church Hall, St Matthews Church, Cotham, BS6
Nadya Webster: 0117 902 1509
astridpestell@hotmail.com
Mon 3.30pm-5.30pm
£2.50 a session

Group for German-speaking parents and
their pre-school children. Lots of toys, craft
activities and songs. Meets at St Matthews
throughout the year except during the
summer holidays when there are informal
meetings at local parks.

### Ecole Française de Bristol

Henbury Village Hall, Church Lane, BS10 7WZ
Estelle Tenant: 0117 959 3311
www.ecolefrancaisebristol.co.uk

Nursery for bilingual and English children aged
3-4yrs. Learning French through play. After
school classes and holiday schemes for 4-10yr
olds. See advertisement on pg 225.

### La Casita Toddler Group

Quakers Society of Friends Building,
300 Gloucester Rd, Horfield, BS7 8PD
Rosabel Portela: 0117 914 6950
Wed 10am-1pm, £2 a session

Relaxed friendly group for Spanish speakers
with children from 0-4yrs. Children use their
knowledge of Spanish in play, songs and
creative activities. Weekly summer outings.

Chapter photography: Neil Phillips, Bristol Museums, Galleries and Archives

# SCHOOLS & EDUCATIONAL SUPPORT

**Emma Woodworth**

## CONTENTS

## INTRODUCTION

As a teacher and parent, I am very aware of how important it is to make the right educational choices for your child. Applying for schools can be very stressful and it's important to make informed decisions. Every child's needs are different and finding the right path for them is one of the most important decisions a parent can make.

This chapter outlines all the options available to you and your child throughout their education. We explain admissions and appeals procedures, from starting school up to sixth form. There are contacts and advice for families with children with special educational needs. In addition, there's a list of useful links to educational organisations and services which give advice and support.

# STATE EDUCATION

Local Education Authorities (LEAs) are part of local councils and they are accountable for early-years education, schools, adult education and youth services. LEAs are also responsible for promoting high standards of education and work to improve standards and tackle failure. They provide support for special educational needs, access and school transport, pupil welfare and educating excluded pupils.

Schools in Bristol and its surrounding area fall under four different LEAs.

### Education & Life Long Learning
PO Box 57, The Council House, College Green, Bristol, BS99 7EB
0117 903 7900, www.bristol-lea.org.uk

### South Gloucestershire Council Education Service
Bowling Hill, Chipping Sodbury, South Gloucestershire, BS37 6JX
01454 868009, www.southglos.gov.uk

### North Somerset Council Education Department
PO Box 51, Town Hall, Weston-s-Mare, BS23 1ZZ
01934 888888, www.n-somerset.gov.uk

### Bath and North East Somerset Council Education Department
PO Box 25, Riverside, Temple St, Keynsham, BS31 1DN
01225 477000, www.bathnes.gov.uk

# TYPES OF LEA SCHOOLS

All LEA-run schools are self-managing and do not charge fees. They work in partnership with other schools and LEAs, and receive LEA funding. Each has its own characteristics.

## Community schools

Community schools are very similar to former county schools and include both primary and secondary schools. The LEA employs the school's staff, owns the school's land and buildings and is the admissions authority.

## Voluntary-aided schools

These primary and secondary schools are run by the Church of England or Catholic Church in partnership with the LEA. The governing body determines admissions. For further details, contact individual schools.

## Voluntary-controlled schools

Management of these primary and secondary schools is shared between the LEA and the Church of England. The LEA is responsible for admissions and allocating school places.

## City Technology Colleges

City Technology Colleges (CTCs) are independent, non fee-paying schools for pupils, 11-18yrs. Their purpose is to offer pupils of all abilities the opportunity to study successfully towards the world of work. All CTCs offer a wide range of vocational post -16 qualifications alongside A-Levels.

## Academies

Academies are publicly-funded, independent, secondary schools that will provide a first class free education for local pupils.

## Special schools

LEAs provide these schools (primary and secondary) for certain children with special educational needs (SEN). The great majority, however, are educated in ordinary schools.

# PRIMARY EDUCATION

Primary education (5-11yrs) is normally provided in primary schools, although in some areas, there are separate infant and junior schools. Children come of compulsory school age the term after their fifth birthday. However children usually attend school the September after their fourth birthday so that all children benefit from 3 years of infant education. Often admissions to this Reception year can be phased in up to the half term holiday in October either on a part-time or full time basis at the discretion of the head teacher. If you wish to delay admission beyond the beginning of the autumn term, there is no guarantee that a place will remain available. Children whose admission to school is delayed start in their age group.

## SECONDARY EDUCATION

Children transfer to secondary school the September after their eleventh birthday.

## CHOOSING SCHOOLS

The most important thing you can do before choosing a school for your child is to do your research. A list of primary and secondary schools can be found in the Yellow Pages or obtained from the LEA admissions department. Allow plenty of time to look around schools before application forms have to be submitted.

### Visit the school

One of the best ways to assess a school is by visiting it in person. This way, you gain first-hand knowledge of where your child will be spending their day. You can learn a lot from touring the school and observing the children, the teachers and the way they work together. Things to consider:

- The location of the school. Will you have to drive or take public transport? Can older children safely walk to school?
- Observe the children's work and check the school's resources. Is it a happy school where everyone is serious about learning?
- Find out how the school involves parents.
- Was the school welcoming? Would it suit your child?

Most secondary and some primary schools hold open days and evenings, where you can meet the staff and view children's work. You could also make an appointment to visit the school and speak with the head teacher. Schools also have Parent Teacher Associations (PTAs) or Friends Associations which may be able to give you extra information.

### LEA booklets

Your Local Education Authority (LEA) produces a booklet, which lists all the schools in your area and has information:

- About the schools and their admission arrangements (including admissions form)
- How many pupils they admit and how popular they are

This can be obtained from any school in the LEA or from the LEA admissions department. They are also available in public libraries.

### The school prospectus

Each year, every school publishes a brochure called a prospectus. It usually tells you more about a particular school than the LEA booklet can, and contains the school's admissions policy in detail.

### The performance tables

Every year the Department for Education and Skills (DfES) publishes performance tables for primary and secondary schools. Though they cannot give a complete picture, they serve as a guide to how well a school is doing.

www.dfes.gov.uk/performancetables

### Ofsted reports

It is helpful to read the Office for Standards in Education (Ofsted) reports, produced by the government's school inspectors. A report is available for every school in the country.

www.ofsted.gov.uk/reports

## ADMISSION & APPEAL PROCEDURES

You have the right to say which school you would prefer your child to attend, regardless of the school's location (even if it does not fall into the LEA in which you live). But your right to express a preference does not guarantee you a place at the school if it is oversubscribed.

## Time your application

LEA booklets are usually available during the summer the year before the child is due to start school. The application form, which must be returned by the given deadline, (usually in the autumn term) will be included in the booklet. Late applications will be processed last and you may not get your preferred choice of school. Arrangements vary in each area so contact your local LEA for advice.

## Find out who handles admissions

Admissions are handled either by the local authority, or by the school itself. If you have not applied, **do not** assume your child will get a place at the school you want. This is true even if your child is at a nursery which is linked to an infant school, or at an infant school which is linked to a junior school. Remember also, that you need to apply for each of your children as they reach school age. Having one child at a school does not automatically mean a place for siblings.

When completing the application form, it is important to state your second and third preferred school in case your first choice is unsuccessful.

If there are sufficient places available, your child will be offered a place at your preferred school. However in schools which are oversubscribed, the LEA uses specific criteria when allocating places. These are usually:

- Siblings already attending the school
- Medical, psychological or special educational reason
- Geographical location to home

## Appeals procedure

If you are not allocated a place at your preferred school, you will be offered an alternative school. You have the right to accept the alternative place or formally appeal to an independent panel for a place at your preferred school. The letter you receive from the admission authority should also provide information about your right to appeal and how to go about it.

## SERVICES PROVIDED BY LEA

### Free transport

Free transport is provided if pupils:

- Attend the nearest appropriate school as determined by the city council and
- The distance between home and school is 2 miles or more for pupils under 8yrs or 3 miles or more for pupils 8-16 yrs

### Free school meals

These are available if you are entitled to Income Support, Income Based Job-seeker's Allowance, support under Part VI of the Immigration and Asylum Act 1999 or Child Tax Credit with an income below £13,910.

### Milk in schools

The LEA provides a free daily carton of milk to all pupils under the age of 5. Some schools run their own scheme for pupils over 5.

### Grants

The LEA may be able to help with costs for families who are in financial difficulty. Contact your LEA for further details.

### Welfare

Child welfare in schools is primarily the concern of the staff and head teacher of the school. A welfare officer also supports schools and parents in ensuring full-time school attendance, promoting good home/school liaison, supporting excluded pupils, special educational needs, bullying and welfare benefits.

### Educational psychology

Schools are allocated an educational psychologist. They may get involved if there are any concerns with children's learning and general development, behaviour and special educational needs.

### School nurse

Each school has a named nurse who works in partnership with parents, teachers and children offering help and support with any emotional/behavioural or physical concerns parents may have. At school entry parents are offered hearing and sight tests and growth measurement for their child.

## SCHOOL YEARS

| | |
|---|---|
| Nursery/Reception | Foundation Stage<br>3-5 years |
| Year 1 & 2 | Infants/Key Stage 1<br>5-7 years |
| Year 3-6 | Juniors/Key Stage 2<br>7-11 years |
| Years 7-9 | Secondary/Key Stage 3<br>11-14 years |
| Years 10 & 11 | Secondary/Key Stage 4<br>14-16 years |

## ASSESSMENT AT SCHOOL

### Foundation stage

Each child is issued with a profile which charts their development across the areas of learning throughout the Foundation stage.

### National testing

Currently at the end of Key Stages 1 (Yr 2), 2 (Yr 6) and 3 (Yr 9) pupil progress is assessed through Standard Attainment Tests (SATs) in English, Maths and Science.

### Key Stage 4

There are a range of options for pupils in years 10 and 11. These include:

- Entry level certificates for pupils that would struggle with GCSEs
- General Certificates for Secondary Education (GCSEs) based on coursework and exams
- GCSE short courses, taking a year, two make up a full GCSE
- General National Vocational Qualifications (GNVQs), studying broad work areas
- National Vocational Qualifications (NVQs) relate to real work
- Vocational Qualifications (VQs) earned through practical work-based placements

Individual schools do not necessarily offer all of these options, so when choosing a school, make sure it suits your preferences.

## EDUCATIONAL WEBSITES

**Allkids**, www.allkids.co.uk

Extensive parent/child directory. Tons of links to educational and safe, fun sites.

**BBC Learning**
www.bbc.co.uk/learning/home

Useful resources and interactive activities.

**At School**
www.atschool.co.uk

**Bookstart**, www.bookstart.co.uk

The Booktrust's national 'books for babies' programme, offering free books to every child.

### For parents

**DfES: The Parent Centre**
www.parentcentre.gov.uk

Information about schools and the curriculum, as well as a facility to search for local schools.

**Educate the Children**, www.educate.org.uk

Guidelines on the education system and information about local schools.

**Reading is Fundamental**
www.rif.org.uk

Top tips to help children read.

**Spelling it Right**
www.spelling.hemscott.net

### For children

**Digger and the Gang**
www.bbc.co.uk/education/schools/digger

A BBC website based on the National Curriculum for primary school children.

**Granada Learning**
www.granada-learning.com

Curriculum software, online resources and multimedia products for all ages and needs.

**Science Line**, www.sciencenet.org.uk/index

### Homework

**Homework High,** www.homeworkhigh.com

Help with main subjects, answers emails.

### Homework Elephant
www.homeworkelephant.co.uk

Help for homework assignments and provides a font of all knowledge, the 'agony elephant'!

### Kidscape, www.kidscape.org.uk
Practical advice to help beat bullying.

## Revision

### GCSE Answers, www.gcse.com
Tips on GCSE coursework and exams.

### GCSE Bitesize
www.bbc.co.uk/education/revision

Brush up on your GCSE skills.

### S-Cool
www.s-cool.co.uk

Revision guides and exam hints.

# SPECIAL EDUCATIONAL NEEDS

Children with special educational needs (SEN) have learning difficulties, or disabilities that make it harder for them to learn than most children of the same age. These children may need extra help.

Special needs could include problems with: thinking and understanding, physical or sensory skills, behaviour and emotions or speech and language.

Help for children with SEN will usually be in the child's ordinary, mainstream early education setting or school, sometimes with help from outside specialists.

### If you are worried your child may be having difficulties

Your child's early years are an important time for physical, emotional, intellectual and social development. When your health visitor or doctor makes a routine check, they might suggest that there could be a problem and give you advice about the next steps to take.

If you think your child may have a special educational need, you should talk to your child's class teacher, the SENCO (the SEN co-ordinator), the head teacher or head of year.

The Independent Panel for Special Education Advice (IPSEA) offers free advice on LEAs' legal duties to assess and provide for children with SEN. www.ipsea.org.uk

# EDUCATIONAL SUPPORT
Also see Special Needs, Advice & Support chapter.

### Advisory Centre for Education
Unit 1C, 22 Highbury Grove, London, N5 2EA
www.ace-ed.org.uk
0808 800 5793, 2pm-5pm

### Support for ADD/ADHD
45 Vincent Close, Broadstairs, Kent, CT10 2ND
support@adders.org, www.adders.org
01843 851145, 24 hr

### AFASIC
2nd Floor, 50-52 Great Sutton St, London, EC1V 0DJ
info@afasic.org.uk, www.afasic.org.uk
020 7490 9410, Mon-Fri 9am-5pm
Helpline 0845 3555577 Mon-Thu 11am-2pm

Association for All Speech Impaired Children.

### Belgrave School
10 Upper Belgrave Road, BS8 2XH
0117 974 3133
www.dyslexiacentre.co.uk

Full time school (24 pupils) for children (7-12 yrs) with dyslexia and related difficulties.

### Bristol Dyslexia Centre
10 Upper Belgrave Road, BS8 2XH
0117 973 9405
www.dyslexiacentre.co.uk

Private tuition for children with learning difficulties.

## British Dyslexia Association

98 London Road, Reading, Berkshire RG1 5AU
www.bda-dyslexia.org.uk
0118 966 2677
Mon-Fri 10am-12.45pm & 2pm-5pm

## The Dyslexia Institute

14 Whiteladies Rd, Bristol, BS8 1PD
0117 923 9166
www.dyslexia-inst.org.uk

Advice, assessments and tuition. Additional teaching centre at Staple Hill.

## Dyspraxia Foundation

8 West Alley, Hitchin, Herts, SG5 1EG
www.dyspraxiafoundation.org.uk
01462 454986

## Parents for Inclusion

Unit 2, 70 South Lambeth Road, London SW8 1RL
020 7735 7735

## Portage Service

Elmfield House, Greystoke Ave, Bristol, BS10 6AY
0117 903 8438

A home-visiting educational service for pre-school children with special needs.

## The National Association for Gifted Children — NAGC

Suite 14, Challenge House, Sherwood Drive, Bletchley, MK3 6DP
www.nagcbritain.org.uk
0845 450 0221

## Supportive Parents, Parent Partnership Service

3rd Floor Royal Oak House, Royal Oak Ave, BS1 4GB
www.supportiveparents.org.uk
0117 989 7724 Admin
0117 989 7725 Helpline, Mon/Wed/Fri 10am-2pm

Term time support for parents of children with any level of special educational need.

# SICK CHILDREN

The LEA and schools must ensure that children who are unable to attend school because of medical needs have access to as much education as their medical condition allows. If a child is hospitalised then staff need to liase with and involve the school early on. Contact your LEA or visit www.dfes.gov.uk/sickchildren

# POST 16 EDUCATION

Our new Freedom Guide (for young people aged 10-18yrs) gives full details on college education. The book is available from outlets across the West or from:

www.freedomguide.co.uk.

# HOME SCHOOLING

While school is not compulsory, parents do have a responsibility to ensure their child has an effective education, which can be at home.

## Education Otherwise

PO Box 7420, London, N9 9SG
Tel: 0870 730 0074
www.educationotherwise.org.uk

A self-help group offering support and information on home education.

## Home Education Advisory Service

www.heas.org.uk

Provides advice and support for families who wish to educate their children at home.

# PRIVATE TUITION

There are many independent tutors or larger agencies (search on the internet under private tuition) providing extra educational support for your child. Tuition can be on a one-to-one basis or in small groups. Independent tutors can also be found in the Yellow Pages, Primary Times (available in schools & libraries), in newspapers and via schools. Check any tutor you find for your child has passed a police check.

## Kumon

www.kumon.co.uk
0800 854 714

This style of educational support is becoming increasingly popular. It was devised 40 years ago by Toru Kumon, a Japanese school teacher. It is based on repeated exercises in maths and English and is about making sure the foundations of learning are solid before moving on to the next level. Parental involvement is essential! There are centres across the West. See advertisement in the Colour Reference Section, pg 129.

# INDEPENDENT EDUCATION

These are private schools which are independent of local or central government control. Most of them have their own board of governors and a bursar who is responsible for financial and other aspects of school management. The head is responsible to the governors but has the freedom to appoint staff, admit pupils and take day-to-day decisions. Independents include day and boarding schools and can be single-sex or co-educational.

## Choosing a school

Most schools advertise in the Yellow Pages, local papers and educational publications. Having obtained a prospectus, arrange a visit. It's worth going to open days, but also try to visit on a normal working day.

## Curriculum

Independent schools are not required to follow the National Curriculum and therefore set their own. Some schools place emphasis on the arts or sciences, whereas some are more sport-oriented.

## Admission and selection

Many junior schools and even some senior schools admit pupils on a first-come-first-served basis. Senior schools usually set some form of entrance test. The difficulty of these and the standards required for admission vary.

## How much?

Basic fees vary widely depending on the age of the child, location and facilities. Approximate fee range per term as at 2006:

| | |
|---|---|
| Pre-Prep (age 2-7) | £1200-£2770 |
| Junior/Prep (age 7-13) | £1325-£3270 |
| Senior (age 11/13-18) | £2200-£4060 |

Many schools include lunches in basic fees. Uniforms, trips and other incidental costs will add to the bill. You may have to pay for books, entries for public examinations, stationery and medical supplies.

## Scholarships and bursaries

Scholarships are awarded to students who have shown academic or sporting excellence. They rarely cover the whole fee.

Many schools also have bursaries, grants from the school, to help you pay the fees. These are often means-tested. Some schools offer grants to children of clergy, teachers and armed forces personnel. Some give concessions for siblings.

## Bristol Independent Schools

www.bristolindependentschools.co.uk

Bristol's independent schools have made it easy to investigate the range of independent education offered. There are links to 11 schools' websites.

## The Independent Schools Council information service (ISCis)

020 7766 7071, www.isc.co.uk

## The Independent Schools Guide

www.gabbitas.net

A complete directory of the UK's independent schools and special schools.

# SHOPPING & SERVICES

**Lu Hersey**

## CONTENTS

# INTRODUCTION

Shopping with children in tow is not always the most relaxing experience. However, knowing the location of the nearest toilets, changing mats, feeding rooms, lifts and refuelling stations can make the outing a little easier! Assume all independent shops have buggy access unless stated otherwise.

Broadmead and the Mall at Cribbs Causeway provide Bristol with a wide selection of shops along with good facilities for parents with small children. And if you can't get out of the house, many big names offer mail order and internet shopping, see table opposite. This chapter includes a listing of the major high street names, but our main aim is to focus on the many independent retailers in Bristol, who offer interesting products, in-depth knowledge and a personal service.

# SHOPPING CENTRES

## The Galleries

0117 929 0569
www.galleries-shopping.co.uk
Mon-Wed 8.30am-6pm, Thu 8.30am- 8pm, Fri-Sat 8.30am-6pm, Sun 11am-5pm

Car park open for one hour after shops close.

## The Mall at Cribbs Causeway

0117 903 0303
www.mallcribbs.com
Mon-Fri 10am-9pm, Sat 9am-7pm, Sun 11am-5pm
Bank Holidays 10am-6pm
John Lewis opening hours vary.
Jct 17, M5

# SUPERMARKETS

Over recent years, supermarkets have increased their non-food ranges significantly. Many of them now offer a one-stop shop for all your needs, stocking maternity wear, nursery equipment, clothing, toys and books. Some stock food ranges specifically manufactured for children. See Supermarket table overleaf.

## ONLINE SHOPPING

Several supermarkets offer an internet shopping and delivery service which can be very useful at any time, not least during the last few weeks of pregnancy and early months with a newborn. Most charge around £5 for delivery, although some waive this charge if you spend above a certain amount.

The following tips may help you when ordering your groceries online:

• Ordering online can take a while at first, so place your first order when you've got a bit of time on your hands and you will reap the rewards as you build up your own personal shopping list. It's best to make a list before you start.

• It is good for heavy items, particularly if you have enough storage to buy in bulk.

• Know the weights/sizes of products that you buy.

After the initial order, it can be a hassle free way to shop particularly if you are ill, have small children or have no car.

# DEPARTMENT AND LARGER STORES SUMMARY TABLE

For stores situated at The Mall or The Galleries, the facilities shown are in addition to those at the shopping centre. All stores have nearby parking and can accommodate single and double buggies

| Department Store | Mail Order | Internet Shopping | Branch Location | Facilities | Clothing (Age Range) | Shoes | Maternity wear | Maternity Underwear | Children's Furniture | Nursery Equipment | Toys | Outdoor Toys | Computer Games | Books |
|---|---|---|---|---|---|---|---|---|---|---|---|---|---|---|
| BHS www.bhs.co.uk | | | The Mall 0117 950 9493 | [WC][✎][✕][♿][CP] | 0-14 | ✓ | | | | | | | | |
| | | | Broadmead 0117 929 2261 | [WC][✎][✕][♿][CP] | 0-14 | ✓ | | | | | | | | |
| Woolworths www.woolworths.co.uk | | | Filton 0117 969 7303 | [WC][✎][✕][♿][CP] | 0+ | ✓ | | | | ✓ | ✓ | ✓ | ✓ | ✓ |
| | ✓ | ✓ | The Galleries 0117 922 7778 | | 0-13 | ✓ | | | | | ✓ | ✓ | ✓ | ✓ |
| Boots (Larger Branches) www.boots.com | | ✓ | The Mall 0117 950 9744 | | 0-4 | | | | | web | ✓ | ✓ | ✓ | |
| | | | Broadmead 0117 929 3631 | [✎] | 0-4 | | | | | web | ✓ | ✓ | ✓ | |
| | | | Avon Meads 0117 972 8056 | [WC][✎] | 0-4 | | | | | web | ✓ | ✓ | ✓ | |
| Debenhams www.debenhams.com | ▯ | ▯ | Broadmead 08445 616161 | [WC][✎][✕][♿][CP][◷][lift] | 0-14 | ✓ | | ✓ | | | ✓ | ✓ | ✓ | ✓ |
| House of Fraser www.houseoffraser.co.uk | | | Broadmead 0117 944 5566 | [WC][✎][✕][♿][CP][lift] | 0-10 | | | ✓ | | | | | | |
| Ikea www.ikea.co.uk | | | Eastville 0845 355 2264 | [WC][✎][✕][♿][CP][◷][restaurant][lift][buggy][lift] | | | | | ✓ | | ✓ | | | |
| John Lewis www.johnlewis.com | | ✓ | The Mall 0117 959 1100 | [WC][✎][✕][♿][lift][access][◷][arrow] | 0-14 | ✓ | | ✓ | ✓ | ✓ | ✓ | ✓ | ✓ | ✓ |
| Marks & Spencer marksandspencer.com | ✓ | ✓ | Broadmead 0117 927 2000 | [WC][✎][✕][♿][CP][lift][access] | 0-12 | ✓ | | ✓ | ✓ | | ✓ | | ✓ | ✓ |
| | | | The Mall 0117 904 4444 | [WC][✎][✕][♿][CP][lift][access] | 0-12 | ✓ | | ✓ | ✓ | | ✓ | | ✓ | ✓ |
| Mothercare World www.mothercare.com | ✓ | ✓ | Avon Meads 0117 971 9815 | [WC][✎][arrow] | 0-8 | ✓ | ✓ | ✓ | ✓ | ✓ | ✓ | ✓ | | ✓ |
| | | | Eastville 0117 951 8200 | [WC][✎][✕][♿][CP][arrow] | 0-8 | ✓ | ✓ | ✓ | ✓ | ✓ | ✓ | ✓ | | ✓ |
| TK Maxx www.tkmaxx.com | | | The Galleries 0117 930 4404 | | 0+ | ✓ | | | | | ✓ | | ✓ | ✓ |
| | | | Cribbs 0117 950 8081 | [lift] | 0+ | ✓ | | | | | ✓ | | ✓ | ✓ |

## SUPERMARKETS

| Supermarket | Mail Order | Internet Shopping | Branch Location | Facilities | Clothing (Age Range) | Open 24 hrs ? | Shoes | Maternity wear | Maternity Underwear | Nursery Equipment | Toys | Books | Computer Games |
|---|---|---|---|---|---|---|---|---|---|---|---|---|---|
| Asda www.asda.co.uk | | ✓ | Cribbs Causeway 0117 317 2400 | WC, mat, feeding, lift, CP | 0-15 | ✓ | ✓ | ✓ | ✓ | ✓ | ✓ | ✓ | ✓ |
| | | | Longwell Green 0117 960 3947 | WC, mat, feeding, lift, CP | 0-15 | ✓ | ✓ | ✓ | ✓ | ✓ | ✓ | ✓ | ✓ |
| | | | Bedminster 0117 923 1563 | WC, mat, feeding, lift, CP | 0-15 | | ✓ | | | | ✓ | ✓ | ✓ |
| | | | Whitchurch 01275 839 431 | WC, mat | 0-15 | | ✓ | | | | ✓ | ✓ | ✓ |
| Tesco www.tesco.com | ✓ | ✓ | Brislington 0117 991 7400 | WC, mat, feeding, lift, CP | 0-13 | ✓ | ✓ | ✓ | ✓ | | ✓ | ✓ | ✓ |
| | | | Eastgate Centre 0117 912 7400 | WC, mat, feeding, lift, CP | 0-13 | ✓ | ✓ | ✓ | | | ✓ | ✓ | ✓ |
| Sainsburys www.sainsbury.co.uk | | ✓ | Ashton Gate 0117 966 3064 | WC, mat, feeding, lift, CP | 0-13 | | | | | | ✓ | ✓ | ✓ |
| | | | Castle Court 0117 977 4887 | WC, mat, chair, feeding, lift, CP | 0-10 | | ✓ | | | | ✓ | ✓ | ✓ |
| | | | Filton 0117 923 6459 | WC, mat, feeding, lift, CP | 0-13 | | | | | | ✓ | ✓ | ✓ |

## INTRODUCTION

Shopping with children in tow is not always the most relaxing experience. However, knowing the location of the nearest toilets, changing mats, feeding rooms, lifts and refuelling stations can make the outing a little easier! Assume all independent shops have buggy access unless stated otherwise.

Broadmead and the Mall at Cribbs Causeway provide Bristol with a wide selection of shops along with good facilities for parents with small children. And if you can't get out of the house, many big names offer mail order and internet shopping, see table opposite. This chapter includes a listing of the major high street names, but our main aim is to focus on the many independent retailers in Bristol, who offer interesting products, in-depth knowledge and a personal service.

## Baby Gap & Gap Kids

The Mall, Cribbs Causeway
0117 950 9698 Baby Gap
0117 950 9667 Gap Kids
&
30-32 The Broadmead, BS1 3HA
0117 922 0657
Mon-Fri 9.30am-6pm, Sat 9am-6pm, Sun 11am-5pm

Good quality, clothing and shoes (American Sizes). Clothing is expensive, but stock is changed regularly and there are great sale rails. Baby Gap sizes from premature baby to 5 years, Gap Kids from 4-15yrs.

## Be Wise Ltd

26-32 Regent St, Kingswood, BS16
0117 935 2239
Mon-Sat 9am-5.30pm, Sun 10am-4pm
&
48 East Street, Bedminster, BS3
0117 963 1652

Sells inexpensive clothes, 0-13 yrs.

## Bishopston Trading Company

193 Gloucester Rd, Bishopston
0117 924 5598
www.bishopstontrading.co.uk
Mon-Sat 9.30am-5.30pm

Workers co-operative set up to create employment in South Indian village of KV Kuppam. Fair trade shop with play area. Specialises in natural fabrics and organic handloom cotton in a range of colours in sizes from 0-13yrs. Also see Mail Order below.

## Born

64 Gloucester Rd, Bishopston, BS7 8BH
0845 1302676
www.borndirect.com
Mon-Sat 9.30am-5.30pm

Most of the products in this shop are natural/organic. They stock a large range of cotton nappies and accessories, soft leather shoes, organic cotton and fairtraded clothing/toys along with a practical range of high quality outdoor wear. Also see their advertisement above along with Nursery Equipment and Maternity Wear sub-chapters.

## Claire's Accessories

The Mall, Cribbs Causeway
0117 959 4779
Broadmead Gallery, Broadmead
0117 922 6657
Mon-Sat 9am-5.30pm, Thu 7pm

A great selection of beauty and hair accessories. Branches in Yate and Weston-super-Mare.

## H&M

The Mall, Cribbs Causeway
0117 950 9590

Fashionable but inexpensive children's clothing from birth to 14yrs. Also see Maternity Wear sub-chapter.

## Monsoon Kids' Store

The Mall, Cribbs Causeway
0117 750 0753

New store selling only childrens' clothes with complete range of clothing for babies, girls (under 12yrs) and boys (under 8yrs). Changing room has toys and games to keep kids amused.

## Monsoon

Unit 7 New Broadmead, Union St, BS1 2DL
0117 929 0870
www.monsoon.co.uk
Mon-Sat 9.30am-5.30pm, Sun 11am-5pm

Girl's clothes including posh frocks and shoes.

## Mothercare World

The Eastgate Centre, Eastville, BS12
0117 951 8200
Mon-Fri 9.30am-8pm, Sat 9am-6pm, Sun 11am-5pm

&
Avon Meads, St Philips Causeway
0117 971 9815
Mon-Fri 9.30am-8pm, Sat 9am-6pm, Sun 11am-5pm

Large range of reasonably priced baby and children's wear. Clothes from 0-8yrs, school wear to 11yrs. Also see Nursery Equipment, Toys and Maternity Wear sub-chapters.

## Next

Broadmead (opposite H & M)
0117 922 6495
Mon-Sat 9am-6pm, Thu until 7pm, Sun 11am-5pm

&
The Mall, Cribbs Causeway
0117 950 9033
www.next.co.uk

Good range of mid-priced clothing and shoes. Stores stock sizes from 0-10yrs, but clothes up to 16yrs available to order in store or from the directory.

## Next Clearance

Abbeywood Retail Park, Station Rd, Filton
0117 906 2280
Mon-Fri 9.30am-8pm, Sat 9am-6pm, Sun 11am-5pm

End of season and clearance stock from Next and Next Directory. Prices are up to 50% off original selling price. Children's clothing and shoes available from birth upwards.

## Oranges and Lemons

20 Princess Victoria Street, Clifton, BS8 4BP
0117 973 7370
Mon-Sat 9am-5.30pm

Wide range of designer clothing, shoes and accessories, including Baby Dior, Diesel and O'Neill. Excellent quality clothes, 0-12yrs.

## Peacocks

50-60 The Horsefair, BS1 3EY
0117 927 9583
www.peacocks.co.uk
Mon-Sat 9am-5.30pm

Large selection of reasonably priced clothing, from 0-15yrs. Branches in Bedminster, Gloucester Road, Keynsham, Nailsea and Weston-super-Mare.

## The Natural Nursery

185 North Street, Southville, Bristol, BS3 1JQ
0117 966 8483
www.naturalnursery.co.uk
Mon-Sat 9am-4pm Thu 6pm
nr junction with Luckwell Road

Organic and fair traded products. Nappies, clothes, bedding, toys, breastfeeding aids, maternity clothes, 'Bugaboo' prams, books, slings and toiletries. See advertisement.

## TinyTots Kids Shop

Abbotswood Shopping Centre, Yate
01454 314 174
Mon-Fri 9am-4pm, Wed 1pm, Sat 9am-12am.

Sells designer and well known chainstore clothing for 0-8yrs at discount prices.

## CHILDREN'S SHOES

There are a wide range of shoes available from birth, suited to each stage of your child's development.

When learning to walk, children use the feel of the floor to balance, so it is best to wait until they are walking confidently before buying their first pair of proper walking shoes' Children's shoes can be expensive, but it is very important to look after their developing feet. Once purchased, it is important to check the fit frequently and good shoe shops will be happy to do so.

Besides the specialist shoe shops listed below, please also see Department Stores, Supermarkets and Factory Outlets.

### Clarks Shoes

The Mall, Cribbs Causeway
0117 959 2290
&
35 Broadmead, BS1 8EU
0117 929 0992
Mon-Sat 9.30am-5.30pm, Sun 11am-5pm

### Clarks at Mothercare World

The Eastgate Centre, Eastville, BS12
0117 951 9917
&
Avon Meads, St Philips Causeway, BS2 0SP
0117 971 9860

Good range of shoes in width fittings starting from size three. Also a range of crawling and cruising shoes for those early months. The staff are helpful and will take a photo of your child in their first pair of shoes!

## Holbrooks

1-2 Boyce's Av, Clifton, BS8
0117 973 8350
Mon-Sat 9am-5.30pm

Good range of Start-rite and Clarks shoes and trainers from size 4. Dance shoes for ballroom, latin, ballet, tap and jazz. Discount available for twins.

## John Lewis

The Mall, Cribbs Causeway
0117 959 1100

Shoe department on the first floor selling many different brands. Also stocks trainers, slippers, sandals and wellies.

When busy, there is an efficient queuing system using bleeping pagers to allow you to shop elsewhere while waiting.

## KBK Shoes

203 Cheltenham Road, Cotham, BS6 5QX
0117 924 3707
Mon-Fri 9.30am-6pm, Sat 9am-6pm

Sells Dr Martens and Birkenstock sandals in summer. Children's feet can be measured accurately in the store.

## Kids at Clinks

At Charles Clinkard, The Mall, Cribbs Causeway
0117 959 2484

A good selection of baby shoes (size 0) and shoes starting at size 2. Brands include Clarks, Start-Rite, Kickers, Hush Puppies, Timberland, Babybotte, Buckle My Shoe and many more. Trained shoe fitters.

## One small step one giant leap

See Shops Outside Bristol (Bath) for further details.

## Oranges and Lemons

20 Princess Victoria Street, Clifton, BS8 4BP
0117 973 7370
Mon-Sat 9am-5.30pm

Shoes stocked from newborn upwards including O'Neill trainers and sandals.

## The Handmade Shoe Company

64 Colston Street, BS1 5AZ
0117 921 4247
Opening hours vary, please call shop for details.

Handmade shoes starting at size 4, available in standard sizes and made to measure. Baby shoes available (not handmade).

## Thomas Ford

The Clarks Shop, Kingschase Shopping Centre, Kingswood, BS15 2LP
0117 961 3807
Mon-Sat 9am-5.30pm
&
12 St Mary's Way, Thornbury, BS35 2BH
01454 419142
Mon-Sat 9am-5.30pm
&
17 Old Church Rd, Clevedon, BS21 6LU
01275 879512
WC at all stores

Full range of Clarks' shoes in width fittings including cruisers, trainers and slippers. Staff are trained Clarks' shoes fitters. Kingschase store also stock discounted children's shoes.

# UNIFORMS

Most department stores and supermarkets sell school uniforms and offer good value ranges. Below are specialist stockists.

## National School Wear Centres

22 Gloucester Rd Nth, Filton Park, BS7 0SF
0117 969 8551
www.n-sc.co.uk
Mon-Fri 9am-5pm, Sat 10am-4pm

Sells generic and some North Bristol State school uniforms. Also clothing for Cubs, Brownies, ballet, bowling and sports wear.

## School Togs Nailsea Ltd

110 High St, Nailsea, BS48 1AH
01275 857 491
Mon-Fri 9am-5.30pm, Sat 9am-5pm

Comprehensive range of uniforms for local schools, along with school sports, Scouts, Guides & dance clothing. 4-16yrs.

## Ikon (UK) Ltd

190 Henleaze Rd, Bristol, BS9 4NE
0117 962 0011
Mon-Fri 9am-5pm, Sat 10am-5pm

Recently opened and keen to help with any sporting equipment/clothing or Scout/school uniforms you may need.

# MATERNITY

There are good ranges of maternity wear available, at varying prices, in the outlets listed below. There are several fastenings designed to accommodate your growing bump and it is a good idea to try, before buying, to find the most comfortable one for you. Well-fitting, comfortable, maternity underwear is a necessary expense during your pregnancy, to support your changing shape. Your bra size can change dramatically during pregnancy and most stockists offer a measuring service. Also see Department Stores, Supermarkets and Nearly New for maternity clothing.

## MAIL ORDER MATERNITY WEAR

If you would like the privacy and convenience of trying your maternity clothes at home before buying, try the companies listed below. All offer maternity wear ordering and delivery via the internet or by phone from a catalogue.

### Argos Additions
0845 304 0008
www.additionsdirect.co.uk

### Blooming Marvellous
0845 458 7406
www.bloomingmarvellous.co.uk

### JoJo Maman Bebe
0870 241 0560
Website: www.jojomamanbebe.co.uk

### Next
0845 600 7000
www.next.co.uk

### Vertbaudet
0845 270 0270
www.vertbaudet.co.uk

## Asda

Asda has recently introduced a range of maternity wear within its George clothing brand. It is stocked at their Cribbs Causeway and Longwell Green branches.

## Blooming Marvellous

5 Saracan Street, Bath, BA1 5BR
0845 458 7425
www.bloomingmarvellous.co.uk
Mon-Sat 9.30am-5.30pm, Sun 10.30am-4.30pm

Although well known for its mail order, it is great to be able to see their range of maternity & baby wear, nursery equipment & toys in store. "This is a great place to start your maternity wardrobe." See advertisement in Healthcare, pg 181.

## Born

64 Gloucester Rd, Bishopston, BS7 8BH
0117 924 5080
www.borndirect.com
Mon-Sat 9.30am-5.30pm

Bravado range of maternity underwear and feeding tops.

**Need to hire a Birthing pool, ObTENS machine, valley cushion or breast pump?**
See Healthcare, pg 181

## Dorothy Perkins

62 Broadmead, Broadmead
0117 927 3790
Mon-Fri 9am-5.30pm, Sat 9am-6pm, Sun 11am-5pm
The Mall, Cribbs Causeway
0117 950 7665

Good range of trousers, jeans, dresses, tops and swimwear in sizes 8 to 22. No underwear. Branches in Yate and Weston-Super-Mare.

## H&M

The Mall, Cribbs Causeway
0117 950 9590

Good range of inexpensive maternity wear in sizes 8 to 20.

## John Lewis

The Mall, Cribbs Causeway
0117 959 1100

A good range of maternity and feeding bras, with a measuring service available. No maternity clothes.

## Mothercare World

The Eastgate Centre, Eastville, BS12
0117 951 8200
&
Avon Meads, St Philips Causeway
0117 971 9815
For Hours & Facilities see Children's Clothing

Both stores have a wide range of maternity wear in sizes from 8 to 22. Swimming costumes and bras (measuring service).

## NCT — Maternity Bra Sales

0117 924 3849

Ruth Bolgar sells maternity bras on behalf of the NCT. She offers a free fitting service. Call her for further details.

## Next Clearance

Abbeywood Retail Park, Station Rd, Filton
0117 906 2280
www.next.co.uk
Mon-Fri 9.30am-8pm, Sat 9am-6pm, Sun 11am-5pm

End-of-season and clearance maternity wear at up to 50% off original price.

## Venus Maternity

56 The Mall, Clifton Village, Bristol, BS8 4JG
0117 973 6400
www.venus-maternity.com
Mon 12pm-5.30pm, Tue-Sat 10am-5.50pm

Venus maternity wear offers a range of affordable fashions for all occasions along with swimwear, underwear and mum & baby gift ideas. Visit the shop or buy online. See adveriisement in Heathcare, pg 179.

**Need some mental preparation for the impending day?** See Parentcraft Classes, pg 180

# MATERNITY SERVICES

During your pregnancy and postnatally, there will be services you may require. Some you may never have thought of! These services are listed in the Healthcare chapter under Maternity Services. They include hiring birthing pools, valley cushions, ObTen machines and breast pumps. See pg 181.

# NAPPY INFORMATION & LAUNDRY SERVICES

After the move away from washable nappies to disposables, the trend is now reversing. Modern washable nappies are different from the old-fashioned Terry toweling ones and there are several types to choose from.

Nappy Laundry Services deliver re-usable nappies to your home and once a week collect the soiled nappies, which are washed according to NHS guidelines. Users rate their service as excellent and you may be surprised to see how little it costs. Companies often offer a trial of their service.

Some parents are coming around to doing the laundry themselves, with modern liners, detergents and a reliable washing machine you may be tempted too!

## Boo coo

Ham Green, Pill
01275 374 909
www.boocoo.co.uk

A friendly, local business run by washable nappy users with a vast experience of cloth nappies. They sell a select range of easy to use modern washables at competitive prices. Their website has cost comparisons and they offer local demos and hire kits so you can try before you buy! Local nappy incentive vouchers, including the Bristol & S. Gloucestershire scheme, can be redeemed. (No laundry service provided.)

## Born

64 Gloucester Rd, Bishopston, BS7 8BH
0845 1302676
www.borndirect.com
Mon-Sat 9.30am-5.30pm

Stock a large range of cotton nappies and accessories.

## Dinky Diapers

Unit 2, 13 Wellsway, Keynsham, Bristol, BS31 1HS
0117 986 6167
www.dinkydiapers.co.uk

All-cotton nappies are delivered to homes in Bristol and Bath. A special lined bin for storing soiled nappies is provided. Weekly collection and delivery, including nappy rental, costs £7.95. A 4-week trial with demonstration is £30. Also sells Tushies, Moltex and Ecover refillable products.

## The Nappy Stash

Unit 2C, Olympia House, Beaconsfield Rd, St George, BS5 8ER
0117 941 4839
www.nappystash.co.uk

Nappies are delivered and collected on a weekly basis in Bristol and North Somerset. You will also be provided with a deodorised, sealed bin. The full-time weekly service costs £8.05, and a month's trial including demonstration is £32. A part-time service is available and costs £2.50 per week plus 18p per nappy. "Very efficient service."

## The Natural Nursery

185 North Street, Southville, Bristol, BS3 1JQ
0117 966 8483
www.naturalnursery.co.uk
Mon-Sat 9am-4pm Thu 6pm
nr junction with Luckwell Road

Stocks a good range of washable nappies.

## The Real Nappy Project

0117 930 4355
www.recyclingconsortium.org.uk

Working with parents, health professionals and community projects to raise awareness of the cost and environmental savings that parents can make by using modern washable nappies. The new styles have poppers, Velcro and wash and dry really easily. Contact them for a list of local stockists.

# NURSERY EQUIPMENT

The independent retailers listed in this section offer a great choice of nursery equipment including prams, car seats and cots. They often stock more unusual brands compared to the high street names and can often order prams etc. in specific colours or fabrics. Staff are usually very helpful and have great product knowledge.

See also Department & Larger Stores, and for repair services see the Services section of this chapter.

## Baby & Co

21 Temple Street, Keynsham, BS31 1HF
0117 986 8184
Mon-Sat 9am-5pm

Large range of prams, highchairs, cots, car seats and clothing up to 3yrs.

## Born

64 Gloucester Rd, Bishopston, BS7 8BH
0117 924 5080
www.borndirect.com
Mon-Sat 9.30am-5.30pm

Stockist of Stokke children's furniture, Tripp Trapp high chair, Sleepi Cot, Sleepy Care changing table and the Xplory pushchair and Bugaboo buggy. Also stocks slings and backpacks.

## Hurwoods

32 Old Market Street, Old Market, BS2 0HB
0117 926 2690
www.hurwoods.co.uk
Mon-Fri 9.30am-5pm, Sat 9am-5pm

Established in 1899, Hurwoods have a huge range of nursery equipment. They stock a large selection of prams, travel systems, three wheelers and buggies, all which are serviced for free within the first twelve months. Good choice of car seats with a 'try before you buy' policy. Nursery furniture, bedding and decor department. Car park nearby. 'Excellent range with good service from knowledgeable staff'.

## John Lewis

The Mall, Cribbs Causeway

Large range of nursery equipment including prams, cots, bedding, car seats, high chairs and nursery furniture. Very helpful staff with good product knowledge. Car seats can be fitted by appointment. They run a nursery advisory service for new mums.

## TinyTots Kids Shop

Abbotswood Shopping Centre, Yate
01454 314 174
Mon-Fri 9am-4pm, Wed 1pm, Sat 9am-12am.

Stocks a full range of nursery equipment and accessories including buggies, bedding, Grobags, buggy boards and Taggies. They also stock a wide range of personalised gifts and clothing for the U8's.

## CAR SEATS

Child safety when travelling by car is of the utmost importance. There is a wide variety of car safety seats to suit each stage of your child's growth.

Important points to remember:

• It is the weight of your child, not the age, which is the determining factor for buying the correct stage seat.

• Car seats should not be used after being involved in an accident, therefore, for safety reasons, it is not advisable to purchase second hand seats.

• Not all seats are suited to all models of car and it is important to check the fit is correct before purchasing an expensive seat.

Recent research by a leading manufacturer of car seats found that many child car seats were fitted incorrectly. Most car seat retailers offer a fitting service, usually by appointment. However, for a completely unbiased opinion, contact Bristol city council who offer a 'try before you buy' scheme.

## Bristol City Council

0117 922 4383
www.bristol-city.gov.uk

The road safety education team within Bristol City Council currently hold stock of 40 different models of car seats, which they place in your car to check for fit and safety. The service usually operates on a Wednesday, you may need to make an appointment. The team are also willing to visit playgroups and give safety talks.

# NEARLY NEW

Children grow so quickly that most clothes, toys and nursery equipment are outgrown before they're outworn. The shops listed in this section specialise in buying and selling good quality, nearly new children's items. This is an ideal way to recycle, save and generate some cash, whilst clearing some space.

**Remember to check all second hand goods for safety before you buy.**

## CAR BOOT SALES

0117 922 4014
www.bristol-city.gov.uk

Toys and other items can be bought cheaply at Car Boot Sales which are held across Bristol. Some are held regularly, others on an ad hoc basis and are mostly advertised in the local press. Bristol City Council markets department can advise you of when and where they are held.

## As New Toys and Togs

99 High Street, Staple Hill, BS16 5FH
0117 940 1214
www.asnewtoys.co.uk
Mon-Sat 9am-5pm

An Aladdin's Cave stocking second hand toys (disinfected and tested for safety), children's clothes, maternity wear and equipment. Also has new equipment, toys and books. Buys selected items from clients with 50% commission. 0-11yrs.

## Caterpillars

8 Alexandra Rd, Clevedon
01275 876 966
Tues-Sat 10am-4.30pm, Wed closes 1pm

High quality second hand nursery equipment, toys & children's clothes. 0-10 yrs.

## Jack & Jill

192 Wells Road, Totterdown
0117 958 8860
Mon-Fri 9am-4.30pm, Sat 11am-4pm

Full range of second hand children's products. Clothing 0-11yrs, nursery equipment, prams, maternity wear, nappies, toys, books. Sellers receive 60% commission on products over £25, and either 40% cash or 50% credit to spend in shop for products under £25.

## NCT Sales

Jane Monaghan
0117 942 5329

The Bristol branch of the NCT organise nearly new sales on a regular basis. They sell clothes, toys, books, nursery equipment, prams, washable nappies and maternity wear. The seller receives 70% commission on sales, with 30% going to the NCT. Sales are busy and you usually need to go early to get the bargains! Call for details.

## Punchinello

133 Gloucester Road, Bishopston, BS7 8AX
0117 944 5999
Mon-Sat 9.30am-5.30pm

A large second hand shop selling good quality children's clothes, toys and equipment. If you wish to sell items, particularly equipment, it is best to ring to find out if they are in demand. Commission for items £30 and under is 50% & 60% for items over this amount. 0-8yrs.

## Roundabout

14 North View, Westbury Park
0117 373 9147
Mon-Sat 9.30am-5pm

A small shop filled with second hand clothing for 0-12yrs, books, toys, nursery equipment

and maternity wear. Commission is 50% on all sales. "Good quality second hand shop with friendly, helpful staff — well worth a visit."

# BOOKS

Bristol has some great book shops, offering a good range from birth upwards. Staff are usually very knowledgeable and helpful, with ordering services offered by the majority. When the reading bug hits a child it can be costly — remember that libraries and second hand books offer a cheaper alternative to keep them going!

There are some excellent books sold through local agents:

www.barefootbooks.co.uk

www.osbornebooksathome.co.uk

See Home Parties in Time Out for Adults.

## Blackwell's

89 Park Street, Clifton, BS1 5PW
0117 927 6602
www.blackwell.co.uk
Mon-Sat 9.30am-7pm, Sun 11.30am-5.30pm

Friendly, expert staff. The various departments are on several levels, staff can help with buggies. The array of books, CDs and academic publications is impressive. Within the shop is the popular Cafe Nero where shoppers can browse books and take refreshments.

There is a good selection of children's books with a separate section for young adults.

## Book Cupboard

361-363 Gloucester Road, Horfield, BS7 8TG
0117 942 8878
www.bookcupboard.co.uk
Mon-Sat 9am-5.30pm

A large area dedicated to children's books with an excellent range. There are easily defined sections displaying picture books, first readers and a reference section divided into topics for older readers. There is a separate section for teenage books, and a wide selection of books on parenting issues. There is also a large range of toys in stock for all ages. Free 24 hour book ordering service. "A book for everyone to be found here."

## Borders

Clifton Promenade, 48-56 Queens Rd, BS8 1RE
0117 922 6959
Mon-Sat 9am-10pm, Sun 12am-6pm

WC ♿ ⊠ ♿

A huge book shop catering for all ages and tastes. There is a large, bright children's section with story time (U8's) at 11am and 3.30pm on Saturdays and 2.30pm on Sundays. There is also a kids' club, contact store for details. This store is very popular with teenagers with its Starbucks Coffee Shop, so you can browse while drinking coffee!

## Durdham Down Bookshop

39 North View, Westbury Park, Bristol, BS6 7PY
0117 973 9095
Mon-Sat 9am-6pm

For a small bookshop, it has a large section of children's books for all ages. Also books on parenting, health and well-being. 24 hour ordering service.

## Family Books

3 Temple Court, Keynsham, BS31
0117 986 8747
Mon-Sat 9am-5pm

Children's books and Christian titles. Ordering service available.

## Stanfords

29 Corn Street, BS1 1HT
0117 929 9966
www.stanfords.co.uk
Mon-Sat 9am-6pm, Tue 9:30 am.

This is a great shop for young explorers. Stanfords specialise in maps, but also stock a wide range of travel and guide books. There is a small children's section with soft baby globes and puzzles for the younger ones, and children's/teen's guide books for the young traveller and those taking gap years abroad. Online ordering is available.

## The Clifton Bookshop

84 Whiteladies Rd, Clifton, BS8 2QP
0117 983 8989
Mon-Sat 9am-5.30pm

A large selection of children's books along with parenting and health sections. Staff are happy for children to look at the books whilst the adults browse. An ordering service is available. Staff will carry buggies upstairs, or watch them downstairs.

## Waterstones

College Green, BS1 5TB
0117 925 0511
www.waterstones.co.uk
Mon-Sat 9am-6pm, Tue 9.30am-6pm,
Sun 11am-5pm
&
The Mall, Cribbs Causeway
0117 950 9813
&
The Galleries, Broadmead, BS1 3XF
0117 925 2274

Full range of books available for children, teenagers and parents. Large children's sections where children are welcome to browse. Ordering service available.

## West Country Travelling Books

0117 932 4173
www.booktime.co.uk

Run book fairs, for nursery and primary age children in schools in the South West, as an aid to fundraising.

## WH Smith

The Galleries, Broadmead, BS1 3XB
0117 925 2152
www.whsmith.co.uk
&
The Mall, Cribbs Causeway, BS34
0117 950 9525

Range of books to suit all ages. Also stocks stationery, CDs and toys. An ordering service is available.

Libraries all over the city run weekly Storytime and Chatterbook sessions, see Out & About in Bristol, pg 14.

# TOYS

Toys can be bought from all sorts of places, from department stores to school fetes. Check that toys are safe for the age of the child you are buying for. Also try nearly new shops, car boot sales or Trade It as many toys, particularly the plastic variety, can be cleaned easily and look brand new.

## Bristol Guild of Applied Art

68-70 Park Street, BS1 5JY
0117 926 5548
www.bristolguild.co.uk
Mon and Sat 9.30am-5.30pm, Tue-Fri 9am-5.30pm
[WC] [♿] [✖]

Large store selling a wide variety of gifts, household goods and furniture (including Tripp Trap highchairs). The toy department sells toys, games and puzzles for all ages. The store is not buggy friendly, with lots of stairs, but staff are happy to mind buggies on the ground floor. "Good quality, gifts and toys".

## Early Learning Centre

The Mall, Cribbs Causeway, BS34
0117 950 8775
www.elc.co.uk
&
The Galleries, Broadmead, BS1 3XJ
0117 926 8645

A range of traditional and modern toys, with an emphasis on learning through play. The majority of stock is aimed at pre-school children but some stock is suitable up to 8yrs. Mail order and outdoor equipment is available. There are also branches in Weston-super-Mare, Bath and within Debenhams (Broadmead).

### Tuesday Playtime (2+yrs)

10am-11am, The Galleries
10am-11.30am, The Mall

Toys and activities are brought out specifically for children's use.

## Just So Toys

12 Regent Street, Clifton, BS8 9AU
0117 974 3600
Mon-Sat 9.30am-5.30pm

A traditional shop selling good quality toys and puppets. Also Tripp Trapp high chairs, soft shoes and blankets. 0-11yrs. "Helpful staff."

## Katze

55 Gloucester Rd, Bishopston, BS7 8AD
0117 942 5625
Mon-Sat 10.00am-5.30pm

Sells wooden toys and children's giftware, along with jewellery popular with teenagers. There is a craft department upstairs selling things llike beads, fabric and knitting dolls.

## Playfull

87 Gloucester Rd, BS7 8AS
0117 944 6767
Mon-Sat 9.30am-5.30pm

This shop sells a wide range of natural toys, puzzles, gifts and some craft materials. They have handmade wooden toys suitable from birth, starting at £4.50. There is a small play area for children to test the toys! Mail order is also available. "A friendly place to buy special, handmade gifts".

## The Entertainer

The Galleries, Broadmead, BS1
0117 934 9522
www.theentertainer.com
Closed Sundays

Toys for all ages (up to adult!) with 6,000 lines. Also branches in Keynsham, Yate and Midsomer Norton. Mail or internet ordering available. Call 01494 737002 for a catalogue.

## Totally Toys

109 Gloucester Rd, Bishopston, BS7 8AT
0117 942 3833
Mon-Sat 9am-5.30pm
[WC]

Friendly shop stocking major brands of toys including Brio, Lego, Play Mobil, Galt and TP (outdoor equipment). Good range of pocket money toys, party bag items as well as play tables for children to use while you browse.

## Toys R Us

Centaurus Road, Cribbs Causeway, BS12 5TQ
0117 959 1430
www.babiesrus.co.uk, www.toysrus.co.uk
Mon-Sat 9am-10pm, Sun 11am-5pm

A warehouse-type shop with a huge range of indoor and outdoor toys, bikes, computers, nursery equipment, prams and car seats. Mail order and internet shopping available.

# OUTSIDE ACTIVITY TOYS

## Child's Play Activity Toys

The Close, Inglesbatch, Bath, BA2 9DZ
01225 314123
www.childsplayatc.co.uk
Opening hours vary, please call for details.

Stocks mainly TP Activity toys, climbing frames with wooden and galvanised metal frames. There is a good range of trampolines, equipment for tennis, indoor play and giant garden games. Larger orders delivered free. See advertisement opposite.

## Eastermead Activity Toy Centre

Eastermead Farm, Eastermead Lane, Banwell, BS29
01934 823926
www.eastermead-activity-toys.co.uk
Mon-Sat 10am-5pm, Sunday am by arrangement

Stocks TP galvanised climbing frames. Also has a wide range of wooden toddler toys including garages, castles, farms and dolls houses. Stocks sledges and ride-on tractors. Will deliver locally, free on orders over £100.

# DANCEWEAR

## Cavalier Dancewear

45 Deanery Rd, Warmley, BS15 9JB
0117 940 5677
Mon-Fri 10.30-5pm, Closed Wed, Sat 10am-4pm

Good range of clothing and shoes for ballet, tap and jazz. Also stocks fancy dress and party wear. Sizes from 2yrs.

## Dance World

52 Bedminster Parade, Bedminster, BS3 4HS
0117 953 7941
www.danceworld.ltd.uk
Mon-Sat 9am-5.30pm

Extensive range of dancewear and dance shoes for ballet, tap and salsa from 3yrs.

## Dancewell

60 Cotham Hill, Bristol, BS6 6JX
0117 973 0120
www.dancewell.com
Mon-Sat 9am-5pm

Supplying Bristol's dancers for 40 years. Dancewear and shoes for all types of dance from 2yrs.

## Holbrooks

1-2 Boyce's Ave, Clifton, BS8
0117 973 8350
Mon-Sat 9am-5.30pm

Dance shoes available for ballroom, latin, ballet, tap and jazz. Adult shoes available.

## Kathy's Dancewear

Alexandra Park, Fishponds, BS16 2BG
0117 965 5660
www.dancestation.org.uk
Mon-Fri 9am-12.30pm,
1.30pm-6pm term time, 5pm sch holidays

Good range of ballet, tap, modern & jazz dance wear, plus shoes & leotards. From 2yrs.

# ARTS & CRAFT SHOPS

### B Delicious

2 Triangle South, Clifton, Bristol
0117 929 1789
Mon 1pm-6pm, Tue-Sat 10am-6pm

Creative fun with beads and feathers, ready made, made to order or even made by you!

### Children's Scrapstore

The Proving House, Sevier St, St Werburghs, BS29LB
0117 908 5644
www.childrensscrapstore.co.uk
Mon-Wed 10am-5pm, Thu 10am-8pm,
Sat 10am-5pm

Registered charity who re-use safe, clean waste for play purposes. There is a members only warehouse and an art and craft shop, Artrageous, which is open to all (members receive 20% discount). Membership is open to any group working in creative play in an educational or therapeutic setting. Items sold include paper, plastic, thread, material ad foam. Please note: for safety reasons, U11's are not allowed in the warehouse.

### Craft Works

355-357 Gloucester Rd, Horfield, BS7 8TG
0117 942 1644
Mon-Fri 9am-6pm, Sat 9am-5pm

Everything for the craft lover including kids crafts, fine art, needle craft and creative craft.

### Creativity

7/9 Worrall Rd, Clifton, BS8 2UF
0117 973 1710
Mon-Sat 9am-5.30pm

Everything creative. They sell decorative mirrors, paints, tapestries, beads, glass and silk paints, candle making kits, ribbons and a lot more.

### Evangeline's

58-61 St Nicholas Market, Bristol, BS1 1LJ
0117 925 7170
www.evangelines.co.uk
Mon-Sat 9.30am-5pm

Small shop stocking most things for those with a flair for arts & crafts. They sell glass paints, acetate sheets, beads, embroidery material, origami paper and much more. They also offer a postal service.

### Harold Hockey

170-174 Whiteladies Road, Clifton, Bristol
0117 973 5988
Mon-Sat 8.45am-5.30

Packed with all things artistic, from easels to sketchpads, pens, cards and picture frames. Also a good selection of puzzles and games.

## Hobbycraft

Centaurus Road, Cribbs Causeway, BS34 5TS
0117 959 7100
www.hobbycraft.co.uk
Mon-Fri 9am-8pm, Sat 9am-6pm, Sun 10am-4pm

Superstore packed with craft and art materials
for children through to professionals!
Occasional in-store demonstrations.

## Rajani's Superstore Ltd

Fishponds Trading Estate, Maggs Lane, BS5 7EW
0117 958 5801
Mon-Fri 9am-6pm, Thu 8pm, Sat 9am-5.30pm,
Sun 10am-4pm

Here you will find artists' materials at very
reasonable prices: paints, canvasses, brushes
and frames. You will also be amazed at the
other household bargains in this huge store.

# FANCY DRESS

Many children love to dress up and once
they start school there are often costumes
to be made. If you want to try your hand at
dress-making, the art and craft stores above
will give you loads of ideas. However below
are some quicker solution to your needs.
Remember many of the super hero costumes
can be found in such shops as Woolworths.

## Christmas Steps Joke Shop

47 Colston St, Bristol, BS1 5AX
0117 926 4703
Tue-Sat 10am-5pm (4.30pm costume hire)

Jokes, wigs, magic tricks and a range of
costumes and accessories for children.
Costume hire for older teens and adults only.

## Dauphine's of Bristol

7 Cleeve Road, Downend, Bristol, BS16 6AD
0117 955 1700
Mon-Sat 9am-5pm

Sells wigs along with face painting and
theatre make-up. There are make-up courses
for children.

## Starlite Costumes

275-277 Lodge Causeway, Fishponds, BS16 3RA
0117 958 4668
www.starlitecostumes.co.uk
Mon-Sat 9.30am-5.30pm, Wed closed

Quality fancy dress hire, theatrical costumes
and wigs. Costume sizes from 18 months to
adult. Face paints and novelties.

# MUSIC SHOPS

## Bristol Music Shop/Hobgoblin

30 College Green, Bristol
0117 929 0390
Mon-Sat 9.30am-5.30pm

A wide range of musical instruments,
accessories and sheet music.

## Clevedon Music Shop

19 Alexandra Rd, Clevedon, BS21 7QH
01275 342 090
Mon-Sat 9.30am-5.30pm
Road is opposite pier, café Scarlett's on corner.

Great selection of instruments and
accessories, particularly guitars. Walls lined
with sheet music. Ordering system.

## Mickleburgh

1-9 Stokes Croft, Bristol, BS1 3PL
0117 924 1151
www.mickleburgh.co.uk
Mon-Sat 9am-5.30pm

Large selection of new and second hand
upright and grand pianos. Also guitars, drums,
violins, amplifiers, brass and woodwind
instruments. Sheet music and accessories.

## Music Room

30 College Green, Bristol, BS1 5TB
0117 929 0390
Mon-Sat 9.30am-5.30pm

A large range of printed sheet music. Also
sell basic school recorders, percussion
instruments, flutes, saxophones, clarinets,

trumpets and keyboards. There is an instrument hire scheme and mail order is available.

### Saunders Recorders

205 Whiteladies Rd, Bristol, BS8 2XT
0117 973 5149
www.saundrecs.co.uk
Mon-Sat 9.30am-1.15pm & 2.30pm-5.30pm, closes pm on Wed from 11.30am & Sat 1.15pm

International supplier of recorders. The walls are lined with a vast selection of recorders. Large range of sheet music for recorders.

# HOBBY TOYS

### Al's Hobbies

438-440 Gloucester Rd, BS7 8TX
0117 944 1144
Tue-Sat 9.30am-5pm

For all hobby and modelling enthusiasts. Large stacks of balsa wood, building materials, paints, clay, brushes, model kits. From 8+yrs.

### Modelmania

13 Clouds Hill Rd, St George, BS5 7LD
0117 955 9819
Tue-Sat 9.30am-6pm

Stocks die cast models, scalextric and plastic model kits. Also new and second hand model railways. 5+yrs.

# SPORTS & OUTDOOR STORES

### Gyles Bros Ltd

188 Whiteladies Rd, Clifton, BS8 2XU
0117 973 3143
Mon-Sat 9am-5.30pm

This is a family-run business, selling quality equipment for most major sports. They offer a racquet restringing service (next day) and on the spot grip replacement. "Helpful and knowledgeable staff."

### Ikon (UK) Ltd

190 Henleaze Rd, Bristol, BS9 4NE
0117 962 0011
www.ikon-uk.com
Mon-Fri 9am-5pm, Sat 10am-5pm

Recently opened and keen to help with any sporting equipment/clothing or Scout/school uniforms you may need. There is a good stock but anything new or unusual can be sourced.

### Marcruss Stores

177-181 Hotwells Rd, Hotwells, BS8 4RY
0117 929 7427
Mon-Sat 9am-5.30pm

Large range of camping equipment and accessories. Family ski and outdoor wear.

### Millets The Outdoor Shop

9-10 Transom House, Victoria Street, BS1 6AH
0117 926 4892
&
10 Broadmead, Bristol BS1 3HH
0117 922 1167
Mon-Sat 9am-5.30pm, Sun 10am-4pm

Well-known chain selling a wide selection of tents, outdoor equipment and clothes.

### Snow & Rock Superstore

Shield Retail Centre, Filton, BS34 7BQ
0117 914 3000
www.snowandrock.com
Mon-Fri 10am-7pm, Thu 8pm, Sat 9am-6pm, Sun 11am-5pmSun 11am-5pm

Packed full of stylish outdoor clothing for all

ages, Snow & Rock stocks a huge selection of ski and rock climbing equipment as well as child carriers and rucksacks.

## Taunton Leisure

38-42 Bedminster Parade, Bedminster, BS3 4HS
0117 963 7640
www.tauntonleisure.com
Mon-Sat 9am-5.30pm, Thu 7pm

Taunton Leisure stocks a broad range of outdoor clothing and camping equipment as well as climbing, cycling and walking gear. It also sells guidebooks and maps, rucksacks and baby carriers. There is a small play area for children to keep them occupied.

# KITES & SKATEBOARDS

## 50/50 Skateboard Supplies

16 Park Row, BS1 5LJ
0117 914 7783
www.5050store.com
Mon-Sat 9am-6pm

Skateboard specialists stocking hardware, footwear, clothing, accessories, videos. From 8+yrs. Mail order available, see website. "Skateboarder owned and operated."

## Bristol Kite Store

39A Cotham Hill, Redland, BS6 6JY
0117 974 5010
www.kitestore.co.uk
Mon-Fri 10am-6pm, Sat 9.30am-5.30pm

Wide range of kites and kite surfing equipment, DIY Kites and spare parts. Also frisbees, yo-yos, juggling and circus equipment, books & videos. From 3yrs.

## UFO Power Kites

See entry in Shopping Outside Bristol - Weston-super-Mare.

# PET SHOPS

The recommended independent pet shops listed below stock smaller animals such as hamsters, rabbits, guinea pigs, fish and birds. It is not possible in the Bristol area to buy puppies and kittens from pet shops — please contact your local vet or rescue centre.

### Bath Cats and Dogs Home (RSPCA)

The Avenue, Claverton Down, Bath BA2 7AZ
01225 466129
www.bathcatsanddogshome.org.uk

### Bristol Dogs and Cats Home (RSPCA)

50 Albert Road, St Philips, Bristol BS2 0XW
0117 9776043
www.bristoldogsandcatshome.org.uk

## Mar-Pet

25 Highridge Rd, Bishopsworth, BS13 8HJ
0117 964 3416
Mon-Sat 9am-1pm & 2pm-5.30pm, closed Wed

Specialises in birds, cold water fish and small animals. Sells cages, hutches, runs, tanks, food and accessories.

## Pet & Poultry Stores

5 Worrall Rd, Clifton, BS8 2UF
0117 973 8617
Mon-Sat 9am-5.30pm, Wed until 3.30pm

Friendly shop with a range of small animals, birds, animal feed and accessories. Specialises in garden bird food and feeders. Free delivery.

## Roxfords

155 Gloucester Road, Bishopston, BS7 8BA
0117 924 8397
Mon-Sat 9am-5.30pm

Large range of small animals, rodents and fish. Pet toys, leads (can engrave discs) and cages. Lodges small animals for the holidays. Free local deliveries for £10 and over.

# MARKETS

Bristol has its fair share of markets where bargains and quality produce can be bought. Crowded markets can make the manoeuvring of buggies and toddlers difficult but children of any age can enjoy the atmosphere, colours and sounds. Non-regular markets and sales are usually advertised in the local press.

## BRISTOL MARKETS

### Craft Market

Corn St, BS1 1LJ
Fri 10am-5pm, Sat 10am-4pm

All kinds of crafts including glass and jewellery.

### Eastville Market

Eastgate Shopping Centre, Eastgate Rd, BS5 6XY
0117 935 4913 / 0117 934 9870
Fri and Sun until 2.30pm

Varied range of inexpensive goods, with an emphasis on clothes and fabrics. "Great for fancy dress and costume fabrics."

### Slow Food Market

Corn St, Bristol, BS1 1JQ
1st Sun of the month

Run in conjunction with Bristol City Council markets. Slow food is about good food production. This market is a monthly treat for everyone who loves real food.

### Southmead Hospital Market

Southmead Road, Southmead, BS10
07050 236 682
Sat 9am-4pm

Good for general bargain hunting. Food, clothing, home wares. Bouncy castle in the summer.

### St Nicholas' Market

St Nicholas St/Corn St, BS1 1LJ
0117 922 4017
Mon-Sat 9.30am-5pm

This is an indoor and outdoor market, situated in the Glass Arcade and the Corn Exchange, selling a wide variety of goods.

### The Farmers' Market

Corn St
Wed 9.30am-2.30pm

Local farm produce including dairy, meat, fruit and veg, as well as wines and preserves.

### The Sunday Market

Alberts Crescent, St Philips Marsh, Bristol
01608 652556
Sun 9am-3pm

In the grounds of the Wholesale Fruit and Veg Market, selling almost everything including inexpensive clothes, with some brand names.

## FARMERS' MARKETS & SHOPS OUTSIDE BRISTOL

### Axbridge Farmers' Market

The Square, Axbridge, Somerset
01458 830801
www.sfmdirect.co.uk
1st Sat of the mth 9am-1pm (check with website)

Canopy market of about 20 stalls in the picturesque market square of this historic town. Mainly local produce on offer, including bread, meat, cheese, chutneys and pickles, ice cream, willow baskets and plants.

### Stroud Farmers' Market

Cornhill Market Place, Stroud, Gloucestershire
01453 758060
www.madeinstroud.org/markets
1st & 3rd Sat every mth: 9am-2pm

Award-winning farmers' market with up to 60 stalls, offering a wide range of local produce and local crafts. A tempting range of hot food available. Entertainment from local musicians adds to the atmosphere. Seasonal events include Apple Day festivities in the autumn and Christmas activities in December.

## Tortworth Estate Shop

Box Walk, Tortworth, Wotton-under-Edge
01454 261633
Mon-Sat 9am-5.30pm, closed B/H's

P ⚒ ⚒ ⚒

Farm shop with locally produced, home-made and speciality foods. Large meat counter and well-stocked freezer cabinets. Mini-baskets for children to help with shopping.

## Wotton Farm Shop

Gloucester Row, Wotton-under-Edge, GL12 7DY
01453 521546
www.wottonfarmshop.co.uk
Apr-Dec, Mon-Sat 9am-4.30pm, Sun: 10am-1pm

P WC ⚒ ⚒

Farm shop, farm kitchen for take-away home-cooked food, pick-your-own and nursery, provising a hanging-basket refilling service. PYO includes a wide variety of seasonal fruit and veg.

# ORGANIC & SPECIALIST FOODSTORES

In recent years, the demand for organic food has grown enormously and many parents are keen to give their children organic food from weaning onwards. The following companies offer good organic and specialist food either from their premises or delivered to your door. Nearly all supermarkets sell organic food in their fresh, frozen and packaged sections.

### Soil Association

Bristol House, 40-56 Victoria Street, Bristol, BS1 6BY
0117 314 5000
www.soilassociation.org

The Soil Association has a wealth of information on organic food and healthy living. It sells the Organic Directory, listing all organic outlets, which is also on their consumer website www.whyorganic.org.

## Bib & Tucker

34 Thingwall Park, Fishponds, BS16 2AE
0117 965 7387
www.bibandtuckerfoods.co.uk

Homecooked children's food, prepared, frozen and delivered to your door, within the Bristol area. Ingredients include organic fruit and vegetables along with free range locally sourced meat. Order over the phone or through their website. Party food and celebration cakes also available.

## Earthbound

8 Abbotsford Rd, Cotham, BS6 6HB
0117 904 2260
Mon-Sat 9am-6pm

Friendly store specialising in locally produced organic foods. Sells a wide range of fresh fruit and veg, basic and luxury organic groceries, wholefoods and fair trade products.

## Fresh & Wild

85 Queen's Rd, Clifton, Bristol, BS8 1QS
0117 910 5930
www.freshandwild.com
Mon-Fri 8am-9pm, Sat 9am-8pm, Sun 11am-5pm

This natural food store has a vast range of fresh produce and dry goods. There is a salad bar for eating in or take-away, an organic range of children's frozen ready meals and environmentally friendly nappies including Moltex compostibles. Helpful friendly staff.

## Harvest Natural Foods

11 Gloucester Road, Bishopston, BS7 8AA
0117 942 5997
www.harvest-bristol.coop
Mon-Sat 9am-6pm

This workers' co-operative sells a wide range of organic products including bread, fresh fruit and veg, beers and wines, suitable for vegans. They also stock a wide range of gluten-free products and have a delicatessen.

## Riverford Organic Vegetables

0845 600 2311
www.riverford.co.uk

This Devon-based company was one of the

first to start delivering organic vegetable boxes to customers' doors. Predominantly seasonal vegetables grown locally, although they do import from France and Spain (nothing via air freight). Boxes start from £7.50 up to £13.50. Order ad hoc or on a regular basis.

### Somerset Organics

Gilcombe Farm, Bruton, Somerset
01749 813710
www.somersetorganics.co.uk

Delivery of a wide range of fresh organic meat, cheese, fish, juices, chutneys & butter to your door. Minimum order £40, deliveries cost £7.50 to any UK address.

### Southville Deli

262 North St, Bedminster, BS3 1JA
0117 966 4507
www.southvilledeli.com
Mon-Sat 9am-5.30pm

Organic whole foods, ground coffee, herbal teas, preserves, goat milk, and a range of baby products including Tushies nappies. "A wonderful shop in the heart of South Bristol."

### Stone Age Organics

01823 432 488
www.stoneageorganics.co.uk

Boxes of 100% organic vegetables priced from £6-£10. Also sells organic Lamb. Delivery is free in Bristol, Clevedon and Weston. Monthly newsletter with recipes.

### Stoneground Health Foods

5 The Mall, Clifton Village, BS8 4DP
0117 974 1260
Mon-Fri 9am-5pm, Sat 9am-3pm

Combination of organic, GM free and natural products, 100% vegetarian. Sells fruit, veg, dairy products and dry goods. Take-away sandwiches, home-made soup, jacket potatoes, smoothies and fresh juice.

### The Bay Tree

176 Henleaze Rd, Henleaze, BS9
0117 962 1115
Mon-Sat 9am-5pm

Stocks a wide variety of natural, organic and gluten-free foods as well as supplements, natural toiletries, Bach Flower and other homeopathic remedies.

### Viva Oliva

30 Oxford St, Totterdown, BS3 4RJ
0117 940 7419, 07980 634926
Mon-Sat 10am-6pm

Friendly delicatessen stocks a variety of Mediterranean delights including breads, olives, sundried tomatoes, handmade sauces and pestos, authentic preserves, cheeses and meats. "The stuffed vine leaves are a must!"

# SHOPS OUTSIDE BRISTOL

Bath and Weston-Super-Mare are great for a day trip from Bristol, both offering a wide range of activities to keep children entertained, see Out & About in the West Country. Whilst you're visiting, why not check out some of the shops recommended below.

## BATH

### Bath Model Centre (The Modellers Den)

2 Lower Borough Walls, Bath, BA1 1QR
01225 460115
www.bathmodelcentre.com
Mon-Fri 9.30am-5.30pm, Sat 9am-5.30pm

This store is crammed from floor to ceiling with all types of models. Ranges include Hornby Trains, Scalextric, die cast cars and pedal cars. Suitable for 4-99 yrs. "For model loving kids and dads!"

## Blooming Marvellous

5 Saracan Street, Bath, BA1 5BR
0845 4587425
Mon-Sat 9.30am-5.30pm, Sun 10.30am-4.30pm

Although well-known for its mail order, it is great to be able to see their range of maternity & baby wear, nursery equipment & toys in store. "This is a great place to start your maternity wardrobe." See advertisement in Healthcare, pg 181.

## Born

134 Walcot Street, Bath, BA1 5BG
0845 1302676
www.borndirect.com
Mon-Sat 9.30am-5.30pm

Most of the products in this shop are natural, organic and/or fairtraded. They stock a large range of cotton nappies and accessories, soft leather shoes, high quality outdoor wear, baby slings, backpacks, Bravado range of maternity underwear and feeding tops. They also have pushchairs and furniture with brands names like Tripp Trapp, Stokke, Sleepi, Xplory and Bugaboo. See their advertisement, pg 245.

## Enkla

21 Broad St, Bath, BA1 5LN
01225 339789
www.enkla.co.uk
Mon-Sat 10am-5.30pm, Sun 11am-4pm

This recently opened shop looks at childhood through work, rest and play. There are toys to help with gardening, cooking and cleaning along with a range of lighting, storage and bedding. The play products are mainly related to craft and science. Age range 3-13yrs, although some lovely gifts for babies.

## Eric Snooks, The Golden Cot

2 Abbeygate St, Bath, BA1 1NP
01225 463739
www.snooksonline.co.uk
Mon-Sat 9am-5.30pm

Wide range of toys on ground floor, including hobby toys (skateboards and rollerblades) for the older child. Upstairs, there are clothes, 0-7yrs, and nursery equipment. There is no lift

but staff will mind buggies. "A great range of good quality, modern and traditional toys."

## Laura Ashley

Bath, BA1 1BE
0871 2231327
www.lauraashley.com
Mon-Sat 9.30am-5.30pm, Sun 11am-4pm

Lovely range of girls' clothes from 2-12yrs.

## One small step one giant leap

5 - 6 Cheap Street, Bath, BA1 1NE
01225 445345
Mon-Fri 9.30am-5.30pm, Sun 11am-5pm

A large range of children's shoes and trainers from size 0. Brands include Start-Rite in width fittings, Replay, Diesel, Timberland, Kickers and Birkenstock. More expensive but unusual ranges include Aster, Mod8, Pom D'api and Ricosta. "Shoe-tail therapy at its best!"

## Roundabout

2-4 Prior Park Road, Bath, BA2 4NG
01225 316696
Mon-Sat 9am-5pm

One mile from city centre. Good quality nearly new and second hand nursery equipment, toys, maternity, adult and children's wear. Clients given 50% commission after sale.

## Routeone

9 Broad Street, Bath, BA1 5LJ
01225 446710
www.routeone.co.uk
Mon-Sat 9.30am-6pm, Sun 11am-5pm

Skate boards and hardware, roller blades, inline skates, power kiting, frisbees and BMX. They also have clothing suitable for 7+yrs.

## Tridias

124 Walcot Street, Bath, BA1 5BG
01225 314 730, 0870 4431300 mailorder
www.tridias.co.uk
Mon-Sat 9.30am-5.30pm, Sat 9am-5.30pm

Unusual and exciting ideas for children's birthday presents and parties. They have a large range of games and toys. If you can't visit the store call for a catalogue or visit their website.

# WESTON-SUPER-MARE

## Adams Childrenswear

Sovereign Centre, High St, Weston-super-Mare
01934 643 501
Mon-Fri 9am-5.30pm, Sun 10.30am-4.30pm

Good selection of reasonably priced clothes for babies and children up to 10yrs.

## Model Masters

International House, Clifton Rd, Weston-s-Mare BS23
01934 629 717
www.modelmasters.co.uk
Mon-Sat 9am-5pm (Display closed between Christmas and Easter)

This shop sells model trains and railways sourced mainly from Germany, Switzerland and Austria. To the rear of the shop there is a model railway layout for customers to see the products in operation. Products suitable for 5+yrs, layout suitable for all!

## Ottakas

Sovereign Centre, High Street, Weston-s-Mare, BS23
01934 642588
www.ottakas.co.uk
Mon-Sat 9am-5.30pm, Tue 9.30am
Sun 10.30am-4.30pm

Books to suit all ages including educational and those for young adults. There is a large, bright, children's department stocking a wide range of books which has a rocking horse for children to ride.

## Peacocks

4-5 Regents St, Weston-super-Mare, BS23 1SE
01934 632553
www.peacocks.co.uk
Mon-Sat 9am-5.30pm, Sun 12pm-4pm

Inexpensive clothing, from 0-15yrs.

## TJ Hughes

17-21 High Street, Weston-s-Mare
01934 414 466
Mon-Sat 9am-5.30pm, Sun 11am-5pm

Discount department store selling brand names at low prices. Children's clothes from birth upwards. Stock changes frequently.

## UFO Power Kites

41 Alexandra Parade, Weston-s-Mare, BS23 1QZ
01934 644 988
Mon-Sat 10am-5.30pm

Large shop selling kites, kite surfing equipment, spare parts, skate boards, inline skates, frisbees, yo-yos, juggling equipment and clothing. 8+yrs.

## Weston Dancewear

32a-34 Orchard St, Weston-super-Mare, BS23 1RQ
01934 419818
Mon-Sat 9am-5pm

Large range of dancewear, gym leotards and shoes for ballet, tap, modern and jazz, from 2+yrs.

# MAIL ORDER

A selection of recommended and mainly regionally based mail order companies where you can order via the internet or by phoning for a catalogue.

## Bishopston Trading Company

193 Gloucester Rd, Bristol, BS7 8BG
0117 924 5598
Also in Bradford-on-Avon, Glastonbury,
Stroud & Totnes
www.bishopstontrading.co.uk

Workers co-operative set up to create employment in South Indian village of KV Kuppam. Catalogue includes children's clothing 0-13yrs, range of colours, mainly produced in organic handloom cloth.

## Blooming Marvellous

0845 458 7406
www.bloomingmarvellous.co.uk

Mail order maternity & baby wear 0-4yrs, nursery equipment & toys. They have a good range of maternity underwear and swimming costumes. New Mini Marvellous range, 2-8yrs, with toys, storage solutions, gifts, sun suits and float jackets. Call for a free 96 page catalogue. See advertisement pg 181.

## Coach House

Unit 2, 21 Broadway, Chilton Polden, Bridgwater
08450 616262 (call for catalogue)
www.coach-house.co.uk

A great range of competitively priced, traditional wooden toys and games. Sales via the website or mail order catalogue. "Traditional but trendy."

## Ethos Baby Care

37 Chandos Rd, Redland, BS6 6PQ
www.ethosbaby.com

Stocks natural products for baby: 100% natural cotton nappies, organic cotton clothing, sleeping bags, natural baby care products and wooden toys. For mum: a range of books and maternity pillows. On-line ordering only.

## Formative Fun

58 High St, Staple Hill, BS16 5HN
0845 8900609
www.formative-fun.com

Educational toys, games and puzzles supporting the National Curriculum and the Early Learning Goals, for ages 0-14 yrs and those with Special Needs. 10% discount cards for schools, nurseries and playgroups.

## Funky Little Feet

07966 500342
www.funkylittlefeet.com

Southville-based company selling bright fun shoes from Vans, Etnies and DC, not previously available in the UK. Sizes start from infants to UK size 13 (stock will soon go up to adult size 2). The website has a printable measuring pattern to assist with sizing.

## Letterbox

PO Box 114, Truro, TR2 5YR
0870 6007878
www.letterbox.co.uk

Original and colourful durable gifts and toys for babies through to young teens.

## Nitty Gritty

1 Oakwood Court, Kensington, London, W14 8JU
0207 460 0166
www.nittygritty.co.uk

This company, created and run by three mums, may not be regionally based but their chemical-free Head Lice Solution and Repellent Spray comes with loads of recommendations. Their award-winning NitFree Comb effectively removes head lice, nits and eggs. At last, a non-toxic solution to ridding your family of head lice! See advertisement on pg 137.

## Raindrops

01730 810031
www.raindrops.co.uk

"There is no such thing as bad weather, just inappropriate clothing." Raindrops sells good quality Scandinavian outdoor clothing. Products include dungarees and jackets, camouflage trousers, wellie boots, ski kit, thermals and swim wear — everything you need come rain, snow or shine. Sizes range from 6mths to 13yrs. See advertisement on pg 130.

## Party Pieces

Childs Court Farm, Ashhampstead Common, West Berkshire, RG8 8QT
01635 201844
www.partypieces.co.uk
Mon-Fri 8.30am-6pm, Sat 9am-5pm

Sells a wide range of top quality products for children's parties. A huge range of themes are in stock and products are competitively priced with a nominal delivery charge.

## The Faerie Shop

01672 515995
wwwfaerieshop.co.uk

Enchanting fairy items: costumes, fairy dolls, sparkly wings and magic dust.

**Need inspiration for your child's birthday party?** See Children's Party Ideas, pg 115.

### Tridias (Mail Order)

The Buffer Depot, Badminton Rd, Acton Turville,
Gloucestershire, GL9 1HE
0870 443 1300 (call for catalogue)
www.tridias.co.uk

Unusual and exciting selection of ideas for
children's birthday presents and parties. They
have a range of games, activities, toys and
party bags suitable for different ages. Order
online or via the catalogue.

# FACTORY OUTLETS

Factory outlet centres are great because you
always feel like you're saving money — even if
you're not! The three listed all have a diverse
range of shops in their complexes, selling
high street and designer labels at a fraction
of their original cost. Each offer good facilities
for children and it can be a good way to save
money while having a day out.

### Clarks Village

Farm Rd, Street, Somerset, BA16 0BB
01458 840064
www.clarksvillage.co.uk
Apr-Oct: Mon-Sat 9am-6pm, Nov-Mar: 5.30pm,
Thu 8pm, Sun 10am-5pm
Jct 23 M5 or A37, excellent sign posting

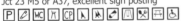

There are now over 80 well known high street
stores selling discontinued lines, last season's
stock and factory seconds. "A good place to
shop for and with children." Street centre also
has several discount shoe shops which are
worth visiting. See Out & About in the West
Country.

### McArthurGlen Designer Outlet, Bridgend

The Derwen, Bridgend, South Wales, CF32 9SU
01656 665 700
www.mcarthurglen.com
Mon-Fri 10am-8pm, Sat 10am-7pm, Sun 11am-5pm
Jct 36, M4.

Offers end of season and excess stock at
discounts of up to 50%. There are more

than 80 stores at Bridgend, which was the
first designer outlet in the UK to be built with
an on-site cinema. As at Swindon, there are
events during school holidays.

### McArthurGlen Designer Outlet, Great Western

Kemble Drive, Swindon, SN2 2DY
01793 507600
www.mcarthurglen.com
Mon-Wed 10am-8pm, Sat 9am-6pm, Sun 11am-5pm
Jct 16, M4 follow brown signs.

Offers end of season and excess stock at
discounts of up to 50%. It has over 100
shops including fashion, toys, home-wares
& sport. Events programme, with children's
fun workshops in the school holidays. It is
situated in a restored grade II building that
once housed the Great Western Railway works
and is next door to the Museum of the Great
Western Railway. See Steam in Out & About in
the West Country pg 54.

# SERVICES

## LATE NIGHT PHARMACIES

Pharmacies have a rota for opening outside normal retail hours. Details can be found in the Bristol Evening Post or by calling NHS Direct. The pharmacies listed below are open after 5.30pm and on Sundays.

### NHS Direct

0845 606 46 47

Gives out of hours pharmacies in your area.

### Asda Walmart

Highwood Lane, Cribbs Causeway
0117 979 0426
Mon-Fri 9am-10pm, Sat 8.30am-10pm,
Sun 10am-4pm

### Boots The Chemists

19 St Augustines Parade, (near to Hippodrome)
0117 927 6311
Mon-Fri 8am-7pm, Sat 8.30am-5.30pm
&
59 Broadmead, Bristol City Centre
0117 929 3631
Mon, Wed, Fri 8.45am-5.30pm, Tue 9am-5.30pm,
Thu 8.45am-7pm, Sat 8.45am-6pm, Sun 11am-5pm
&
Upper Mall, Cribbs Causeway
0117 950 9744
Mon-Fri 10am-9pm, Sat 9am-7pm, Sun 11am-5pm
B/Hs 10am-6pm

### Morrisons

688-718 Fishponds Road, Fishponds
0117 965 3014
Mon-Sat 8.30am-8.00pm, Sun 10am-4pm

### Sainsbury's

Sainsbury's, Winterstoke Road, Ashton
0117 953 7273
Mon-Fri 8am-10pm, Sat 7.30am-10pm,
Sun 10am-4pm
&
Fox Den Road, Stoke Gifford, S Glos
0117 923 6459
Mon-Sat 8am-8pm, Sun 10am-4pm

### Tesco

Callington Road, Brislington
0117 991 7400
Mon-Sat 8.30am-8pm, Sun 10am-4pm
&
Eastgate Centre, Eastville
0117 951 1156
Mon-Sat 8am-8pm, Sun 10am-4pm

## EQUIPMENT REPAIR

The companies listed here can repair prams and buggies. For problems with other baby equipment it is probably best to contact your supplier or go direct to the manufacturer. For the safety of you and your child, car seats should be replaced and not repaired.

### Baby & Co

21 Temple Street, Keynsham, BS31 1HF
0117 986 8184
Mon-Sat 9am-5pm

The workshop, which is on the premises, can repair all major makes of prams/buggies and carries many spare parts. If available, buggies can be loaned to you.

### Hurwoods

32 Old Market Street, Old Market, BS2 0HB
0117 926 2690
www.hurwoods.co.uk
Mon-Fri 9.30am-5pm, Sat 9am-5pm

All major makes of prams and buggies can be repaired, mostly on site.

### John Lewis

The Mall, Cribbs Causeway, BS34
0117 959 1100

Will arrange for the repair of any pram or buggy bought at John Lewis.

### Mothercare World

Eastgate Centre, Eastville, BS5 6XZ
0117 951 8200
Mon-Fri 9.30am-8pm, Sat 9am-6pm, Sun 11am-5pm

Most types of prams and buggies can be repaired here. The repair man is in the store on Mon, Wed and Fri. You must book your repair in advance.

**Housebound, need a hairdresser to come to your home?** See Time Out for Adults, pg 168.

# HAIRDRESSERS

The following are salons with staff that are experienced in cutting children's hair, plus they have a few tools for distracting the child while they do it.

## Bonomini

22 Alma Vale Road, Clifton, BS8
0117 923 9169
£12 U5's, £16 5-9yrs, £25 10-14yrs

Despite being a sophisticated salon, Bonomini welcomes children and the staff are experienced in cutting children's hair, toys available for distraction. An appointment is not always needed.

## Illusions Hair

22 Gloucester Road, The Promenade, Bishopston, Bristol, BS7 8AE
0117 907 7447
Tue-Wed 9am-5.30pm, Thu/Fri 7pm,
Sat 8.30am-5.30pm
U4's £7.70, 4-8yrs £12.10

Child seats and gowns. From 8yrs hair is washed and cut wet. Appointment usually necessary. Prices given are discretionary.

## Jon Hurst Hairdressing

18 Cotham Hill, Cotham, Bristol, BS6 6LF
0117 373 0044
Mon-Fri: 10am-7pm Sat: 9am-5pm
Baby's First Haircut £10

Offering a relaxed atmosphere for your baby's first haircut. Take home the curls in a gift box along with a framed photo of your baby's new look! Full range of hairdressing services available to children, teenagers and adults. See advertisement above.

## Moda Hairdressing

205a Gloucester Rd, Bishopston
0117 924 1006
£6 preschool, £10 5+yrs to adult
 WC

Tina use to be listed as one of our mobile hairdressers. She has now opened this friendly Italian salon.

## Pink Hair Designs

282 Gloucester Rd, Horfield
0117 944 4080
Mon & Thu 10am-8pm, Tue 10am-4pm,
Fri 10am-5pm, Sat 7.30am-2.30pm
From £3.50 depending on age

These people just love children! There is a toy box, a selection of videos and often a treat for good behaviour.

## Pride Hair and Beauty Salon

236 Stapleton Rd, Easton, BS5 0NT
0117 951 9518
Tue-Wed 9am-5.30pm, Thu 10am-6pm,
Fri 11.30am-8pm, Sat 8.30am-4.30pm
£11.50 girls, £7 infants & boys under 12yrs
WC

Cuts all types of hair but specialises in Afro hair. An appointment is required.

## Supercuts

The Mall, Cribbs Causeway
0117 959 2597
Mon-Fri 10am-9pm, Sat 9am-7pm, Sun 11am-5pm
&
In-store at Asda Walmart, Cribbs Causeway
0117 923 6180
Mon-Fri 9am-6pm, Sat 8.30am-4.30pm
&
7 Union Gallery, Broadmead
0117 929 2184
£7.95 U8's, £11.95 over 8's (& all children at w/e's)

A national chain of salons geared to cutting children's hair. Opening times vary between stores. You do not need an appointment.

## Reflections

Branches: Clifton, Bedminster, Broadmead, Fishponds, Kingswood, Knowle, Keynsham, Nailsea, Thornbury and Yate
From £5.50 U6's, £13 boys 6-16yrs, £15.40 girls 6-16yrs
Trim priced at discretion of management

All salons across Bristol welcome children. Toys and lollipops sometimes available!

## The Business Hair Studio

69 Islington Road, Southville, BS3
0117 966 6618
Mon & Wed 9am-5pm, Tue closed, Thu/Fri 9am-8pm, Sat 8.30am-4.30pm
£4.50 U10's

This is a child-friendly salon with toys. An appointment is usually required.

# PHOTOGRAPHERS

The photographers listed here have been recommended for their expertise in children's photography.

## James Nicholas Photography

27 Pool Road, Kingswood, Bristol
0117 985 9520
www.jamesnicholasphotography.co.uk
From £14.95 for 7"x5" print.

Free studio fee, or £25 for a venue anywhere in Bristol.

## Mark Simmons

The Fire Station, 82-84 York Rd, Bedminster, BS3
0117 914 0999
www.marksimmonsphotography.co.uk
Appointment only
Studio Fee is £85, prints start at £8 for a 7"x5" print

Mark is an established Bristol portrait photographer with a warm, spacious and comfortable studio. He is friendly, relaxed and favours an informal style of portraiture. See website for examples of his work.

## Michael Rich Studios

3 Prospect Lane, Frampton Cotterell, BS36 2DR
01454 778816
www.richphotos.com
£25 for 8"x 6", studio fee £25

Mike offers a free Little Angels scheme for babies up to one year old. Your child will have three sittings and one 5"x4" print from each sitting will be included in a folio. Family portraits in colour or back and white.

## James Owens Studios

Charlton Studio, 18 Charlton Road, Keynsham
0117 986 5114
www.jamesowens.co.uk
£15 1 hr studio session, there is no minimum order, prints start at £25

A family-run photographic studio with 25 years experience. Examples of previous work are shown on the website.

## Paul Burns Photography

72 Shirehampton Road, Bristol, BS9 2DU
0117 968 6300
www.paulburns.co.uk
From £25, includes studio fee and one 8x6 print

Photographs for all occasions. Friendly family-run business. Contemporary style portraits from a photographer with a royal warrant!

## Phil McCheyne Photographers

5 St. Austell Close, Nailsea, Bristol, BS48 2US
01275 858 545
Flexible opening times

This friendly photographer specialises in school, nursery and playgroup photography along with portraits and passport photos.

## Portrait Place

Debenhams, 1-5 St James Barton, Broadmead
0117 922 5960

Vouchers for free Baby photo sessions are found inside Bounty Packs. Otherwise a photo session costs £10 which includes a 12"x10" portrait. Additional prints start at £20.

# ADVICE & SUPPORT

**Nicola O'Brien**

# CONTENTS

# INTRODUCTION

Family life does not always run smoothly. At times of trouble, we often find it difficult to know where to turn. Whatever your concerns, there is help out there. There is an incredible network of charities and support agencies in th UK, offering a huge range of services both regionally and nationally. In this chapter, we have created a directory which lists many organisations and charities that can either help you or advise you on where to find help. It's by no means exhaustive, but we cover most bases and it should point you in the right direction.

Contact details frequently change and new support services are starting up all the time. Please let us know any updates via our website.

# FOR FAMILIES & INDIVIDUALS

## GENERAL SUPPORT

### Bristol City Council

Social Services and Health Department, Amelia Court
PO Box 30, Bristol, BS99 7NB
0117 922 2000
Mon-Fri 8.30am-5pm (until 4.30pm on Fri)
Emergency out of hours: 01454 615 165

Services include: social workers, family support workers, special needs provision, respite care, adoption and fostering, child protection, services and support for disabled children and their families.

They also work closely with Children's Information Services, who will advise on: registered childminders, nurseries, Social Services day nurseries. See listing in Babies & Children below.

### Easton Community Children's Centre

Russell Town Ave, Bristol, BS5 9JF
0117 939 2550
easton-childrens-centre@yahoo.co.uk

Provides childcare services, information on learning opportunities and offers support for inner-city families.

### Fulford Family Centre

237-239 Gatehouse Avenue, Withywood, Bristol, BS13 9AQ
0117 978 2441
Mon-Fri 9am-5pm

For families with pre-school children. Provides parent and toddler support groups, individual and family counselling, play therapy, welfare rights advice, holidays and outings.

### Home-Start Bristol

St Matthews Rd, Kingsdown, Bristol, BS6 5TT
www.home-start.org.uk
0117 942 8399 Mon-Thu 9am-3pm
(answerphone out of hours)

Voluntary home-visiting scheme for families with children under five, where there are difficulties or stress.

### Parentline Plus

520 Highgate Studios, 53-79 Highgate Road, London, NW5 1TL
centraloffice@parentlineplus.org.uk
www.parentlineplus.org.uk
Freephone 0808 800 2222
Textphone 0800 783 66783

Call centres run by parents, offering a confidential, anonymous listening ear and practical help. The lines are often busy so keep trying!

**Totterdown office**
0117 971 4831

Offers a range of parenting courses.

### Working Families

1-3 Berry Street, London, EC1V 0AA
www.workingfamilies.org.uk
020 7253 7243
0800 013 0313 legal advice for low income families

Offering help to children, working parents/ carers and their employers to find a better balance between responsibilities at home and work.

## BABIES & CHILDREN

### Children's Information Service

The Proving House, Sevier St, Bristol, BS2 9LB
0845 129 7217
www.cisbristol.co.uk
enquiries@cisbristol.co.uk
Mon/Fri: 8am-4pm, Tue-Thu: 8am-8pm

Provides free, impartial and confidential information/guidance on a full range of childcare, children's services and resources in Bristol. See Childcare 0-4 Years.

### Bristol City Council Child Protection

Citywide services are provided for:
www.bristol-city.gov.uk
Adoption 0117 954 8545
Disabled Children's Service 0117 903 8250

The telephone directory provides a list of all

local Child Protection offices, to contact the nearest to the child's home.

## ChildLine

Childline, 45 Folgate Street, London, E1 6GL
www.childline.org.uk
Children's correspondence address:
Childline, Freepost, NATN1111, London, E1 6BR
Admin 020 7650 3200
Helpline 0800 1111

UK's free helpline for children and young people. It provides a confidential telephone counselling service for any child with any problem, 24/7. It comforts, advises, protects. Now part of the NSPCC.

### The Line
For children living away from home

| | |
|---|---|
| 0800 884444 | Mon-Fri 3.30pm-9.30pm |
| | Sat-Sun 2pm-8pm |
| Textphone 0800 400222 | Mon-Fri 9.30am-9.30pm |
| | Sat-Sun 9.30am-8pm |

## Childtime

The Old Treasury, 30A College Green, BS1 5TB
www.childtime.org.uk, info@childtime.org.uk
0117 929 1533 answerphone out of hours
Helps children who are experiencing emotional or psychological difficulties, in partnership with parents and relevant professionals. Subsidised fees on sliding scale.

## CRY-SIS

BM Cry-sis, London, WC1N 3XX
www.cry-sis.org.uk, info@cry-sis.org.uk
Helpline 08451 228669
9am-10pm

A helpline that gives emotional and practical support to parents whose babies cry excessively. Helpline gives local contacts available out of hours.

## Educational Special Needs

See Schools & Educational Support chapter.

## NSPCC (National Society for the Prevention of Cruelty to Children)

www.nspcc.org.uk, info@nspcc.org.uk
Helpline 0808 800 5000 24hr
Child Protection Helpline 0808 800 5000 24hr
Textphone 0800 056 0566 24 hr

### NSPCC Asian Child Protection Helpline
0800 096 7719                    Mon-Fri 11am-7pm

## Sure Start Units

www.surestart.gov.uk

Government programme supporting families from pregnancy until children are 14. Aiming to increasing the availability of childcare, improve health and emotional development of young children and support parents.

### Sure Start Easton
178 Easton Rd, Easton, Bristol, BS5 0PR
0117 941 3400
info@surestarteaston.org.uk

### Sure Start Hartcliffe Early Years Centre (Children's Centre)
Hartcliffe Early Years Centre, Hartcliffe Rd, BS13 0JW
0117 903 8633
hartcliffeearlyyears@bristol-city.gov.uk

### Sure Start Redliffe Nursery School (Children's Centre)
Spencer House, Ship Lane, Bristol, BS1 6RK
0117 903 0334
redcliffe-n@bristol-city.gov.uk

### Sure Start Four Acres (Children's Centre)
Four Acres Primary School, Four Acres, Withywood, Bristol, BS13 8RB
maggie.proom@barnardos.org.uk
Local Programme Manager: 0117 944 6474

Providing integrated education, care, family support and health services. Covering Hartcliffe, Highridge and Withywood.

### Sure Start Knowle West
The Park, Daventry Rd, Knowle, Bristol, BS4 1QD
lil_bowers@bristol-city.gov.uk
0117 903 9781

## Multiple Births

### Twins and Multiple Births Association (TAMBA)
2 The Willows, Gardner Road, Guildford, GU1 4PG
www.tamba.org.uk, enquiries@tamba.org.uk

| | |
|---|---|
| 0870 770 3305 | Mon-Fri 9.30am-5pm |
| Twinline: 0800 138 0509 | Daily 10am-1pm |
| | & 7pm-10pm |

Information and mutual support network for families of twins, triplets and more and the professionals involved in their care. Details of local groups can be obtained from the helpline.

### Little Saplings

Oakfield Road Day Nursery, 17 Oakfield Rd, BS8 2AW
0117 377 2270
Meet Thu 2pm-3.30pm

A free service run for parents/carers of multiple births. The group offers activities, trips and speakers. Qualified staff are available to support families.

## ADOPTIVE, FOSTER, STEP & ONE PARENT FAMILIES

### Adoption UK

46 The Green, South Bar St, Banbury, OX16 9AB
01295 752240
www.adoptionuk.org.uk
**Helpline** 0870 7700 450                    11am-4pm

Supporting families before, during and after adoption or long-term fostering. Online community provides information and support.

### Bristol Family Placement Team (Recruitment)

Social Services, Avonvale Road, Redfield, BS5 9RH
www.bristol-city.gov.uk/fostering
0117 954 8545

This team offers information, training and support to anyone interested in fostering children or young people. They welcome applicants from all sections of the community. See their advertisement in the Colour Reference Section, pg 136.

### Child Support Agency (CSA)

www.dss.gov.uk/csa
National enquiries 08457 133 133
Textphone 08457 138924

Aims to support families with the cost of raising children, while recognising that the primary responsibility rests with parents.

### Gingerbread (Association for One-Parent Families)

307 Borough High St, London, SE1 1JH
www.gingerbread.org.uk
Helpline 0800 018 4318

Self-help association for lone parent families. Provides advice, local contacts and activities.

### One-Parent Families' Services

255 Kentish Town Rd, London, NW5 2LX
www.oneparentfamilies.org.uk
Helpline 0800 018 5026                    Mon-Fri 9am-5pm

Provides help and advice for lone parents on benefits, work, education, relationship breakdown and child maintenance, children and holidays.

### Our Place

139 Fishponds Road, Eastville, Bristol, BS5 6PR
ourplace1@btconnect.com
0117 951 2433

Offering foster and adoptive families the opportunity to mix with others and share experiences. Fun activities, seminars and workshops run by professionals, no charges.

### Single Parent Action Network UK (SPAN)

Millpond, Baptist St, Easton, BS5 0YW
www.spanuk.org.uk, info@spanuk.org.uk
www.singleparents.org.uk (interactive site)
0117 951 4231

Campaigns to improve the lives of one parent families. Supports development of single parent self-help groups around the UK.

**SPAN Study Centre**
www.spanstudy.org.uk
0117 952 0626/2712                    Mon-Fri 9am-5pm

Focuses on training and support for single parents, further education and employment.

### South West Adoption Network (SWAN)

Leinster House, Leinster Avenue, Knowle, BS4 1NL
www.swan-adoption.org.uk
Helpline 0845 601 2459                    Tue-Thu 10am-2pm
                    Tue 7pm-9pm

A post-adoption centre offering advice, counselling, support groups and workshops.

# YOUNG PEOPLE & YOUNG PARENTS

## Brook Young People's Services

1 Unity Street, College Green, Bristol, BS1 5HH
www.brook.org.uk
0117 929 0090
Helpline  0800 018 5023          Mon-Fri 9am-5pm
Walk-in Mon-Tue 1-3pm, 4-6pm
Appt only Wed & Fri 12am-2pm,
Walk-in Wed/Thu 4-6pm, Sat 10-12pm

Expert counselling and advice on sexual health for under 25's. Provides all methods of contraception and emergency contraception; screening and testing. Connexions advice, and ACCSEX — a project aimed at young disabled people. Extremely informative website.

## Off the Record

2 Horfield Road, St Michael's Hill, Bristol, BS2 8EA
www.otrbristol.org.uk
Helpline 0808 808 9120
Mon-Wed 9.30am-8pm
Drop-in Mon-Wed 11.30am-5pm

Free, confidential information, advice and informal support for all ages. Free, counselling via appointments for 11-25's.

## The Young Mothers Group and Information Project

c/o The Mill Youth Centre, Lower Ashley Rd, BS5 0YJ
group@ymgt.fsnet.co.uk
0117 935 5639

Offers advice, support and out-reach visits to mothers under 25yrs. The Information Project is peer-led: trained volunteers talk in schools, colleges & youth clubs about the realities of young parenthood.

### Young Mothers' Group Trust

Unit 31/32, Easton Business Centre, Felix Rd,
BS5 0HE
0117 941 5838

Provides housing and advice for single homeless mothers (16-24yrs) or those facing homelessness.

# RELATIONSHIPS

## The Bridge Foundation

12 Sydenham Rd, Bristol, BS6 5SH
0117 942 4510
www.bridgefoundation.org.uk

A consultation and therapy service for couples, young children and families. Fees are charged but are discretionary for some.

## Bristol Family Mediation

Alexander House, Telephone Av, Bristol, BS1 4BS
www.bristolfamilymediation.org.uk
0117 929 2002                    Mon-Fri 9am-5pm
                              appointments available

Help pre or post-separating/divorcing couples make mutual decisions or resolve issues. A not-for-profit organisation. Outreach offices in Bath and Weston-super-Mare, see website.

## Marriage Care

58 Alma Rd, Clifton, Bristol, BS8 2DQ
www.marriagecare.org.uk
0117 973 3777
Fees by donation

Free, confidential counselling service for adults, whether single or in relationships.

## Relate Avon

133 Cheltenham Rd, Bristol, BS6 5RR
relateavon@compuserve.com
0117 942 8444                Mon-Fri 9.30am-9pm
Fees on a sliding scale.

Counselling people with relationship difficulties along with psycho-sexual therapy for people in committed relationships.

# DRUGS AND ALCOHOL

## Advice and Counselling on Alcohol and Drugs (ACAD)

15/16 Lower Park Row, Bristol, BS1 5BN
www.acad.org.uk, info@acad.org.uk
0117 929 3028
Group drop-in Mon-Thu 9am-5pm, Fri 9am-4pm

Free advice and counselling by appointment (or drop-ins) for people directly or indirectly affected by alcohol-related problems.

## Al-Anon Family Group

Al-Anon Family Group, 61 Great Dover St, London, SE1 4YF
www.al-anonuk.org.uk, alanonuk@aol.com
Helpline 0207 403 0888          Daily 10am-10pm

Confidential understanding and support for family and friends of problem drinkers. Details of local support groups.

**Alateen**, a service for young people (12-20yrs) who have been affected by someone else's drinking.

## Alcoholics Anonymous

Alcoholics Anonymous, PO Box 42, Bristol, BS99 7RJ
0117 926 5520/926 5926 24hr
National helpline 0845 769 755

Frequent meetings held in various parts of Bristol. Free to join, the only requirement for membership is a desire to stop drinking.

## Bristol & District Tranquilliser Project

88 Henleaze Road, Bristol, BS9 4JY
Helpline 0117 962 8874          Mon-Thu 10am-4pm

Advice and support to people taking prescribed psychotropic medication. Runs withdrawal groups and offers individual counselling.

## Bristol Drugs Project

11 Brunswick Square, Bristol, BS2 8PE
0117 987 1500 answerphone out of hours
www.bdp.org.uk, info@bdp.org.uk
Drop-in &/or needle exchange:
Mon-Sat 9.30am-12.30pm

Free and confidential advice and counselling for anyone concerned about drug use. Crèche facilities on Wednesday mornings.

## Narcotics Anonymous

www.ukna.org.uk
National Helpline 0845 7730 0009
0117 924 0084 or 07949 429 567
Answerphone out of hours

Information on fellowship meetings throughout the West Country and Wales, as well as nationally. Check website for meetings.

# BEREAVEMENT

## ARC

73 Charlotte St, London, W1T 4PN
www.arc-uk.org, info@arc-uk.org
Helpline 0207 631 0285          Mon-Fri 10am-5pm

Antenatal Results and Choices provides information and support through the ante-natal testing process and when an abnormality is diagnosed; impartial help when making a decision about a pregnancy's future.

## Cruse Bereavement Care

9A St James Barton, Bristol, BS1 3LT
www.crusebereavementcare.org.uk
National Helpline                    0870 167 1677
0117 926 4045                  Mon-Fri 10am-2pm
Answerphone out of hours

Provides free 1:1 or family counselling.

## FSID

Artillery House, 11-19 Artillery Row, London, SW1P 1RT
www.sids.org.uk, fsid@sids.org.uk
Admin 020 722 8001
Helpline 020 7233 2090          Mon-Fri 9am-11pm
                                Sat-Sun 6pm-11pm

Foundation for the Study of Infant Death funds research, promotes baby health and supports grieving families.

## Miscarriage Association

c/o Clayton Hosp, Northgate, W Yorkshire, WF1 3JS
www.miscarriageassociation.org.uk
Admin 01924 200 795
Helpline 01924 200 799          Mon-Fri 9am-4pm
(Answerphone out of hours)

Support for those who have suffered a miscarriage or are worried that they might. Newsletters, leaflets and local contacts.

## SANDS

28 Portland Place, London, W1B 1LY
www.uk-sands.org, helpline@uk-sands.org
Enquiries 0207 436 7940
Helpline 0207 436 5881     Mon-Fri 9.30am-5.30pm

Stillbirth and Neonatal Death Society supports parents who are faced with the loss of a baby before, during or after birth.

## The Compassionate Friends

53 North St, Bristol, BS3 1EN
www.tcf.org.uk, info@tcf.org.uk
Helpline 0845 1232304 24hr
Admin 08451 203786    10am-4pm & 6.30-10.30pm

Self-help befriending organisation offering support to families after the death of a child.

## Twins and Multiple Birth Association (TAMBA)

Runs a support group led by parents who have themselves experienced a loss within a multiple birth. See Babies & Children above for contact details.

## Winstons Wish

Clara Burgess Centre, Bayshill Rd,
Cheltenham, GL50 3AW
www.winstonswish.org.uk
01242 515157
Helpline 0845 2030405         Mon-Fri 9am-5pm
Answerphone out of hours

Helping bereaved children and their families rebuild their lives. Also assists schools and carers with the needs of bereaved children.

# FOR WOMEN

## WOMEN'S HEALTH

### Wellwomen Information

6 West Street, Old Market, St Philips, BS2 0BH
0117 941 3311         Mon/Wed 9.30am-12.30pm
www.wellwomeninformation.co.uk

Drop-in and helpline available for women in distress or other health problems. Counselling for women on low incomes.

**Sehatmand Aurat (Asian Women's Health Project)**
176 Easton Road, Bristol, BS5 0ES
0117 941 5186

Complementary therapy sessions fortnightly, Mon 9.30am-12.30pm.

## PRECONCEPTION & ANTENATAL

### Pre-conception care

GPs give advice on pre-conception and fertility problems, and will refer you to specialists if necessary. There are also organisations that help with pre-conception healthcare outside the NHS.

### Foresight

178 Hawthorn Rd, W Bognor, W Sussex, PO21 2UY
www.foresight-preconception.org.uk
01243 868 001

Offers dietary & life-style advice and general support to help couples conceive. For further information send an SAE (35p) or see website.

### Life

125 Cheltenham Rd, Bristol, BS6 5RR
0800 068 5028 (local helpline)
www.lifeuk.org
Helpline 0800 849 4545         7am-7pm
Free/donations welcome

Pro-life counselling service for women facing unplanned pregnancy, termination, miscarriage, still birth or infertility.

### National Childbirth Trust (NCT)

The NCT, Alexandra House, Oldham Terrace, Acton, London, W3 6NH
www.nctpregnancyandbabycare.com
0870 770 3236
Enquiry Line 0870 444 8707
Membership Line 08709 908040
Breastfeeding Line 0870 444 8708 8am-10pm

Information and support in pregnancy, childbirth and early parenthood. See listing in Healthcare for ante-natal classes, breastfeeding counsellors.

### The National Endometriosis Society

Artillery Row, London, SW1P 1RR
0207 222 2781
www.endo.org.uk, nes@endo.org.uk
Helpline 0808 808 2227         7pm-10pm

Provides support, information and local branch phone numbers.

## Well-Being Eating for Pregnancy Helpline

Univ. of Sheffield, Dept of Reproductive Medicine, The Jessop Wing, Tree Root Walk, Sheffield, S10 2SF
www.shef.ac.uk/pregnancy_nutrition/
0845 1303646

The helpline offers scientifically valid information on nutrition for women who are pregnant, planning to be or are breast-feeding.

## POSTNATAL

### Association for Post Natal Illness

145 Dawes Rd, London, SW6 7EB
www.apni.org, info@apni.org
0207 386 0868                    Mon-Fri: 10am-2pm

Telephone one-to-one support for mothers with post-natal illness. Callers are matched with a local volunteer who has experienced the illness. The line is very busy, keep trying, answerphone messages are responded to within 24hrs.

### Meet A Mum Association

54 Lillington Rd, Radstock, BA3 3NR
www.mama.co.uk
National Helpline 0845 120 3746
Mon-Fri 7pm-10pm

Offers moral support, friendship and practical help (local groups) to women suffering from post-natal illness, or who feel lonely or isolated after birth of a child.

## Mothers for Mothers

82 Colston St, Bristol, BS1 5BB
0117 904 0065                    Mon-Thu 9.30am-12.30pm
0117 975 6006                    up to 9pm

Befriending and support for women suffering post-natal illness. Holds coffee mornings for mothers to meet. Counselling and home visits available. Groups in Bedminster and Barton Hill.

## IN CRISIS

### Avon Sexual Abuse Centre

PO Box 665, BS99 1XY
www.napac.org.uk
National Helpline 0800 0853 330
0117 935 1707                    Mon/Wed/Thu 9.30am-4pm
Answerphone at all other times

A free and confidential counselling service available to adults, children and their families.

### Bristol Crisis Service for Women

PO Box 654, Bristol, BS99 1XH
www.users.zetnet.co.uk/bcsw
Admin 0117 927 9600
Helpline 0117 925 1119            Fri, Sat 9pm-12.30am
Answerphone out of hours          Sun 6-9pm

Support for women in any emotional distress; specialises in those who have suffered childhood abuse, and those who self injure.

### Gloucester Rape Crisis Centre

Helpline 01452 526770

### Next Link Domestic Abuse Services

5 Queen Sq, Bristol, BS1 4JQ
0117 925 1811
www.nextlinkhousing.co.uk
Mon-Fri 9am-5pm, answerphone out of hours

Safe temporary accommodation for women and children experiencing and fleeing domestic abuse. Offers other support services including resettlement and tenancy.

# FOR MINORITY GROUPS

## GENERAL SUPPORT

### Bangladesh Association

Bangladesh House, 539 Stapleton Rd, Eastville, Bristol, BS5 6PE
0117 951 1491

Advice, information and library service for the Bangladeshi community in English and Bengali.

### Bristol & Avon Chinese Women's Group

St Agnes Church, Thomas St, St Pauls, BS2 9LL
www.bacwg.org.uk, bacwg2@onetel.net.uk
0117 935 1462     Mon-Fri 9.30am-4.30pm, Fri 4pm

Provides support, advice and information to Chinese women.

### Bristol Gay & Lesbian Switchboard

8 Somerville Rd, Bishopston, Bristol, BS7 9AA
www.bristolblag.org. uk, mail@bristolblags.org.uk
0117 942 0842                    Daily 8pm-10pm

Provides information and support to gay, lesbian, transgender and tranvestite people.

### Bristol Pakistani Women's Organisation

454 Stapleton Rd, Easton, Bristol, BS5 6PA
0117 952 3031

Organises social, cultural, educational, religious and recreational activities especially for women and children.

### Bristol Racial Equality Council

Colston House, Colston St, Bristol, BS1 5AQ
bristolrec@aol.com
0117 929 7899

Advice on racial discrimination. Produces a directory of organisations and contacts for black and other ethnic minority groups, and a monthly newsletter and weekly news bulletin.

### KHAAS

St Werburgh's Community Centre, Horley Rd, BS29TJ
0117 955 4070

Provides services to Asian families who have children with disabilities and special needs.

### Overseas Chinese Association

11-13 Lower Ashley Rd, St Agnes, BS2 9QA
overseaschineseassociation@southwest.fslife.co.uk
0117 955 5225

Support for the local Chinese community. There is a club for the elderly, a Chinese language group, courses and workshops.

### Support Against Racist Incidents (SARI)

PO Box 2454, Bristol, BS2 2WX
www.sariweb.org.uk, sari@sari.freeserve.co.uk
0117 952 0060

Support for people under racial attack or suffering harassment.

### Unity Group

Fulford Family Centre, 237-239 Gatehouse Ave, Withywood, BS13 9AQ
0117 978 2441
www.barnardos.org.uk/newfulfordfamilycentre
Thu 1-3pm

Informal support group with crèche, for black multi-racial families living in Hartcliffe, Withywood, Highridge and Bishopsworth.

# MEDICAL CONDITIONS & SPECIAL NEEDS

## GENERAL SUPPORT GROUPS

### Break

1 Montague Rd, Sheringham, Norfolk, NR26 8WN
www.break-charity.org, office@break-charity.org
01263 822161

Provides special care services for children, adults and families with special needs, including subsidised holidays and respite care.

## Bristol Family Link Scheme

Family Placements, Avonvale Rd, Redfield, BS5 9RH
www.sharedcarenetwork.org.uk
0117 954 8502

Family-based short breaks for disabled children and young people.

## Contact a Family

209-211 City Rd, London, EC1V 1JN
www.cafamily.org.uk, info@cafamily.org.uk
Admin 020 7608 8700
Helpline 0808 808 3555
Textphone 0808 808 3556

Supports families with disabled children, including those with health conditions and rare disorders. Supplies information on eductional needs, benefits and local support.

## Disabled Living Centre, West of England

The Vassall Centre, Gill Ave, Fishponds, BS16 2QQ
www.dlcbristol.org, info@dlcbristol.org
0117 965 3651 (also Minicom)
For appts: Mon-Fri 10am-4pm (some Sats)

Consultation by appointment providing professional, impartial information and advice on products and equipment to aid independent living. Also has a Multimedia Resource Area, coffee shop and garden.

## Disabled Parents Network

Unit F9, 89-93 Fonthill Rd, London, N4 3JH
www.disabledparentsnetwork.org.uk
0870 2410 450

A national network of disabled people who are parents or hope to become parents. Peer support, information, advice, contact register, a quarterly newsletter (available on tape) and a helpline. Local and national events.

## Hop Skip & Jump

Grimsbury Road, Kingswood, Bristol, BS15 9SE
www.hopskipandjump.org.uk
0117 967 7282
Mon-Fri: 9am-5.30pm, Sat 10am-4pm
Donations welcome

Charity-run play centre for children, 0-16yrs, with special needs, where parents can relax

while children are looked after by qualified care workers, siblings welcome.

## Parkway Parent and Child Project

Parkway Methodist Church, Conduit Place, St Werburghs, BS2 9RU
enquiries@parkwaypcp.free-online.co.uk
0117 935 0205

Playgroup, crèche, parent and toddler sessions. Informal advice and counselling, courses and workshops.

## The Care Forum

The Vassall Centre, Gill Ave, Fishponds, BS16 2QQ
0117 965 4444
www.thecareforum.org.uk

Provides support, co-ordination and information services for voluntary groups enabling them to deliver local health and social care services. Direct services includes The Complaints Procedure Advocacy Service (CPA), complaints about Social Services; The Disability Information Service (DIS).

### Purple Pages Helpline

info@purplepage.org.uk
0808 808 5252                    Mon-Fri 9.30am-4.30pm

A friendly and up-to-date helpline for disabled people, older people, carers and their friends, family and professionals in Bristol and the surrounding areas.

## The Yellow Book

Consumer Services Manager at South Gloucestershire Council
www.southglos.gov.uk
01454 866 345

A definitive guide book giving information and services relevant to caring for children with special needs in South Gloucestershire. Download guide from website.

## Time 2 Share

Unit 55, Easton Business Centre, Felix Rd, BS5 OHE
www.time2share.org.uk, info@time2share.org.uk
0117 941 5868                    Mon-Fri 9.30am-2.00pm
Answerphone out of hours

Support for families who care for children with learning difficulties. Provides sitters and caters for individual needs. Families are matched on a one to one basis with a volunteer; support and training is available.

### West of England Centre for Disabled Living

Leinster Avenue, Knowle, Bristol, BS4 1AR
www.wecil.co.uk, reception@wecil.co.uk
Helpline & Minicom 0117 903 8900
Admin 0117 983 2828

Phone service provided by disabled people, offering free, confidential advice covering all aspects of disability — especially welfare rights, DLA and AA form-filling service.

# A-Z SUPPORT FOR SPECIFIC SPECIAL NEEDS & MEDICAL CONDITIONS

## ALLERGIES

### Allergy UK

3 White Oak Sq, London Rd, Swanley, BR8 7AG
www.allergyuk.org, info@allergyuk.org
Helpline 01322 619 898          Mon-Fri 9am-5pm
Membership £20

Aims to increase understanding and awareness and assist in allergy management. Information, advice and support.

## ARTHRITIS

### Arthritis Care South England

18 Stephenson Way, London, NW1 2HD
www.arthritiscare.org.uk
020 7380 6509
Helplines 0808 800 4050          Mon-Fri 12pm-4pm
The Source 0808 808 2000          Mon-Fri 12pm-2pm
for sufferers under 26yrs

Aims to empower people with arthritis to take control of their arthritis and their lives.

## ASTHMA

### Asthma UK

Summit House, 70 Wilson St, London, EC2A 2DB
www.asthma.org.uk, info@asthma.org.uk
Advice Line 020 7786 4900
Helpline 08457 010203          Mon-Fri 9am-5pm

Helpline staffed by asthma nurses. Publishes fact sheets and lists of support groups.

## AUTISM

### Autism (National Autistic Society)

393 City Rd, London, EC1V 1NG
www.nas.org.uk
Admin 0207 833 2299
Helpline 0845 070 4004          Mon-Fri 10am-4pm
Minicom 0845 0704003
Local contact 0117 939 0141

The local group meets regularly and there are family social events throughout the year.

## BED WETTING

### ERIC Education & Resources for Improving Childhood Continence

34 Old School House, Brittania Rd, BS15 8DB
www.eric.org.uk, info@eric.org.uk
0845 370 8008          Mon-Fri 10am-4pm

Provides advice and information on bedwetting, day-time wetting, constipation and soiling.

## BIRTH DEFECTS

### Newlife

BDF Centre, Hemlock Way, Cannock, WS11 2GF
www.bdfcharity.co.uk, info@bdfnewlife.co.uk
Helpline 08700 70 70 20          Mon-Fri 9.30am-5pm
Answerphone out of hours

Dedicated to improving child health by combating birth defects and supporting those affected or at risk.

# BLOOD DISORDERS

## Haemophilia Society

Petersham House, 57a Hatton Garden, EC1N 8JG
www.haemophilia.org.uk, info@haemophilia.org.uk
Admin 0207831 1020
Helpline 0800 018 6068          Mon-Fri 10am-4pm

Patient group for people with haemophilia, von Willebrand's and related bleeding disorders. Information and advice, run special projects for families, young people and women. 17 local groups across the UK.

## OSCAR (Sickle Cell and Thalassaemia Centre, Bristol)

256 Stapleton Road, Easton, Bristol, BS5 0NP
www.sicklecellsociety.org
0117 951 2200

Providing information, support and counselling.

# BRAIN INJURIES

## Cerebra

13 Guild Hall Sq, Carmarthen, Wales, SA31 1PR
www.cerebra.org.uk
Admin 0126 724 4200
Helpline 0800 328 1159

Information, contact and support network for families and carers of brain-injured children. Also funds research.

# CEREBRAL PALSY

## Scope Bristol (Cerebral Palsy)

Unit 13 The Greenway Centre, Doncaster Rd, Southmead, Bristol, BS10 5PY
www.scopebristol.co.uk
0117 950 5099          Mon-Thu 9am-3pm, Fri 9-12am
Answerphone out of hours

Services include; information, grants scheme, evening club, Connexions Young People's Information Point (YPIP), Lifestyles Project, newsletter, physiotherapy and equipment.

# CLEFT LIP & PALATE

## CLAPA (Cleft Lip and Palate Association)

Greenman Tower, 332 Goswell Rd, London EC1V 7LQ
www.clapa.com, info@clapa.com
020 7783 34883, answerphone out of hours

Information and support to all those affected by cleft lip or palate. Specialist feeding bottles, information leaflets, lists of local contacts.

# CYSTIC FIBROSIS

## Cystic Fibrosis Trust

11 London Road, Bromley, Kent, BR1 1BY
www.cftrust.org.uk, enquiries@cftrust.org.uk
Admin 020 8464 7211
Helpline 0845 8591000, answerphone out of hours

Information, advice and support for those affected by CF and their families and carers. Lists of local contacts.

# DEAFNESS

## Acorns Resource for Families of Deaf Children

Elmfield House, Greystoke Ave, Bristol, BS10 6AY
sue_horne@bristol-city.gov.uk
Voice/minicom 0117 903 8442

For families with pre-school deaf children. Drop-in centre for parents, access to advice on sign language and communication. There is a crèche, Wed in term time.

### BUDS Group

Sensory Support Service (0117 903 8442)

Beginning to Understand Deafness for families with newly-diagnosed, hearing-impaired children.

## Avon Deaf Child Society & Bristol Centre for Deaf People

16-18 King Sq, Bristol, BS2 8JL
www.ndcs.org.uk
Helpline 0808 800 8880 (voice & textphone)
Textphone 0117 924 9868    Mon-Fri 8.30am-5pm
Minicom 0117 944 1344

Provides support, information and advice for deaf children and their families. Sign language and lip-reading taught to hearing-impaired parents or to those with hearing-impaired children.

## Family Centre (Deaf Children)

Family Centre (Deaf Children), Frome House, Cranleigh Court Rd, Yate, BS37 5DE
www.fcdc.org.uk, office @fcdc.org.uk
Minicom 01454 315405
01454 315404    Mon/Wed-Fri 9am-5.30pm
answerphone out of hours

Support, information, educational and social activities for hearing families with deaf children across the Avon area.

## Sense (The National Deafblind and Rubella Association)

The Woodside Family Centre, Woodside Rd, Kingswood, BS15 8DG
www.sense.org.uk
0117 967 0008
Local Branch 0117 908 9400

Provides support to the families of multi-sensory impaired children. Running groups for babies, toddler and children. Facilities include toy library, crèche and sensory stimulation room.

## Social Services Sensory Services Team

Centre for Deaf People, 16-18 King Square, BS2 8JL
brssmc@bristol-city.gov.uk
0117 924 0484
Minicom 0117 944 2168

Advice and social work services for deaf and hearing-impaired people.

## DIABETES

### Diabetes UK

10 Parkway, London, NW1 7AA
www.diabetes.org.uk, info@diabetes.org.uk
0207 424 1000    Mon-Fri 9am-5pm
Care line 0845 1202960

Specially trained staff offering advice to those with diabetes.

**Local Contact**

Diabetes UK South West 01823 324 007

## DOWNS SYNDROME

### Downs Syndrome Association

Langdon Down Centre, 2A Langdon Park, Teddington, London, TW11 9PS
www.downs-syndrome.org.uk
0845 230 0372

**South West Development Officer**

vr_dsasouthwest@hotmail.com
01275 858230

**BADSS (local parent support group)**

www.dsa-bristol.org.uk, info@dsa-bristol.org.uk
0117 986 7992

Information library, parents support network and mother & toddler group. Outings, events.

## DYSLEXIA

See Schools & Educational Support pg 238

## EPILEPSY

### Epilepsy (British Epilepsy Association)

New Antsey House, Gateway Drive, Yeadon, Leeds, LS19 7XY
www.epilepsy.org.uk, epilepsy@epilepsy.org.uk
Admin 0113 210 8800 admin
Helpline 0808 800 5050    Mon-Thu 9am-4.30pm
Fri 9am-4pm

Information, local support groups and a newsletter.

## HIV

### Aled Richards Centre

8-10 West St, Old Market, BS2 0BH
0117 955 1000
www.tht.org.uk, info@thtwest.org.uk

The Terrence Higgins Trust has a wide range of publications and information on HIV, AIDS and sexual health for professionals and the public.

## HYPERACTIVE CHILDREN

### Hyperactive Children's Support Group

71 Whyke Lane, Chichester, Sussex, PO19 7PD
www.hacsg.org.uk, web@hacsg.org.uk
01243 539966                    Mon-Fri 10am-1pm

Including allergic/ADD children. Advice and support with a dietary and nutrition approach for parents, carers and professionals.

## LIMB DISABILITIES

### Reach

PO Box 54, Helston, TR13 8WD
www.reach.org.uk, reach@reach.org.uk
0845 130 6225                    Mon-Fri 9.30am-5pm

Association for children with hand or arm deficiency. Parent support group offering information and lists of local contacts. Membership £20 per year.

### STEPS

Warrington Lane, Lymm, Cheshire, WA13 0SA
www.steps-charity.org.uk, info@steps-charity.org.uk
Helpline 0871 7170044
Admin 0871 717 0045

Association for people with lower limb conditions which offers information and support with local contacts.

## MENINGITIS

### Meningitis Research Foundation

Midland Way, Thornbury, Bristol, BS35 2BS
www.meningitis.org, info@meningitis.org.uk
01454 281811
Helpline 0808 800 3344 24hr

Funds vital scientific research into the prevention, detection and treatment of meningitis and septicaemia. Offers support through in-depth information and befriending.

### The Meningitis Trust

Fern House, Bath Rd, Stroud, GL5 3TJ
01453 768 000 (admin and info) Mon-Fri 9am-5pm
www.meningitis-trust.org
Helpline 0845 6000 800 24 hr

Financial, emotional and practical support to sufferers and their families. Information and local contacts available on admin line.

## MENTAL ILLNESS

### MENCAP Avon North

Kingswood House, South Rd, Kingswood, BS15 8JF
www.avonnorthmencap.org.uk
0117 961 4372

Support, advice and information for people with learning disabilities and their families.

### Mind

174 Cheltenham Rd, Bristol, BS6 5RE
www.bristolmind.org.uk
Mindline 0808 8080 330          Wed-Sun: 8pm-12am

Drop-in, advocacy, information services and helpline for those with mental health or emotional support needs.

## METABOLIC DISEASES

### CLIMB (Metabolic diseases)

CLIMB Building, 176 Nantwich Rd, Crewe, CW2 6BG
www.climb.org.uk
0870 7700325
Helpline 0800 6523181

Children Living with Inherited Metabolic

Diseases (CLIMB) provides information to parents, carers and professionals. Local contacts and magazine.

# PREMATURE BABIES

## BLISS (The Premature Baby Charity)

68 South Lambeth Rd, London, SW8 1RL
www.bliss.org.uk, information@bliss.org.uk
Parent Support Line 0500 618 140
Mon-Fri 10am-5pm
Answerphone out of hours

Support and information for parents and families with babies on, or recently returned home from, special care baby units.

# SKIN DISORDERS

## Eczema (National Eczema Society)

Hill House, Highgate Hill, London, N19 5NA
www.eczema.org, helpline@eczema.org
Helpline 0870 241 3604          Mon-Fri 8am-8pm

Help and support for those people affected by eczema. Also provides list of local support groups.

## Psoriasis Association

7 Milton St, Northampton, NN2 7JG
www.psoriasis-association.org.uk
Helpline 0845 676 0076
Mon-Thu 9.15am-4.45pm, Fri 9.15am-4.15pm

Offers support and advice to children and adults suffering from psoriasis.

# SPINA BIFIDA & HYDROCEPHALUS

## ASBAH

Asbah House, 42 Park Road, Peterborough, PE1 2UQ
01733 555988
www.asbah.org, info@asbah.org

Information, support and practical help for those affected and their families including local group contacts.

# VISUALLY IMPAIRED

## Look West

c/o RNIB Bristol, Stillhouse Lane, Bristol, BS3 4EB
01225 421 717
www.look-uk.org.uk

Parent self-help group of visually impaired children and their families. Has its own holiday caravan equipped to meet the needs of a visually impaired child. Children's groups include The Explorers and Discoverers.

## RNIB Bristol

10 Stillhouse Lane, Bedminster, Bristol, BS3 4EB
www.rnib.org.uk, rnibbristol@rnib.org.uk
Helpline 0845 766 9999
Voice/minicom 0117 953 7750
Mon-Fri 10am-4pm

Support and facilities for those with any level of visual impairment, including combined sight and hearing loss. Sells a range of equipment; offers information (education and employment issues — New Deal, Access to Work) on tapes and leaflets. Many other services.

# SERIOUS & TERMINAL ILLNESSES

## ACT (Association for Children with Life Threatening or Terminal Conditions and their Families)

Orchard House, Orchard Lane, Bristol, BS1 5DT
www.act.org.uk, info@act.org.uk
Helpline 0117 922 1556          Mon-Fri 8.30am-5pm
Answerphone out of hours

Information on support services available for families. ACT campaigns for the development of children's palliative care services. Online discussion group.

## CLIC Sargent (Cancer and Leukaemia in Childhood)

Abbeywood, Bristol, BS34 7JU
www.clicsargent.org.uk, info@clic-charity.org.uk
0117 311 2600          Mon-Fri: 8.30am-5pm
Helpline 0845 301 0031          Mon-Fri 9am-5pm
Answerphone out of hours

CLIC and Sargent Cancer Care merged in 2005. Provides specialist clinical care, family support, family accommodation close to paediatric oncology centres, holidays, financial help and advice, research.

## Leukaemia Care Society

1 Birch Court, Blackpole East, Worcester, WR3 8SG
www.leukaemiacare.org.uk
01905 755 977          Mon-Fri 9am-5pm
Helpline 0800 169 6680 24hr

Support through a national befriending scheme. Provides information, limited financial assistance and organises caravan holidays. Lists local contacts. Helpline staffed by those with direct experience of leukaemia.

## The Jessie May Trust

35 Old School House, Kingswood Foundation Estate, Britannia Rd, Kingswood, Bristol, BS15 8DB
www.jessiemaytrust.org.uk
Admin 0117 961 6840
Care Team 0117 958 2172

Providing a palliative care service for children and young people who are not expected to live beyond the age of 19. Respite, support, advice, terminal nursing care and bereavement support.

## The Rainbow Centre

27 Lilymead Avenue, Bristol, BS4 2BY
www.rainbowcentre.org.uk
0117 985 3343

Aims to provide the highest quality support and help to children with life-threatening illness, and their families. Also bereavement support, art and play therapy, and complementary therapies.

# LEGAL & FINANCIAL ADVICE

## ADVICE ON ALL ISSUES

## Citizens Advice Bureau

www.citizensadvice.org.uk

Provides free, confidential, impartial and independent advice. They advise on almost any subject including: debt, benefits, employment, housing problems, relationship breakdown and immigration. Operates on a first-in-line basis.

### Bristol CAB
12 Broad Street, Bristol BS1 2HL
0870 121 2134
Drop-in, telephone and appointments:
Mon/Thu/Fri 10am-3.30pm, Wed/Sat 10-12am
Appt service only: Tue 10am-1.30pm

### Outreach:
The Meeting Rooms, Greystoke Avenue, Southmead
Wed 10am-1pm (drop-in only)

### Hartcliffe Health Centre
1st & 3rd Mon of month by appt

### South Gloucester (Yate) CAB
Kennedy Way, Yate, BS37 4DQ
0870 121 2019

### Outreaches:
Town Hall, 35 High St, Thornbury
Patchway Community Centre, Rodway Rd, Patchway

### Keynsham CAB
Town Hall, Keynsham, BS31 1EF
BANES residents only: Mon/Thu 10am-2pm

## North Bristol Advice Centre

2 Gainsborough Square, Lockleaze, Bristol, BS7 9XA
www.northbristoladvice.org.uk
0117 951 5751
Minicom 0117 987 4339

Free, independent and confidential legal advice and assistance in social welfare law and general advice on debt, housing and employment issues. Drop-in and appointment advice sessions available throughout the week in Lockleaze, Southmead, Horfield, Patchway, Little Stoke, Lawrence Weston and Sea Mills.

## South Bristol Advice Service

Leinster House, Leinster Avenue, Knowle, BS4 1NL
Minicom 0117 909 9705
0117 985 1122 answerphone out of hours
www.southbristoladvice.org.uk

Advice, representation, specialist debt and benefit services. Advice points across south Bristol. Home visits for house-bound clients.

## St Pauls Advice Centre

146 Grosvenor Rd, St Paul's, Bristol, BS2 8YA
stpaulsadvice@btconnect.com
0117 955 2981
Mon-Fri (closed Wed) 10am-12pm, appt or drop-in

Advice on benefits, housing, debt and rights issues. Tribunal representation available.

# DEBT

## Bristol Debt Advice Centre

2nd Floor, 48-54 West Street, St Philips, BS2 0BL
www.bdac.org.uk, mail@bdac.org.uk
Helpline: 0117 954 3990
Minicom 0117 954 3991
Mon/Tue/Thu 9.30am-12.30pm

Free professional advice over the phone to people in debt. Also sessions in Lawrence Weston, Knowle West, St Pauls & Lockleaze. Appointments for more complex problems.

# HOUSING

## Bristol City Council Housing Services

Neighbourhood & Housing Customer Services,
The Hub, 13-17 Cumberland St, BS2 8NL
0117 909 6000
Mon/Tue/Thu/Fri 10am-4pm, Wed 12pm-4pm

Advice to council tenants on housing problems including homelessness and money advice.

## Shelter Housing Aid Centre

Kenham House, Wilder St, Bristol, BS2 8PD
www.england.shelter.org.uk
0808 800 4444, 0117 924 9500
Mon-Fri (closed Wed) 10am-1pm

A drop-in and telephone service providing advice and help on housing issues.

## South Glos and North Bristol Housing Aid Centre

Rodway Rd, Patchway, Bristol, BS34 5DQ
www.england.shelter.org.uk
01454 865 560

A drop-in and telephone service providing advice and help on housing issues.

## The SPACE Trust

St Nicholas House, Lawfords Gate, Bristol, BS5 0RE
spacetrust@hotmail.co.uk
Enquiries 0117 907 5355
Outreach 0117 907 3012

Christian charity working with families (from all cultures) housed in temporary accommodation. Organises outreach clubs in hostels and finds families free furniture amd household goods when rehoused.

# LEGAL

## Avon and Bristol Law Centre

2 Moon St, Stokes Croft, BS2 8QE
www.avonandbristollawcentre.org.uk
0117 924 8662 Mon-Fri 9am-5pm

Free legal advice and advocacy service. Advice on immigration, employment (including discrimination), housing, debt, welfare benefits and community groups. By appt.

## Resolution (First for Family Law)

PO Box 302, Orpington, Kent, BR6 8QX
www.sfla.co.uk
01689 850 227

Provides local lists of solicitors who are members of the Association. Promotes non-confrontational resolutions to family problems.

## The Law Shop

48 Gloucester Rd, Bishopston, BS7 8BH
www.lawshopbristol.co.uk
0117 944 1966
Mon-Fri 9am-5pm, Sat 9.30-12.30am
Duty solicitor: £10 per 10 minutes

Provides support to people handling simple legal matters themselves. Services include legal forms, books and CDs. Provides free access to the legal library, workstations for

## CHILDREN'S INFORMATION SERVICE FOR BRISTOL

Registered Charity No: 1053854

Are you looking for childcare?

Would you like to know about different types of childcare and what to look for when choosing childcare?

Would you like information on the Nursery Education Grant or Tax Credits?

### THEN WE CAN HELP!
### We have the answers to all these questions PLUS lots more......

Call our friendly helpline on 0845 129 7217
8am-4pm Monday & Friday
8am-8pm Tuesday-Thursday

enquiries@cisbristol.co.uk
www.cisbristol.co.uk

people who want to do the work themselves (which can be checked by the duty solicitor) and low cost internet access. The Law Shop does not give advice by phone or email.

## SOCIAL SECURITY & TAX

### Citizens Advice Bureau

Provides free, confidential, impartial and independent advice on social security and tax issues. See listings above.

### Inland Revenue

www.hmrc.gov.uk
See telephone book for full range of helplines

**Child Benefits**
0845 302 1444         Daily 8am-8pm
Textphone 0845 302 1474

**Working Tax Credit**
Textphone 0845 300 3909
0845 300 3900        Mon-Fri 8am-8pm

**Self assessment**
0845 900 0444        Daily 8am-8pm

**Bristol & North Somerset area**
Norfolk House, Temple Street, BS1 6HS
0845 302 1443    Mon-Fri 8am-8pm, Sat 9am-4pm

Local office providing help and advice.

### Social Security

Bristol Office 0117 991 3000
www.jobcentreplus.gov.uk or www.dwp.gov.uk
Jobseeker Direct 0845 60 60 234
Textphone 0845 605 5255
Mon-Fri 8am-6pm, Sat 9am-1pm

Jobcentre Plus offers help for those seeking work, also with Jobseeker's Allowance, social security benefit and NI number applications.

| | |
|---|---|
| Benefit enquiry line | 0800 882 200 |
| (Textphone | 0800 24 33 55) |
| Disability Living Allowance | 0845 712 3456 |
| Attendance Allowance | 0845 712 3456 |
| National Insurance enquiries | 0845 302 1479 |
| Carers' Allowance | 01253 856123 |

## ACKNOWLEDGEMENTS

It is impossible to credit all the contributors to Titch Hikers over the last 25 years but we are very grateful to: Tricia Phoenix and Sally Stanley who came up with the original idea back in the early 1980s; to Emily Shepherd who helmed the 7th and 8th Editions with help from Flora Pearce and Dr Simon Atkins and to all those involved in the 9th Edition.

### Special thanks from the Editor to the following:

The fourteen-strong team of researchers, for their enthusiasm, humour and attention to detail, please see their credits below. To all those readers, friends and relatives who have fed back information and sent in their fan mail! Titch Hikers exists because of you.

### Contributors

Bertie Ellis, Kate Fisher, Rob Furness, Suneetha Goring, Mary Griffin, Anita Long, Simon McMurtrie, Fiona & Rory MccGwire, Vanessa Meakin, Tracy Moyle-Maton, Cathy Panter, Angela & Keith Potter, Carol Portlock, Ruth Revell, Kath Sidaway, Jo Smart, Mark Stonham, Julia Swan and Madelyn White.

### Photographs

Ian, Ella and Theo Beavon, Chris Dickinson, Caroline Doran, Karen and Marina Painter, Alison Simmonds, Monica Worsley and all the researchers' children. See also credits in the inside front cover or beside individual photographs.

### Sport & Leisure Centre research

Alison Simmonds

### Schools & Educational Support

Cathy Panter

### Database

Mark Furnevall, www.sunspace.ltd.uk

### Cover Design

karen painter design, karenpainter@blueyonder.co.uk

### Personal thanks

To Tim for his inspired IT support and coolness in keeping this mammoth task in perspective. To Sophia Denham, who helped with data entry and research. To Diana Beavon for taking on quite a bit extra! To Rachel Miller who unstintingly contributed so much more than her chapter.

### Individual researchers' profiles and thanks

#### Diana Beavon — Childcare 0-4 Years, Eating Out, Transport

Would like to thank all those people who completed questionnaires, in particular the Mums (and some Dads too) at Imps in Henleaze, Ebenezer Rendezvous in Filton, Sunbeams in Bedminster, Kings Tots Parent & Toddlers in Kingswood plus Jack and Jill Pre-school. Having researched so many new recommendations, she is keen to try many of them out with Ella and Theo.

She would also like to thank her family for their understanding and allowing her to lock herself away to write the chapters. She will see you again for the next edition!

#### Paula Brown — Time Out for Adults

Mother of 2 boys, Gabriel and Jude. Paula sells Barefoot children's books and runs Tatty Bumpkin yoga. She has a personal interest in the Time Out section, believing that doing something for yourself is vital to your well-being and therefore your families, no matter how hard it is.

### Lu Hersey — Shopping & Services

Has four teenagers and works as a freelance copywriter to keep them supplied in Clearasil and trainers.

### Rachel Miller — Activities and clever sub-editing

Is a freelance journalist who moved to Bristol five years ago from London and has never looked back. She is married to Chris and has two children, Sam and Zoë. Huge thanks to all three as they've been incredibly encouraging and supportive during the researching of the book. Her idea of the perfect day with her family is going on a walk with a lovely lunch somewhere on the way.

### Nicola O'Brien — Out & About in the West Country, Advice & Support

Is married to John, with three children — Megan, Cerys and Francesca. Their idea of a perfect family day out includes a beach, some good surf and a barbecue!

### Elspeth Pontin — Healthcare

Mother to William, Dominic and Anna, and wife of Ben (all of whom she would like to thank). Elspeth's interest in publicising local healthcare services of relevance to families comes both from her work in psychology (she works on the mother and baby unit in Bristol and also with child protection), and her involvement with the NCT. Elspeth also works as a freelance writer.

### Alex Reed — Out & About in Bristol, Playgroups & Early Education

Arriving in Bristol, from New Zealand, with a lively 1½yr old in one hand and another one on the way, was a daunting prospect. Fortunately the Mum's of Bristol welcomed them with open arms and encouraged them to buy the Titch Hikers' Guide! She has loved working on such a well-loved local institution and found it a perfect way to settle in.

### Lucy Saunders — Family Holidays & Weekends Away

As mother to Megan, Lucy would like to thank her husband and mother for all their childcare support. Also thanks to Lindsey for giving her a chapter which she thoroughly enjoyed researching and got the old grey cells going! She is an instructor in Tatty Bumpkin Yoga classes, based in North Bristol.

### Sharon Wagg — general research

A freelance writer based in Bristol, Sharon combines part-time work with looking after her two daughters Jessica, aged three and Abigail, aged one. She has a love for the outdoors — taking Jessica camping when she was only seven weeks old — and enjoys finding great places to take children, whether it's a child-friendly tea room or a beautiful location for a walk.

### Jane Wisbey — West Country research

A freelance writer and editor based in the South Cotswolds, Jane combines part-time work with looking after her daughter Hazel, aged three. She loves sharing her passion for wildlife and the natural world with Hazel, seeking out child-friendly places in the rural areas around Bristol.

# INDEX

# Index

# Index

# Index

# Index

## QUICK INDEX